Distributed System Concepts

Distributed System Concepts

Prof. Munesh Chandra Trivedi

M.Tech., Ph.D.

Institute of Management Studies

Ghaziabad (NCR)

KHANNA BOOK PUBLISHING CO. (P) LTD.

Publisher of Engineering and Computer Books

4C/4344, Ansari Road, Darya Ganj, New Delhi-110002

Phone: 011-23244447-48 **Mobile:** +91-99109 09320

E-mail: contact@khannabooks.com

Website: www.khannabooks.com, www.khannapublishers.com

Dear Readers,

To prevent the piracy, this book is secured with HIGH SECURITY HOLOGRAM on the front title cover. In case you don't find the hologram on the front cover title, please write us to at contact@khannabooks.com or whatsapp us at +91-99109 09320 and avail special gift voucher for yourself.

Specimen of Hologram on front Cover title:

Moreover, there is a SPECIAL DISCOUNT COUPON for you with EVERY HOLOGRAM.

How to avail this SPECIAL DISCOUNT:

Step 1: Scratch the hologram
Step 2: Under the scratch area, your "coupon code" is available
Step 3: Logon to www.khannabooks.com
Step 4: Use your "coupon code" in the shopping cart and get your copy at a special discount
Step 5: Enjoy your reading!

Thanks,
Khanna Publishing House

Price: ₹ 695.00

ISBN: 978-93-80016-41-2

DISTRIBUTED SYSTEM CONCEPTS
by **Munesh Chandra Trivedi**

Edition: 2025

To view complete list of books, please scan the QR Code:

Published by:
Khanna Book Publishing Co. (P) Ltd.
CIN: U22110DL1998PTC095547

Visit us at: www.khannabooks.com
Write us at: contact@khannabooks.com

Printed in Bharat.

Contents

CHAPTER 1

Process Concept

1.1 CONCEPT OF PROCESS

The process is a program in execution, process includes the program counter & number of registers. A program counter is a register, which contains the address of current instruction. A program by itself is not a process. A program is a passive entity, such as the contents of a file stored on the disk, where as process is an active entity, with a program counter specifying the next instruction to execute and a set of associated resources.

Processes are among the most useful abstractions in operating systems (OS) theory and design, since they offer a unified framework to describe all the various activities of a computer as they are managed by the OS. The term process was (allegedly) first used by the designers of Multics in the '60s, to mean something more general than a job in a multiprogramming environment. Similar ideas, however, were at the heart of many independent system design efforts at the time, so it's rather difficult to point at one particular person or team as the originator of the concept.

As is common for concepts discovered and re-discovered many times on the field before being put on theory books, several definitions have been proposed for the term *process*, including picturesque ones like "the animated spirit of a program". We'd rather draw upon the very general ideas of system theory instead, and regard a process as a *representation* of the *state* of an *instance* of a program in execution.

In this definition, the word *instance* (also "image", "activation") refers to the fact that in a multiprogramming environment several copies of the same program (or of a piece of executable common to different programs) may be concurrently executed by different users or applications. Instead of mantaining in main memory several copies of the executable code of the program, it is often possible to store in memory just one copy of it, and mantain a description of the current status (program counter position, values of the variables, etc.) of each executing activation of it. Main memory usage is in this way maximized. This tecnique is called *code reentrance*, and its implementation requires both careful crafting of the reentrant routines, whose instructions constitute the permanent part of the activation, and provisions in the OS in order to mantain an *activation record* of the temporary part relative to each activation, such as program counter value, variable values, a pointer back to the calling routine and to its activation record ,etc.

Similarly to the way in which activation records allow distinguishing between different activations of the same piece of executable code, by mantaining information about their status, a process description allow an OS to manage, without ensuing chaos, the concurrent execution of different programs all sharing the same resources in terms of processors, memory, peripherals. Again, the keyword here is *state* i.e., in system theory parlance, all the information that, along with the knowledge of the current and future input values, allows predicting the evolution of a deterministic system like a program.

What information is this? Obviously the program's executable code is a part of it, as is the associated data needed by the program (variables, I/O buffers, etc.), but this is not enough. The OS needs also to know about the *execution context* of the program, which includes -at the very least- the content of the processor registers and the work space in main memory, and often additional information like a priority value, whether the process is running or waiting for the completion of an I/O event, etc.

Consider the scheme in Fig. 1.1, which depicts a simple process implementation scheme. There are two processes, A and B, each with its own instructions, data and context, stored in main memory. The OS maintains, also in memory, a list of pointers to the above processes, and perhaps some additional information for each of them. The content of a "current process" location identifies which process is currently being executed. The processor registers then contain data relevant to that particular process. Among them are the base and top adrresses of the area in memory reserved to the process: an error condition would be trapped if the program being executed tried to write in a memory word whose address is outside those bounds. This allows process protect in and prevents unwanted interferences. When the OS decides, according to a predefined policy, that time has come to suspend the current process, the whole process registers content would be saved in the process's context area, and the registers would be restored with the context of another process. Since the program counter register of the latter process would be restored too, execution would restart automatically from the previous suspension point.

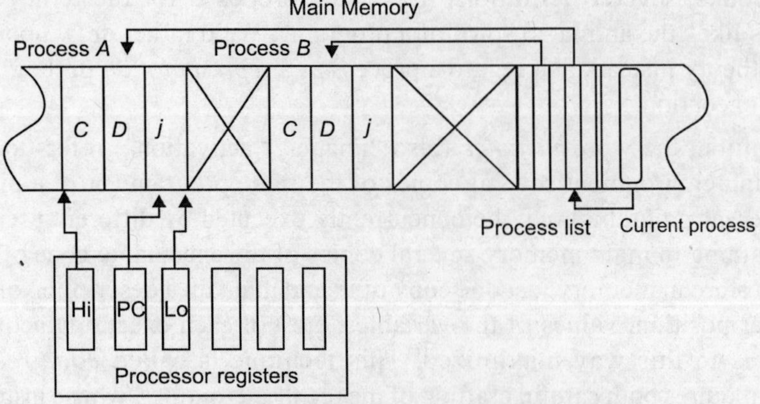

Fig. 1.1 A simple process implementation scheme

1.2 PROCESS STATE

The process state is defined in part by the current activity of that process. Each process may be in one of the following state-

New: The process is being created.

Running: The instruction are being executed.

Waiting: The process is waiting for some event to occur, such as an input/output completion.

Ready: Process is ready for execution waiting for CPU scheduling.

Terminated: The process has finished execution.

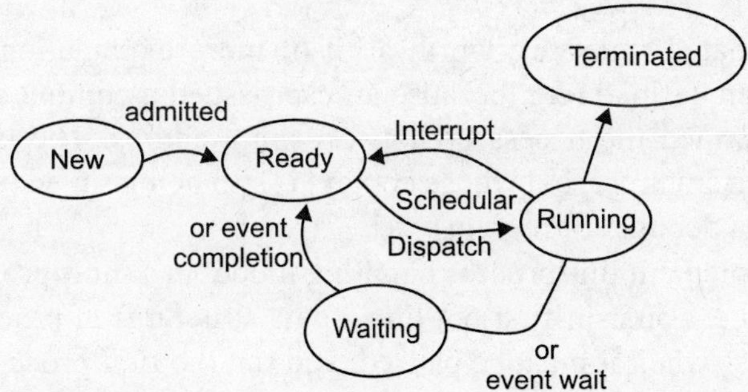

Note: Each process is represented in the operating system by a process control block also called task control block. i.e. A data structure associated with each process which stores all information about process

Carefully reconsider the simple process implementation scheme of the previous section from the point of view of the individual programs, or *tasks*, being executed in each process. Do they need to know about their execution context, or about their being repeatedly suspended and restarted by the OS? Of course not, as long as they can rely upon the OS providing them the resources they need. The OS needs context information to perform its job of allocating resources among tasks according to a certain policy, and the application programmers who write the tasks usually don't want (and sometimes must not be allowed) to care about that policy. Moreover, as long as the OS represents faithfully and completely the state of a suspended task in its context, that task can be restarted at any time without it taking notice of the past suspension.

So far we have considered only two possible conditions (or states) for a process, namely *running* and *not-running* (we'll use the term suspended in another well-defined sense later on): a running process has control of the machine's CPU and is executing its task, a not running process is in the OS process list, and will crunch some CPU time when the OS think it should. We have already noticed, among the reasons that can cause the OS to switch a running process into non-running state, the need to wait for the completion of an I/O event, and the expiration of a quantum of CPU time allotted to the process.

It's useful, at this point, to identify the possible transitions between process states. We can, for example draw (do it) a state transition diagram with four nodes, one for each of the so far identified states, plus one to point at a *new* process and one to a *terminated* process, and call *admission* the creation of a new process, which is put into not-running state, *dispatch* its transition into running state, *pause* its transition from running into not-running, and *exit* the termination of a running process. This way of dealing with the two transitions which are not between running/not-running states, namely the admission and the exit, makes apparently sense, since

- a running process may be disposed immediately as a consequence of an arror condition, without further need to pass it into not-running state;
- a new process must at least wait for the current process to be paused before gaining control of the CPU (here we obviously refer to a single processor architecture).

The new and terminated states are worth a bit of more explanation. The former refer to a process that has just been defined (e.g. because an user issued a command at a terminal), and for which the OS has performed the necessary housekeeping chores. The latter refers to a process whose task is not running anymore, but whose context is still being saved (e.g. because an user may want to inspect it using a debugger program).

A simple way to implement this process handling model in a multiprogramming OS would be to mantain a queue (i.e. a first-in-first-out linear data structure) of processes, put at the end the queue the current process when it must be paused, and run the first process in the queue.

However, it's easy to realize that this simple two-state model does not work. Given that the number of processes that an OS can manage is limited by the available resources, and that I/O events occur at much larger time scale that CPU events, it may well be the case that the first process of the queue must still wait for an I/O event before being able to restart; even worse, it may happen that *most* of the processes in the queue must wait for I/O. In this condition the scheduler would just waste its time sifting the queue in search of a runnable process.

A solution is to split the not-running process class according to two possible conditions: processes *blocked* in the wait for an I/O event to occur, and processes in pause, but nonetheless *ready* to run when given a chance. A process would then be put from running into blocked state on account of an *event wait* transition, would go running to ready state due to a *timeout* transition, and from blocked to ready due to *event occurred* transition.

This model would work fine if the OS had an very large amount of main memory available and none of the processes hogged too much of it, since in this case there would always be a fair number of ready processes. However, because the costs involved this scenario is hardly possible, and again the likely result is a list of blocked processes all waiting for I/O .

Modern architectures rely on a hyerarchical organization of the available memory, only part of which exists in silicon on the machine board, while the rest is *paged* on a high speed storage peripheral like a hard disk. We will address this topic in detail later on; for now it will sufice to say that while the processor has the capability to address memory well above the amount of available RAM, it physically accedes the RAM only, and dedicated hardware is used to copy (or *page*) from the disk to RAM those pieces of memory which the processor refers to and are not available on RAM, and copy back areas of RAM onto disk when RAM space needs be made available. In particular, the act of copying entire processes back and forth from RAM to disk and viceversa is called *swapping*. As we'll see further on, swapping is often mandated by efficiency considerations even if paged memory is available, since the performance of a paged memory system can fall abruptly if too many active processes are mantained in main memory.

The OS could then perform a *suspend* transition on blocked processes, swapping them on disk and marking their state as *suspended* (after all, if they must wait for I/O, they might as well do it out of costly RAM), load into main memory a previously suspended process, *activating* into ready state and go on, However, swapping is an I/O operation in itself, and so at a first sight things might seem to get even worse doing this way. Again the solution is to carefully reconsider the reasons why processes are blocked and swapped, and recognize that if a process is blocked because it waits for I/O, and then suspended, the I/O event might occur while it sits swapped on the disk, We can thus classify suspended processes into two classes: *ready-suspended* for those suspended process whose restarting condition has occurred, and *blocked-suspended* for those who must still wait instead. This classification allows the OS to pick from the good pool of ready-suspended processes, when it wants to revive the queue in main memory. Provisions must be made for passing processes between the new states. In our model this means allowing for new transitions: *activate* and *suspend* between ready and ready-suspended, and between blocked-suspended and blocked as well (why also the activation?), end *event-occurred* transitions from blocked to ready, and from blockes-suspendedto ready-suspended as well. The final scheme thus obtained is sketched in Fig. 2.

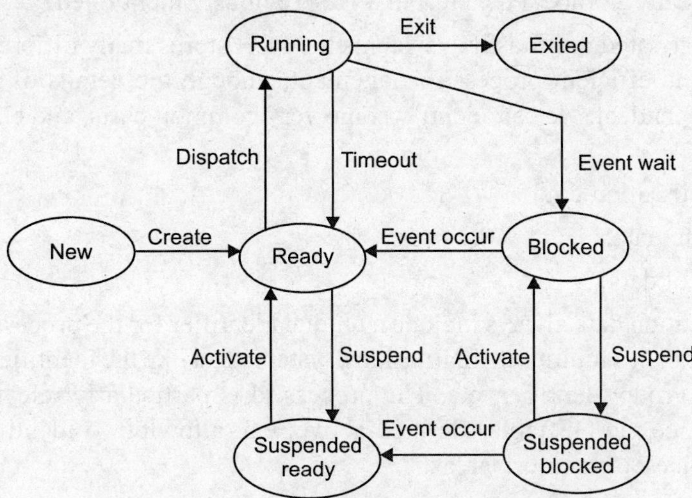

Fig. 1.2 A 7-state process model

1.3 ESS DESCRIPTION AND CONTROL

1.3.1 Process Control Blocks

If the mission of the operating system is to manage computing resources on behalf of processes, then it must be continuously informed about the status of each process and resource. The approach commonly followed to represent this information is to create and update status tables for each relevant entity, like memory, I/O devices, files and processes. Memory tables, for example, may contain information about the allocation of main and secondary (virtual) memory for each process, authorization attributes for accessing memory areas shared among different processes, etc. I/O tables may have entries stating the availability of a device or its assignment to a process, the status of I/O operations being executed, the location of memory buffers used for them, etc. File tables provide info about location and status of files (of course, what else? more on this later). Finally, process tables store the data the OS needs to manage processes. At least part of the process control data structure is always maintained in main memory, though its exact location and configuration varies with the OS and the memory management technique it uses. In the following we'll refer by *process image* to the complete physical manifestation of a process, which includes instructions, program data areas (both static and dynamic - e.g. at least a stack for procedure calls and parameter passing) and the process management information. We'll call this last set the *process control block* (PCB).

The role of the PCBs is central in process management: they are accessed and/or modified by most OS utilities, including those involved with scheduling, memory and I/O resource access and performance monitoring. It can be said that the set of the PCBs defines the current state of the operating system. Data structuring for processes is often done in terms of PCBs. For example, pointers to other PCBs inside a PCB allow the creation of those queues of processes in various scheduling states ("ready", "blocked", etc.) that we previously mentioned.

In modern sophisticated multitasking systems the PCB stores many different items of data, all needed for correct and efficient process management. Though the details of these structures are obviously system-dependent, we can identify some very common parts, and classify them in three main categories:

- Process identification data;
- Processor state data;
- Process control data;

Process identification data always include a unique identifier for the process (almost invariably an integer number) and, in a multiuser-multitasking system, data like the identifier the parent process, user identifier, user group identifier, etc. The process id is particularly relevant, since it's often used to cross-reference the OS tables defined above, e.g. allowing to identify which process is using which I/O devices, or memory areas.

Processor state data are those pieces of information that define the status of a process when it's suspended, allowing the OS to restart it later and still execute correctly. This always include the content of the CPU general-purpose registers, the CPU process status word, stack and frame pointers etc.

Process control information is used by the OS to manage the process itself. This include

- The process scheduling state (different from the task state above discussed), e.g. in terms of "ready", "suspended", etc., and other scheduling information as well, like a priority value, the amount of time elapsed since the process gained control of the CPU or since it was suspended. Also, in case of a suspended process, event identification data must be recorded for the event the process is waiting for.
- Process structuring information:process's children id's, or the id's of other processes related to the current one in some functional way, which may be represented as a queue, a ring or other data structures.
- Interprocess communication information: various flags, signals and messages associated with the communication among independent processes may be stored in the PCB.
- Process privileges, in terms of allowed/unallowed access to system resources.
- Accounting information.

1.3.2 Process Control and System Execution Modes

The management of (user) process activity is the first and foremost task accomplished by an operating system, since the management of all computing resources available on a machine is done on behalf of running processes.

1.3.3 Privileged Execution Modes

In order to perform effectively its process management tasks, an operating systems must control the execution of each process and ensure that all the information used for management purposes is protected from direct access by a process. Otherwise a process might ensue chaos by messing with OS data structures, possibly defeating the resource utilization policies the OS is supposed to enforce.

Furthermore, in order to ensure the correct execution of each process, a multitasking operating system must protect each process's private information (executable code, data, stack) from uncontrolled interferences from other processes. As remarked before, this is accomplished by suitably restricting the memory address space available to a process for reading/writing, so that the OS can regain CPU control through hardware-generated exceptions whenever a process violates those restrictions. At the same time, multitasking OS which offer inter-process communication facilities, provide these communication resources to all processes that need them, so they can "interfere" with each other in a controlled and fruitful fashion.

All the above implies that the OS code needs to execute in a privileged condition with respect to "normal": to manage processes, it needs to be enabled to execute operations which are forbidden to "normal" processes. The approach commonly followed to implement these privileges takes advantage of the fact that:

1. Most modern CPUs have a subset of machine instructions that can be executed only in a "supervisor" (or "protected", or "kernel") mode, indicated by the the status of one or more of the PSW bits. Among the privileged instructions there may be the access to special registers,

used as pointers to OS data structures, the execution of special memory management operations, the possibility to access the whole memory address space available to the CPU.

2. A change of status from CPU "normal" (or "user") mode to "supervisor" mode can be accomplished only by means of hardware interrupts (e.g. timer, I/O) or by executing in software dedicated interrupt/trap/exceptions instructions.

The interruption mechanism needed to switch execution modes allows the enforcement of OS privileges in a simple and elegant way. In fact, each interruption (both HW or SW) generally causes the CPU to branch the execution flow to memory to a fragment of executable code (exception or interrupt handler) which:

1. is not under the control of the currently executing process; indeed, it is often stored outside the process's own address space;
2. is executed with the CPU in supervisor mode

Hence an application program cannot inadvertently mess with the OS code or data: the interrupt handler is part of the OS code, not of the application's, and the application cannot modify this code because it resides outside the application's own allowable address space. If it tried to, an exception would be trapped by the hardware, thus causing the OS to regain control by the above mechanism, and possibly remove the faulty process (incidentally, this is what causes a process-killer "Segmentation Fault" exception in UNIX).

1.3.4 Process Creation and Execution

From the above discussion it should be clear that the creation of a process involves on the OS side

- the creation of a process image in a certain address space, which typically involves the loading of the executable code for the task from some mass storage medium;
- the creation and initialization of a PCB for the process, and its insertion in one of the process control queues (typically the "ready" one).

Process creation is only the first management action performed by the OS on the process. Since the process will use the resources made available by the OS, further OS activity will typically be needed to manage those resources on behalf of the process. This involves the release of the CPU control from the process to the OS. This release is triggered by various conditions, that can usually be classified as follows:

- Explicit request: the process branches to one of the OS routines (in particular, it could explicitly request to be suspended). Appropriate steps be taken in order maintain through the branch the OS's exclusive on privileged execution mode. Typically such a branch will involve the execution of an appropriate SW interrupt instruction, so that the process yields CPU control to the OS code which provides the needed service. We shall say more about this when talking about "kernels executing in the context of a process".
- Hardware interrupt: an hardware event generated outside the CPU that needs be serviced asynchronously. Example: I/O interrupts from DMA or peripherals. Particularly important in this class is the clock (or "timer") interrupt, that allows an OS to periodically regain control of the CPU no matter what the current process is doing.

- Exceptional condition originated from “inside” the CPU while executing the current task (e.g. attempt to execute unallowed operations, arithmetical errors, etc.)

It is at this point important to analyze the in detail the operations involved in the above CPU release/regain events. From the point of view of an OS managing several processes, in particular, it’s important to differentiate between two different scenarios:

- A process is interrupted; some OS service is performed; the process is continued thereafter.
- A process is interrupted; the OS gives control to another process.

Note carefully that the first scenario can be treated similarly to a subroutine call within one process: in order to resume correctly the process after the OS actions it’s necessary that only a *context switch*, i.e. the saving/resuming of the processor state data, be performed before and after the interruption. The second scenario implies a *process switch*, which is typically a much more time-consuming sequence of operations on the OS side, since it involves the update of process tables and queues, the loading of suspended processes if no ready one are available, etc. It’s consequently important for efficiency reasons that the OS be able to identify what services can be provided by a simple context switch (e.g., a memory block allocation in main memory), and which ones it’s better to delay, allowing CPU access to another process.

Two interesting consequences derive from the above observation. One, leading to the distinction between processes and *threads* will be treated later. The second is of interest here, since it leads to understand in greater detail *how* the OS services are performed from a process’s point of view.

1.4 PROCESS CONTROL: ARCHITECTURAL DESIGN ISSUES

Several architectural choices are possible for the implementation of the OS subsystem responsible for process management and control. The same goals of address space protection and controlled access to OS resources can be achieved through the same mechanisms (separation between privileged and user execution modes), yet via radically different designs.

From an historical perspective, we observe a continuing tendency toward “lighter”, smaller kernels or, putting it in a different way, toward kernels that delegate as much as possible of their functionality to the processes. The reasons for this line of development lie mainly in the ever increasing sophistication of the operating systems themselves, and consequently in an attempt to manage effectively the complexity of their design, implementation and maintenance by making them more and more modular.

Hence, from monolithic OS kernels, whose code executes outside all processes, we pass to kernels which execute mainly in the context of the processes, to microkernels, which push the modularization to the ultimate end by making the OS itself a collection of inter-operating “special” processes.

In the following sections we shall consider in some detail these basic architectures in some detail (see Fig. 1.3).

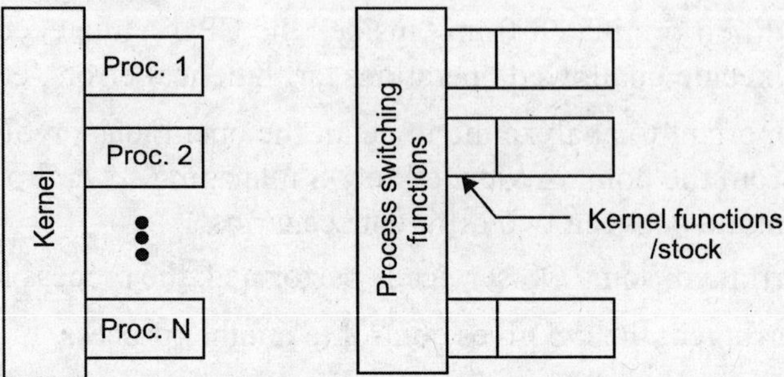

Fig. 1.3 A schematic view of two possible OS execution models:nonprocess kernel (left), kernel executed in a process's context (right)

1.4.1 Non-process Kernel

This approach is quite traditional, and views the OS kernel as a program whose execution is qualitatively different from a process's one. The kernel resides in its own region of memory, has its own stack for managing procedure calls, etc. When its services are requested, due to an interrupt, a trap or a system call from a process, it gains CPU control and operates a context or a process switch depending on the scheduling policy. The key point in this scenario is that the concept of process does not apply to the kernel, which operates in its own privileged mode.

1.4.2 Kernel Executed within a Process

In this case (which is common for OSs designed for small machines, e.g. minicomputer, PCs) the OS provides almost all its services within a user process's context, as if they were obtained through "normal" subroutine calls. However, these calls must be differentiated by some mechanism for this scheme to work correctly, This allows the implementation (in software) of system subroutines that put the processor in protected mode on entering, thus gaining access to all system resources, and return it in user mode on return. If the system is well designed, an attempt to gain privileged access by-passing the OS can be detected (and punished) because it invariably causes an interrupt, thus allowing the OS the gain CPU control once more.

In Fig. 1.4 this scheme is represented in detail, as it is implemented in the UNIX operating system. Here a part of the PCB, called "user area", is stored in the process image: it contains those PCB data which are used only when the process is running, hence not needing to be stored in global kernel process tables. In particular, it contains a *kernel stack*, i.e. a stack used to manage kernel subroutines calls and parameter passing. Although a part of the process image, the user area *cannot* be addressed by the process: simply put, it's outside the range of valid addresses the process can generate (the "user address space"), and an exception would be trapped if it tried to. When the process is running, the kernel accesses those data by remapping the the process image in a part of a shared memory area, the *system address space*, in which the kernel routines are executed.

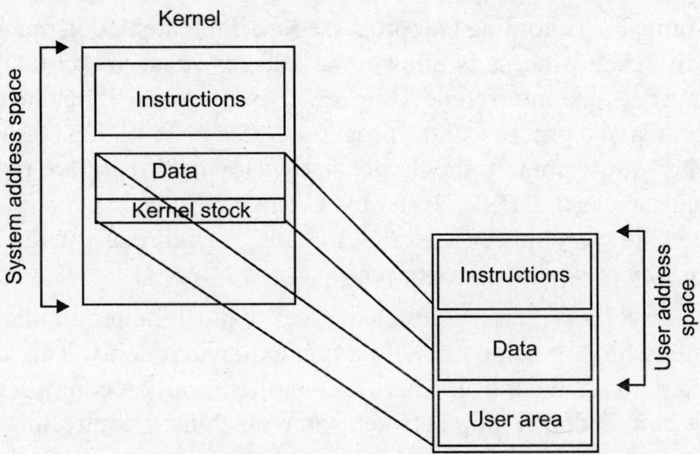

Fig.1.4 Logical view of the process image in the UNIX OS

1.5 THREADS

In previous sections the concept of context switch has been differentiated from that of process switch, and it has been remarked that performing an OS service, while usually requiring a context switch, not always makes a process switch necessary, depending on the scheduling policy adopted by the OS.

A different way to regard the same issue consists in differentiating between two independent attributes involved by the concept of process, namely:

- Unit of resource utilization (for resources other than CPU time);
- Unit of dispatching;

The former refers to the fact that the management of a process involves, on the OS side, the "investing" of resources in terms of allocated main memory, OS table update, availability of I/O streams and devices.

The latter points at the process as being the execution of a program, which may be interleaved with that of other processes in a multiprogramming environment, and involves the management of process states, priority, queues, etc.

Now it should be noted that, even if in traditional operating systems the above attributes uniquely coexist within one process, nothing in the above forbids considering a *collection of programs*, all sharing resources, as a unit of dispatching. The recognition of the independence of these two aspects has lead to the invention of *threads* or *lightweight processes*.

Though the relatively recent concept of thread has found different implementation in various operating system, the most common one in an arrangement in which multiple threads coexist within one process. In this case threads can be easily visualized as as parallel traces of the same process independently executed (think of something like having multiple program counters on the same instruction list - that of the process). This approach has been implemented in OS/2, Sun OS, Lynx and, most notably, Mach.

In Linux, a real-time, Posix abiding OS, processes are implemented in much the same way as is usual in UNIX family: each process is allowed an address space in (virtual) memory which is protected from other processes' interference, the kernel executes mostly in the user process context and keeps in the user area of a process all the process-related information that is needed only when the process is running - most notably the kernel stack. However there are two major differences with other "traditional" unices (e.g BSD, System V, Ultrix, USD, etc.): Lynx is a real-time operating system and allows for the spawning of "parallel threads", or pthreads, within a process (because this is about the only way to be real-time for real).

Real-time means essentially that the OS guarantees that it'll honor an interrupt request within a fixed response time, which is comparable to a context-switch delay. This is essential for most application involving automatic control, where a computer (really a controller program sitting on top of the OS) is put in a feedback loop between some machinery controlling a plant and devices sensing the plant's behaviour. An unpredictable response time for the controller makes the control design problem very difficult, if not altogether impossible. Yet traditional unices *cannot* be interrupted while executing in kernel mode (disabling the CPU's interrupt pins is about the first thing that both system calls and system utilities do when they gain control), and hence the interrupt response time can be as long as the execution time of the longest system routine. Lynx can be interrupted in kernel mode, instead, and also offers some quite sophisticated "timer" system calls for finely tuning the timing of the application's operations.

Since fast controller's are always welcome in control application (you can always slow them down if you want, while boosting a FIAT into a Ferrari is still the subject of basic research...), Lynx also offer pthreads, which allow a designer to nicely decompose the control application in parallel time-bound tasks (maybe operating at radically different time scales), without incurring in a process switch overhead, and with the bonus of fast inter-thread communication through a shared memory area. Each pthread has the following attributes:

- Thread's execution state (Running, Ready, etc.);
- Saved thread processor context when not running (so there's one context per thread, plus the process context).
- Thread's execution stack and local variables;
- Pointers to resources (memory, I/O buffers, timers, etc.) shared with all the other pthreads within the same process.

Note that operations like suspension (i.e. swapping to disk) are still performed at the process level, and they affect all the pthreads within a process when they occur.

A very common application of threads outside real-time control is on the server side of client-server application over computer networks. In a typical scenario for these applications, a server program sits idle listening to a communication port, waiting for service requests from remote clients. When one arrives, according to how it's designed, it can:

- Service the request by itself, in the meantime denying service to other clients. Obviously this works only for very simple & quick kinds of services, and when only a small number of service requests may arrive within one service time interval.

- Spawn a child process which does the servicing. This initially improves the response time on the client side, since the creation of a process is a quick event on a network's time scale. Yet with an increasing number of active processes the burden can become excessive, with the OS wasting too many a cycle switching between them. For this very reason, many OSs impose quite stingy limits on the maximum allowable number of active processes, refusing to spawn new ones when the limit is exceeded.
- Delegate the service to one of a pre-defined number of *worker threads*. This has the same response time advantage as the previous solution, without the process switch burden. Moreover, threading the services allows way more flexibility in the servicing application design. For example, one can make use of the cheap inter-thread communication for chaining threads that compute only parts of the service.

1.6 PROCESS CREATION IN UNIX

The seven-state logical process model we considered in a previous lecture can accommodate the UNIX process model with some modifications, actually becoming a ten state model.

First, as we previously observed, UNIX executes most kernel services within a process's context, by implementing a mechanism which separates between the two possible modes of execution of a process. Hence our previously unique "Running" state must actually be split in a "User Running" state and a "Kernel Running" state. Moreover a process preemption mechanism is usually implemented in the UNIX scheduler to enforce priority. This allows a process returning from a system call (hence after having run in kernel mode) to be immediately blocked and put in the ready processes queue instead of returning to user mode running, leaving the CPU to another process. So it's worth considering a "Preempted" state as a special case of "Blocked". Moreover, among exited processes there's a distinction between those which have a parent process that waits for their completion (possibly to clean after them), and those which upon termination have an active parent that might decide to wait for them sometime in the future (and then be immediately notified of its children's termination). These last processes are called "Zombie", while the others are "Exited". The difference is that the system needs to maintain an entry in the process table for a zombie, since its parent might reference it in the future, while the entry for an exited (and waited for) process can be discarded without further fiddling. So the much talked about "Zombie" processes of UNIX are nothing but entries in a system table, the system having already disposed of all the rest of their image. This process model is depicted in Fig. 1.5.

All processes in UNIX are created using the fork() system call. System calls in UNIX can be best thought of as C functions provided with the standard C library. Even if their particular implementation is depends on the particular UNIX flavor (and on hardware, for many of them), a C API is always provided, and is consistent among the different unices, at least in the fundamental traits.

UNIX implements through the fork() and exec() system calls an elegant two-step mechanism for process creation and execution. fork() is used to create the image of a process using the one of an existing one, and exec is used to execute a program by overwriting that image with the program's one. This separation allows to perform some interesting housekeeping actions in between.

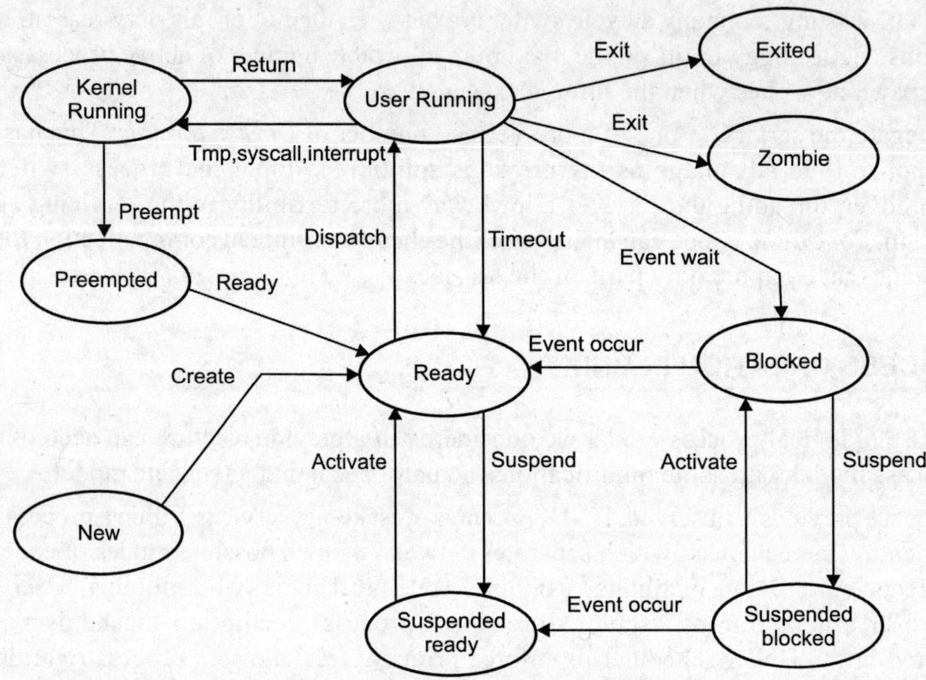

Fig. 1.5 UNIX process state model

A call to fork() of the form:

```
#include <sys/types.h>
pid_t childpid;
...
childpid = fork(); /* child's pid in the parent, 0 in the child */
...
```

creates (if it succeeds) a new process, which a child of the caller's, and is an exact copy of of the (parent) caller itself. By exact copy we mean that it's image is a physical bitwise copy of the parent's (in principle, they *do not* share the image in memory: though there can be exceptions to this rule, we can always thing of the two images as being stored in two separate and protected address spaces in memory, hence a manipulation of the parent's variables won't affect the child's copies, and vice versa). The only visible differences are in the PCB, and the most relevant (for now) of them are the following:

- The two processes obviously have two different process id.s. (pid). In a C program process id.s are conveniently represented by variables of pid_t type, the type being defined in the sys/types.h header.

- In UNIX the PCB of a process contains the id of the process's parent, hence the child's PCB will contain as parent id (ppid) the pid of the process that called fork(), while the caller will have as ppid the pid of the process that spawned it.
- The child process has its own copy of the parent's file descriptors. These descriptors reference the same under-lying objects, so that files are shared between the child and the parent. This makes sense, since other processes might access those files as well, and having them already open in the child is a time-saver.

The fork() call returns in both the parent and the child, and both resume their execution from the statement immediately following the call. One usually wants that parent and child behave differently, and the way to distinguish between them in the program's source code is to test the value returned by fork(). This value is 0 in the child, and the child's pid in the parent. Since fork() returns -1 in case the child spawning fails, a catch-all C code fragment to separate behaviours may look like the following:

```
#include <sys/types.h>
#include <errno.h>
#include <stdio.h>
...
pid_t childpid;
...
childpid=fork();
switch(childpid)
{
  case -1:
    fprintf(stderr,'ERROR: %s\n", sys_errlist[errno]);
    exit(1);
    break;
  case 0:
    /* Child's code goes here */
    break;
  default:
    /* Parent's code goes here */
    break;
}
```

The array of strings char *sys_errlist[] and the global integer variable int errno are defined in the errno.h header. The former contains a list of system error messages, and the latter is set to index the appropriate message whenever an error occurs. For each system call several possible error conditions are defined. Each of them is associated to an integer constant - defined via a #define directive in one system header file - whose value is exactly the one that errno takes when an error occurs. A sample definition (from the sys/errno.h header) is:

```
...
#define ENOMEM 12
...
```

which defines the error that might occur when a process creation fails because there's not enough memory available.

Note that a child (i.e. a process whatsoever, since they are all children of some other process, with the exception of processes 0, swapper and 1, init) cannot use the value returned by fork() to know its pid, since this is always 0 in the child. A system call named getpid() is provided for this purpose, and another one, named getppid() is used to ask the system about the parent's id. Both functions take no arguments and return the requested value in pid_t type, or -1 in case of failure.

In the above program fragment, a system call to exit() is made in case of failure, which causes the program to abort (you might want to deal with the errors in a smoother way, depending on your application, and perform some application-dependent error recovery action). We'll see later that the exit() call returns the lower 8 bits of its argument (1, in the above example) to a waiting parent process, which can use them to determine the child's exit status and behave accordingly. The usual convention is to exit with 0 on correct termination, and with a meaningful (for the parent) error code on abort.

It is often the case that a parent process must coordinate its actions with those of its children, maybe exchanging with them various kind of messages. UNIX defines several sophisticated inter-process communication (IPC) mechanisms, the simplest of which is a parent's ability to test the termination status of its children. A synchronization mechanism is provided via the wait() system call, that allows a parent to sleep until one of its children exits, and then get its exit status. This call actually comes in three flavors, one simply called wait() and common to all version of UNIX (that i know of), one called waitpid(), which is a POSIX extension, and one called wait3(), and it's a BSD extension.

Here's an example call to wait(): a program spawns two children, then waits for their completion and behaves differently according to which one is finished. Try to compile and execute it (no need to type: you can cut and paste from your web browser...).

```
#include <sys/types.h>
#include <sys/wait.h>
#include <stdio.h>

int main(int argc, char *argv[])
{
    pid_t whichone, first, second;
    int howmany;
    int status;

    if ((first=fork())==0) /* Parent spawns 1st child */
```

```
{
   printf("Hiya, I am the first child, "
         "and my id is %d\n",
         getpid()
         );
   sleep(10); /* Sleep 10 sec, then exit */
   exit(0);
}
else if (first == -1)
{
   perror("1st fork: something went bananas\n");
   exit(1);
}
else if ((second=fork())==0) /* Parent spawns 2nd  child */
{
   printf("Hiya, I am the second child, "
         "and my id is %d\n",
         getpid()
         );
   sleep(15); /* Sleep 15 sec, then exit */
   exit(0);
}
else if (second == -1)
{
   perror("2nd fork: something went bananas\n");
   exit(1);
}

printf("This is the parent\n");

howmany=0;
while (howmany < 2) /* Wait twice */
{
   whichone=wait(&status);
   howmany++;

   if (whichone==first)
```

```
        printf('First child exited ');
      else
        printf('Second child exited ');

      if ((status & 0xffff)==0)
        printf("correctly\n");
      else
        printf("uncorrectly\n");
    }

    return 0;
}
```

The first part of this example, up to the howmany=0 statement, contains nothing new: just make sure you understand what the instruction flow is in the parent and in the children. The parent then enters a loop waiting for the children's completion. The wait() system call blocks the caller process until one of its immediate children (not children's children, or other siblings) terminates, and then returns the pid of the terminated process. The argument to wait() is the address on an integer variable or the NULL pointer. If it's not NULL, the system writes 16 bits of status information about the terminated child in the low-order 16 bits of that variable. Among these 16 bits, the *higher* 8 bits contain the *lower* 8 bits of the argument the child passed to exit(), while the *lower* 8 bits are all zero if the process exited correctly, and contain error information if not (see the wait(2) man page for details). Hence, if a child exits with 0 all those 16 bits are zero. To reveal if this is actually the case we test the bitwise AND expression (status & 0xffff), which evaluates as an integer whose lower 16 bits are those of status, and the others are zero. If it evaluates to zero, everything went fine, otherwise some trouble occurred. Try changing the argument passed to exit() in one of the children.

The Posix and BSD extensions to wait() are useful when a parent must not block waiting for children, but still wants to know about the children's termination status values via the wait mechanism. We'll treat only the Posix waitpid() call, and you are referred to the man page for the BSD call.

The waitpid() call is declared as follows in the sys/wait.h header:

```
pid_t waitpid(pid_t pid, int *statptr, int options);
```

Here the meaning of the the return value and of the pointer to the status statptr is exactly the same in wait(). However this call allows to specify which children should be waited for and how. Specifically, the first argument pid specifies the process(es) that must be waited for. The relevant (for now) cases are:

- pid == -1: all children are waited for;
- pid > 0: it specifies the pid of a single child that should be waited for (an error occurs if that process does not exist or is not one of the caller's children);

The relevant (for now) value for the third argument is a constant called WNOHANG, that causes the function not to suspend the caller's execution if status is not immediately available for one of the child processes. This allows to implement a loop in which the parent can do something useful and periodically poll the children's status as well.

Note that the use of a loop also allows to use wait() and yet wait for one particular child: try to figure out yourself how.

1.7 CONCURRENCY

Under the heading of "Concurrency" goes the analysis of the problems that in a multiprogramming environment may occur when processes share resources like the content of a shared memory area, files, devices. In general, these are all problems due to lack of proper synchronization in the access to the shared resources, which may cause data corruption or evil situations, known as deadlocks, in which processes are stalled waiting to access a shared resource, and never being allowed to. These problems are often pretty subtle in that their manifestation is often unpredictable, depending on the actual operations performed by the processes, hence they typically defy common, source-oriented debugging techniques, requiring an overall vision of the system behaviour. It then follows that specific system design techniques must be employed in order to provide application programmers with tools by which these problems can be avoided.

A general treatment of concurrency problems starts with the definition of the concept of "critical section" of a program: it's simply a code fragment in which a shared resource is accessed, and encapsulation in the source of these code fragments is of vital importance for the fruitful use of the above mentioned tools.

The theory then goes on by requiring that efficient solutions to conflict problems must be characterized by a synchronization among processes, so that they have to wait for executing a critical section if another process is accessing the shared resource that critical section is for. This kind of synchronization is named "mutual exclusion" (from running the critical section at the same time).

The following design guidelines should be followed:

- No two processes may be simultaneously in their critical sections related to the same shared resource.
- No assumptions can be made on the number of available CPUs.
- No process running outside its critical sections may block any other process from running its own ones.
- No process should have to wait (potentially) forever to enter its critical section.

Among the simplest ways to enforce mutual exclusion, we observes that a "hard" approach like a user program disabling interrupts when entering a critical section is certainly a solution, since processes must be interrupted in order for other processes to gain CPU control and possibly access a shared resource, but it's certainly a bad one, since it leaves too much control to the user program itself: means that not even the kernel can gain CPU control if something goes astray in the user program.

The use of simple shared variables or files to signal that a process is in a critical section is wrong in principle: they would simply be new shared resources, and an access to them without proper synchronization would simply add a new problem. A strict alternation among processes is deemed to be highly inefficient.

1.7.1 Basic Concepts

Concurrency is the execution of two or more independent, interacting programs over the same period of time; their execution can be interleaved or even simultaneous. Concurrency is used in many kinds of systems, both small and large.

1.7.2 Example 1

The typical home computer is full of examples. In separate windows, a user runs a web browser, a text editor, and a music player all at once. The operating system interacts with each of them.

Almost unnoticed, the clock and virus scanner are also running. The operating system waits for the user to ask more programs to start, while also handling underlying tasks such as resolving what information from the Internet goes to which program.

1.7.3 Example 2

Using a web-based airline reservation system, Joe and Sue each want to buy a ticket. Each has a separate computer, and thus a separate web browser. Their two web browsers plus the airline's web server together comprise the concurrent program.

As this example illustrates, the term *concurrent system* might be more appropriate. However, for verification purposes, we will view them as a single, distributed entity to be modeled.

A concurrent system may be implemented via *process*es and/or *thread*s. Although details can vary upon platform, the fundamental difference is that processes have separate address spaces, whereas threads share address spaces. We will follow the common theoretical practice and ignore this distinction, using shared variables when desired, and using the two terms interchangeably.

We view these threads as executing relatively independently. However, since they are acting together towards some goal, they must need to communicate and coordinate. The two most common communication techniques in processes and threads are through, respectively, *message passing* and *shared variables*. In order to communicate at the right times, they must *synchronize*, together arriving at agreed-upon control points. Often, one or more threads *block*, or stop and wait for some external event. In this module, we will use only shared variables, although the tools we use also allow message passing.

Even though we have multiple flows of control, that doesn't imply we need multiple processors. Concurrent programs may be executed on a single processor by interleaving their control flows. In order to understand what happens in a concurrent program over time, we must understand how the individual operations of the threads can interleave. This is independent of how many processesors we use, although it is convenient to think of only having one processor. To consider the possible interleavings, we need to know which actions are *atomic*, or indivisible. If an atomic operation begins, we know that it won't be interrupted by a context switch until it is done. We generally assume that each hardware machine instruction is atomic, but a programming language might guarantee that even more complicated operations are atomic as well.

***Definition:* State**

A state captures all the current information in a program. This includes all local and global variables' values and each thread's current program counter. More generally, this includes all the memory and register contents.

***Definition:* Trace**

A trace is the sequence of operations (and their data) performed in a particular run of a concurrent program. Equivalently, it is the sequence of states during a run — i.e., the collection of variable and program counter values.

***Definition:* Atomic**

An atomic operation is indivisible. A context switch to another process cannot happen during this operation

1.7.4 Example: Statement-level Atomicity

Let's examine the possible interleaving of the code fragments for two threads. First, let's assume that each assignment statement is atomic.

```
thread0:
{
x=x+1
}
thread1:
{
x=x*2
}
```

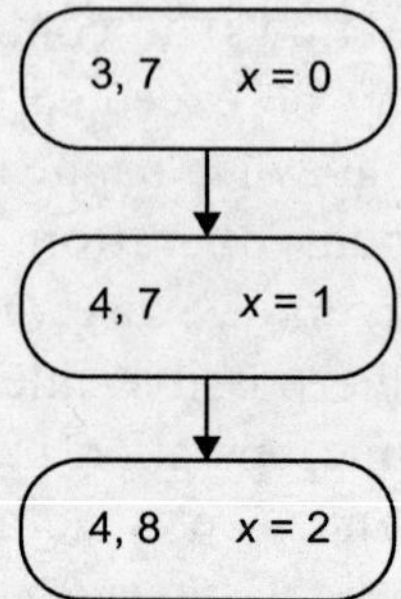

Fig. 1.6: There are two possible traces, as either thread's statement could execute first. Bold type highlights anything modified or assigned to each step

Here, each trace is a timeline, representing one possible interleaving of operations. From top to bottom, each state represents one point in time, with a current line number for each thread, plus the value of each variable. The first state is the starting point, before execution begins. Here, we assume that x is initially zero. We will use traces and their timeline diagrams throughout this module to understand concurrent programs.

1.7.5 Example: Instruction-level Atomicity

For contrast, let's change what is atomic. Now, assume that each machine instruction operation, such as loading, adding, or storing a register, is atomic. Again, we assume x is initially zero. Observe that with finer-grained atomicity, there are many more ways to interleave the threads, and (in this case) more possible result values for x.

```
thread0:
{
r0 = x
r0 += 1
x = r0
}
thread1:
{
r1 = x
r1 <<= 1 /* Shifting left one position multiplies by 2. */
x = r1
}
```

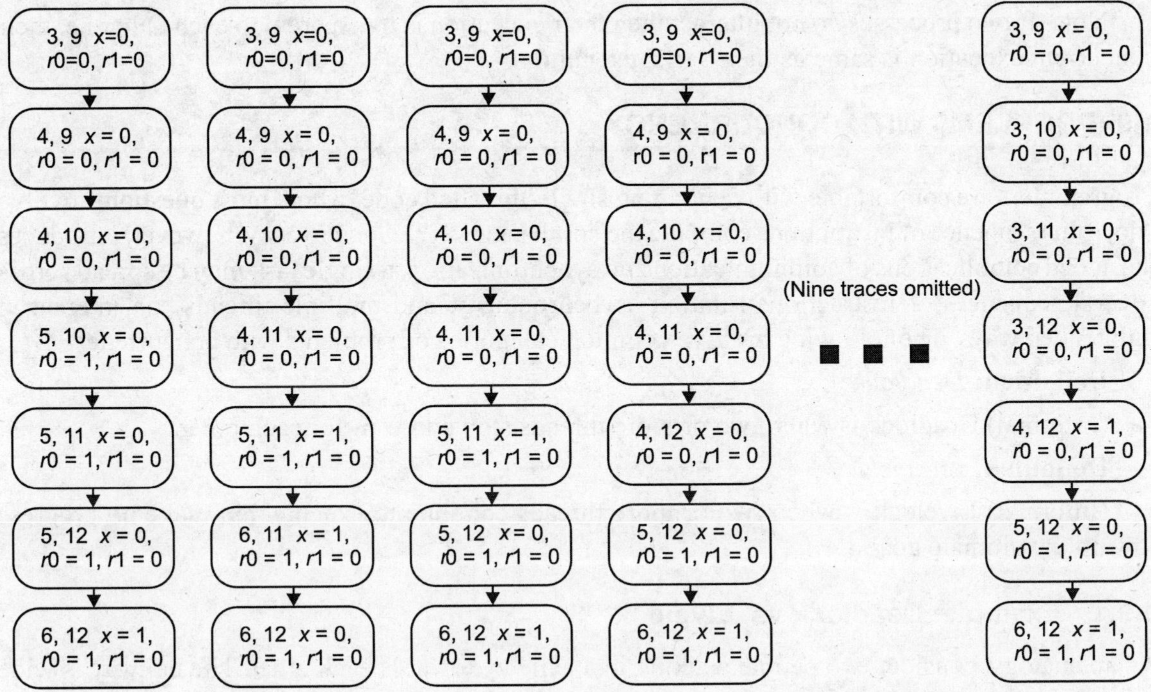

Fig. 1.7 With finer-grained atomicity, there are many more ways to interleave the threads.

Both the syntax and semantics of the concurrency primitives can vary among programming languages and concurrency libraries.

1.8 CONCURRENT PROCESS

Two processes are concurrent if execution can overlap in time i.e. the execution of the second process starts before the first process completes. In multiprocessor systems, since CPUs can simultaneously executed different processes. The concept of concurrency is concrete and easy to visualize.

In a single CPU system, Physical concurrency can be due to concurrent execution of the CPU and an I/O. Two processes are serial if the execution of one must be completer before the execution of the other can starts. Normally two processes are said to be concurrent if they are not serial. Concurrent processes generally interacts through either of the following mechanisms-

Shared Variable

The processes access (read/write) a common variable/common data.

Message Passing

The processes exchange information with each other by sanding and receiving messages.

Note–If two processes do not interact then their execution is transparent to each Other i.e. their concurrent execution is same as their serial execution.

1.9 PROBLEMS WITH CONCURRENCY

Programmers are comfortable with debugging single-threaded code, where most questions involve "does this sequence of instructions compute the correct answer?" Concurrency, however, introduces the added complications of communication and synchronization; a single task may be spread across several sequences of instructions running asynchronously, and multiple threads can interact in unintended ways. The following are five common categories of problems with concurrency.

Definition: *Deadlock*

(Informal) Deadlock is when two or more threads stop and wait for each other.

Definition: *Livelock*

(Informal) Livelock is when two or more threads continue to execute, but make no progress toward the ultimate goal.

1.9.1 Example: Deadlock vs. Livelock

As an analogy, consider two people walking in a hallway towards each other. The hallway is wide enough for two people to pass. Of interest is what happens when the two people meet. If on the same side of the hallway, a polite strategy is to step to the other side. A more belligerent strategy is to wait for the other person to move. Two belligerent people will suffer in deadlock, glaring face to face in front of each other. Two polite people could suffer from livelock if they repeatedly side-step simultaneously. (No conclusions on morality are to be inferred from the fact that one polite and one belligerent person don't have any problems.)

Definition: *Fairness*

(Informal) Fairness is the idea that each thread gets a turn to make progress.

There are more specific notions of fairness that describe when and how often threads are guaranteed to get a turn. For example, do we expect that each thread should be executed as often as any other, or is it acceptable if one runs a hundred steps for each step of any other thread? When considering fairness, one must also consider the system code implementing the threads. The implementation includes a scheduler that determines how to interleave the threads, and the scheduler might or might not provide any fairness guarantees.

Definition: *Starvation*

(Informal) Starvation is when some thread gets deferred forever.

1.9.2 Example : Fairness and Starvation

Assume we are modeling a store. Consumers buy products, reducing the shelf inventory. Meanwhile, employees restock the shelves, increasing the shelf inventory. More simply, let thread *C* be a loop that repeatedly decrements a counter, and thread *P* be a loop that repeatedly increments that same counter.

Unless our scheduler (which may be nature) otherwise gives some guarantees, this system does not ensure that the two threads execute fairly. In particular, it is possible for one thread to starve the other.

1.9.3 Example: The Express Checkout Line, and the Woes of Grover

A Sesame Street skit has Grover in line at the grocery store, his basket heaped full of animal crackers and other essentials. A little old lady gets in line behind him, holding only a single candle, muttering how she is late for her grandson's very first birthday party. Grover muses that she has to wait a long time for his big basket to be rung up, whereas if she went first it's hardly any delay at all for him. So he invites her to get in front of him in line, and she gratefully accepts.

The scheduler, in this case, is the social protocol at the checkout line (which includes Grover's politeness). This input situation demonstrates how Grover gets starved. The alternate protocol of having an additional express checkout line (without allowing any butt-ins) is an attempt to minimize customers' wait-delay without introducing starvation.

Definition: *Race Condition*

A race condition is when some possible interleaving of threads results in an undesired computation result. A race condition is when some possible interleaving of threads results in an undesired computation result.

Typically, a race condition is an oversight by the programmer who did not realize the interleaving was possible. Race conditions are notoriously hard to debug and test for because they can well occur in highly unlikely situations. More generally, these and other issues are categorized as being either *safety* or *liveness* issues.

- Safety properties are those that say "bad things never happen". Examples are the lack of deadlock, the lack of livelock, and the lack of race conditions. For a particular program, a safety property might be that inventory levels never become negative, or that customers can't cut ahead in line.
- Liveness properties are those that say "good things eventually happen". An example is fairness. For a particular program, a liveness property might be that each customer is served, or that after each program error, an error message is printed. Typically, liveness issues can't be detected by looking at a program at a particular moment, but instead require considering an entire (infinite) trace.

In this module, we will concentrate on the four issues of deadlock, livelock, race conditions, and fairness. We will see how to write and automatedly detect these problems in some concurrent programs, using the tools Promela and SPIN. We will also learn how to formally specify more intricate properties using temporal logic.

1.10 AVOIDING AND DETECTING PROBLEMS WITH CONCURRENCY

There are known programming techniques to avoid certain problems such as deadlock and some kinds of race conditions. Some of these techniques—notably locks and semaphores—are so common that they are often embedded into programming languages. While the details of such techniques are outside the scope of this module, it is important to recognize that although they greatly help writing concurrent problems, they don't mean that concurrency problems can't arise.

Given concurrent code, how can we determine if it behaves as expected? Certainly we can test it on various inputs, but we can never try every possible input. Neither can we test every possible interleaving on every possible input. As always, testing can reveal errors, but it can't demonstrate the lack of errors.

Since concurrency problems can lead to programs that don't terminate, it's clear that detecting concurrency problems can't be any easier than the Halting Problem, which is itself unsolvable. So we can't write a checker which takes a concurrent program as input and always determines whether it's free of (say) deadlock.

But just as we can study individual programs and conclude whether or not they will halt, for many real-world concurrent programs, we *can* determine whether or not they are susceptible to deadlock. For example, communications protocols generally have a finite number of options and are amenable to automated checking. Thus automated tools (such as SPIN) are valuable aid in catching and eliminating real-world bugs.

1.11 SEMAPHORES

A semaphores S is an integer variable which can be accessed to two standard atomic functions-

Wait (s)

Signal (s)

```
Wait (s) :
          While (s <= 0 )
          s=s-1;              // no operation i.e. wait
signal (s):
          s=s+1;
```

An alternative approach, that must make use of specific system facilities is the use of the "semaphore" variables proposed by Dijkstra. Semaphores are a pair composed of an integer variable, called the semaphore counter, and of a queue (FIFO) of id.s of processes waiting to get synchronized access to the shared resource the semaphore controls. The counter is initialized to a positive value upon semaphore instantiation, and only two *atomic* operations can be performed on the semaphore by a process:

- *wait*: decrease the counter by one; if it gets negative, block the process and enter its id in the queue.
- *signal*: increase the semaphore by one; if it's still negative, unblock the first process of the queue, removing its id from the queue itself.

The atomicity of the above operations is an essential requirement: mutual exclusion while accessing a semaphore must be strictly enforced by the operating system. This is often done by implementing the operations themselves as uninterruptible system calls.

It's easy to see how a semaphore can be used to enforce mutual exclusion on a shared resource: a semaphore is assigned to the resource, it's shared among all processes that need to access the resource, and its counter is initialized to 1. A process then waits on the semaphore upon entering the critical section for the resource, and signals on leaving it. The first process will get access. If another process arrives while the former is still in the critical section, it'll be blocked, and so will further processes. In this situation the absolute value of the counter is equal to the number of processes waiting to enter the critical section. Every process leaving the critical section will let a waiting process use the resource by signaling the semaphore.

1.11.1 Semaphores in System V UNIX

The System V specification of the UNIX operating system introduces semaphores among the other facilities for Inter-Process Communication (IPC). This implementation is a (rather messy) generalization of the above described scheme. Three features contribute to this unnecessary complication:

- A semaphore counter is not just a single value. It's rather a set of one or more values, and the exact number of values is specified upon semaphore creation.
- The creation of a semaphore is independent of its initialization. This is a fatal flaw, since we cannot atomically create a new semaphore set and initialize all the values in the set: a competing process may sneak in and access the semaphore after creation but before initialization, thus finding semagarbage.
- A semaphore must be explicitly destroyed when the shared resource is no longer necessary, since the systemwide total number of semaphore sets is limited.

Moreover, semaphore counters are always nonnegative, a zero causing the waiting process to be put to sleep

A semaphore is created by the semget(3) system call, whose synopsis is:

```
#include <sys/types.h>
#include <sys/ipc.h>
#include <sys/sem.h>
int semget(key_t key, int nsems, int flag);
```

This system call returns an integer id for the semaphore (analogous to a file descriptor), or -1 in case of error.

The key argument is analogous to a file name, and is used to identify exclusively a semaphore set (and other IPC objects as well) all over the system, while the semaphore id is - like a file descriptor - known only by one process and by its siblings that inherit it through variables after a fork(). Cooperating processes wishing to access the semaphore set must use the same key, much like a file name is used to store on disk shared data by cooperating processes. A key is implemented as an integer (whose size is specified by the key_t type), and a library function called ftok() is provided for the purpose of generating meaningful keys.

The value of nsems specifies the number of semaphores in newly created semaphore set.

The value of flag is a bit mask obtained ORing constants that specify:

- The access permissions for the semaphore set, in the same way as for a file;
- The creation mode, which can be:
- IPC_PRIVATE: if this is specified, the value of the key is ignored, and a private semaphore set is created, that can be used by a process and its siblings through semaphore id inheritance. Since there's no key, other unrelated processes have no way to access the semaphore set.
- IPC_CREAT: if this is specified, and a semaphore with the given key does not exist, it is created, otherwise the call returns with -1, setting the appropriate errno value.

For example, to create one semaphore with key 333, readable an writable by an user and his group, you'd use a code fragment like:

```
int sid;
...
sid=semget((key_t)333, 1, SEM_R|SEM_W|(SEM_R>>3)|(SEM_W>>3)|IPC_CREAT);
if (sid<0)
{
   perror("Semaphore 333");
   exit(1);
}
...
```

Once a semaphore has been created, a process accesses it either directly via its id, if its a private semaphore and the id has been inherited from a creating ancestor, or by calling semget() to get its id in exchange for the right key, much like opening an already existing file. In this case the IPC_PRIVATE and IPC_CREAT bits are not set.

1.11.2 Implementation of Semaphore

A process must be in a busy waiting loop, while performs wait ( ), such semaphore are called spin lock semaphore . so define semaphore as-

```
        Struct semaphore
        {       int value ;
                list L;
        }       s;
        wait (s):
                s. value =s. value -1;
                if(s. value < 0)  //wait
        {       add this process to list L;
                block ;                    // process enters in waiting state release CPU.
    Signal (s) ;
                s. value =s. value+1;
                if(s. value <= 0 )
                {
                        remove a process P from L;
                        wake up (P);    // move to ready state.
                }
```

1.12 MESSAGES

Messages are yet another form of shared resource, through which cooperating processes can communicate data to each other. intuitively, we can think of implementing them by means of two primitives like

- *send(dest, msg)*: to send a message to a designated process, destination of the message;
- *receive(source, msg)*: to receive a message from a designated process;

The implementation of this rather simple idea raises a number of design issues, namely:

- Synchronization: the primitives can cause the destination or source of the message to block until the delivery is completed (successfully or not). In this case they are called blocking, and nonblocking otherwise. The reception can also be either explicitly confirmed through the use of the analog of a return receipt or not.

- Addressing. It can be either direct or indirect. In a directly addressed send the destination is specified directly via the recipient(s) pid(s). This scheme is obviously very rigid: since pid(s) are unpredictable, their values should be communicated through some sort of message or in some other way too. A direct reception can be either explicit, when the source a message is expected form is declared via a pid, or implicit, when the source is actually returned along with the message. In the other general approach, indirect addressing, communicating processes share a common storage area, called a *mailbox* or *message queue*, into which the deposit messages or from which they pick up messages to be received. This scheme is very flexible, for example allowing for one-to-many and/or many-to-one relationships between senders and receivers.
- Format. How the message data should be organized, whether they should have a fixed length or a variable one, if they should have a header specifying content information, and how, etc.
- Queuing discipline. In what order should messages to the same destination be delivered. Commonly used disciplines use a FIFO scheme, or a priority mechanism via multiple FIFO queues.

1.13 PROCESS SYNCHRONIZATION

A situation where several process access and manipulate the same data concurrently and outcome of the execution depends on takes place is called "race condition". A solution to this problem requires that be synchronized access the variable at any one time.

1.13.1 Critical Section Problem

When concurrent processes interacts through a shared variable, the integrity of the variable may be violated. If access to the variable is not coordinated. Let there are n processes and each process has a segment of code called a critical selection, in which the process may be changing common variables, updating a common table, a common files and so on.

The critical selection problem is to design a protocol that the processes can use to cooperate. A solution to the critical section problem must satisfy the following requirement-

- Mutual exclusion.
- Progress
- Bound waiting.

Each process must request permission to enter its critical section. The section of code implementing this request is the entry section. The critical section may be followed by an exit section. The remaining code is the remaining section.

```
Do
{
                        Entry section
```

```
                              Critical section;
   Exit section

          Remainder section;
                         } while(1);
```

Fig: General Structure of a process

Two process solution:-

Algorithms:

```
int turn; // globle,initialize to 0.
Do
{          while (turn=/=1) // no operation
                critical section;
           turn=0;
           remainder section;
} while(1);
```

This algorithms does not satisfy the process requirements, since if requires strict alternation between two processes.

Multiple Process Solutions

Let us develop an algorithm for solving the critical section problem for n process this algorithm is known as backery algorithm and it is based on a scheduling algorithm commonly used in bakeries i.e. ice- cream parlours etc. on entering in the parlour. Each customer receives a number, number is serviced first, if two processes i.e. customers receives the same number then the process with the lowest name is serviced first.

Algorithms:

```
Boolean choosing [n] ; //initialize to false
Int number [n] ; // initialize to 0.

Do
{
        choosing [i] = true;
        number [i]  = max (number)+1;
        choosing [i] = false;
        for ( j= 0  to n-1)
```

```
        {
                while (choosing (j))
                while (number(j)=/=0&(number(i),j)<number (i),i))
                        critical section;
                        number (i)=)
                remainder section }
                while (1);
```

Critical section problem using Semaprore

```
                Semaphore mutex ;                   //global
                Do
                {       wait (mutex);
                        critical section;
                        signal(mutex);
                        remainder section ;

                } while(1);
```

Note: A semaphore is a class containing two functions wait (s) and signal (s)

```
                        Semaphore
                        {       wait( );
                                signal( );
                        }
```

1.13.2 Dining Philosopher Problem

Let five philosophers who spend their lives thinking and eating. The philosopher share a common circular table surrounded by five circular table surrounded by five chairs, each belonging to one philosopher. In the center of the table a bowl of rice and the table is laid with five single chopsticks. When a philosopher thinks, he does not interact with his colleages. From time to time a philosopher gets hungry and tries to pick the two chopsticks that are closest to him.

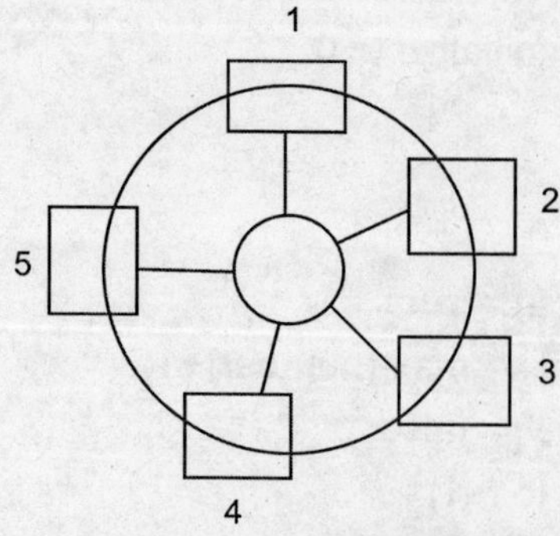

```
semaphore chopstick (5);
do
{           wait (chopstick(i));
            wait (chopstick(i+1)mod5);
            cat;
            signal(chopstick (i));
            signal (chopstick(i+1)mod5);
}           while (i);
```

Although this solution guarantee that no two neighbors are eating simultaneously, it neverthess must be rejected because it has the possibility of creating deadlock. A solution to the dining philosopher problem that ensures freedom from deadlocks-

- Allow at most four philosophers to be sitting simultaneously at the table.
- Allow a philosopher to pick up his chopstick only if both the chopsticks are available.
- Use an asymmetric solution, i.e. an odd philosophers picks up first his left chopsticks then his right chopsticks, whereas an even philosophers picks first right then left.

1.13.3 Producer Consumer Problem

A producer process produces information that is consumed by a consumer process. For ex- A print program produces characters that are consumed by the printer device. A compiler may produce Assembly code, which is consumed by an assembler. To allow procedure and consumer processes to run concurrently, we must have available a buffer of items that can be filled by the producer & consumed by consumer.

The producer and consumer must be synchronized, so that the consumer does not try to consumer an item that has not yet been produced. The unbounded buffer producer consumer problem places no practical limit on the size of buffer. The consumer may have to wait for new items, but the producer can always produce new items. The bounded buffer producer consumer problem assumes a fixed buffer size, in this case the consumer must wait. If the buffer is empty and the producer must wait if the buffer is full.

The buffer may either be provided by the operating system through the use of an inter process communication facility or by explicitly coded by the application programmer with the use of shared memory.

Unbounded buffer

```
Producer()
    {
    while(1)
        {
```

```
while((in+1)mod n==out) // do nothing
          {
          produce an item in next p;
          buffer(in)=next p;
          in=(in+1)mod n;
          }
}
                    consumer ( )
          {
                    while ( in= =out) // do nothing
                    next  = buffer (out);
                    out  = (out+1) mod n;
                    consume an item in next c;
                    }
          }
```

Bounded buffer

```
                    Producer  buffer- consumer
          —wait when buffer full    —wait when buffer empty.
          —wait when consumer is            —wait when producer is using
                    using buffer.                      Buffer.

          Semaphore full, empty , mutex;

          // mutex provides mutual exclusion initialize to1
          // empty counts the no. of empty buffer & initialize to n
          // full counts the no. of full buffer & initialize to 0.
                    Producer ( )
                    Do
                    {
                              Produce an item in temp;
                              Wait (empty);
                              Wait (mutex);
                              Add item to buffer;
                              Signal (mutex);
                              Signal (full);
                    }    while (1);
                              consumer ( )
```

```
do
{       wait (full);
        wait (mutex);
        remove an item from buffer in temp;
        signal (mutex);
        signal(empty);
        consume the item in temp;
} while (1);
```

1.13.4 Readers-Writers Problems

A date object such as a file/record is to be shared among several concurrent processes. Some of these processes may wait only to object, where as the shared object, where as other want to update the shared object. We distinguish between these two types of processes that are referring to those processes that are interested in only reading as reading as readers and to the rest as writer.

First Readers/Writers Problem: Reader has given a priority i.e. no. reader should wait for other reader to finish simply because a writer is waiting.

Second Reader/Writers Problem: Writer is given a priority i.e. if a writer waiting to access the object, no new recorders may start ready.

```
Semaphore mutex,wrts;
Int read count;  // to count no. of readers
Writer ( )
Do {
        Wait (wrt);
        Writing the files;
        Signal (wrts);
    } while(i);
Reader( )
Do
{       wait (mutex);
        read count ++;
        if (read count = =1)
        wait (wrt);
        signal(mutex);

        reading is Performed;
        wait (mutex);
        read count —;
```

```
        if (read count = =0)
        signal(wrt);
        signal(mutex);
    } while(1);
```

1.14 PROCESS DEADLOCKS

A deadlock is a situation where a process or a set of processes is blocked, waiting an event that will never occur. A processes request resources if the resources are not available at that time the processes enters a wait state. It may happen that waiting processes will never again change state because the resources they have requested are hold by another waiting process this situation is called deadlock.

Example: If you are locking more than one RIN at a time in your program, there is a chance that you can cause a deadlock between two or more processes. Deadlock occurs when two or more processes are mutually blocked, waiting for each other to release a needed resource.Example 2-6 illustrates how a deadlock can occur between two processes, Process A and Process B. Assume that both processes in the example are executing concurrently, line by line.

```
{ PROCESS A EXECUTING }                 { PROCESS B EXECUTING }
          .                .
          .                .
          .                .
LOCKGLORIN (1);                         LOCKGLORIN (2);
LOCKGLORIN (2);                         LOCKGLORIN (1);
PROCESS A REMAINS BLOCKED               PROCESS B REMAINS BLOCKED
UNTIL RIN 2 IS UNLOCKED                 UNTIL RIN 1 IS UNLOCKED
BY PROCESS B. PROCESS A                 BY PROCESS A. PROCESS B
CANNOT UNLOCK RIN 1 WHILE               CANNOT UNLOCK RIN 2 WHILE
BEING BLOCKED                           BEING BLOCKED
```

Example 2-6. Deadlock.

In Example 2-6, Process A successfully locks global RIN 1, then attempts to lock global RIN 2 (already locked by Process B). Process A is blocked until it can successfully lock global RIN 2. While Process A is blocked, it cannot unlock global RIN 1, thus making global RIN 1 unavailable for locking by Process B.

Process B, meanwhile, has locked global RIN 2 and has been blocked attempting to lock global RIN 1 (locked, or course, by Process A). Global RIN 2 remains unavailable to Process A.

Both Process A and Process B find themselves mutually blocked and in the state of deadlock. Even if subsequent code in both program files unlocks one or both global RINs, neither process can execute that code.

One way to avoid deadlocks is by ranking the RINs used by cooperating processes. In Example 2-5, cooperating processes agree to first attempt to lock RIN 1 before attempting to lock RIN2. In addition, the processes that have successfully locked both RINs agree to unlock the two RINs in the reverse order, first RIN 2, then RIN 1. Because cooperating processes must lock RINs in ascending order and unlock them in descending order, deadlock cannot occur.

If you have only standard user capabilities and deadlock occurs between two or more processes in your program's process structure, you must abort your program to resolve the deadlock.

If you have Multiple RIN (MR) Capability and deadlock occurs between your program and processes located in different jobs/sessions, you must immediately contact your System Manager to resolve the deadlock.

1.14.1 Deadlock Vs Starvation

Starvation occurs when a process wait for a resource that continuously becomes available but is never assigned to that process because of priority or a flow in the design of the scheduler. There are two major differences between deadlocks & starvation.

1. In starvation, it is not certain that a process will ever get the required resources, whereas a deadlocked process is permanently blocked because the required resource never becomes available.
2. In starvation the resources under contention is in continuous use, where as this not true in a dead lock. Starvation is easier to take them deadlock

1.14.2 Fundamental Causes of Deadlock

The Following Four condition are necessary for deadlock to occurs in a computer system-

Execution Access: Process request exclusive access to resources.

Wait and hold: Process hold previously acquired while waiting for additional resources.

No Pre emption: A resource can not be preempted from a process with out aborting the process.

Circular Wait: There exists a set of blocked processes involved in a circular wait.

A System is in deadlock only if it satisfies all of the above conditions.

1.15 MODELS OF DEADLOCKS

Depending upon the type of resources requests of processes, there are four Types of deadlocks. For example –a process may request and need only one resourse, many resources or a few of many resources. Deadlock models are distinguished by the type of request. The type of request models are-

- Single unit request model.
- The AND request model.
- The OR request model.

- The AND-OR request model.
- The P. out of Q model.

These models are represents a broad spectrum of systems and applications and have different conditions for deadlocks.

1.15.1 Single Unit Request Model

The single unit request model is the simplest request model since a Process is restricted to requesting only one unit of a resource at a time. Thus in this model, the out degree of nodes in the wait for graph is 1. A deadlock in this model corresponds to cycle in the wait for graph, provided that there is only one unit of every resource in the system.

1.15.2 And Request Model

In the AND Request model, a Process can simultaneously request multiple resources and if remains blocked until it is grated all of the requested resources. Clearly , the single unit request model is a special case of AND request model. The AND request model is more powerful and allow more concurrently as a process can request several resources simultaneously rather than requesting resources one by one.

The out degree of nodes in the wait for graph can be greater than one in this model. A dead lock in this model corresponds to a cycle in the wait for graph provided that there is only one copy of resources on the system.

1.15.3 OR-request Model

In the OR-request model a process can simultaneously request multiple resources and it remains blocked until it is granted any one of the requested resources. The single until request model is also a special case of the OR request model. The OR request model is more flexible than the single unit request model.

A cycle in the wait for graph is not a sufficient condition for a dead lock in an OR request model, even if there is only one copy of each resource in the system. The presence of a knot the wait for graph is a sufficient condition for dead lock. A knot is a subset of a graph, such that starting from any node in the subset, it is impossible to leave the knot by following the edges of the graph.

1.15.4 And-or Request Model

The AND-OR Request model is a generalized of the AND and OR request models. In the AND-OR request model, process request are specified by using a predicate whose items or variables are the resources. For example, a request "R1 and (R2 or R3)" can be satisfied with either R1 and R2 or R1 and R3 . a knot is a wait for graph is a sufficient condition for a deadlock in the AND-OR request model.

1.15.5 P out of Q Request Model

In the P out of Q request model, a process simultaneously request Q resources and remains blocked until it is granted any P of these resources. When P = Q it is the and request model. A knot in the wait for graph is a sufficient condition for a deadlock in the P out Q request model.

1.16 MODELS OF RESOURCES

The modeling of resources is important in understanding deadlocks because processes interact with each other by requesting and blocking for resources. A resource is any object that processes can request and wait for. Processes can requests of any numbers of identical units of resource.

Types of resources

1.16.1 Reusable Resources

A reusable resource does not vanish as a result of its use but can be used over and over again. In a system a reusable resource has a fixed number of units and these units can neither be created nor destroyed. A process requests a unit, hold it during usage and then release it on completion of usage the units of reusable resource can then be assigned to another waiting process if any example- CPU, main memory, I/O devices.

1.16.2 Consumable Resources

A consumable resource vanishes as a result of its use. When a unit of consumable resources is allocated to a process, it is consumed and eases top exit. There is no fixed number of units of a consumable resource in a system, since the resource units can be created & consumed. There are one or more producers of a consumable resource. When a procedure of a resource is not blocked, it can produce any number of units of that resource. Example, messages, interrupts signals & the +v operations in semaphores.

1.17 TYPES OF RESOURCE ACCESS:

A resource can be access in two modes

- Exclusive access mode.
- Shared access mode.

1.17.1 Exclusive access mode

In the exclusive access mode, a resource can be accessed by only one process at a time. Two or more processes can not simultaneously access a resource in the exclusive access mode.

1.17.2 Shared access mode

In the shared access mode, a resource can be accessed by any number of processes simultaneously.

Note: Exclusive & shared access modes are mutually incompatible i. e. a resource can not be accesses in both simultaneously.

1.18 A GRAPH THEORETIC MODEL OF A SYSTEM STATE:

A general resource system is characterized by the following entities-

A nonempty set of processes

T T = { P1, P2,...........Pn}

A nonempty set of resources

T = { R1, R2,...........Rn}

A T can be partitioned into two disjoint set Tr a set of reusable resources and Tc a set of consumable resources.

- For every reusable resource Ri, there exits a non negative integer ti, denoting the total number of units of the resource presents in the syatem.
- For every consumable resource Ri there exits a non empty subset of processes of T T called the produces of Ri

1.18.1 General Resource Graph

The state of a system is modeled by a direct graph whose nodes correspond to rocesses and whose edges represent interaction among these processes and resources. A process is denoted by a rectangle and resource by a circle, A consumable resource is denoted by a thick line circle.

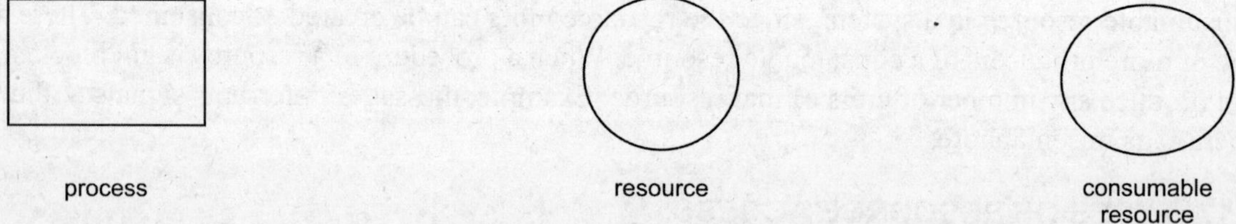

A general resource graph is a bipartite directed graph, whose disjoint set of nodes are Đ = {P1,P2, ...Pn} and T = {R1, R2,..............Rn}. A non negative integer vector {r1, r2,...........rm} called the available units vector denotes the number of units of the resources available in any states.

An edge denoted node P to a resource node R is called request edge, it indicate that the process is requesting one unit of that resource. An edge (R, P) directed from a reusable resource R to a process node P is called an assignment edge. It indicates that the process has been assigned one unit of that resource.

An edge (R, P) directed from a consumable resources node R to a process node P is called a producer edge. It indicates that process is a procedure of that resource.

Let

(P, R) – denotes the number of outgoing edges from node P to node R.

(R, P) – denotes the number of outgoing edges from node R to node P.

(P, *) – denotes the total number of outgoing edges from node P.

(R, *) – denotes the total number of outgoing edges from node R.

A general resource graph must satisfy the following condition:

(i) For every reusable resource Ri

 # (Ri, *) d" ti

i.e. at any instant a process can not results more than total units of reusable resource.

(ii) For every consumable resource Ri

There is an edge from Ri to a process P jiff is a producer of Ri

Ri e" 0

Example

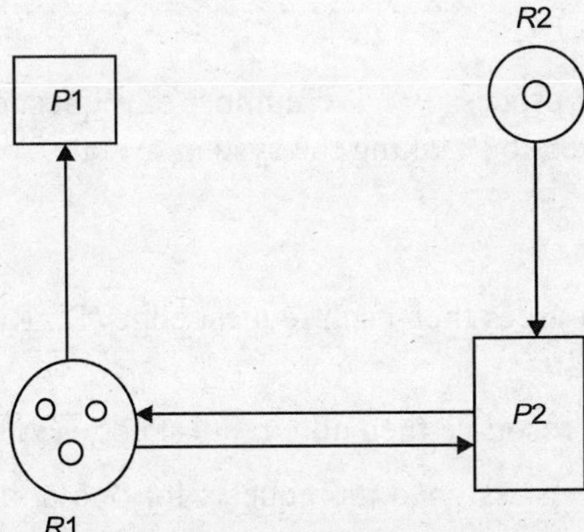

Above figure. shows the general resource graph of a state of a system with two processes and two resources. Process P1 holds one units of R1 and process P2 holds one units of R1, process P1 is active and P2 is waiting to be assigned a unit of R1. P2 is a producer of consumable resource R2 one unit of both of resources is available.

Note: a little circle inside a resource node denotes the resources units.

1.18.2 Operations on General Resource Graph

The system state and the corresponding general resource graph changes as the processes execute operations. A process can perform three operations:

- Request a resource
- Acquire a resource
- Release a resource

Request: If a process Pi is active in a state S then it can request one or more number of units of resource Rj taking the system to state T such that state T has e number of edges from node Pi to node Rj where e is the number of units of Rj requested by Pi.

Example: If P1 makes requests for one units of R1 and R2 then the resulting state is

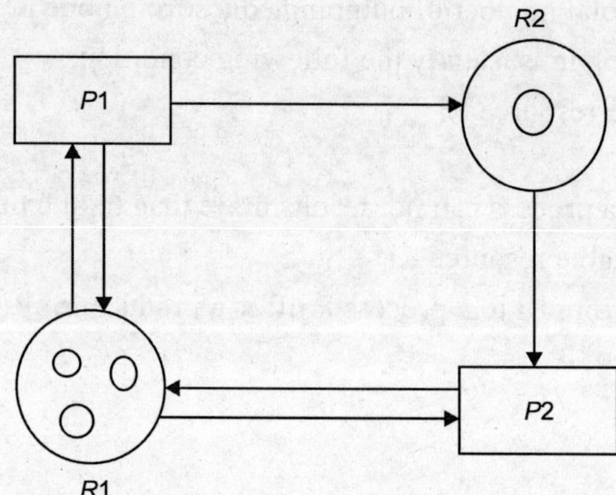

Acquisition: In state S, it a process Pi has e number of request edges to resource Rj and rj e" e then e units of Rj can be assigned to Pi taking the system to state T which is obtained from S in the following way:

(i) rj is decreased by e.

(ii) if Rj is a reusable resources then each request edge (Pi, Rj) is replaced by an assignment edge (Rj, Pi)

(iii) If Rj is a consumable resource then all e request edge (Pi, Rj) are deleted.

Example: After P1 has been assigned its requests for one units of R1 and R2 each, then the resulting state is

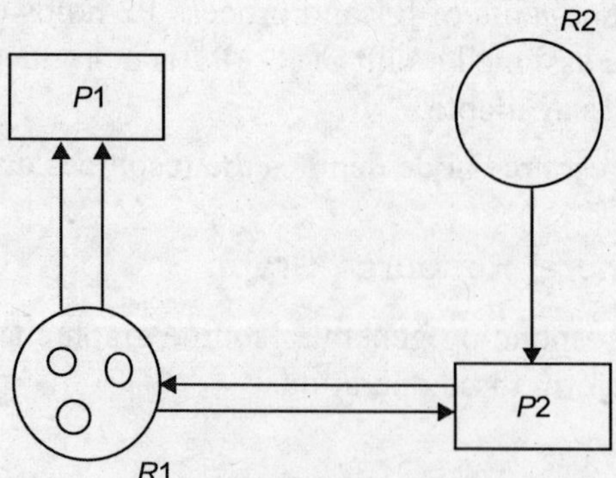

Release- If in state S, no request edges are directed from Pi and some edges are directed from Rj to Pi then Pi can system to a state T in which rj the available units of Ri are increased.

If Rj is a reusable resource then rj is incremented by a quantity equal to the number of (Rj, Pi) assignment edges deleted in T.

If Rj is a consumable resource than rj is incremented by any number of units in T (i.e. producer of rj can produce any number of units of Rj).

Example: After P1 released one units of R1

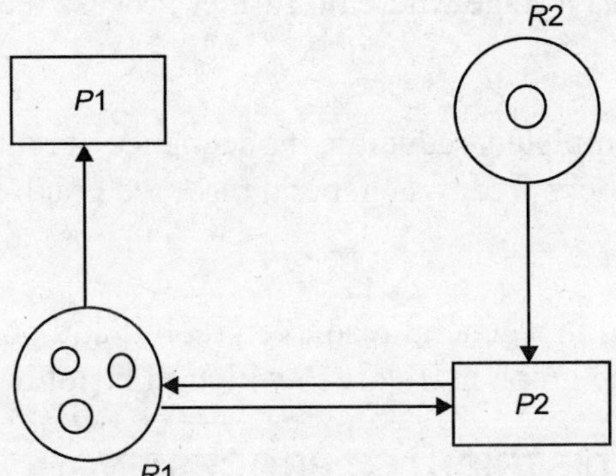

Note: If (Pi, Rj) rj process Pi blocked

1.19 NECESSARY AND SUFFICIENT CONDITION FOR A DEADLOCK

A blocked process is not dead locked if and only if we can find a sequence of operations that leaves the process unlocked. A blocked process is deadlocked if and only if there is no way for it to become unblocked. A graph reduction method corresponds to the best possible set of operations that can be executes in a system to unblock the blocked process. The graph reduction method is an optimistic method since it assumes that a process does not make additional request for a resource.

If a process for a resource as a request of the graph reduction method, it means that in the current state, the process is not involved in a deadlock. If a process can not be made unblocked by the graph reduction method, then the process is deadlocked in the current state.

1.19.1 Graph Reduction Method

A general resource graph can be reduced in the following way by a process Pi, whch is not blocked—

(i) For each reusable resource Rj, detects all edges (Pi, Rj) and (Rj, Pi) from the graph. For each assignment edge (Rj, p) deleted increase rj by one.

(ii) For each consumable resource Rj

- Decrement rj by the number of edges (Pi, Rj)
- If Pi is a producer of Rj, then set rj to á.
- Delete all edges (Pi, Rj) and (Rj, Pi)

After a general resource graph has been reduced by a process, some additional resources are freed. Consequently more processes become unblocked, which can then be used in the next reduction and so on. In general, the final outcome depends on the sequence in which the processes have been reduced. The final outcome can be one of the following:

– All the processes are reduced.

– The graph reaches a stage where no further process reduction is possible.

Definition

A general resource graph is completely reducible if a sequence of reductions deletes all edges in the graph. A system state is deadlocks free if its general resource graph is completely reducible.

Theorem

A process Pi is not deadlocked in a general resource graph if and only if a sequence of reductions applied to that graph leaves the graph in a state in which Pi is not blocked.

1.20 INTRODUCTION TO DISTRIBUTED PROCESSING

A variety of computer systems that use more than one computer, or processor, to run an application. This includes parallel processing, in which a single computer uses more than one CPU to execute programs. More often, however, distributed processing refers to local-area networks (LANs) designed so that a single program can run simultaneously at various sites. Most distributed processing systems contain sophisticated software that detects idle CPUs on the network and parcels out programs to utilize them.

Another form of distributed processing involves distributed databases, databases in which the data is stored across two or more computer systems. The database system keeps track of where the data is so that the distributed nature of the database is not apparent to users.

The term distributed system is used to describe a system with the following characteristics. It consists of several computers that do not share a memory or clock. The computers communicate with each other by exchanging messages over a communication network and each computer has its own memory and run its own operating system.

1.20.1 What is Distributed Processing?

The distribution of applications and business logic across multiple processing platforms. Distributed processing implies that processing will occur on more than one processor in order for a transaction to be completed. In other words, processing is distributed across two or more machines and the processes are most likely not running at the same time, i.e. each process performs part of an application in a sequence. Often the data used in a distributed processing environment is also distributed across platforms.

The resources owned and controlled by a computer are said to be local to it, while the resources owned and controlled by other computers and those that can only be accessed through the network are said to be remote. Accessing remote resources is more expensive than accessing local resources because of the communication delay that occur in the network & the CPU overhead incurred to process communication protocols. Distributed system divided into two parts—

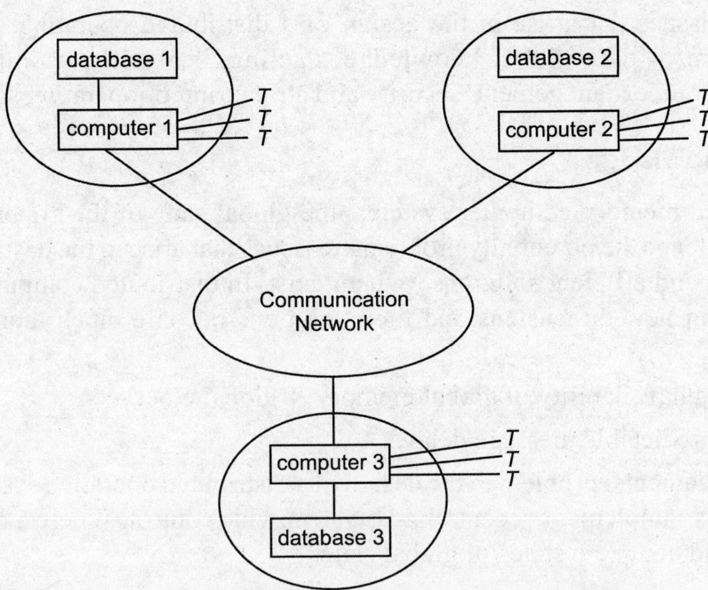

Fig 1.8 Architecture of Distributed System

- Distribution
- Logical correlation

In this there are two types of transactions—

1. Local transaction
2. Global transaction

1.20.2 Distribution

In distributed system this is the fact that the data are not resident at the same site or processes so that we can use distinguish a distributed system from a single centralized system. In distributed system the data are distributed on number of processes or site, the use remote information or data

1.20.3 Logical Correlation

In distributed system since the data are distributed on the different site, so to make accessible remote data, it is necessary or fact that the data reside on different sites must have logical correlation.

1.21 ISSUES IN DISTRIBUTED SYSTEM

A distributed operating system extends the concepts of resource management and user friendly interface for shared memory computers a step further: A distributed operating system appears to its users as a centralized operating system for a size machine but it runs on multiple independent computers. An identical copy of the operating system may run at every computer.

The important issues that arise in the design of a distributed operating system include the unavailability of up to date global knowledge, naming, scalability, compatibility, process synchronization, resource management, security and structuring of operating system.

1.21.1 Global Knowledge

In the case of shared memory computer systems, the global state of the system is completely & accurately known. Hence the potentially problematic issues that arise in the design of these systems are well understood and efficient solutions to them exist. In distributed computing systems, these same issues takes on new dimensions and their solutions become much more complex for the following reason—

(i) Due to the unavailability of global memory & global clock.

(ii) Due to unpredictable message delay.

Therefore a fundamental problem in the design of a distributed operating system is to determine efficient techniques to implement decentralized system wide control. Where a computers does not know the current and complete states of global state.

1.21.2 Naming

Names are used to refer to objects. Objects that can be named in computer system include computers, printers, services files and users. An example of a service is a name service. A name service maps a logical name into a physical address by making use of a table look up, an algorithm or through a combination of two. In the implementation of a table look up, tables are used for mapping names to their addresses.

In the distributed systems, the directories may be replicated and store at many different locations to overcome a single point increase the availability of name services. The two main draw backs of replication are:

(i) It requires more storage capacity.

(ii) Synchronization requirements need to be meet when directories are updated, as the directory at each location would need an updated copy.

Another issue in naming is the method of naming objects such that an object can be located irrespective of its logical name.

1.21.3 Scalability

System generally grows with time. The techniques used in designing a system would not result in the system unavailability or degrades performance when growth occurs. Example—broadcast based protocols work well for small systems but not for large system. As the number of users increase and system gets larger, the number of file location queerness will increase & overhead will grow larger as well, hurting the performance of every computer. In general, any design approach in which the requirement of a scare resources increases linearly in the system, is likely to be too costly to implement.

1.21.4 Compatibility

Compatibility refers to the notion of interoperability among the resources in a system. The three different levels of compatibility that exit in distributed system are—

- Binary level
- Execution level
- Protocol level

In a system that is compatible at the binary level, all processors execute the same binary instruction even though the processors may differ in performance and in input- output. A significant advantage of binary level compatibility is that it is easier for system development. Execution level compatibility is said to exist in a distributed system if the sane source code can be compiled and executed properly on any computer in the system.

Protocol level compatibility is the least restrictive form of compatibility. It achieves interoperability by requiring all system components to support a common set of protocols. A significant advantage of protocol level compatibility is that individual computers can run different operation system while not sacrificing their interoperability.

1.21.5 Process Synchronization

The synchronization of processes in distributed systems is difficult because of the unavailability of shared memory. A distributed system has to synchronize processes running at different computers when they try to concurrently access a shared resource such as file directory. For correctness, it is necessary that the shared resource be accessed by a single at a time.

1.21.6 Resource Management

Resource management in distributed system is concerned with making both and remote resources available to users in an effective manner. Users of a distributed operating system should be able to access remote resources as easily as they can access local resources. In other words, the specific location of resources should be hidden from the users. The resource of a distributed operating system are made available to users in following ways—

- Data migration
- Computation migration
- Distributed scheduling

1.21.7 Security

The security o a system is the responsibility of its operating system. Two issues that must be considered in the design of securing for computer system are

- Authentication
- Authorization

Authentication is the process of guaranteeing that an entity is what it claims to be.

Authorization is the process of deciding what privileges an entity has and making only these privileges available.

1.22 SUMMARY

- A process is a program in execution.
- Process includes the program counter and number of registers.
- Two processes are said to be concurrent if their execution can overlap in time.
- A situation where several process access and manipulate the same data concurrently and outcomes of the execution depends on particular order in which the access take place is called race condition.
- A Semaphore S is an integer variable which can be accessed to two standard atomic functions wait (s), signal (s).
- A deadlock is a situation where a process or a set of processes is blocked; waiting an event that will never occurs.
- Starvation occurs when a process wait for a resource that is continuously become available but is never assigned to that process because of Priority or a flow in the design of a scheduler.
- Starvation is easier to tackle than deadlock.
- A reusable resource does not vanish as a result of its use but can be used over and over again.
- A consumable resource vanishes as a result of its use.
- In Exclusive access mode, a resource can be accessed only by one process at a time.
- In shared access mode, a resource can be accessed only by any number of processes at a time simultaneously.
- A graph reduction method corresponds to the best possible set of operations that can be executed in a system to unblock the blocked process.
- A general resource graph is completely reducible if a sequence of reductions deletes all the edges in the graph.
- A distributed system consists of several computers that do not share a memory or clock.
- In distributed system, the computers communicate with each other by exchanging messages over a communication network.
- Names are used to refer to objects.
- A name service maps a logical name into a physical address.
- Compatibility refers to the notion of interpretability among the resources in the system.

1.23 REVIEW QUESTIONS

1. Explain concept of process and its state.
2. What do you mean by concurrent process explain with examples.
3. What do you mean by process synchronization? Explain it with critical section problem.
4. Explain the term process deadlock and differentiate deadlock with starvation.
5. Explain models of deadlock & models of resources.
6. Explain types of resources access.
7. Discuss a graph theoretic model of system state.
8. Discuss the necessary band sufficient condition for a deadlock.
9. Explain distributed processing & discuss the terms distribution and logical correlation.
10. write short notes on
    (i) Global knowledge
    (ii) Naming
    (iii) Scalability
    (iv) Compatibility
    (v) Process synchronization
    (vi) Resources management
    (vii) Security

CHAPTER 2

Limitation of Distributed System

2.1 LIMITATION OF DISTRIBUTED SYSTEM

The distributed systems also have the limitations. The internet limitations of a distributed system are as following

- Absence of a Global Clock
- Absence of Shared Memory

2.1.1 Absence of a Global Clock

In a distributed system, there exists No system wide common clock or global clock. The limitation problem can not be solved by having common clock or by having synchronized clock. The reason are if a global clock is available for all processes in the system, in that case two different process can observe a global clock value at different instance due to unpredictable message information delay, therefore two different process may falsely perceives two different instance in simple time to bear single instance.

On the other hand, if we provide each computer in the system a physical clock and try to synchronize them, these physical clocks can drift from the physical time and drift rate may vary from clock to clock due to the technological limitation. So again to process running at different computers may perceives two different instances in physical time as a single instance. So the absence of global clock makes it harder to collect updatable information on the state of the system.

2.1.2 Absence of Shared Memory

The computers in distributed system do not share common memory. So an up to date state of the entire system is not available to any individual process because an up to state of system is necessary for reasoning about the system behavior, debugging, discovery from failures.

A process in distributed system can obtain a coherent but partial view of the system or complete but incoherent view of the system. A view is said to be coherent if the all the observations of different processes are made at the same physical time. A complete view encompasses the local view at all the computers and any messages that are in transit in the distributed system. A complete view is also referred to as global state. The global state of the distributed computation encompasses the local states of all the processes and any messages that are in transit between the processes.

2.2 LAMPORTS LOGICAL CLOCK

Lamport proposed the following schemes to order events in a distributed system using logical clocks. The execution processes is characterized by sequence of events. Due to the absence of perfectly synchronized clocks and global time in distributed systems, the order in which two events occur at two different computers can not be determined based on the local time at which they occur. However, under certain condition, it is possible to ascertain the order in which two events occur based on the behavior exhibited by the underlying computation.

Happened before Relation (→)

The happened before relation capture the casual dependencies between events i.e. whether two events are casually related or not

- a →b, if a and b are events in the same process and a occurred before b.
- a → b, if a is the event of sending a message m in a process and b is the event of reaccept of the sane message m by another process.
- If a → b, b →c

  Then a → c

  i.e. relation is transitive

Casually related Events

Event a casually affects event b

If a → b

Concurrent Events

Two distinct events a and b are said to be concurrent if

a /→b, b/→a

2.2.1 Logical clocks

In order to realize the → relation, Lamport introduced the following system of clocks. There is a clock Ci at each process Pi in the system. The clock Ci can be thought of as a function that assign number Ci(a) to any event a called the timestamp of event a at Pi. The numbers assigned by the system of time and hence the name logical clock. The logical clock takes monitory Increasing values. These clocks can be implemented by the counts.

2.2.2 Conditions Satisfied by System of Clocks

For any events a and b

If a → b then

C(a) < C(b)

The happened before relation→ can now be realized using the logical clocks if the following two conditions are met

C1 for any events a and b in a process Pi if a occurs before b, then

Ci(a) < Ci(b)

C2 if a is the event of sending a message m in process Pi, and b is the event of receiving the same message m at process Pi then

Ci(a) < Ci(b)

The following implementation rules (IR) for the clocks guarantee that the clocks satisfy the correctness conditions C1 and C2:

IR1 clock Ci is incremented between any two successive events in process Pi

Ci = Cied (d>0)

i.e. if a and b are two successive events in Pi and aàb then

Ci(b) = Ci(a) + d

IR2 if event a is the sending of massage m by process Pi then message m is assigned a timestamp

Tm = Ci(a)

On receiving the same message m by process Pj, Cj is the set of its present value & greater than Tm

Cj = max (Cj, Tm = d), d>0

Where Ci is calculated from IR1.

Lamports happened before relation → defines an irreflexive partial order among the events. The set of all the events in a distributed computation can be totally ordered using the above system of clocks as follows:

If a is any event at process Pi and b is any event at process Pj then

a => b if and only if

either Ci(a) < Cj(b)

or Ci(a) = Cj(b) and Pi <.. Pj

where <.. is any arbitrary relation that totally orders the processes to break tie.

Note: A simple way to implement <.. is ton assign unique identification on number to each process and then

Pi <.. Pj if i<j

Example:

Find the Lamport clock value

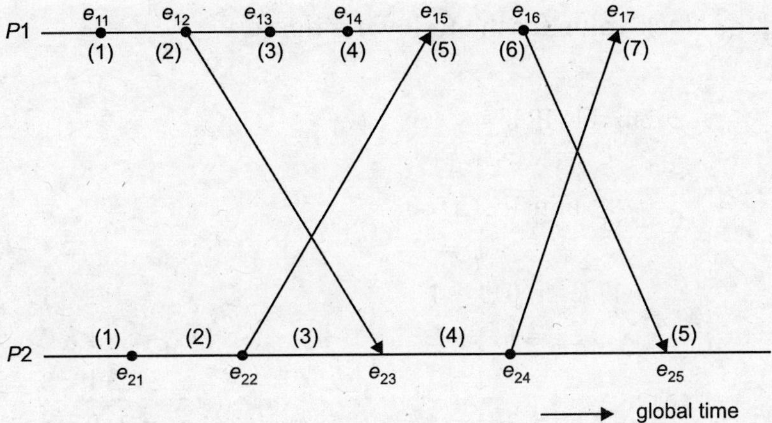

Solution:

From rule IR1

$e_{11} = 1$

$e_{12} = 1+1 = 2$

$e_{13} = 2+1 = 3$

$e_{14} = 3+1 = 4$

$e_{15} = 4+1 = 5$

$e_{16} = 5+1 = 6$

$e_{17} = 6+1 = 7$

$e_{21} = 1, e_{22} = 2$

$e_{23} = 3$

$e_{24} = 4$

$e_{25} = 5$

From rule IR2

$Cj = \max(Cj, Tm+d)$

For event e_{15}

$Cj = \max(4+1, 2+1)$

$= 5$

For event e_{23}

$Cj = \max(2+1, 2+1)$

$= 3$

For event e_{17}

$Cj = \max(6+1, 4+1)$

$= 7$

For event e_{25}

$Cj = \max(4+1, 6+1)$

$= 7$

Example: Find the clock value for the following figure

Solution:

From rule IR1

$Ci = Ci + a$

Initially $Ci = 0$

$D = 1$

$e_{11} = 0+1 = 1$ $e_{21} = 0+1 = 1$

$e_{12} = 1+1 = 2$ $e_{22} = 1+1 = 2$

$e_{13} = 2+1 = 3$ $e_{23} = 2+1 = 3$

$e_{14} = 3+1 = 4$ $e_{24} = 3+2 = 4$

$e_{15} = 4+1 = 5$

$e_{16} = 5+1 = 6$

$e_{17} = 6+1 = 7$

From rule IR2

For event e_{17}

$Cj = \max (Cj, Tm+d)$

$= \max (6+1, 3+1)$

$= 7$

For event e_{24}

$Cj = \max (Cj, Tm=d)$

$= \max (3+1, 5+1)$

$= 6$

2.3 VIRTUAL TIME

Lamports system of logical clocks implements an approximation to global/physical time, which is referred to as virtual time. If no events occur in the system virtual time stops, unlike physical time which continuously programs. Therefore to wait for a virtual time instant to pass is risks as it may never occur.

2.4 LIMITATION OF LAMPORTS CLOCK

$$\text{If } a \rightarrow b$$

$$\text{Then } C(a) < C(b)$$

However, the reverse is not necessarily true, if the events are occurred in different processes i.e. if a and b are events in different processes and C(a) < C(b) then aàb is not necessarily true. Events a and b may be casually related or may not be casually related.

Example:

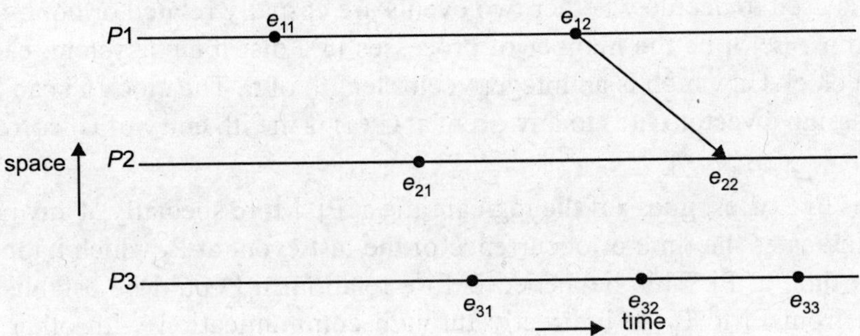

Find the casual relationships between events and given reason

Solution:

From rule IR1

$e_{11} = 0+1 = 1$

$e_{12} = 1+1 = 2$

$e_{21} = 0+1 = 1$

$e_{22} = 1+1 = 2$

$e_{31} = 0+1 = 1$

$e_{32} = 1+1 = 2$

$e_{33} = 2+1 = 3$

From rule IR2

For event e_{22}

$e_{22} = \max(1+1, 2+1)$

$= 3$

$C(e11) < C(e_{22})$

$e_{11} \rightarrow e_{22}$

because $e_{11} \rightarrow e_{12}$

$e_{12} \rightarrow e_{22} \Rightarrow e_{11} \rightarrow e_{22}$

$C(e_{11}) < C(e_{32})$

But we can not say e_{11} is casually related to e_{32} because there is no path between e_{11} and e_{32}c

Note: Using the timestamps assigned by Lamports clocks, we can not reason about the casual relationship between two events occurring in different process by just looking at the timestamps of the events.

2.5 VECTOR CLOCK

This technique is used to decide whether two events are casually related or not by simply looking at their timestamps. Let **n** be the number of processes in a distributed system, each process Pi is equipped with a clock Ci, which is an integer vector length of **n**. The clock Ci can be thought of as a function that assign a vector Ci(a) to any event a. Ci(a) is the ith entry of Ci corresponds to Pi on logical time.

Ci(i), j != i is Pi.... Best guess of the logical time at Pj. More specially at any point in time, the jth entry of Ci indicates the time of occurrence of the last event at Pj which happened before the current point in time at Pj. This happened before relationship could be established directly by communication from Pi to Pj or indirectly through communication with other processes. The implementation rule for the vector clocks are as follows

IR1 clock Ci is incremented between any two successive events in process Pi

$$Ci(i) = Ci(i) + d \qquad (d>0)$$

IR2 if event a is the sending of the message m is assigned a vector timestamp

$$Tm = Ci(a)$$

on receiving the same message m by process Pi, Cj is updated as follows

for all (V).... k , Cj(k) = max (Cj(k), Tm(k))

i.e. on the receipt of message, a process learn about the more recent clock values of the rest of the processes in the system.

Note: In the rule IR1, we treat message send and message receives by a process as events. In rule IR2 , a message is assigned a timestamp after the sender process has incremented its clock value due to IR1 If it is necessary to allow for propagation time for a message then IR2 can be performed after the following step

If Cj(i) <= Tm(i) then

Cj(i) != Tm(i) + d $\qquad$ (d>0)

Example: Find the vector function

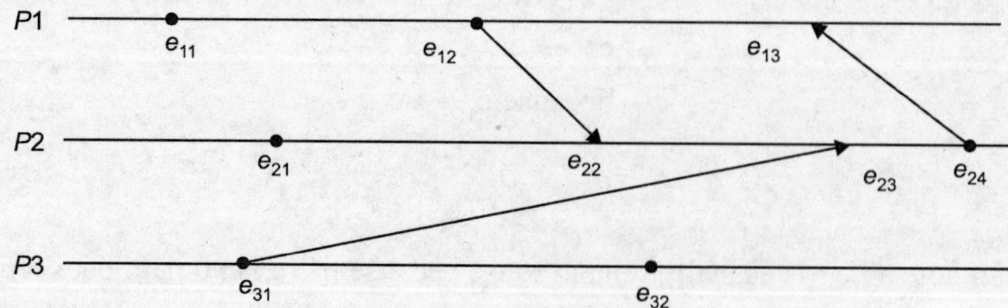

Solution:

By the IR1 for first event of all process is written as

$Ci(i) = Ci(i) + d$

Initially $Ci(i) = 0$ $d = 1$

For $Ci(i) = 0+1 = 1$

So vector function of $e_{11} = (1, 0, 0)$

Similarly for event e_{21}

$C_2(2) = 0+1 = 1$

Vector function = (0, 1, 0)

Foe event e_{31}

$C_3(3) = 0+1 = 1$

Vector function = (0, 0, 1)

From the rule IR2

For event e_{12}

$Ci(2) = 1+1 = 2$

Vector function = (2, 0, 0)

For event e_{22}

$Cj(k) = \max (Cj(k), Tm(k))$

$C_2(1) = \max (C_2(1), 2)$

$= \max (0, 2) = 2$

Vector function = (0, 2, 0)

For event e_{23}

$C_2(3) = \max (C_2(3), 1)$

$= \max (0,1) = 1$

Vector function = (2, 3, 1)

Vector function of e_{24} = (2, 4, 1)

For event e_{13}

$C_1(2) = \max (C_1(2), tm)$

$= \max (0, 4) = 4$

Vector function of e_{13}

= (3, 4, 1)

Example: Find the vector function

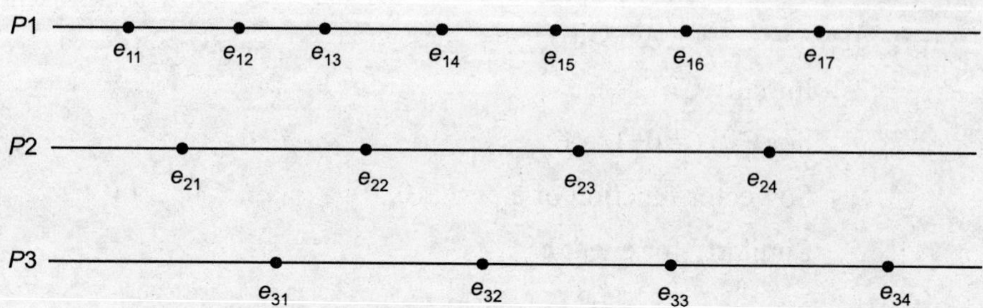

Solution:

By rule IR1 for first events of all process

all processes	vector functions
$C_{11} = 0+1 = 1$	(1, 0, 0)
$C_{12} = 0+1 = 1$	(0, 1, 0)
$C_{31} = 0+1 = 1$	(0, 0, 1)
$C_{12} = 1+1 = 2$	(2, 0, 0)
$C_{13} = 2+1 = 3$	(3, 0, 0)
$C_{14} = 3+1 = 4$	(4, 0, 0)
$C_{15} = 4+1 = 5$	(5, 0, 0)
$C_{16} = 5+1 = 6$	(6, 0, 0)
$C_{17} = 6+1 = 7$	(7, 0, 0)
$C_{22} = 1+1 = 2$	(0, 2, 0)
$C_{23} = 2+1 = 3$	(0, 3, 0)
$C_{24} = 3+1 = 4$	(0, 4, 0)
$C_{32} = 1+1 = 2$	(0, 0, 2)
$C_{33} = 2+1 = 3$	(0, 0, 3)
$C_{34} = 3+1 = 4$	(0, 0, 4)

For rule IR2

For event e_{23}

$$C_2(1) = \max(C_2(1), tm)$$
$$= \max(0, 4) = 4$$

Vector function = (4, 3, 0)

Vector function of e_{24} = (4, 4, 0)

For event e_{16}

$$C_1(2) = \max(C_1(2), tm)$$
$$= \max(0, 4) = 4$$

Vector function of e_{16} = (6, 4, 0)
Vector function of e_{17} = (7, 4, 0)
For event e_{32}

$$C_3(2) = \max(C_3(2), tm)$$
$$= \max(0, 2) = 2$$

Vector function of e_{32} = (0, 2, 2)
Vector function of e_{33} = (0, 2, 3)
Vector function of e_{34} = (0, 2, 4)
Now for event e_{17}

$$C_1(3) = \max(C_1(3), Tm)$$
$$= \max(0, 4) = 4$$

So vector function of e_{17}

$$= (7, 4, 4)$$

2.6 CASUAL ORDERING OF MESSAGES

The casual ordering of messages deals with notion of marinating the same casual relationships that hold among 'message send events with the corresponding 'message receive events.

If send (M1) $\rightarrow$ send (M2)

Where send (M) is the event of sending message M.

Then every recipient of both messages M1 and M2 must receive M1 before M2, the casual ordering of messages should not be confused with the casual ordering of events. In a distributed system, the casual ordering of messages is not automatically guaranteed.

Techniques for the casual ordering of message are useful in developing distributed algorithms and may simply the algorithms themselves. For example, like application such as replicated database system, it is important that every process in charge of updating a replication receives the updates in same order, to maintain the consisting of the database. In the absence of casual ordering of message, each and every update must be checked to ensure that it does not violate the consistency constraints.

Example: Examples of the violation of casual ordering of message are

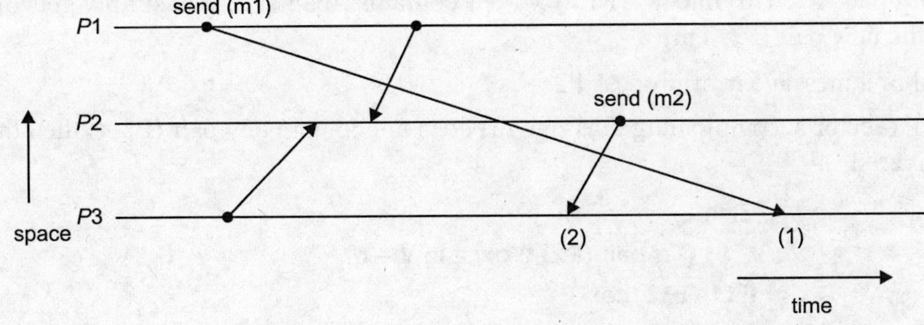

The two protocols that make use of vector clocks for the casual ordering of message in distributed systems.

2.6.1 Birman-Schiper-Stephenson Protocol

- Before broadcasting a message M, a process Pi, increments the vector time VTPi(i) and timestamps Tm.
- A process Pj != Pi upon receiving message M timestamps VTm from Pi delays its delivery until both the following conditions are satisfied—

  (a) VTPj(i) = VTm(i)-1

  (b) VTPj(k) >= VTm(k)

For all..... k (- {1, 2, 3, ..., n} – (i)

Where n is the total number of process.

Delayed message are queued at each process in a queue that is sorted by vector time of the messages. Concurrent messages are ordered by the time of their receipt.

- When a message is delivered at a process Pj VTPj is updated according to the vector check rule IR2.

Since the event ordering relation '→ imposed by vector clocks is acidic, the protocol as deadlock free. The Birman-Schipper-Stephenson casual ordering protocol requires that the process communicate through broadcast messages.

2.6.2 Schiper-Eglli-Sendoz Protocol

Each process P maintains a vector denoted by V-P of size (N-1), where N is the number of processes in the system. An element of V-P is an ordered pair (p, t), where p is the id of the destination process of a message and t is a vector timestamps. The processes in the system are assumed to use vector clocks. The following notations, are used in describing the protocol

Tm = logical time at the sending of message m

Tpi = present/current logical time at process pi

Sending of a message m from process P1 to process P2:

- Send message m (timestamp Tm) along with V – P to process P2.
- Insert pair (P2, Tm) into V – P1. if V – P1 contains a pair (P2, t), it simply gets over written by the new pair (P2, Tm).

Arrival of a message m at process P2:

If V – P (vector accomplishing message m) does not contain any pair (P2, t) then the message can be delivered

Else

{* a pair (P2, t) exist in V – M *}

If t /< tP2 then

The message can not be delivered

Else

The message can be delivered

If a message m can be delivered at process P2, then the following three action are taken—

2.7 GLOBAL STATE

Due to absence of global clock and shared memory recorded data is inconsistent. In the following banking system example there was an inconsistency in data (Rs 50 was in access or loss)

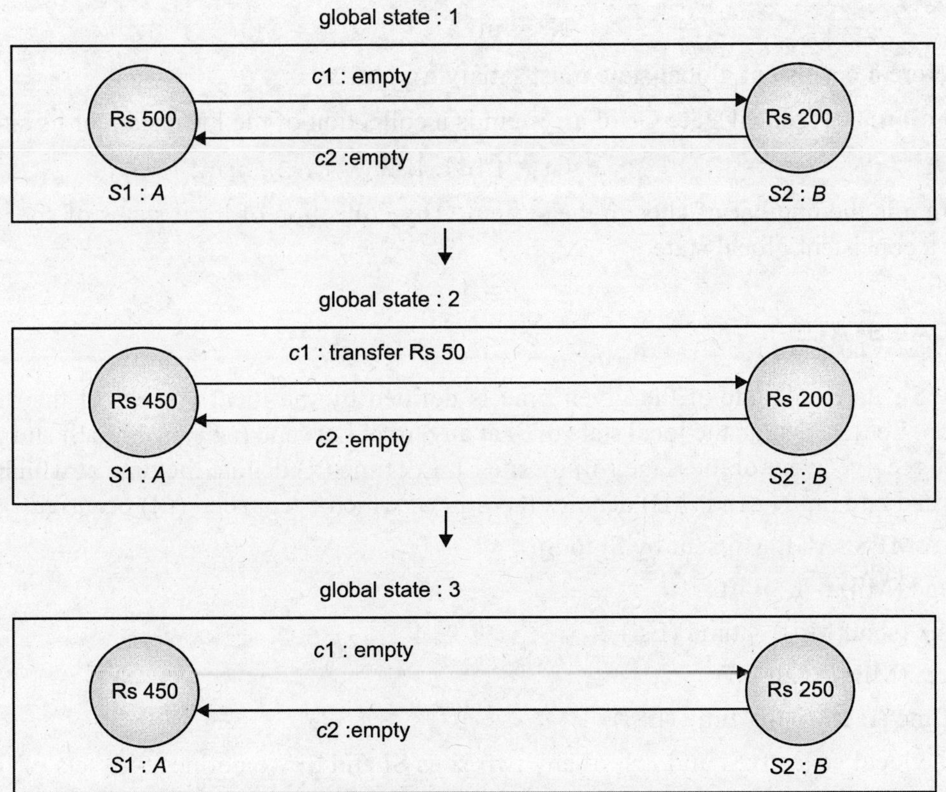

Fig. 2.1 Global state & their transition

The reason for this inconsistency is that As state recorded before the message was sent and channel Cs state was recorded after the message was sent.

Let n be the number of messages sent by A along the channel before As state was recorded and n is the number of message sent by A along the channel before channel state was recorded. The global state may be inconsistency if $n < n$ or $n > n$. Hence a consistent global state requires

$$n = n \qquad (1)$$

Let m is the number of message received along the channel by B before the channel state was recorded and m is the number of messages received along the channel before Bs state was recorded. Similarly in this case for consistent global state

m = m (2)

Since in no system the number of messages sent along the channel can be less than the number of message received along that channel

We have

n > = m (3)

From eq. (1) and eq. (3) we have

N >= m

Therefore a consistent global state must satisfy n >= m

Definition:— A global state Gs of a system is a collection of the local state of its sites.

i.e. Gs = { Ls1, Ls2,.........., Lsn }

Where n is the number of sites in the system. Any collection of local states of sites need not represent a consistent global state.

2.8 LOCAL STATE

For a site Si, its local state at the given time is defined by the local context of the distributed application. Let LSi denote the local state of Si at any time. Let send (Mij) by Si to Sj and rec. (Mij) denote the receive event of message Mij by site Sj. Let time (x) denote the time at which state (x) was recorded and time (send (M)) denotes the time at which event send (M) occurred.

FOR A MESSAGE Mij sent by Si to Sj

- Send (Mij) (- LSi iff
  time (send(Mij)) < time (Lsi)
- Rec. (Mij) (- LSi iff
  Time (rec(Mij)) < time (LSi)

For the local states L:Si and LSj of any two sites Si and Sj we defines two sets of messages. These set contains messages that were sent from Si to Sj.

Transit:

Transit (LSi, LSj)

= { Mij | send(Mij) (- LSi ^ rec(Mij) (- LSj }

Inconsistent:

Inconsistent (LSi, LSj)

'= { Mij | send(Mij) !(- LSi ^ rec(Mij) (- LSj }

Consistent Global State—

A global state Gs = { LS1, LS2,........, LSn} is consistent iff

For all... I, for all... j : 1 <= I, j < = n ::

Inconsistent (LSi, LSj) = ...

Thus, in a consistent global state, for every received message a corresponding send event is recorded in the global state. In a inconsistent global state, there is at least one message whose receive event is recorded but its send event is not recorded in the global state.

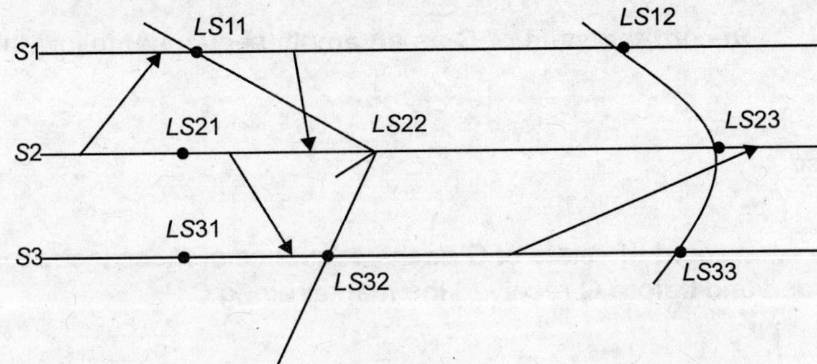

The global state {LS12, LS23, LS33} and {LS11, LS22, LS32} corresponding and inconsistent states respectively.

Transit less global state:-

A global state is transit less iff

• i, • j : 1 d" i, j d" n ::

Transit (LSi,LSj) = ϕ

Thus all communication channel are empty in a transit less global state.

Strongly Consistent global State

A global state is strongly consistent if it is consistent and transits less. In strongly consistent state, not only the send event of the recorded received events are recorded, but the receive events of all the recorded sent events are also recorded. Thus a strongly consistent state corresponds to a consistent global state in which all channel are empty. The global state in figure {LS11, LS21, LS31}is a strongly consistent global state.

2.9 CHANDY – LAMPORTS GLOBAL STATE RECORDING ALGORITHM

Algorithm: The algorithm uses a marker (a special message) to initiate the algorithm and marker has no effect on the underlying computation. The communication channels are assumed to be FIFO. The recorded global state is also referred to as a snapshot of the system state.

Marker sending rule for a process P:

- Process P recorded its state.

- For each outgoing channel C from P on which a marker has not been already C before P sends further message along C.

Marker receiving rule for a process Q:

On receipt of a marker along a channel C

If Q has not recorded its state

Then

{

record the state of C as an empty sequence, follow the marker sending rule

}

Else

{

record the state of C as the sequence of message received along C after Qs state was recorded and before Q received the marker along C

}

The global state recording algorithms can be initiated by any process by executing the marker sending rule. Also, the global state recording algorithm can be initiated by process getting its own version of a consistent global state.

2.10 TERMINATION DETECTION

A distributed computation generally consists of a set of corresponding processes which communicate with each other by exchanging massages In the case of a distributed computation, it is important to know when the computation has terminated. The problem of termination detection arises in many distributed algorithms and computations.

For examples, how to determine when an election, a deadlock detection, a deadlock resolution, or a token generating algorithm has terminated. Termination detection in fact is an example of the usage of the coherent view (consistent global state) of a distributed system.

System Model

A process may be either in an active state or idle state. Only active process can send messages. An active process may become idle at any time. An idle process can become active on receiving a computation messages. A computation is said to have terminated iff all the processes are idle and there are no messages in transit. The messages sent by the termination detection algorithm are referred to as control messages. The following notations are used in algorithm—

- B (D ω) = computation message sent as a part of the computation and D ω is the weight assigned to it.
- C (D ω) = control message sent from the processes to controlling agent and D ω is the weight assigned to it.

2.10.1 Huangs Termination Detection Algorithms

Rule 1: The controlling agent or an active process having weight ù may send a computation messages to a process P by doing

Derive ω1, and ω2 such that

$$\omega 1 + \omega 2 = \omega \qquad \omega 1 > 0 \qquad \omega 2 > 0$$

$$\omega := \omega 1;$$

Send B (ω2) to P;

Rule 2: On receipt of B (D ω), a process P having weight ù does

$$\omega := \omega + D\,\omega$$

If P is idle, P becomes active.

Rule 3: An active process having weight ù may become idle at any time by doing

Send (ù) to controlling agent;

$$\Omega := 0$$

The process become idle,

Rule 4: On receiving C (D ω), the controlling agent having weight ù takes the following actions

$$\omega := \omega + D\,\omega$$

If ω = 1,

Computation has terminated.

2.11 DISTRIBUTED MUTUAL EXCLUSIVE

The problem of mutual exclusion frequency arises, in distributed system whenever concurrent accesses to shared resources by several sites are involved. For correctness, it is required (or necessary) that the shared resources be accessed by a single site at a time.

Over the cast decode, the problem of mutual exclusion has received considerable attention and several algorithms to achieve mutual exclusion in distributed system have proposed. They tend to differ in their communication topology and in the amount of informatio9n maintained by each site about other sites. These algorithms can be group into two classes—

2.11.1 Non Token based algorithm

These algorithm required two or more successive round of message exchanges among the sites. These algorithms are assertion based because a site can never enter its critical section. Mutual exclusion is enforced because the assertion becomes true only at one at any given time.

2.11.2 Token based algorithm

In these algorithms, a unique token is shared among the sites. A site is allowed to enter its critical section if it processes the token and it continues to hold the token until the execution of the critical section is over. These algorithms essentially differ in the way a site carries out the search for the token.

2.11.3 Requirements of Mutual Exclusion

The primary objective of a mutual exclusion algorithm, is to maintain mutual exclusion i.e. to guarantee that only one request access the critical section at a time. The following characteristics are considered important in a mutual exclusion algorithms:

- **Freedom from deadlocks**: Two or more sites should not endlessly wait for messages that will never arrive.
- **Freedom from starvation**: A site should not be wait indefinitely to execute critical section while other sites are repeatedly executing critical section i.e. every requesting site should get an opportunity to execute critical section in a finite time.
- **Fairness:** Fairness dictates that request must be executed in the order they are arrive in the system. Since a physical global clock does not exit, time is determined by logical clocks Fairness imply freedom from starvation but not vice versa..
- **Fault Tolerance:**A mutual exclusion algorithm is fault tolerance if in the wake of a failure it can recognize itself so that it continues to function without any disruptions.
- **How to measure the performance:** The performance of mutual exclusion algorithm is generally measured by following four metrics:

(i) The number of message necessary per critical section invocation.

(ii) The synchronization delay, which is the time required after a site enters in the critical section and before the next site enters the critical section.

(iii) The response time which is the time interval a request waits for its critical section execution to be over after its request messages have been sent out. Thus, response time does not include the time a request waits at a site before its messages have been sent out.

(iv) The system throughput, which is the rate at which the system executes request for the critical section.

If sd is the synchronization delay and E is the average critical section execution time, then the throughput is given by—

$$\text{System throughput} = 1 / sd+E$$

2.12 LOW & HIGH LOAD PERFORMANCE

Performance of a mutual exclusion algorithm depends upon the loading conditions of the system and is often studied under two special loading conditions—

- Low load
- High load

Under low load condition, there as seldom more than one request for mutual exclusion simultaneously in the system. Under high load condition, there is always a pending request for mutual exclusion at a site.

2.13 NON TOKEN BASED ALGORITHMS

In non token based mutual exclusion algorithm, a site communicates with a set of other sites to arbitrate who should execute the critical section next. Non token based mutual exclusion algorithm use timestamps to order request for the critical section and to resolve conflict between simultaneous requests for the critical section.

In all these algorithms, logical clock are maintained and updated according to Lamports scheme. Each request for the critical section gets a timestamps, and smaller timestamps requests have priority over larger timestamps request.

(1) Lamports Algorithm

In Lamports algorithms—

¥ I : 1d"I d"N :: Ri = {S1, S2,…………,Sn}

Every site Si keeps a queue, request queue i which contains mutual exclusion requests ordered by their timestamps.

Requesting the critical section

- When a site Si wants to enter the critical section, it sends a requests (TSi, i) message to all the sites in its request set Ri and places the request on request- queue i.
- When a site Si receives the request (TSi, i) messages from site Si, it returns a timestamps REPLY message to Si and places site Sis request on request-queue j

Executing the critical section

Site Si enters the critical section when the two following conditions hold

[L1] Si has received a message with timestamps larger than (TSi, i) from all other sites.

[L2] Sis request is at the top of request-queue.

Releasing the critical section

- Site Si upon exiting the critical section, removes its request from the top of its request-queue and sends a time stamped RELEASE messages to all the sites in its request-set.
- When a site Sj receives a RELEASE messages from the site Si , it removes Sis requests from its request-queue.

When a site removes a request from its request-queue, its own request may come at the top of the queue, enabling it to enter the critical section. Te algorithm executes critical section requests in the increasing order of timestamps.

Performance Lamports algorithm requires 3(N–1) messages per critical section invocation (N–1) request, (N–1) reply, and (N–1) release messages. N is the number of sites.

2.14 CHARACTERIZATION OF DISTRIBUTED SYSTEM

A distributed system is one in which components located at networked computers communicates and coordinate their actions only by passing messages the sharing of resources is a main motivation for constructing distributed system. Resources may be managed by servers and accesses by clients or they may be encapsulated as objects and accessed by other client object. We define a distributed system as a collection of autonomous computers linked by a network, with software designed to produce an integrated computing facility.

What others think about distributed systems

- A distributed system is one that stops you from getting any work done whenever a machine you ve never even heard of crashes.
- A distributed system is a collection of autonomous computers linked by a network, with software designed to produce an integrated computing facility.

The characteristics of distributed systems are:

- Resource sharing
- Openness
- Concurrency
- Scalability
- Redundancy
- Modularity
- Integration

Object oriented programming is usually used to program distributed systems. The real challenge of distributed system is to design the architecture of a distributed system and to model the software in order to get a system that guarantees the required quality of service.

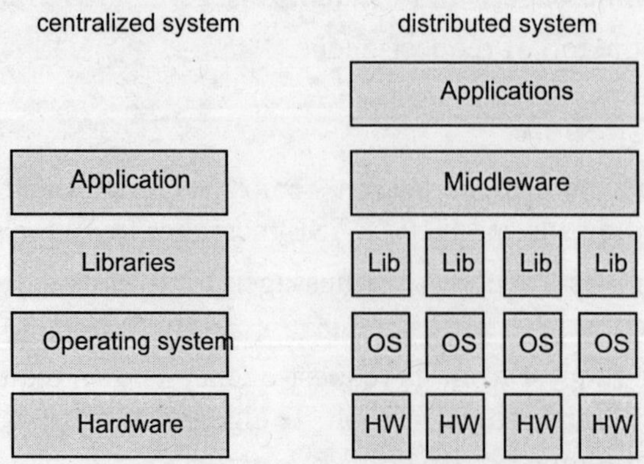

Fig. 2.2 Centralized and distributed systems

Computers that are connected by network may be spatially separated by any distance. They may be on separate continents. The motivation for constructing and using distributed system stems from a desire to share resources. The term resource is a rather abstract one, but it best characterizes the range of things that can usefully be shared in a networked computer system.

2.14.1 Resource Sharing

Users of centralized and distributed systems are so accustomed to the benefits of resource sharing that they may easily overlook their importance:

- Hardware sharing: Printers, plotters and large disks and other peripherals are shared to reduce costs.
- Data sharing is important in many applications
- Software developers working in a team need to access each others code and share the same development tools.
- Many commercial applications enable users to access shared data objects in a single active database.
- The rapidly growing area of *group-ware tools* enables users to cooperate within a network.

Resources of a multi-user system are shared between all of its users. But users of a networked workstation or a personal computer do not automatically gain the benefits of resource sharing. Resources in a distributed system are encapsulated within one computer and can only be accessed from other computers by communication. For effective sharing each resource must be managed by a program called *resource manager* offering a communication interface enabling the resource being accessed, manipulated and updated consistently and reliably. There are two interesting models for distributing systems: the *client-server* model and the *object* model.

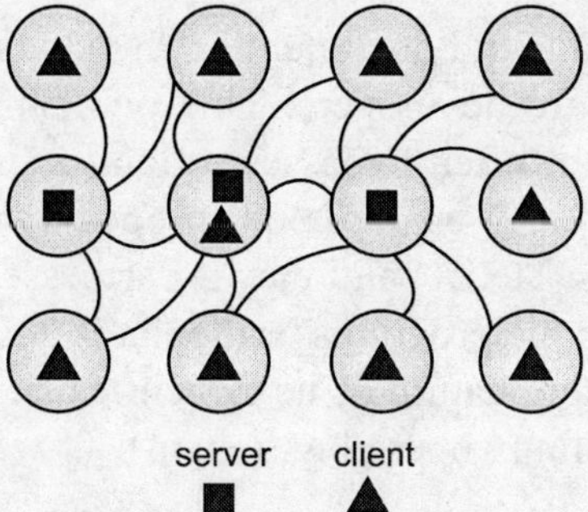

Fig. 2.3 client-server

The *client-server* model is actually the best known and the most widely-adapted model for distributed systems. The executing software is split into separate processes: *clients* ans *servers*. Servers provide services and the clients use these services. Clients usually initiate the communication with a server, whereas the servers passively wait. Servers typically may serve many clients. The clients must not be aware of the location of the servers. Typical examples are:

- nfs servers
- database servers
- WEB servers

In the object model, every entity in a running program is viewed as an object with a message-handling interface providing access to its operations. In the object based model for distributed systems, each shared resource is an object. Objects are uniquely identified and may be moved anywhere in the network without changing their identities. This simple and flexible model is illustrated in Fig. 2.4.

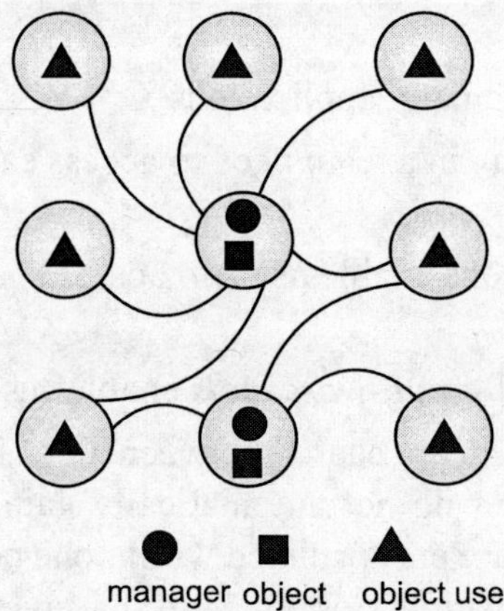

Fig. 2.4: objects and managers

2.14.2 Openness

Openness is achieved by specifying and documenting the key software interface of a system and making them available to software developers. This publishing of interfaces is similar to the standardization of interfaces, but it often bypasses official standardization procedures which are often slow moving. UNIX is an early example of an open system design. All the resources are managed by the operating system (UNIX) and they are accessed by a set of system calls, that are fully documented and available to the programs written in C and other languages. The openness of UNIX is limited by the inextensible nature of its system calls. Today Open Software means free access to source code (Example: linux operating system).

2.14.3 Concurrency

When several processes exist in a single computer, we say that they are executed concurrently. In a distributed system there are many computers, each has one or more processors. Parallel execution arises naturally in distributed systems due to separate activities of users, independence of the resources and the location of server processes in separate computers. Concurrent access to resources must be synchronized.

2.14.4 Scalability

The system and application software should not need to change when the scale of the system increases. This characteristic is achieved to a significant extent in most current distributed systems but it is an area in which further research is required. The demand for scalability in distributed systems has led to a design philosophy in which no single resource - hardware or software - is assumed to be in restricted supply. Rather, as the demand grows, it should be possible to extend the system to meet it. For example the frequency with which files are accessed is likely to grow as the number of users and workstations in a distributed system increases. It must be possible to add server computers to avoid the bottleneck that would arise if a single file server had to handle all the file access requests. In this case these files must be replicated in several servers and the system must be designed so that updates to replicated files are applied to all of the replicas. To a certain extent scalability can also be achieved by **caching** relevant data.

2.14.5 Non-issue: Location Transparency

It was often argued, that the place where an object is located in a distributed system should be completely transparent, i.e. the decision, which parts of a software run local or remote can be taken after the software has been deployed. It was argued, that the programmers should not have to care where the objects run. We do not completely agree to this argumentation. We claim, that a communication between objects across process and computer boundaries is completely different to in-process communication. Thus the distribution of objects has to be a design decision and cannot be hidden from the programmer.

2.14.6 Redundancy

In the field of distributed systems we use redundant resources for fault-tolerance and load-balancing. To build a RAID system we can use disks as *hot standbys*. Whenever a disk fails the standby disk replaces the failing one. In distributed systems, redundancy can be planned at a finer grain - individual servers that are necessary to the continued operation can be replicated. The allocation of redundant hardware is normally exploited for non-critical activities when no faults are present. Distributed systems provide a high degree of *availability* in the face of hardware faults. The network on which distributed systems are based are normally not redundant. Failure of the network causes programs that use the network to hang until communication is restored. The service to users is interrupted during network failure. Efforts are made to exploit concurrency fully and to obtain a higher degree of fault tolerance. A new approach for the construction of replicated programs has been developed as a result of recent research in the field of *group communication*. A number of concurrent processes cooperate by sharing a single communication mechanism called **multicasting**.

2.14.7 Modularity

In a distributed system modularity is enforced by the distribution itself. The granularity of the basic distributed entities is a key factor for making the distributed system *scalable*. Because the object approach promotes encapsulation and modularity, distributed objects are a major trend in today's software industry.

2.14.8 Integration

A distributed system provides an integrated access to various shared resources in the network. An example of a well known distributed system is the web: it is much easier to use a web browser than to use isolated utilities like telnet, ftp and news- or mail readers.

2.15 SIMPLE EXAMPLE OF DISTRIBUTED SYSTEM

One of the simple distributed systems is systems in our network:

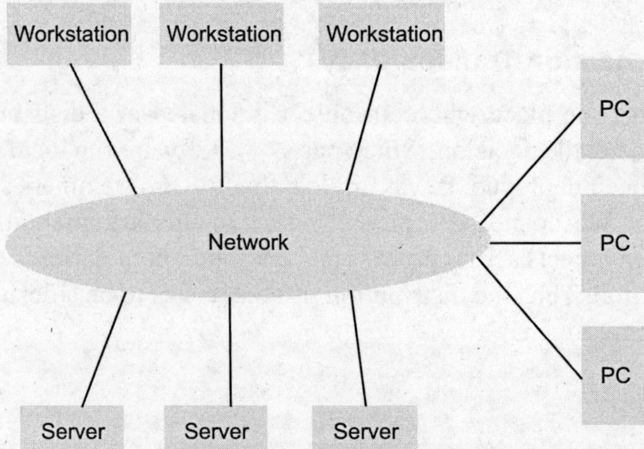

Fig. 2.5 Simple distributed system

Before having distributed systems there existed multi-user systems built around a single time shared computer. UNIX is one of the best-known operating systems for multi-user systems.

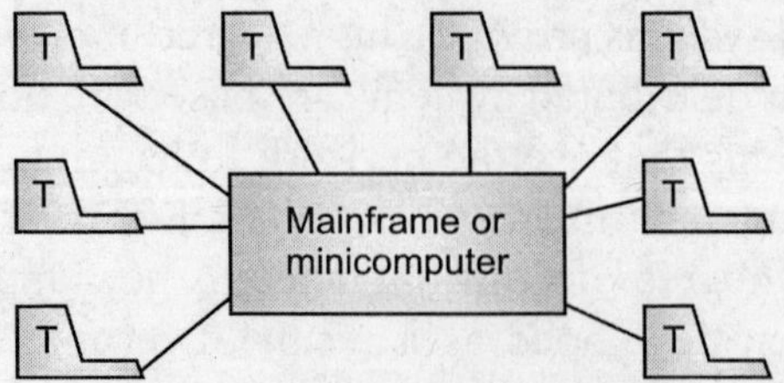

Fig. 2.6 Centralized system

Since UNIX was already in widespread use and easily available, a lot of distributed system researchers extended UNIX as a basis for distributed systems. The first extension, developed at the University of California at Berkeley (BSD) in the late 1970s, was interprocess communication. The distributed UNIX model outlined in figure 2.6 above is the result of the extension contributed by Sun Microsystems: the remote procedure call (RPC) that led to the development of the network file system (NFS) and network information system (NIS). Although the development of distributed UNIX systems offers obvious commercial and technical advantages, UNIX was originally designed to meet a restricted range of requirements in a time when the limitations of computer hardware restricted the scope of the designers' ambitions. In the recent past a new generation of distributed operating systems has been developed. Mach, Chorus and Amoeba are operating systems which have been developed as true distributed systems.

2.16 EXAMPLES OF DISTRIBUTED SYSTEM

The examples of distributed system are

1. **Internet**
2. **Intranet**
3. **Mobile computing**

1. **Internet:** The internet is very large distributed system. It enables uses wherever they are, to make use of services such as the word wide web, email and file transfer. The implementation of internal and the services that if supports has entailed the development of practical solution to many distributed system issues.
2. **Intranet:** An intranet is a portion of the internet that is separating administered and has a boundary that can be configured to enforce local security policies. The network configuration of a particular intranet is the responsibility of the organization that administers it and may vary widely—ranging from a LAN on a single site to a connected set of LANs belonging to branches of a company or other organization in different countries.

   An intranet is connected to the internet via a router, which allows the users inside the intranet to make use of services elsewhere such as the web or Email. It also allows the users in other intranets to access the services it provides.
3. **Mobile Computing:** The portability of many devices, together with their ability to connect conveniently to networks in different places, makes the mobile computing possible. Mobile computing is the performance of the computing tasks while the users is on the move, or visiting places other then their usual environment.

In the mobile computing, users who are away from their 'home intranet are still provided with access to resources via the devices they carry with them. They can continue to access the internet; they can continue to access resources in their home intranet and there is increasing provision for users to utilize resources such as printers. That are conveniently nearly as they move rounds the latter is also known as location aware computing.

2.17 DESIGN GOALS OF DISTRIBUTED SYSTEMS

In this section we focus on the system architecture of distributed systems, on technical issues that must be addressed in their design and on components to meet these issues.

Key design goals for distributed systems

- Performance
- Reliability
- Scalability
- Consistency
- Security

2.17.1 Technical Design Issues

Here we restrict our discussion to design issues that arise specifically because of the distributed nature of the systems:

Naming

Distributed systems are based on shared resources and on the fact that these resources are distributed in the network. The names assigned to resources or objects must have a global meaning which is independent of the locations of the objects. There must be a name interpretation system that can translate names in order to enable programs to access these resources. The design issue is to design naming schemes that will scale to the appropriate degree.

Communication

The performance and reliability of the communication techniques used for the implementation of distributed systems are critical for the system to be built. The design issue here is to optimize the implementation while maintaining a high-level, convenient programming model for its use.

Software structure

Well defined interfaces are necessary to achieve the *openness* (and evolvability) of the software. The design issue is to structure a system so that new services can be introduced that will interwork fully with existing services without duplicating existing service elements.

Workload allocation

Good performance is required for most software products, and it is a major concern for most programmers and system designers. The design issue here is how to deploy the processing and communication resources in an network to optimize the effects of a changing workload.

Maintenance of consistency

The significance of consistency is its impact on the performance of distributed systems and applications. The maintenance of consistency at a reasonable cost is perhaps the most difficult problem encountered in the design of distributed systems.

Naming

A process that requires access to a resource which it does not manage, needs a name or identifier for it. We use the the term *name* to refer to names that can be interpreted by users or by programs and the term *identifier* to refer to names that are interpreted or used by programs only. We say a name is *resolved* when it is translated into a form in which it can be used to invoke an action on the resource or object to which it refers. In distributed systems a resolved name is usually an **object or resource identifier** that is required to perform an action in the system. Naming in distributed systems involves the following design considerations:

- Choice of an appropriate name space for each type of resource. A name space may be finite or potentially infinite, it may be structured or flat. In an object based system, all objects are usually in the same namespace.
- Resource names must resolve to *identifiers*. Access to the resources is only possible through these identifiers. The identifiers of frequently used resources are usually kept in a local cache.

Examples of existing name services are the *BIND* (Berkeley Internet Name Domain) or the UNIX file system, both are hierarchic and potentially infinite. Naming schemes can be designed to protect the resources that they identify from unauthorized access.

Communication

Basic constructs used for the communication are the primitives *send* and *receive*. The *send* can be **synchronous** or blocking, meaning that the sender waits until the receiving process has performed the receive operation or it may be **asynchronous** or non blocking meaning that the message is placed in a message queue and the sending process can continue immediately. In distributed systems we distinguish two different communication models:

Client-server communication:

This Model is oriented towards service provision and consists of:

1. sending the request to the server
2. processing the request by the server
3. sending the reply to the client

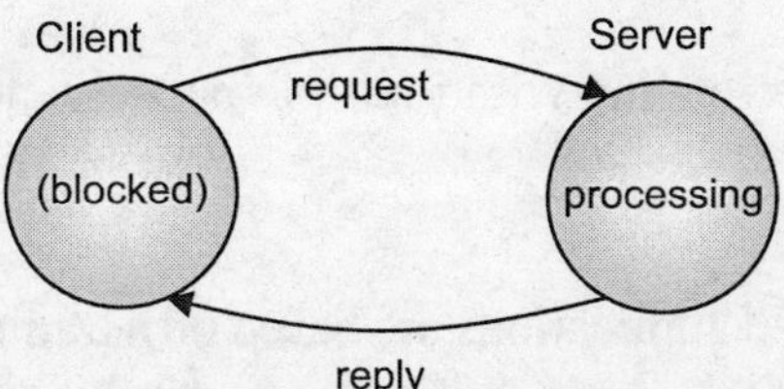

Fig. 2.7 Client-server model

The client server model can be represented at the language level with **remote procedure calls (rpc), remote method invocation (rmi), CORBA or DCOM**.

Example: loading a page from a WEB-server.

Multicast

In this model processes interact using message passing, but in this case the target of the message is a group of processes. To a singe *send* operation there corresponds a *receive* operation by each member of the group.

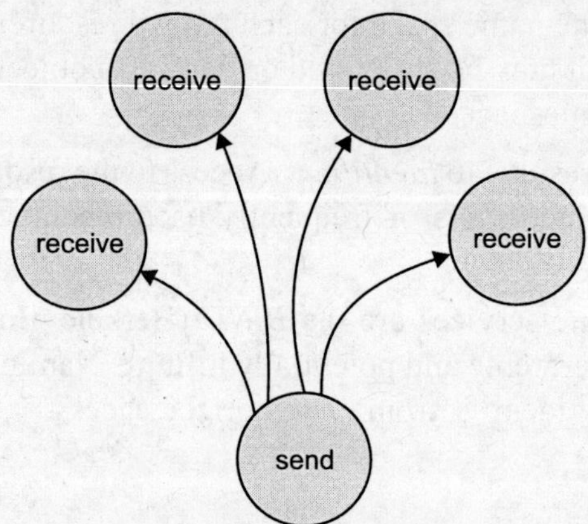

Fig. 2.8: Multicasting

Multicasting can be a solution for the following problems:

Locating an object:

A process multicasts a message containing a name of a resource to a group of server processes. Only the process that holds the resource responds to the message.

Fault tolerance

A process multicasts its request to a group of identical server processes. The group of servers can continue to provide their service even if one of its members fails.

Multiple update

Used for example in video conferencing with multiple participants.

Software structure

The majority of todays distributed applications are based on a traditional operating system enhanced by some middleware.

Many of the services provided by a traditional operating systems like UNIX can also be supplied by open services. This can result in duplication of functions since the kernel functions are immutable. This has led to the development of **micro kernels**. These kernels contain the strict minimum of services on which the other services can be built.

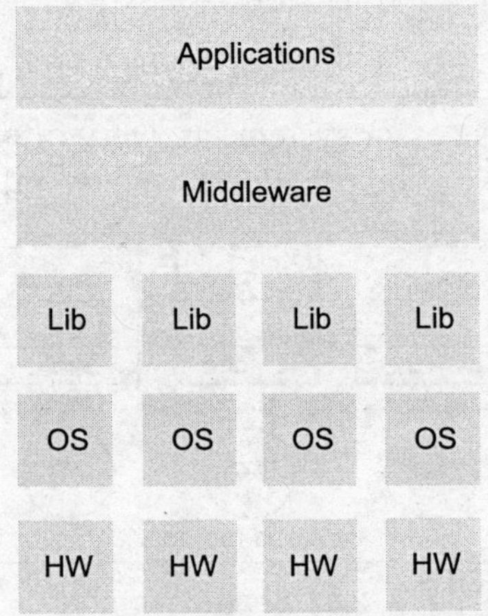

Fig. 2.9 Traditional distributed systems

Workload allocation

The following four models for workload allocation are presented here:

- Processor pool model
- Shared memory multiprocessors
- Parallel virtual machines
- Distributed shared memory

Processor pool model

Processors are allocated to processes for their lifetime. This results in sharing the processors at the granularity of the processes. A single user with an appropriate task can use several processors simultaneously.

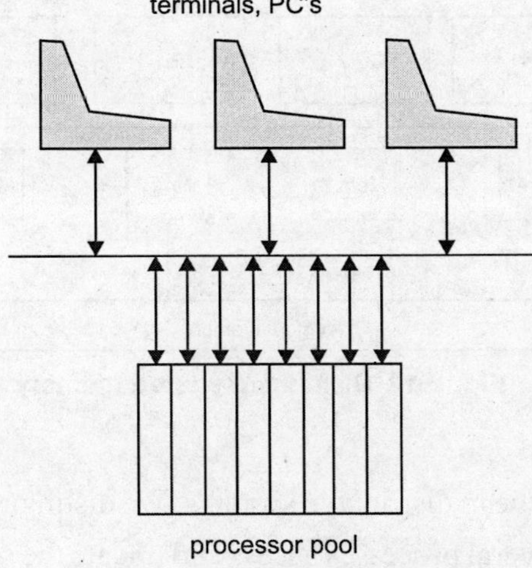

Fig. 2.10 Processor pool

Shared memory multiprocessors

Figure 2.10 illustrates the processor and memory architecture of a shared memory multiprocessor computer. Shared memory multiprocessor systems are very often used as server machines in open distributed systems because of their good price/performance ratio.

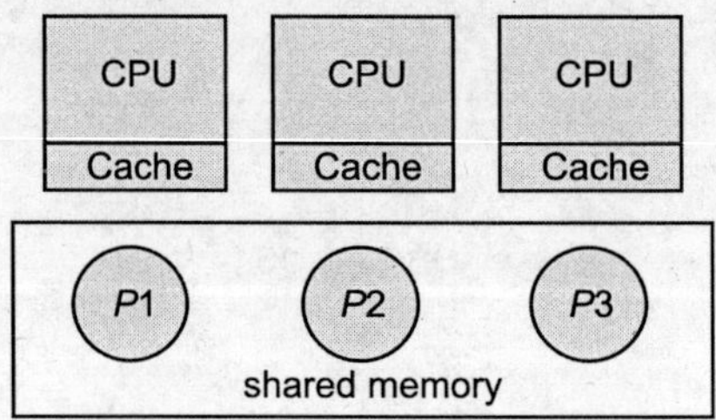

Fig. 2.11 Shared memory

Parallel virtual machines (PVM)

PVM is an integrated set of software tools and libraries that emulates a general-purpose, flexible heterogeneous concurrent computing framework on interconnected computers of varied architecture. The overall objective of the PVM system is to enable a collection of computers to be used cooperatively for concurrent or parallel computation.

Distributed shared memory (DSM)

DSM provides a global shared address space across the different machines on a cluster (Figure 2.12). The shared address space distinguishes it from packages such as PVM that provide a message passing interface between machines. There is a growing consensus in the parallel computing community that a shared memory interface is more desirable from the application programmer's viewpoint, allowing him to focus on algorithmic development rather than on managing communication.

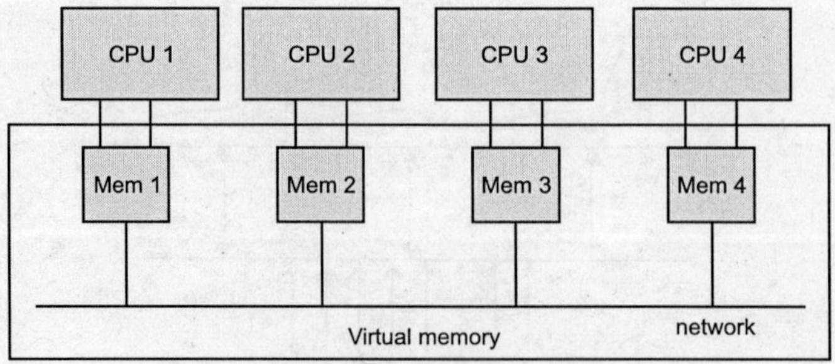

Fig. 2.12 Distributed shared memory

Consistency maintenance

Consistency is an important issue in distributed systems. We distinguish the following consistencies:

Update consistency: If several processes access and update the same data we have a consistency problem if the updates are not performed with an atomic action.

Replication consistency: If data derived from a single source has been copied to several computers and is subsequently modified at one or more of them, then the data items on the other machines might be inconsistent.

Cache consistency: The term *caching* refers to a mechanism, implemented by software in the client computer, for the retention in the client's environment of a copy of the data values for subsequent reuse, avoiding the need to request them again when the resource is accessed again. A consistency problem arises when data that has been accessed by one client is updated by another.

Failure consistency: When a centralized computer fails, all of the programs that are running on it fail simultaneously - there is a single mode of failure. In a distributed system when one component fails, the others, including any with which it was cooperating, will normally continue to run. But if they depend on the continued operation of the failed computer then they may fail later. This is the problem of **multiple failure modes** in distributed systems. To insure consistency recovery procedures are necessary to cause the data to be *rolled back* to a known state before the failure.

Clock consistency: Many algorithms depend on the use of *time stamps*. In distributed systems the physical time of the different computers are not necessarily the same. This can can cause inconsistencies.

2.17.2 *User requirements*

The designer must consider the needs of their users. In this section we highlight some of the more important requirements in practical systems. We consider the following topics:

- Functionality: what should the system do for the users.
- Quality of service: issue containing performance, reliability and security.
- Reconfigurability: the need to accommodate changes without causing disruption of the actual service.

Functionality

The minimal requirement for a distributed system is that the functionality provided by a distributed system should not be less than the user can expect from a single computer. The stronger requirement is that a distributed system should bring an improvement over the services provided by a single computer-through one or both of the following enhancements:

- Sharing across a network can bring a richer variety of resources to resolve the problem.
- Utilization of the advantages of *distributed application programming* so that fault-tolerant, sharing or or parallel applications can be built.

Reconfigurability

The scalability of distributed system design and its ability to to accommodate heterogeneity are relevant features of these systems. There are two timescales in distributed systems on which changes are potential causes for disruption that should be addressed in the design of the software:

Short-term changes

The runtime system should handle the following conditions: A failing process, computer or network component has to be replaced by a working counterpart. Computational load is shifted from the overloaded to a less loaded computer in order to increase the total throughput of the system (load balancing).

Network communication has to be minimized by transferring activities or data to make an activity's data locally available.

Medium to long term evolution

In addition to the changes due to the expansion in scale, an existing system may be assigned new roles in a network.

Quality of service

The question is: *what is the added value arising from distribution*? We discuss it under the following three areas:

Performance: When a service is is accessed, the speed at which the response is generally determined by the performance of all the software components involved: the network services of the operating system, the middleware and the software that implements the service.

Reliability and availability: Distributed systems are not automatically better in terms of *reliability and availability*. The design of the software has a strong influence on it. Highly reliable services in distributed systems often give worse response times than those without these features. The distinction between whether reliability is a convenience or a an absolute requirement is thus an important one. Distributed systems offer some resilience against hardware failures as an automatic consequence of their architecture: the failure of a workstation interrupts the work of a single user but does not affect the service provided to other users. Even the failure of a server may not have critical impact on the service if there are several instances of of the same service running in the system.

Security: There are known weaknesses in the security provided by distributed systems. Distributed systems are less secure than centralized systems unless special precautions are taken. The security problem stems from two main threads that are consequences of the distribution itself:

1. The network: the user's data is traveling over the network. It is often difficult or impossible to secure a network against tampering and modifying the data as it passes over the network.
2. The openness: not all machines in a network can be made physically secure. The openness to interfere with system software at the individual systems opens a possibility for potential intruders to attack the system.

2.18 RESOURCES SHARING AND WEB CHALLENGES

Users are so accustomed to the benefits of resource sharing that they may easily overlook their significant .users are concerned with the sharing data in the form of shared database or a set of web pages not the disc or processors. Patterns of resources sharing vary widely in there scope and how closely users work together .at one extreme, a search engine on a web browser provides a facility to the users throughout the world, users who need never come into contact with one another directly. The pattern of sharing and the geographic distribution of particular users determine what mechanisms the system must supply to coordinate users actions. Resources in distributed system are physically encapsulated within computers and can only be accessed from other computers by communication.

The web is an open system can be extended and implemented in new ways without disturbing its exiting functionality. Its operation is based on communication standards and document standards that are freely published and widely implemented. The web is open with respect to the types of resources that can be published and shared on it. The web has moved beyond these sample data resources to encompass services, such electronics purchasing of goods. It has evolved without changing its basic architecture, the web is based there main standard technological components—

- Hypertext markup language
- Uniform resource locaters
- Client-system architecture

The internet enables users to access services and run application over a homogeneous collection of computers and networks. The major challenges are

- Heterogeneity
- Openness
- Security
- Scalability
- Failure handling
- Concurrency
- Transparency

2.19 SYSTEM MODELS

Systems that are intended for use in the real world environment should be designed to function correctly I the widest possible range of circumstances and threats. Each model is intended to provide an abstract, simplified but consistent description of the relative aspect of distributed systems design. Two types of system models are

- Architectural model
- Fundamental model

2.19.1 Architectural Model

An architectural model of a distributed system is concerned with the placement of its parts and relationship between them. Examples includes the client- server model and the peer process model. The client server model can modified by

- The partition of data or replication of cooperative servers
- The caching of data by proxy servers and clients
- The use of mobile code and mobile agent
- The requirement to add and remove mobile device in a convenient manner.

There are several widely used patterns for allocation of work in distributive systems that have an important impact on the performance and effectiveness of resulting system. The architectural model provides only simplified view of the more important pattern of distribution. The main types of architectural model are

1. Clients invoke individual servers.
2. A service provided by multiple servers.
3. web proxy server

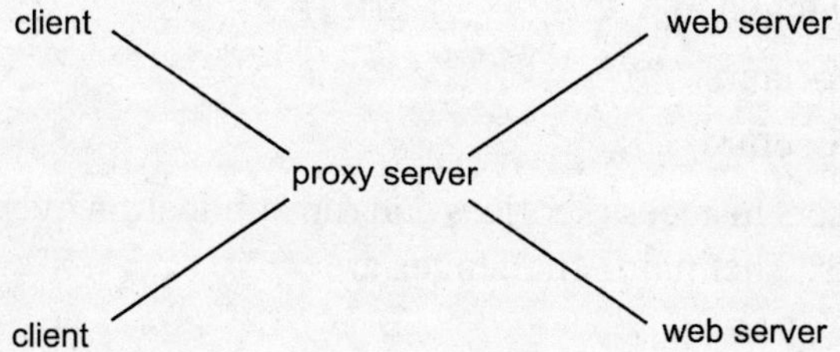

4. A Distributed application based on peer process.

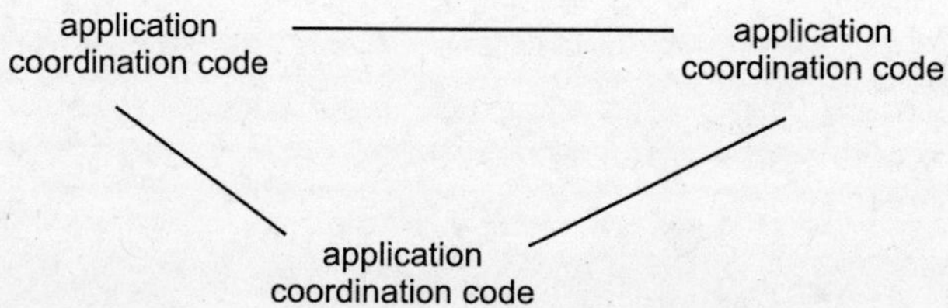

2.19.2 Fundamental Models

Fundamentals models are concerned with a more formed description of the properties that are common in all of the architectural models. There is no global time in a distributed system. So the clocks on different computers do not necessarily give the same time as one another. All communication between processes is achieved by means of messages. Message communication over a computer network can be affected by delays, can suffer from a variety of failures and is vulnerable to security attacks these issues are addressed by three models—

(i) The **interaction models** deals with the performance and with the difficulty of setting time limits in a distributed system, for example, for message delivery.

(ii) The **failure model** attempts to give a precise specification of the faults that can be exhibited by processes and communication channels. It defines reliable communication and correct processes.

(iii) The **security models** discuss the possible threats to processes and communication channels. It introduces the concept of a secure channel, which is secure against these threats.

Integrity is a property of reliable communication- it requires that a message received be identical to one that was sent and that no message be sent twice. Validity is another property—it requires that any message put in the outgoing buffer be delivered eventually to the incoming message buffer.

2.20 SUMMARY

- Distributed systems are arranged according to architectural models.
- Services such as the DNS that have large numbers of users and manage a great deal of information are based on multiple servers and use data partition and replication to enhance availability and fault tolerance.
- In peer process models, distributed application processes communicate directly with one another without using a server as an intermediary.
- In client server model, the web and other internet services are based, the ability to move code from are process to another has resulted in same variant of the client server model.
- The existence of portable computers, PADs and other digital devices and their integration in to distributed systems allow users to access and local and internet services when they are away from their desktop computer.
- The presence of computing devices with wireless communication capability in everyday objects.
- A characteristic of mobile devices in distributed system is that they connect and disconnect unpredictably.
- The integration model is concerned with the performance of processes and communication channels and absence of a global clock.
- The failure model classifies the failure processes and basic communication channels in a distributed systems
- The security model; identifies the possible threats to processes and communication channels in an open distributed system

2.21 REVIEW QUESTIONS

1. Discuss the limitation of a distributed system.
2. Explain Lamports logical clock and limitation of Lamports clocks.
3. Explain virtual time and the vector clocks.
4. Discuss the casual ordering of messages.
5. Differentiate Global state and Local state.
6. Explain termination detection & algorithms for implementing.

7. Explain Lamports algorithm for non token based.
8. Explain characteristics of a distributed system and its examples.
9. Discuss the concept of resources sharing and web challenges.
10 Explain system model and the functionality of architecture models.
11. Explain different types of fundamental models.
12. Suggest some application for the peer process models, distinguishing between cases when all the states of all peers needs to be identical and cases that demands less consistency.
13. List the types of local resources that are venerable to an attack by an entrusted program that is download from a remote site and run in a local computer

CHAPTER 3

Distributed Deadlock Detection

A distributed system consists of a number of sites connected by a network. Each site maintains some of the resources of the system. Processes with a globally unique identifier run on the distributed system. They make resource requests to a controller. There is one controller per site. If the resource is local, the process makes a request of the local controller. If the desired resource is at a remote site, the process sends a message. After a process makes a request, but before it is granted, it is blocked and said to be *dependent* on the process that holds the desired resource.

The controller at each site could maintain a WFG on the process requests that it knows about. This is the local WFG. However, each site's WFG could be cycle free and yet the distributed system could be deadlocked. This is called *global deadlock*. This would occur in the following situation:

1. Process A at site 1 holds a lock on resource X.
2. Process A has requested, but has not been granted, resource Y at site 2.
3. Process B at site 2 holds a lock on resource Y.
4. Process B has requested, but has not been granted, resource X at site 1.

Both processes are blocked by the other one. There is a global deadlock. However, the deadlock will not be discovered at either site unless they exchange information via some detection scheme.

3.1 SYSTEM MODEL

The problem of deadlock has been generally studied in distributed systems under the following model:

- The system has only reusable resources.
- Processes are allowed only exclusive access to resources.
- There is only one copy of each resources.

A process can be in two states running or blocked. In the running state a process has all the needed resources and is either executing or is ready for the execution. In the blocked state, a process is waiting to acquire some resources.

3.2 RESOURCE VS COMMUNICATION DEADLOCK

Two types of deadlocks:

- Resource deadlock
- Communication deadlock

In *resource deadlocks*, processes are simultaneously wait for several resources and can not proceed until they have acquired all these resources. A set of processes is resource deadlocked if each process in the set request resource held by another process in the set and it must receive all of the requested resource before it can become unblocked.

In the communication deadlocks, processes wait to communicate with other processes. A waiting process can unblock on receiving a communication from any one of these processes. A set of processes is communication deadlocked if each process in the set is waiting to communicate with another process in the set and no process in the set ever initiates any further communication, until it receives the communication for which it is waiting.

3.3 DEADLOCK

Deadlock can occur whenever two or more processes are competing for limited resources and the processes are allowed to acquire and hold a resource (obtain a lock) thus preventing others from using the resource while the process waits for other resources.

Two common places where deadlocks may occur are with processes in an operating system (distributed or centralized) and with transactions in a database. The concepts discussed here are applicable to any system that allocates resources to processes.

Locking protocols such as the popular Two Phase Locking (see concurrency control) give rise to deadlock as follows: process A gets a lock on data item X while process B gets a lock on data item Y. Process A then tries to get a lock on Y. As Y is already locked, process A enters a blocked state. Process B now decides to get a lock on X, but is blocked. Both processes are now blocked, and, by the rules of Two Phase Locking, neither will relinquish their locks.

This is a deadlock: process A is waiting for a resource held by process B and process B is waiting for a resource held by process A. No progress will take place without outside intervention. Several processes can be involved in a deadlock when there exists a cycle of processes waiting for each other. Process A waits for B which waits for C which waits for A.

Four conditions must hold for deadlock to occur:

1. **Exclusive use:** when a process accesses a resource, it is granted exclusive use of that resource.
2. **Hold and wait:** a process is allowed to hold onto some resources while it is waiting for other resources.

3. **No preemption:** a process cannot preempt or take away the resources held by another process.
4. **Cyclical wait:** there is a circular chain of waiting processes, each waiting for a resource held by the next process in the chain.

The structure of the system may allow additional complexities in the deadlock problem. The simplest model, *single-resource*, requires that a process have no more than one unfulfilled request. Thus a blocked process is waiting for only one other process and can be involved in at most one deadlock cycle.

In the AND model (also called the multiple-resource model), a process is allowed to make several resource requests, and it is blocked until all of the requests are granted. Processes in this model can be involved in several deadlock cycles at once.

In the OR model (also called the communication model), a process makes several requests and is blocked until any one of them is granted. The AND-OR model allows a combination of request types, such as a request for resource X and either Y or Z. Unless specifically stated, this article assumes the AND model.

The problem of deadlocks can be handled in several ways: Prevention, Avoidance, and Detection. In prevention, some requirement of the system makes deadlocks impossible so that no runtime support is required. Avoidance schemes require decisions by the system while it is running to insure that deadlocks will not occur. Detection requires the most sophisticated runtime support: the system must find deadlocks and break them by choosing a suitable *victim* that is terminated or *aborted* and restarted if appropriate.

3.4 DEADLOCK PREVENTION

Prevention is the name given to schemes that guarantee that deadlocks can never happen because of the way the system is structured. One of the four conditions for deadlock is prevented, thus preventing deadlocks. One way to do this is to make processes declare all of the resources they might eventually need, when the process is first started. Only if all the resources are available is the process allowed to continue. All of the resources are acquired together, and the process proceeds, releasing all the resources when it is finished. Thus, *hold and wait* cannot occur.

The major disadvantage of this scheme is that resources must be acquired because they might be used, not because they will be used. Also, the pre-allocation requirement reduces potential concurrency.

Another prevention scheme is to impose an order on the resources and require processes to request resources in increasing order. This prevents *cyclic wait* and thus makes deadlocks impossible.

One advantage of prevention is that process aborts are never required due to deadlocks. While most systems can deal with rollbacks, some systems may not be designed to handle them and thus must use deadlock prevention.

Deadlock prevention is commonly achieved by either having a process acquire all the needed resources simultaneously before it begins execution or by preempting a process that holds the needed resources. In the former method, a process requests or release a remote resource by sending a request message or release message to the site where the resource is located. This method has a number of drawbacks.

I. It is inefficient, as it deceases the system concurrency.

II. A set of processes can become deadlocked in the resource enquiring phase. For example, suppose process.

3.5 DEADLOCK AVOIDANCE

In deadlock avoidance the system considers resource requests while the processes are running and takes action to insure that those requests do not lead to deadlock. Avoidance based on the *banker's algorithm*, sometimes used in centralized systems, is considered not practical for a distributed system. Two popular avoidance algorithms based on timestamps or priorities are *wound-wait* and *wait-die*. They depend on the assignment of unique global timestamps or priority to each process when it starts. Some authors refer to these as prevention.

In wound-wait, if process A requests a resource currently held by process B, their timestamps are compared. B is *wounded* and must restart if it has a larger timestamp (is younger) than A. Process A is allowed to wait if B has the smaller timestamp. Deadlock cycles cannot occur since processes only wait for older processes. In wait-die, if a request from process A conflicts with process B, A will wait if B has the larger timestamp (is younger). If B is the older process, A is not allowed to wait, so it *dies* and restarts.

In timeout based avoidance, a process is blocked when it requests a resource that is not currently available. If it has been blocked longer than a timeout period, it is aborted and restarted. Given the uncertainty of message delays in distributed systems, it is difficult to determine good timeout values.

These avoidance strategies have the disadvantage that the aborted process may not have been actually involved in a deadlock.

3.6 DEADLOCK DETECTION

Deadlock detection attempts to find and resolve actual deadlocks. These strategies rely on a Wait-For-Graph (WFG) that in some schemes is explicitly built and analyzed for cycles. In the WFG, the nodes represent processes and the edges represent the blockages or dependencies. Thus, if process A is waiting for a resource held by process B, there is an edge in the WFG from the node for process A to the node for process B.

In the AND model (resource model), a cycle in the graph indicates a deadlock. In the OR model, a cycle may not mean a deadlock since any of a set of requested resources may unblock the process. A *knot* in the WFG is needed to declare a deadlock. A knot exists when all nodes that can be reached from some node in a directed graph can also reach that node.

In a centralized system, a WFG can be constructed fairly easily. The WFG can be checked for cycles periodically or every time a process is blocked, thus potentially adding a new edge to the WFG. When a cycle is found, a victim is selected and aborted.

3.7 DISTRIBUTED DEADLOCK

A distributed system consists of a number of sites connected by a network. Each site maintains some of the resources of the system. Processes with a globally unique identifier run on the distributed system. They make resource requests to a controller. There is one controller per site. If the resource is local, the process makes a request of the local controller. If the desired resource is at a remote site, the process sends a message. After a process makes a request, but before it is granted, it is blocked and said to be *dependent* on the process that holds the desired resource.

The controller at each site could maintain a WFG on the process requests that it knows about. This is the local WFG. However, each site's WFG could be cycle free and yet the distributed system could be deadlocked. This is called *global deadlock*. This would occur in the following situation:

1. Process A at site 1 holds a lock on resource X.
2. Process A has requested, but has not been granted, resource Y at site 2.
3. Process B at site 2 holds a lock on resource Y.
4. Process B has requested, but has not been granted, resource X at site 1.

Both processes are blocked by the other one. There is a global deadlock. However, the deadlock will not be discovered at either site unless they exchange information via some detection scheme.

3.8 DISTRIBUTED DEADLOCK DETECTION SCHEMES

A detection scheme is evaluated by two criteria:

1. If there exists an actual deadlock, it must be detected in a finite amount of time.
2. The scheme must not find a deadlock that is not actually there.

One way to detect deadlocks in distributed systems is for each site to construct a local Wait for Graph on the part it knows about. A site that suspects deadlock initiates a global snapshot protocol that constructs a consistent global state of the distributed system. The global state corresponds to a deadlock if the union of the local WFGs has a cycle. This algorithm is correct because deadlock is a stable property.

3.8.1 The Probe Scheme

The Wait for Graph is used to detect local deadlocks and *probes* to determine the existence of global deadlocks. If the controller at a site suspects that process A, for which it is responsible, is involved in a deadlock it will send a probe message to each process that A is dependent on. When A requested the remote resource, a process or *agent* was created at the remote site to act on behalf of process A to obtain the resource. This agent receives the probe message and determines the dependencies at the current site.

The probe message identifies process A and the path it has been sent along. Thus, the message probe (i, j, k) says that it was initiated on behalf of process i and was sent from the controller for agent j (which i is dependent on) to the controller for agent k. When an agent whose process is not blocked receives a probe, it discards the probe. It is not blocked so there is no deadlock. An agent that is blocked sends a probe to each agent that it is blocked by. If process i ever receives probe(i,j,i), it knows it is deadlocked.

This popular approach, often called "edge-chasing", has been shown correct in that it detects all deadlocks and does not find deadlocks when none exist. In the OR model, where only one out of several requested resources must be acquired, all of the blocking processes are sent a query message and all of the messages must return to the originator in order for a deadlock to be declared. The query message is similar to a probe, but has an additional identifier so the originator can determine whether or not all the paths were covered. There are several variations to these algorithms that seek to optimize different properties such as: number of messages, length of messages, and frequency of detection.

3.9 ISSUES IN DISTRIBUTE DEADLOCK DETECTION

3.9.1 Deadlock Detection

- Deadlock prevention is achieved by denying the existence of one or more of the necessary conditions for deadlock. Commonly adopted strategies include: (1) having a process acquire all needed resources simultaneously before it begins execution, or (2) using a liner ordering scheme for resource acquisition to prevent circular waits. Unless information about resource availability and process requests are maintained centrally on one site, such an approach is impractical for a distributed system.
- In deadlock avoidance, a resource is granted to a process if the resulting state is safe. For a distributed system, the safe state checking must examine the global state that involves all processes and resources in all sites. This approach is impractical for distributed systems because: (a) The need to maintain information on the global state for every site leads to huge storage requirements and extensive communication costs, (b) the safe state checking will be computationally expensive due to the potentially large number of processes and resources involved, and (c) the safe state checking for the global state must be mutually exclusive. If we allow multiple sites to perform safe state checking concurrently, each site for a different request, they may find the state safe but the net global state may not be.
- In light of the difficulty in deadlock detection for the general resource system, the study of deadlock problems in distributed systems usually adopts a simpler system model assuming:
  (a) Reusable resources only
  (b) Only exclusive accesses to resources
  (c) Each resource has only one instance
- With the simpler system model as defined above, deadlock detection can be achieved by finding a cycle in the Wait For Graph (WFG) of the resource system.
- One major difficulty in deadlock detection in distributed systems is the Potential for detecting phantom deadlocks.

3.9.2 Deadlock Resolution

A deadlock is resolved by aborting one or more processes involved in the deadlock and granting the released resources to other processes involved in the deadlock. The efficient resolution of a deadlock requires knowledge of all the processes involved in the deadlock and all the resources held by these processes. Resolution of deadlocks detected using distributed control is complicated due to the following issues:

- A process that detects a global deadlock does not know all the processes involved in a deadlock and the resources held by them.
- Two or more processes may independently detect the same deadlock and then independently resolves it. Consequently several processes will be aborted (likely more than necessary) in an attempt to resolve a deadlock, resulting in inefficiency.

Obermarck's suggestion of assigning unique priorities to transactions/processes and using these priorities in detection as well as resolution as follows has helped resolved these problems.

- Each deadlock is detected only by the highest priority process in the deadlock (i.e., deadlock detections initiated by all other processes involved in the deadlock are suppressed).
- When the highest priority process detects a deadlock, it knows the lowest priority processes in the cycle, which can be aborted to resolve the deadlock.

It should be noted that deadlock resolution is a nontrivial procedure that involves the following steps:

- The victim must be aborted, all the resources held by it must be released, the state of all the released resources must be restored to their states prior to the allocation, an the released resources must be granted to other processes involved in the deadlock.
- All the deadlock detection information concerning the victim must be cleaned at all the sites.

3.10 CONTROL ORGANIZATION FOR DISTRIBUTED DEADLOCK DETECTION

The following three control organizations are common for deadlock detection in distributed systems:

3.10.1 Centralized Control

In centralized deadlock detection algorithms, a designated site (often called a control site) has the responsibility of constructing the global WFG and searching it for cycles. The control site may maintain the global WFG constantly or it may build it whenever a deadlock detection is to be carried out by soliciting the local WFG from every site.

Advantages of centralized algorithms include: detection as well as resolution are conceptually simple and easy to implement since the control site has complete information of the WFG and the deadlock cycle. Disadvantages include: single point of failure, congestion likely at the control site and at communication links near that site, design not scalable to growth of system.

3.10.2 Distributed Control

In distributed deadlock detection algorithms, the responsibility of detecting a global deadlock is shared equally among all sites. A deadlock detection is initiated only when a waiting process is suspected to be part of a deadlock. When the detection of a global deadlock is to be carried out, several sites participate in the detection and the WFG is spread over many sites.

Distributed control is not vulnerable to a single point of failure, no site will become a bottleneck due to deadlock activities, and the design is much more scalable than the centralized organization. However, distributed deadlock detection algorithms are difficult to implement due to the lack of globally shared memory. Additional problems include: several sites may initiate detection of the same deadlock, deadlock resolution is often cumbersome since several sites may detect the same deadlock without being aware of it, and the proof of correctness of these algorithms is difficult.

3.10.3 Hierarchical Control

In hierarchical deadlock detection algorithms, sites are arranged in a hierarchical fashion, and a site detects deadlocks involving only its descendent sites. If the hierarchy structure coincides with resources access patterns local to clusters of sites, this approach can provide efficient detection of deadlocks and rip the benefits of both the centralized and the distributed control organizations. On the other hand, if deadlocks are not mostly localized to a few clusters but often span several clusters, this approach will be inefficient.

3.11 CENTRALIZED DEADLOCK-DETECTION ALGORITHMS

3.11.1 The Completely Centralized Algorithm

The completely centralized algorithm is the simplest centralized deadlock detection algorithm, wherein a designated site called the control site, maintains the WFG of the entire system and checks it for the existence of deadlock cycles. All sites request and release resources (even local resources) by sending request resource and release resource messages to the control site, respectively. When the control site receives a request resource or a release resource message, it correspondingly updates its WFG. The control site checks the WFG for deadlocks whenever a request edge is added to the WFG.

3.11.2 The Ho-Ramamurthy Algorithms

3.11.2.1 The Two-Phase Algorithm

In the two-phase algorithm, every site maintains a status table that contains the status of all processes initiated at that site. The status of a process includes all resources locked and all resources being waited upon. Periodically, a designated site requests the status table from all sites, constructs a WFG from the information received, and searches it for cycles. If there is no cycle, then the system is free from deadlocks, otherwise, the designated site again requests status tables from all the sites and again reports. If the same cycle is detected again, the system is declared deadlocked.

3.11.2.2 The One-Phase Algorithm

The one-phase algorithm requires only one status report from each site; however, each site maintains two status tables: *a resource status* table and *process status* table. The resource status table at a site keeps track of the transactions that have locked or are waiting for resources stored at that site. The process status table at a site keeps track of the resources locked by or waited for by all the transactions at that site. Periodically, a designated site requests both tables from every site, constructs a WFG using only those transactions for which the entry in the resource table matches the corresponding entry in the process table, and searches the WFG for cycles. If no cycle is found, then the system is not deadlocked, otherwise a deadlock is detected.

The one-phase algorithm is faster and requires fewer messages as compared to the two-phase algorithm. However, it requires more storage because every site maintains two status tables and exchanged bigger messages because a message contains two tables instead of one.

3.12 DISTRIBUTED DEADLOCK DETECTION ALGORITHMS

Global state detection based deadlock detection algorithms exploit the following facts:

- A consistent snapshot of a distributed system can be obtained without freezing the underlying computation.
- A consistent snapshot may not represent the system state at any moment in time, but if a stable property holds in the system before the snapshot collection is initiated, this property will still hold in the snapshot.

Therefore, distributed deadlocks can be detected by taking a snapshot of the system and examining it for the condition of a deadlock.

3.12.1 A Path-Pushing Algorithm

In path-pushing deadlock detection algorithms, information about the wait-for dependencies is propagated in the form of paths. Obermarck's algorithm is chosen is illustrate a path-pushing deadlock detection algorithm.

Obermarck's algorithm has two interesting features:

- The nonlocal portion of the global Transaction Wait-For (TWF) graph at a site is abstracted by a distinguished note (called External or EX) which helps in determining potential multisite deadlocks without requiring a huge global TEF graph to be stored at each site.
- Transactions are totally ordered, which reduces the number of messages and consequently decreases deadlock detection overhead. It also ensures that exactly one transaction in each cycle detects the deadlock.

The Algorithm

Deadlock detection at a site follows the following iterative process:

1. The site waits for deadlock-related information (produced in Step 3 of the previous deadlock detection iteration) from other sites. (Note that deadlock-related information is passed by sites in the form of paths.)
2. The site combines the received information with its local TWF graph to build an updated TWF graph. It then detects all cycles and breaks only those cycles which do not contain the node 'Ex'. Note that these cycles are local to this site. All other cycles have the potential to be a part of global cycles.
3. For all cycles 'Ex T_1 T_2 Ex' which contain the node 'Ex' (these cycles are potential candidates for global deadlocks), the site transmits them in string form 'Ex, T_1, T_2, Ex' to all other sites where an agent of T_2 is waiting for a resource being held by another transaction. The algorithm reduces message traffic by lexically ordering transactions and sending the string 'Ex, T_1, T_2, T_3, Ex' to other sites only if T_1 is higher than T_3 in the lexical ordering. Also, for a deadlock, the highest priority transaction detects the deadlock.

3.12.2 An Edge-Chasing Algorithm

Chandy et al.'s algorithm uses a special message called a probe. A probe is a triplet (i, j, k) denoting that it belongs to a deadlock detection initiated by process P_i and it is being sent by the home site of process P_j to the home site of process P_k. A probe message travels along the edges of the global TWF graph, and a deadlock is detected when a probe message returns to its initiating process. The system maintains a Boolean array, dependent, for each process P_i, where $dependent_i(j)$ is true only if P_i knows that P_j is dependent on it. Initially, $dependent_i(j)$ is false for all i and j.

The Algorithm

To determine if a blocked process is deadlocked, the system executed the following algorithm:

if P_i is locally dependent on itself
then declare a deadlock
else for all P_j and P_k such that
 (a) P_i is locally dependent upon P_j, and
 (b) P_j is waiting on P_k, and
 (c) P_j and P_k are on different sites, send probe (i, j, k) to the home site of P_k

On the receipt of probe (i, j, k), the site takes the following actions:

if
 (a) P_k is blocked, and
 (b) dependent$_k(i)$ is false, and
 (c) P_k has not replied to all requests of P_j

then

begin

dependent$_k(i)$ = true;
if $k = i$
then declare that P_i is deadlocked
else for all P_m and P_n such that
(a) P_k is locally dependent upon P_m, and
(b) P_m is waiting on P_n, and
(c) P_m and Pn are on different sites,
end.

Thus, a probe message is successively propagated along the edges of the global TWF graph and a deadlock si detected when a probe message returns to its initiating process. Chandy et al.'s algorithm sends one probe message (per deadlock detection initiation) on each edge of the WFG, which spans two sites. Thus, the algorithm at most exchanges $m(n–1)/2$ messages to detect a deadlock that involves m processes and spans over n sites. The size of messages exchanged is fixed and very small (only 3 integer words). The delay in detecting the deadlock is $O(n)$.

3.12.3 A Diffusion Computation Based Algorithm

In diffusion computation based distributed deadlock detection algorithm, deadlock detection computations is diffused through the WFG of the system. Chandy et al.'s distributed deadlock detection algorithm for the OR request model [5] is discussed to illustrate the technique of diffusion computation based algorithms.

A process determines if it is deadlocked by initiating a diffusion computation. The messages used in diffusion computation take the form of a query (i, j, k) and a reply (i, j, k), denoting that they belong to a diffusion computation initiated by a process P_i and are being sent from process P_j to process P_k. A process can be in two states: active or blocked. In the active state, a process is executing and in the blocked state, a process is waiting to acquire a resource. A blocked process initiates deadlock detection by sending query messages to all the processes from whom it is waiting to receive a message (these processes are called the *dependent set* of the process).

If an active process receives a query or reply message, it discards it. When a blocked process P_k receives a query (i, j, k) message, it takes the following actions:

- If this is the first query message received by Pk for the deadlock detection initiated by P_i (called the *engaging query*), then it propagates the query to all the processes in its dependent set and sets a local variable $num_k(i)$ to the number of query messages sent.
- If this is not an engaging query, then P_k returns a reply message to it immediately, provided P_k has been continuously blocked since it received the corresponding engaging query. Otherwise, it discards the query.

3.12.4 A Global State Detection Based Algorithm

There are three deadlock detection algorithms to detect generalized distributed deadlocks using global state detection approach. The algorithm by Bracha and Toueg [2] consists of two phases. In the first phase, the algorithm records a snapshot of a distributed WFG and in the second phase, the algorithm simulates the granting of requests to check for generalized deadlocks. The second phase is nested within the first phase. Therefore, the first phase terminates after the second phase has terminated. The algorithm by Wang et al. [30] also consists of two phases. In the first phase, the algorithm records a snapshot of the distributed WFG. In the second phase, the static WFG recorded in the first phase is reduced to detect any deadlocks. Both the phase occur serially.

The Kshemkalyani-Singhal algorithm [20] has a single phase, which consists of a fan-out sweep of messages outwards from an initiator process and a fan-in sweep of messages inwards to the initiator process. A *sweep* of a WFG is a traversal of the WFG in which all messages are sent in the direction of the WFG edges (an outward sweep) or all messages are sent against the direction of the WFG edges (an inward sweep). Both the outward and the inward sweeps are done concurrently in the algorithm. In the outward sweep, the algorithm records a snapshot of a distributed WFG In the inward sweep, the recorded distributed WFG is reduced to determine whether the initiator is deadlocked. This algorithm deals with the complications introduced because the two sweeps can overlap in time at nay process, i.e., the reduction of the WFG at a process can begin before al the WFG edges incident at that process have been recorded.

System Modes

The system has n nodes, with every node connected to every other node by a logical channel. An event in a computation can be an internal event, a message send event, or a message receive event. Events are assigned timestamps as per Lamport's clock scheme [21]. The timestamp of an event that occurs at time t on node i is denoted by t_i.

The computation messages can either be REQUEST, REPLY or CANCEL messages. A node i sends q_i REQUESTs to q_i other nodes when it blocks (goes from an active to a blocked state) on a p_i-out-of-q_i request. When node i blocks on node j node j becomes a successor of node i an node i becomes a predecessor of node j in the WFG. A REPLY message denotes the granting of a request. A node i unblocks when p_i out of its q_i requests are granted. When the node unblocks, it sends CANCEL messages to withdraw the remaining $q_i - p_i$ requests it had sent.

The sending and receiving of REQUEST, REPLY, and CANCEL messages are *computation events*. The sending and receiving of deadlock detection algorithm messages are *algorithm events*.

A node i has the following local variables to record its state:

$wait_i$: boolean (:= *false*); /*records the current status.*/

t_i: integer (:= 0); /*current time.*/

$in(i)$: set of nodes whose requests are outstanding at i

$out(i)$: set of nodes on which i is waiting.

p_i: integer (:= 0); /*the number of replies required for unblocking.*/

w_i: real (:= 1.0); /*weight to detect termination of deadlock detection algorithm.*/

REQUEST_SEND(*i*).

/*Executed by node *i* when it blocks on a p_i-out-of-q_i request.*/

For every node *j* on which *i* is blocked do

$out(i) \leftarrow out(i)$ 4 $\{j\}$;

send REQUEST(*i*) to *j*;

set p_i to the number of replies needed;

$wait_i \leftarrow true$;

REQUEST_RECEIVE(*j*).

/*Executed by node *i* when it receives a request made by j */

$in(i) \leftarrow in(i)$ 4 $\{j\}$;

REPLY_SEND(*j*).

/*Executed by node *i* when it replies to a request by *j*.*/

$in(i) \leftarrow in(i) - \{j\}$;

send REPLY(*i*) to *j*;

REPLY_RECEIVE(*j*).

/*Executed by node *i* when it receives a reply from *j* to its request.*/

if valid reply for the current request

then begin

$out(i) \leftarrow out(i) - \{j\}$;

$p_i \leftarrow p_i - 1$;

$p_i = 0 \rightarrow$

$\{wait_i \leftarrow false$;

$\forall$ □□$k \in out(i)$, **send** CANCEL(*i*) to *k*;

$out(i) \leftarrow \emptyset$.}

end

CANCEL_RECEIVE(*j*).

/*Executed by node *i* when it receives a cancel from j.*/

$in(j) \in in(i)$ then $in(i) \leftarrow in(i) - \{j\}$.

When a not *init* blocks on a P-out-of-Q request, it initiates the deadlock detection algorithm. The algorithm records part of the WFG that is reachable from init (henceforth, referred to as *init*'s WFG) in a distributed snapshot [4]; such a distributed snapshot includes only those dependency edges and nodes that from *init*'s WFG. When multiple nodes block concurrently, they may each initiate the deadlock detection algorithm concurrently. Each invocation of the deadlock detection algorithm is treated independently and is identified by the initiator's identity and initiator's timestamp when it is blocked. Every node maintains a local snapshot for the latest deadlock detection algorithm initiated by every other node. We will describe only a single instance of the deadlock detection algorithm.

3.13 AGREEMENT PROTOCOL

In distributed systems, *where sites (or processor) often compete as well as cooperate to achieve a common goal, it is often required that sites reach mutual agreement*. For example, in distributed database systems, data managers at sites must agree on whether to commit or to abort a transaction [11]. Reaching an agreement typically requires that sites have knowledge about the values of other sites. For example, in *distributed commit*, a site should know the outcome of *local commit* at each site.

When the system is free from failures, an agreement can easily be reached among the processors (or sites). For example, processors can reach an agreement by communicating their values to each other and then by taking a majority vote or a minimum, maximum, mean, etc. of those values. However, when the system is prone to failure, this method does not work. This is because faulty processors can send conflicting values to other processors preventing them from reaching an agreement. In the presence of faults, processors must exchange their values with other processors and relay the values received from other processors several times to isolate the effects of faulty processors. A processor refines its value as it learn of the values of other processors (This entire process of reaching an agreement is called an agreement protocol.)

In this chapter, we study agreement protocols for distributed systems under processor failures. A very general model of faults is assumed. For example, a faulty processor may send spurious messages to other processors, may lie, may not respond to received messages correctly, etc. Also, nonfaulty processors do not know which processors are faulty.

In agreement problems, nonfaulty processors in a distributed system should be able to reach a common agreement, even if certain components in the system are faulty. The agreement is achieved through an agreement protocol that involves several rounds of message exchange among the processors.

3.14 SYSTEM MODEL OF AGREEMENT PROTOCOL

Agreement problems have been studied under the following system model:

- There are n processors in the system and at most m of the processors can be faulty.

- The processors can directly communicate with other processors by message passing. Thus, the system is logically fully connected.
- A receiver processor always knows the identity of the sender processor of the message.
- The communication medium is reliable (i.e., it delivers all messages without introducing any errors) and only processors are prone to failures.

For simplicity, we assume that agreement is to be reached between only two values, 0 and 1. Results can easily be extended to multivalue agreement [23].

Early solutions to agreement problems assumed that only processors could be faulty and that communication links did not fail. Limiting faults solely to the processors simplifies the solution to agreement problems. Recently, agreement problems have been studied under the failure of communication links only [24] and under the failure of both processors and communication links [25]. In this chapter, we limit the treatment of agreement problems solely to processor failures.

3.15 SYNCHRONOUS VS. ASYNCHRONOUS COMPUTATIONS

In a synchronous computation, processes in the system run in lock step manner, where in each step, a process receives messages (sent to it in the previous step), performs a computation, and sends messages to other process (received in the next step). A step of a synchronous computation is also referred to as a *round*. In synchronous computation, a process knows all the messages it expects to receive in a round. A message delay or a slow process can slow down the entire system or computation.

In an asynchronous computation, on the other hand, the computation at processes does not process in lock steps. A process can send and receive messages and perform computation at any time.

In this chapter, synchronous models of computation are assumed. The assumption of synchronous computation is critical to agreement protocols. In fact, the agreement problem is not solvable in an asynchronous system, even for a single processor failure [10].

3.16 MODEL OF PROCESSOR FAILURES

In agreement problems, we consider a very general model of processor failures. A processor can fail in three modes: *crash fault, omission fault* and *malicious fault.* In a crash fault, a processor stops functioning and never resumes operation. In an omission fault, a processor 'omits' to send messages to some processors. (These are the messages that the processor should have sent according to the protocol or algorithm it is executing.) For example, a processor is supposed to broadcast a message to all other processors, but it sends the message to only a few processors. In a malicious fault, a processor behaves randomly and arbitrarily. For example, a processor may send fictitious messages to other processors to confuse them. Malicious faults are very broad in nature and thus most other conceivable faults can be treated as malicious faults. Malicious faults are also referred to as *Byzantine faults*.'

Since a faulty processor can refuse to send a message, a nonfaulty processor may never receive an expected message from a faulty processor. In such a situation, we assume that the nonfaulty processor simply chooses and arbitrary value and acts as if the expected message has been received [16]. Of course, we assume that such situations, where a processor refuses to send a message, can be detected by the respective receiver processors. In synchronous systems, if the duration of each round is known, then this detection is simple — all the expected messages not received by the end of a round were not sent.

3.17 AUTHENTICATED VS. NO-AUTHENTICATED MESSAGES

Note that to reach an agreement, processors have to exchange their values and relay the received values to other processors several times. The capability of faulty processors to distort what they receive from other processors greatly depends upon the type of underlying messages.

There are two types of messages: *authenticated* and *non-authenticated.* In an authenticated message system, (a faulty) processor cannot forge a message or change the contents of a received message (before it relays the message to other processors). A processor can verify the authenticity of a received message. An authenticated message is also called a *signed* message [14].

In a non-authenticated message system, a (faulty) processor can forge a message and claim to have received it from another processor or change the contents of a received message before it relays the message to other processors. A processor has no way of verifying the authenticity of a received message. A non-authenticated message is also called an *oral* message [14]. It is easier to reach agreement in an authenticated message system because faulty processors are capable of doing less damage.

3.18 PERFORMANCE ASPECTS

The performance (or the computational complexity) of agreement protocols is generally determined by the following three metrics: *time*, *message traffic*, and *storage overhead*. Time refers to the time taken to reach an agreement under a protocol. The time is usually expressed as the number of rounds needed to reach an agreement. Message traffic is measured by the number of messages exchanged to reach an agreement. Sometimes the message traffic is also measured by the total number of bits exchanged to reach an agreement [5]. Storage overhead measures the amount of information that needs to be stored at processors during the execution of a protocol.

Next, we discuss three agreement problems for non-authenticated messages under processor failures.

3.19 A CLASSIFICATION OF AGREEMENT PROBLEMS

There are three well known agreement problems in distributed systems: the *Byzantine agreement problem*, the *consensus problem*, and the *interactive consistency problem*. In the Byzantine agreement problem, a single value, which is to be agreed on, is initialized by an arbitrary processor and all nonfaulty processors have to agree on that value. In the consensus problem, every processor has its own initial value and all nonfaulty processors must agree on a single common value. In the interactive consistency problem, every processor has its own initial value and all nonfaulty processors must agree on a set of common values.

In all three problems, all nonfaulty processors must reach a common agreement. In the Byzantine agreement and the consensus problem, the agreement is about a single value. Whereas in the interactive consistency problem, the agreement is about a set of common values. In the Byzantine agreement problem, only one processor initializes the initial value. Whereas in the consensus and the interactive consistency problems, every processor has its own initial value. Whereas in the consensus and the interactive consistency problems, every processor has its own initial value. Table 3.1 summarizes the starting values and final outcomes of the three problems.

Next, we define these three agreement problems in a precise manner.

3.19.1 The Byzantine Agreement Problem

In the Byzantine agreement problem, an arbitrarily chosen processor, called the *source processor*, broadcasts its initial value to all other processors. A solution to the Byzantine agreement problem should meet the following two objectives:

Agreement. All nonfaulty processors agree on the same value.

Validity. If the source processor is nonfaulty, then the common agreed upon value by all nonfaulty processors should be the initial value of the source.

Table 3.1 : The Three Agreement Problems

Problem →	Byzantine Agreement	Consensus	Interactive Consistency
Who initiates the value	One processor	All processors	All processors
Final agreement	Single value	Singly value	A vector of values

Two points should be noted: (1) If the source processor is faulty, then all non-faulty processors can agree on *any* common value. (2) It is irrelevant what value faulty processors agree on or whether they agree on a value at all.

3.19.2 Consensus Agreement Protocol

In the consensus problem, every processor broadcasts its initial value to all other processors. Initial values of the processors may be different. A protocol for reaching consensus should meet the following conditions:

Agreement. All nonfaulty processors agree on the same single value.

Validity. If the initial value of every nonfaulty processor is υ, then the agreed upon common value by all nonfaulty processors must be υ.

Note that if the initial values of nonfaulty processors are different, then all non-faulty processors can agree on *any* common value. Again, we don't care what value faulty processors agree on.

3.19.3 Interactive Consistency Agreement Protocol

In the interactive consistency problem, every processor broadcasts its initial value to all other processors. The initial values of the processors may be different. A protocol for the interactive consistency problem should meet the following conditions:

Agreement. All nonfaulty processors agree on the same vector, $(\upsilon_1, \upsilon_2, \ldots, \upsilon_n)$.

Validity. If the *i*th processor is nonfaulty and its initial value is υ_i, then the *i*th value to be agreed on by all nonfaulty processors must be υ_i.

Note that if the *i*th processors is faulty, then all non-faulty processors can agree on *any* common value for υ_j. It is irrelevant what value faulty processors agree on.

3.20 RELATIONS AMONG THE AGREEMENT PROBLEMS

All three agreement problems are closely related [7]. For example, the Byzantine agreement problem is a special case of the interactive consistency problem, in which the initial value of only one processor is of interest. Conversely, if each of the *n* processors runs a copy of the Byzantine agreement protocol, the interactive consistency problem is solved. Likewise, the consensus problem can be solved using the solution of the interactive consistency problem. This is because all nonfaulty processors can compute the value that is to be agreed upon by taking the majority value of the common vector that is computed by an interactive consistency protocol, or by choosing a default value if a majority does not exist.

Thus, solutions to the interactive consistency and consensus problems can be derived from the solutions to the Byzantine agreement problem. In other words, the Byzantine agreement problem is primitive to the other two agreement problems. For this reason, we will focus solely on the Byzantine agreement problem for the rest of the chapter.

However, it should by no means be concluded that the Byzantine agreement problem is weaker than the interactive consistency problem or that the interactive consistency problem is weaker than the consensus problem. In fact, there is no linear ordering of this sort among these agreement problems. For example, the Byzantine agreement problem can be solved using a solution to the consensus problem in the following manner [7]:

1. The source processor sends its value to all other processors, including itself.
2. All the processors, including the source, run an algorithm for the consensus problem using the values received in the first step as their initial values.

The above two steps solve the Byzantine agreement problem because (1) if the source processor is nonfaulty, then all the processors will receive the same value in the first step and all nonfaulty processors will agree on that value as a result of the consensus algorithm in the second step, and (2) if the source processor is faulty, then the other processors may not receive the same value in the first step; However, all nonfaulty processors will agree on the same value in the second step as a result of the consensus algorithm. Thus, the Byzantine agreement is reached in both cases. However, the n — 1 extra messages are sent at the first step.

3.21 SOLUTIONS TO THE BYZANTINE AGREEMENT PROBLEMS

The Byzantine agreement problem was first defined and solved (under processor failures) by Lamport et al. [14, 16]. Recall that in this problem, an arbitrarily chosen processor (called the source processor) broadcasts its initial value to all other processors. A protocol for the Byzantine agreement should guarantee that all nonfaulty processors agree on the same value and if the source processor is nonfaulty, then the common agreed upon value by all nonfaulty processors should be the initial value of the source.

It is obvious that all the processors must exchange the values through messages to reach a consensus. Processors send their values to other processors and relay received values to other processors [16]. During the execution of the protocol, faulty processors may confuse other processors by sending them conflicting values or by relaying to them fictitious values.

The Byzantine agreement problem is also referred to as the Byzantine generals problem [4.14] because the problem resembles a situation where a team of generals in an army is trying to reach agreement on an attack plan. The generals are located at geographically distant positions and communicate only through messengers. Some of the generals are traitors (equivalent to faulty processors) and try to prevent loyal generals from reaching an agreement by deliberately transmitting erroneous information.

3.21.1 The Upper Bound on the Number of Faulty Processors

In order to reach an agreement on a common value, nonfaulty processors need to be free from the influence of faulty processors. If faulty processors dominate in number, they can prevent nonfaulty processors from reaching a consensus. Thus, the number of faulty processors should not exceed a certain limit if a consensus. Thus, the number of faulty processors should not exceed a certain limit if a consensus is to be reached.

Pease et al. [16] showed that in a fully connected network, it is impossible to reach a consensus if the number of faulty processors, m, exceeds $[(n-1)/3]$. Lamport et al. [14] were the first to give a protocol to reach Byzantine agreement that requires $m + 1$ rounds of message exchanges (m is the maximum number of faulty processors). Fisher et al. [8] showed that m + 1 is the lower bound on the number of rounds of message exchanges to reach a Byzantine agreement in a fully connected network where only processors can fail.

However, if authenticated messages are used, this bound is relaxed and a consensus can be reached for any number of faulty processors.

3.21.2 An Impossibility Result

We now show that a Byzantine agreement cannot be reached among three processors, where one processor is faulty [14]. For a rigorous treatment of this impossibility result for a higher number of processors, readers are referred to [9] and [16].

Consider a system with three processors, p_0, p_1, and p_2. For simplicity, we assume that there are only two values, 0 and 1, on which processors agree and processor p0 initiates the initial value. There are two possibilities: (1), p_0 is not faulty or (2) p_0 is faulty.

Case I: p_0 is not faulty. Assume p_2 is faulty. Suppose that p_0 broadcasts an initial value of 1 to both p_1 and p_2. Processor p_2 acts maliciously and communicates a value of 0 to processor p_1. Thus p_1 receives conflicting values from p_0 and p_2. (This scenario is shown in Fig 3.1. A faulty processor is depicted by an oval and a nonfaulty processor is denoted by a circle.) However, since p_0 is nonfaulty, processor p_1 must accept 1 as the agreed upon value if condition 2 (of Sec. 8.3.1) is to satisfied.

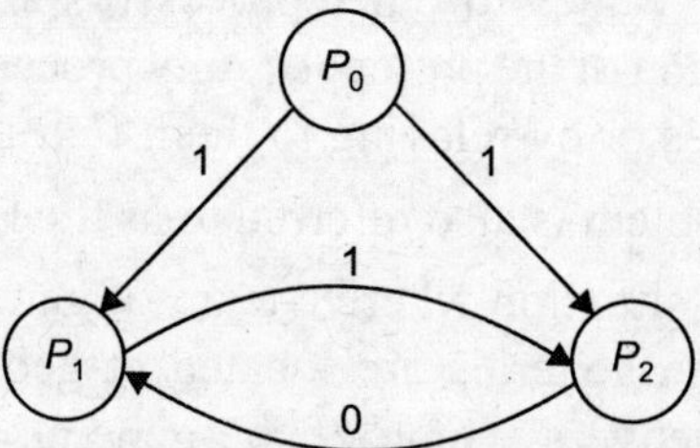

Fig. 3.1 Processor p_0 is Non-Faulty

Case II: p_0 is faulty. Suppose that processor p_0 sends an initial value of 1 to p_1 and 0 to p_2. Processor p_2 will communicates the value 0 to p_1. (This scenario is shown in Fig 3.2. As far as p_1 is concerned, this case will look identical to Case I. So any agreement protocol which works for three processor cannot distinguish between the two cases and must force p_1 to accept 1 as the agreed upon value whenever p_1 is faced with such situations (to satisfy condition 2). However, in Case II, this will work only if p_2 is also made to accept 1 as the agreed upon value.

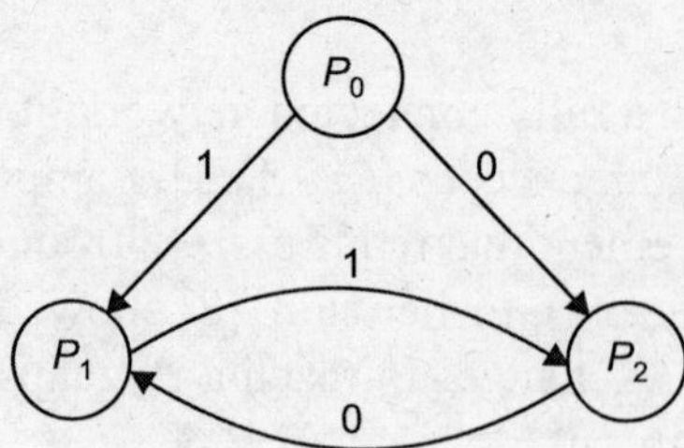

Fig. 3.2 Processor p_0 is Faulty

Using a similar argument, we can show that if p_2 receives an initial value of 0 from p_0, then it must take 0 as the agreed upon value, even if p_1 communicates a value of 1. However, if this is followed in Case II, p_1 will agree on a value of 1 and p_2 will agree on a value of 0, which will violate condition 1 (Sec. 8.3.1) of the solution.

Therefore, no solution exists for the Byzantine agreement problem for three processors, which can work under single processor failure.

3.21.3 Lamport-Shostak-Pease Algorithm

Lamport et al.'s algorithm [14], referred to as the Oral Message algorithm OM(m), $m > 0$, solves the Byzantine agreement problem for $3m + 1$ or more processors in the presence of at most m faulty processors. Let n denote the total number of processors (clearly, $n \geq 3m + 1$). The algorithm is recursively defined as follows:

Algorithm OM(0).

1. The source processor sends its value to every processor.
2. Each processor uses the value it receives from the source. (If it receives no value, then it uses a default value of 0.)

Algorithm OM(m), m > 0.

1. The source processor sends its value to every processor.
2. For each i, let v_i be the value processor i receives from the source. (If it receives no value, then it uses a default value of 0.) Processor i acts as the new source and initiates **Algorithm OM(*m*–1)** wherein it sends the value v_i to each of the n – 2 other processors.
3. For each i and each j ($\neq i$), let v_j be the value processor i received from processor j in Step 2 using Algorithm OM(m – 1). (If it receives no value, then it uses a default value of 0.) Processor i uses the value majority (v_1, v_2, ..., v_{n-1}).

This algorithm is evidently quite complex. The processor are successively divided into smaller and smaller groups and the Byzantine agreement is recursively achieved within each group of processors (Step 2 of 'Algorithm OM(m–1)'). Step 3 is executed during the folding phase of the recursion, where a majority function is applied to select the majority value out of the values received in a round of message exchange (Step 2). The function majority (v_1, v_2, ..., v_{n-1}) computes a majority value of the values v_1, v_2, ..., v_{n-1} if it exists (otherwise, it returns the default value 0).

3.22 APPLICATION OF AGREEMENT PROTOCOLS

Algorithm for agreement problems finds applications in problems where processor should reach an agreement regarding their values in the presence of malicious failures. Two such applications are—

- Clock synchronization in distributed system
- Atomic commit in distributed database

3.22.1 Fault Tolerant Clock Synchronization

In distributed system, it is often necessary that sites maintain physical clocks that are synchronized with one another. Since physical clocks have a drift problem. They must be periodically synchronized. Such periodic synchronization becomes extremely difficult if the Byzantine failures are allowed.

Thus is because a faulty processor can report different clock values to different processors. The following assumptions regarding system are:

A1: All clocks are initially synchronized to approximately same values.

A2: A non faulty processors clock runs at approximately correct rate.

A3: A non faulty process can read the clock value of another non faulty process with at most a small error.

A clock synchronization algorithm should satisfy the following two conditions:

1. At any time, the value of the clocks of all non faulty processors must be approximately equal.
2. There is a small bound on the amount by which the clock of a non faulty process is changed during each resynchronization.

Resynchronization does not cause a clock value to jump arbitrary far, thereby preventing the clock rate being too far from the real time.

3.22.2 Atomic Commit in Distributed Database

In the problem of atomic commit, sites of a distributed database system must agree whether to commit or about a transaction. In the first phase of the atomic commit, sites execute their part of a distributed transaction and broadcast their decision to all other sites. In the second phase, each site based on what it received from other sites in the first phase, decides whether to commit, or abort its part of the distributed computation.

Since every site receives an identical response from all other sites, they will reach same decision. However, if same sites behave maliciously they can send conflicting response to other sites, causing them to make conflicting decision. In these situations, use algorithm for the Byzantine agreement to reach common decision—

1. After sites common decision, it stands the Byzantine agreement.
2. Processes determine a common decision based on agreed vector of values.

3.23 SUMMARY

- In resource deadlocks, processes can simultaneously wait for several resources and can not proceed until they have acquired all those resources.
- In communication deadlocks processes wait to communicate with other processes among a set of processes.
- Deadlocks prevention is commonly achieved by either having a process acquire all the needed resource simultaneously before it begins execution or by preempting a process that holds the needed resource.
- Deadlocks resolution involves breaking existing wait for dependencies in the system WFG to resolve the deadlock.
- In centralized deadlock detection algorithm, a control site has the responsibility of constructing the global WFG and searching it for cycles.
- In distributed deadlock detection algorithm, the responsibility for detecting a global deadlock is shared equally among all the sites.

- In hierarchical deadlock detection sites are arranged in a hierarchical fashion and a site detects deadlock involving only its descendent sites.
- The entire process of reaching an agreement is called an agreement protocol.
- In crash fault, a processor stops functioning and never resumes operation.
- In an omission fault a processor omits to send message to some processors.
- In a malicious fault, a processor behaves randomly & arbitrarily.
- In an authenticated message system, a faulty processor can not forge a message or change the content of a message.
- In a non – authenticated message system a faulty processor can forge a message or change the content of a message before it relay message to other processors.
- In Byzantine agreement problem, an arbitrarily chosen processor called the source processor broadcasts its initial value to all other processors.
- In consensus agreement problem, every processor broadcast its initial value to all other processors. Initial values of the processors may be different then all non faulty processors agree on any common value.
- In interactive consistency problem, every processor broadcast its initial value to all other processors. The initial value of the processors may be different they must agree on vector $(\upsilon_1, \upsilon_2, \upsilon_3, \ldots\ldots\ldots\ldots\upsilon_n)$
- In an atomic commit sites executes their part and broadcasts their decision to all other sites based on what it received from other sites decides whether to commit or abort its part of distributed transactions.

3.24 REVIEW QUESTION

1. Discuss the impact of a message loss on the various deadlock detection algorithms.
2. Give an example to show that in the AND request model, false deadlocks can occur due to deadlock resolution in distributed system. Can something be done about it or they are bound to happen.
3. Discuss the deadlock avoidance approach.
4. Discuss the system model of the deadlock detection.
5. Discuss Resource Vs communication deadlocks.
6. Discuss control organization for distributed deadlock detection.
7. Show that Byzantine Agreement can not always be reached among four processor if two processor are faulty.
8. Show how a solution to the consensus problem can be used to solve the interactive consistency problem.
9. Prove that in dolevetals algorithm for case $n > 3m + 1$, if the active processors agree on the value 1, then the passive processors will also agree on the value of 1.

CHAPTER 4

Distributed File System

4.1 DISTRIBUTED FILE SYSTEM

Distributed file system is a resource management component of a distributed operating system. In distributed files system common can be shared by the entire autonomous computer in the system.Two important goals of distributed file system are-

- Network transparency
- High availability

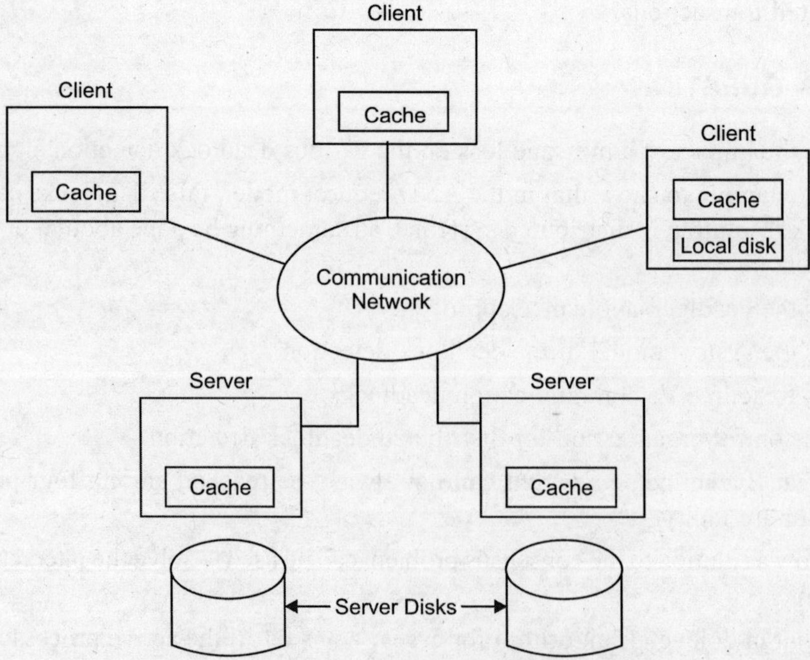

Fig. 4.1 Architecture of distributed file system

A distributed file system is a file system where data is distributed across multiple nodes.

Distributed file system can also refer to:

- Shared disk file system, a different approach, also known as cluster file system.
- Distributed File System (Microsoft), the Microsoft distributed file system (DFS)
- DCE Distributed File System, the distributed file system from The Open Group
- Distributed data store

A shared disk file system

Also known as clustered file system or SAN file system, is an enterprise storage file system which can be shared (concurrently accessed for reading and writing) by multiple computers. Such devices are usually clustered servers, which connect to the underlying block device over an external storage device. Such a device is commonly a storage area network (SAN).

Shared disk file systems are necessary because with regular file systems, if multiple instances (servers) were to attempt concurrent access to the same physical device, the data would rapidly become corrupt, because there is nothing to prevent two devices from performing a modification of the same part of the file system at the same time. Conventional file locking is no aid in this, as file locking operates above the file system level; file locking can protect files against concurrent access but offers no protection when server / operating system manipulates the file system directly. Directly means the server manipulates blocks of storage device. The files in the file system consist of these blocks.

A shared file system extends the file system concept by adding a mechanism for concurrency control. It provides each device accessing the file system with a consistent and serializable view of the file system, avoiding corruption and unintended data loss. Such file systems also usually employ some sort of a fencing mechanism to prevent data corruption in case of node failures.

There are different architectural approaches to a shared disk file system. Some distribute file information across all the servers in a cluster (fully distributed). Others utilize a centralized metadata server. Both achieve the same result of enabling all servers to access all the data on a shared storage device.

Examples of such file systems include:

- Veritas Cluster File System
- Xsan
- Global File System
- Oracle Cluster File System
- VMware VMFS
- IBM General Parallel File System

Distributed file system (DFS) is a set of client and server services that allow an organization utilizing Microsoft Windows servers to organize many distributed SMB file shares into a distributed file system. DFS provides location transparency and redundancy to improve data availability in the face of failure or heavy load by allowing shares in multiple different locations to be logically grouped under one folder, or DFS root.

The **DCE Distributed File System** (DCE/DFS) is the remote file access protocol used with the Distributed Computing Environment. It was based on the AFS Version 3.0 protocol that was developed commercially by Transarc Corporation. AFS Version 3.0 was in turn based on the Andrew File System Version 2.0 protocol (also used by the Coda disconnected file system) originally developed at Carnegie Mellon University.

DCE/DFS consisted of multiple cooperative components that provided a network file system with strong file system semantics, attempting to mimic the behavior of POSIX local file systems while taking advantage of performance optimizations when possible. A DCE/DFS client system utilized a locally managed cache that would contain copies (or regions) of the original file. The client system would coordinate with a server system where the original copy of the file was stored to ensure that multiple clients accessing the same file would re-fetch a cached copy of the file data when the original file had changed.

The advantage of this approach is that it provided very good performance even over slow network connections because most of the file access was actually done to the local cached regions of the file. If the server failed, the client could continue making changes to the file locally, storing it back to the server when it became available again. DCE/DFS also divorced the concept of logical units of management (Filesets) from the underlying volume on which the fileset was stored. In doing this it allowed administrative control of the location for the fileset in a manner that was transparent to the end user. To support this and other advanced DCE/DFS features, a local journaling file system (DCE/LFS also known as Episode) was developed to provide the full range of support options.

IBM was working on a replacement for DCE/DFS called ADFS (Advanced Distributed File System). One major goal of this project was to decouple DFS from the complexities of DCE's cell directory services (CDS) and security services (secd). Another key feature would have been the elimination of enctype limitations associated with DCE/RPC. No public mention of this effort has been made since 2005, leading many to believe the project has been killed.

A **distributed data store** is a network in which a user stores his or her information on a **number of peer network nodes**. The user also usually reciprocates and allows users to use his or her computer as a storage node as well. Information may or may not be accessible to other users depending on the design of the network.

Most of the peer to peer networks do not have distributed data stores in that the user's data is only available when their node is on the network. However, this distinction is somewhat blurred in a system such as BitTorrent, where it is possible for the originating node to go offline but the content to continue to be served. Still, this is only the case for individual files requested by the redistributors, as contrasted with a network such as Freenet where all computers are made available to serve all files.

Distributed data stores typically use an error detection and correction technique. Some distributed data stores (such as Parchive over NNTP) use forward error correction techniques to recover the original file when parts of that file are damaged or unavailable. Others try again to download that file from a different mirror.

Example data store networks

- Chord project
- GNUnet
- Freenet
- NNTP (the distributed data storage protocol used for Usenet news)
- Mnet
- PowerFolder
- Storage@home
- Wuala

4.1.1 Network transparency

It provides the same function as capability to access files distributed over a network as the file system of a timesharing mainframe system does to access files residing at one location.

4.1.2 High Availability

It signifies that users should have same easy access to files, Irrespective of their physical location. System failures or regularly scheduled activities such as backups or maintenance should not result in the unavailability of files.

Ideally, in a distributed file system files can be stored at any machine and the computation can be performed at any machine file services are dedicated to storing files and performing storage and retrieval operation. The clients are used for computational purposes and they can access the file storage on server. Some client machine may also be equipped with local disk storage that can be used for caching remote files, as a swap area or storage area. Two most important services present in the distributed file system are.

- Name server
- Cache manager

Name server is a process that maps names specified by client to store objects such s files directories.

Cache manager is a process that implements file caching in which a copy of data stored at a remote file server is brought to client machine when referenced by client. The data access in distributed file system is shown in failure.

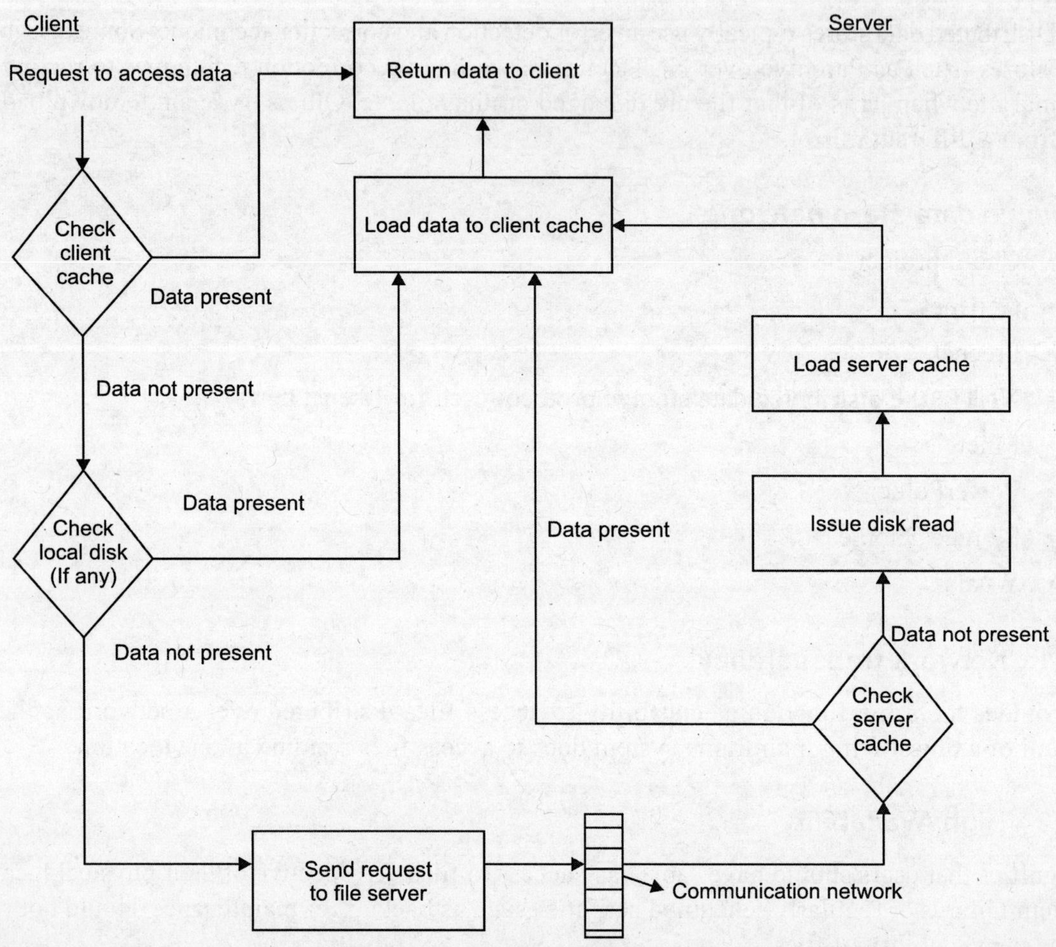

Fig 4.2 Data access actions in DFS

4.2 MECHANISM FOR BUILDING DISTRIBUTED FILE SYSTEM

There are different techniques available to build distributed file systems.

4.2.1 Mounting

This mechanism allows to binding together of different file name space to form a single hierarchical structured name space. A name space can be mounted at an internal node or leaves node of a name space tree. A node onto which a name space is mounted is known as mount point.

In case distributed file system, file system maintain by remote server are mounted at the client there one two approaches to maintain a mount information.

(i) Mount information can be maintained at client; in this case each client has to individuals mount every required file system.

(ii) Mount information can be maintained at server, in this case it is possible that every client sees and identical file name space, if files are known to different server, then mount information need only be updated at server. But in first case every client needs to update its mount tables.

4.2.2 Caching

Caching is commonly employed in distributed file system to reduce delays in the accessing of data. In file caching, a copy of data stored at a remote file server is brought to the client when referenced by the client. Subsequent access to data is performed locally at the client, thereby reducing access delays due to network latency. Caching exploits the temporal locality of reference exhibited by program.

The temporal locality of reference refers to the fact a file recently accessed is likely to be a accessed again in near future. Data can either be cached in the main memory or on the local disks of the clients. Also, data is cached in the main memory (server cache) at the servers to reduce disk access latency. The file system performance can be improved by caching, since accessing remote files is much slower than accessing local memory or local disks. In addition, caching reduces the frequency of access to the file servers and the communication networks thereby improving the scalability of a file system.

4.2.3 Hints

Caching improves file system performance by reducing delay in accessing data, but when multiple clients cache and modify shared data, the problem of cache consistency arises. An alternate approach is to treat the cache data is hints. In this, cached data are not expected to be completely accurate; however, valid cache entries improve performance substantially without incurring the cost of maintaining cache consistency. The classes of applications that can utilize hits are those which can recover after discovering that the cached data are invalid.

For example, after the name of a file or a directory is mapped to the physical object, the address of the object can be stored as a hint in the cache. If the address fails to map to the object in following attempt the cached address is purged from the cache. The file server consults the name server to determine the actual location of the file or directory and updates the cache.

4.2.4 Bulk data Transfer

The bulk of delay in transforming data over a network is due to the high cost of executing communication protocols. Transforming data is bulk reduces the protocol processing overhead at both clients and servers.

In bulk data transfer, multiple consecutive data blocks are transferred from servers to client instead of just the block referenced by clients. A bulk transfer reduces file access overhead through obtaining a multiple number of blocks with a single seek. By formatting and transmitting a multiple number of large packets in a single context switch and by reducing the number of acknowledgements that needs to be sent.

4.2.5 Encryption

Encryption is used for enforcing security in distributed systems. In this, two entities wising to communicate with each other establish a key for conversion with the help of an authentication server. It is important that conversion key is determined by authentications server but is never sent in plain text to either of entities.

4.3 DESIGN ISSUES

The design issues are studied to better understand the intricacies of a distributed file system. The most important design issues are—

4.3.1 Naming and Name Resolution

A name in file systems is associated with an object. Name Resolution refers to the process of mapping a name to an object or in the case of replication, to multiple objects. A name space is a collection of names which may or may not share an identical resolution mechanism. There have been traditionally three approaches to name files in a distributed environment.

1. Concatenate the host name to the names of files that are stored on that host.

   Disadvantage This approaches guarantee that a file name is unique system wide, but it conflicts with the goal of network transparency. Moving a file from host to another requires changes in the file name and in the applications accessing that file i.e. this naming scheme is not location in dependent.

   Advantage Name resolution is very simple as a file can be located with out consulting any other host in the system.

2. To mount remote directories on to local directories.

   Mounting a remote directory requires that the host of the directory be known. Once a remote directory is mounted, its file can be referenced in a location transparent manner. This approach can also resolve a file name without consulting any host.

3. To have a single global directory where all the files in the system belong to a single name space.

   Disadvantage Limited to one computing facility or a few cooperating computing facilities. This limitation is due to requirement of system wide unique filenames which requires that all the computing facilities involved cooperate.

4.3.2 Name Server

In a centralized system, Name resolution can be accomplished by maintaining a table that maps names to objects. In distributed systems, name servers are responsible for name resolution. A name server is a process that maps names specified by client to stored objects such as files and directories. The easiest approach to name resolution in distributed systems is for all clients to send their queries to a single name server which maps names to objects.

Disadvantage

- If name server is crashes, the entire system is affected.
- The name server may become a bottleneck and degrade the system performance.

4.3.3 Cache on Disk or Main Memory

The advantages of having the cache in the main memory are

- Diskless workstation can also take advantage of caching
- Accessing a cache in main memory is much faster than accessing a cache on local disk
- The server cache is in the main memory at the server, and hence a single design for a caching mechanism is applicable to both clients & servers.

The main disadvantage of having client cache in main memory is that it competes with the virtual memory system for physical memory space. Thus a scheme to deal with the memory contention between cache and virtual memory systems necessary.

4.3.4 Writing Policy

The writing policy decides when a modified cache block at a client should be transferred to the server. In this write through policy, all writers requested by the applications at clients are also carried out at the server immediately.

The main advantage of write through policy is reliability. In the event of a client crash, little information is lost. A write through policy, however does not take advantage of cache. An alternate writing policy, delayed writing policy delay writing at the servers. In this, modifications due to write are reflected at the servers after some delay.

Another writing policy delays the updating of files at the server until the file is closed at the client. In this policy, the traffic at the server depends on the average period that files are open. If the average period is short then policy does not benefit from delaying updates, on other hand if the average period is long, this policy is also susceptible to losing data in the event of a client crash.

4.4 DISTRIBUTED SHARED MEMORY

Distributed shared memory system is a resources management component of a distributed operating system that implements that shared memory model in distributed systems, which have no physical shared memory. The shared memory model provides a virtual address space that is shared among all nodes in a distributed system.

4.4.1 Architecture & Motivation

With distributed shared memory program access data in the shared address space just as they access data in traditional virtual memory. In system that support distributed shared memory data moves between secondary memory and main memory as well as between main memories of different nodes. Each node can own data stored in the shared address space, and the ownership can change when data moves from one node to another.

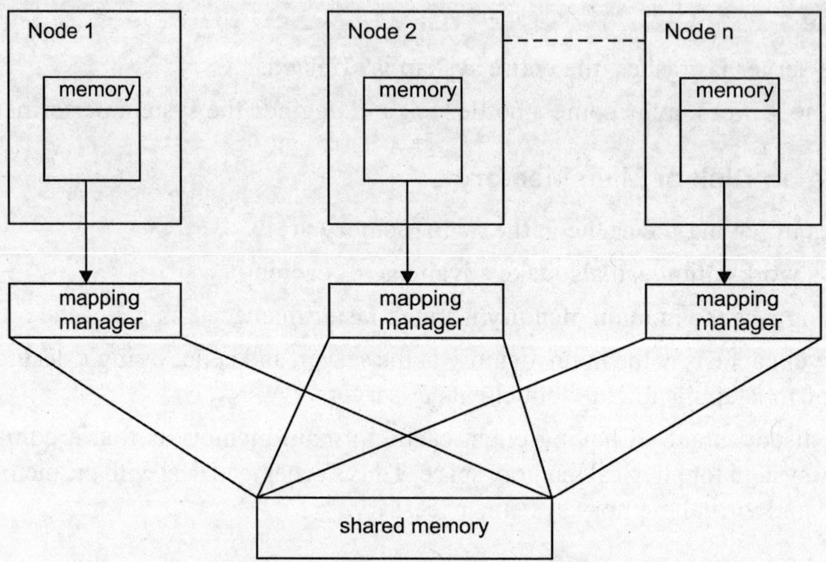

Fig 4.3 Distributed shared momory

When a process data in the shared address space, a mapping manager maps the shared memory address to the physical memory .the mapping manager is a layer of software implemented either in operating system kernel or as a library routine. Advantages of distributed shared memory are-

1. DSM hides explicit data movement and provides a simpler abstraction for sharing data that programmer is already well versed with.
2. It is easier to design and write parallel algorithms using DSM rather than explicit message passing.
3. In the message passing model, data moves between two different address spaces, this makes it difficult to pass complex data structures between two processes, DSM allows complex structures to be passed by reference, thus simplifying the development of algorithms for distributed applications.
4. Distributed shared memory forces advantage of the locality of reference, exhibited by programs and there by cuts down on the over headed of communicating over the network.
5. DSM systems are cheaper to build than tightly coupled multiprocessors system.
6. The physical memory available at all the nodes of a DSM system combined together is enormous.
7. Program written for shared memory multiprocessors can in principle be run on DSM systems without any changes. Such programs can be easily being ported to DSM system.

4.4.2 Algorithms for Implementing DSM

The central issues in the implementation of distributed shared memory are

1. How to keep track of location of remote data.

2. How to overcome the communication delay and high overhead associated with the execution of communication protocols in distributed systems when accessing remote data.
3. How to make shared data concurrently accessible at several nodes in order to improve system performance.

1. **Central Server Algorithms:** In central server algorithms, a central server maintains all the shared data. It services the read requests from other nodes or clients by returning the data items to them. It updates the data on write requests by clients and acknowledgement messages. A timeout can be employed to resend the requests in case of failed acknowledgement. Duplicate write requests can be detected by associating sequence numbers with the write requests.

   Advantage: Simple to implement.

   Disadvantage Central server can become a bottleneck.

   To overcome this problem, shared data can be distributed among several servers. In such a case, clients must be able to locate the appropriate servers for every data access.

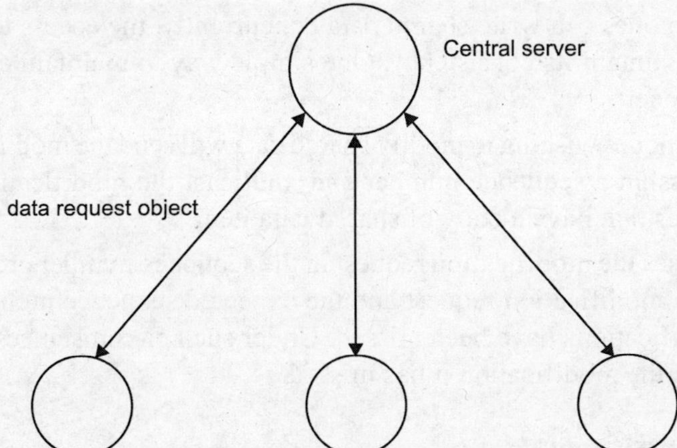

Fig 4.4 Central Server Algorighm

2. **Migration Algorithm:** In contrast to central server algorithm, where every data access request is forwarded to the location of data, data in the migration algorithm is shipped to the location of the data access request, allowing subsequent access to the data to be performed locally. The migration algorithm allows only one node to access a shared data at time. Typically, the whole page or block containing the data items migrates instead of an individual item requested. This algorithm takes the advantages of the locality of reference exhibited by programs by amortizing the cost of migration over multiple accesses to the migrated data. However this approach is susceptible to thrashing where pages frequently migrate between nodes while serving only a few requests.

   To reduce thrashing, the migrate system uses a tunable parameter that determines the duration for which a node can passes a shared data item. This allows a node to make number of accesses to the page before it is migrate to another node. To locate a data block, the migration algorithm can make use of a server that keeps track of the location of pages or through hints maintained at nodes. These hints direct the search for a page toward the node currently holding the page or a query can be broadcast to locate page.

3. **Read Replication Algorithm:**The read replication algorithm extends the migration algorithm by replicating data blocks and allowing multiple nodes to have read access or pone node to have read write access.

   Read replication can improve system performance by allowing multiple node to access data concurrently. However the write operation is expensive as all the copies of a shared block at various nodes will either have to be invalidated or updated with current value to maintain the consistency of the shared date block.

   In the read replication algorithm, distributed shared, memory must keep of the location of all the copies of data blocks.

4. **Full replication Algorithm:** The full replication algorithm is an extension of read replication algorithm. It allows multiple nodes to have both read and write access to shared data block, because many nodes can write shared data concurrently, the access to shared data must be controlled to maintain its consistency. One simple way to maintain consistency is to use a gap free sequencer.

In this scheme, all nodes wishing to modify shared data will send the modification to a sequencer. The sequencer will assign a sequence number and multicast the modification with the sequence number to all the nodes that have a copy of shared data item.

Each node processes the modification request in the sequence number order, A gap between the sequence number of a modification request and the expected sequence number at a node indicate that one or more modifications have been missed. Under such circumstances the node will ask for the retransmissions of the modification it has missed.

4.5 MEMORY COHERENCE

A memory is coherence if the value returned by a read operation is always the value that the programmer expected. To maintain the coherence of shared data items a mechanism that controls or synchronization the accesses is necessary. Also to write correct programs, a programmer needs to understand how the concurrent updates, to shared memory are carried out.

The most intuitive semantics for memory coherence is strict consistency defined as a read returns the most recently written value. Strictly consistency requires the ability to determine the latest write, which in turn implies a total ordering of requests. The total ordering of requests leads to inefficiency due to more data movement and synchronization requirement that what a program may really.

To counter this problem, some distributed shared memory systems attempt to improve the performance by providing relaxed coherence semantics. Following are several form of memory coherence

1. **Sequential Consistency:** A system is sequentially consistent if the request of any execution of the operations of all the processors is the same as if they were executed in a sequential order and the operation of each individual processor appear in this sequence in the order specified by its program.
2. **General Consistency:** A system support general consistency if all the copies of a memory location eventually contain the same data when all the writes issued by every processor have completed.
3. **Processor Consistency:** Writes issued by a processor are observed in the same order in which they issued. However, the order in which writes from two processor occur as observed by themselves or a third processor need not be identical i. e. two simultaneous reads of the same location from different processor may yield different request.
4. **Weak Consistency:** Synchronization accesses are sequentially consistency. Before synchronization access can be performed, all previous regular data accesses must be completed. Before a regular data access can be performed all previous synchronization accesses must be completed. The memory will be consistent immediately after a synchronization problem.
6. **Release Consistency:** Release consistency is same as weak consistency, but synchronization accesses must only be processor consistent with respect to each other. Synchronization operations are broken down into acquires and release operations. All pending acquire must be done before a regular access is done, and all regular access must be done before a release is done.

4.6 COHERENCE PROTOCOLS

To provide concurrent access, DSM systems make use of data replication, but the fundamental problem with data replication is the difficulty in ensuring that all copies have the same information and that nodes do not access state data. A protocol to keep replies coherent is needed. Two basic protocols

(i) **Write invalidate protocols:** In write invalidate protocol, a write to a shared data cause the invalidation of all copies expect one before the writes can proceed. Once invalidated copies are no longer accessible. A major disadvantage is that invalidations are sent to all nodes that have copies, irrespective of whether they will use this data or not. This protocol is better suited for application where several updates occur between reads as well as when a program exhibits a high degree of per node locality of reference.

(ii) **Write updates protocols:** In write update protocol, a write to a shared data causes all copies of that data to be updated this approach is more difficult to implement than previous, as a new value has to be sent instead of involution messages , this protocol can be expected to generate considerable network traffic.

4.7 DISTRIBUTED SCHEDULING

Because wide area networks have high communication delays, distributed scheduling is more suitable for distributed systems based on local area network. A locally distributed system consists of a collection of autonomous computers, connected by local area communication networks. Users submit tasks at their host computers for processing. The need for load distributing arises in such environments because due to random arrival of tasks and their random CPU service time requirement there is a good possibility that several computers are heavily loaded while others are idle or lightly loaded.

4.8 ISSUES IN LOAD DISTRIBUTING

There are several central issues in load distributing.:

1. **Load:** Resource queue length and CPU queue length good indicators of load because they correlate well with the task transfer time. Measuring CPU task queue length is fairly simple and carries little overhead. If a task transfer involves significance delays, however, simply using the current CPU queue length as a load indicates can result in a node accepting task, while other tasks is accepted earlier are still in transit.
2. **Classification of Load Distributing Algorithm:** The basic function of load distributing algorithm is to transfer load from heavily loaded computers to idle or lightly loaded computers. Load distributing algorithms can be categorized as static, dynamic or adaptive. In static load distributed algorithm decision are hard wired in the algorithm using a priori knowledge of the system. Dynamic load distributing algorithm use system state information at least in part to make load distribution decisions. Dynamic load distributing algorithms have the potential to outperform static load distributing algorithm because they are able to exploit short term fluctuation in the system state to improve performance.

   Adaptive load distributing algorithm are a special class of dynamic load distributing algorithms in that they adapt their activities by dynamically changing the parameters of the algorithm to suit the changing system state.
3. **Load Balancing Vs Load Sharing:** Load balancing attempting to equalize loads at all computers because a load balancing algorithm transfers tasks at a higher rate than a load sharing algorithm. The higher overhead incurred by load balancing algorithm. May overweigh this potential performance improvement. Load balancing is a special case of load sharing, performing a particular load of anticipating task transfers.
4. **Distributed Deadlock Detection Preemptive Vs Non Preemptive transfers:** Preemptive task transfer involves the transfer of a task that is partially executive this transfer is an expensive operation as the collection of a tasks state can be difficult. Typically, a task state consists of a virtual memory image, a process control block, unread I/O buffers and messages, file pointers, times that have been set etc.

Non preemptive task transfers involve the transfers of tasks that have not begun execution and hence do not require the transfer of tasks state.

4.9 COMPONENTS OF LOAD DISTRIBUTING ALGORITHM

A load distributing algorithms has four components

- Transfer Policy
- Selection Policy
- Location Policy
- Information policy

1. **Transfer policy:** A large number of transfer policies that have been proposed are threshold policies. Thresholds are expressed in units of load. When a new task originates at a node and the load at that node exceeds a threshold T the transfer policy decides that the node is a sender. If the load at a node falls below T, the transfer policy decides that the node can be a receiver for a remote task.
2. **Selection Policy:** A selection policy selects a task for transfer, once the transfer policy decides that the node is a sender, should the selection policy fail to find a suitable task to transfer, the node is no longer considered sender until the transmission policy again. The factors for selection of the task are
   - The overhead incurred by the transfer should calls made by selected.
   - The number of location dependent system calls made by selected tasks should be minimal.
3. **Location Policy:** The responsibility of a location policy is to find suitable nodes to share load. A widely used method for finding a suitable node is through polling. In policy, a node polls another node to find out whether it is a suitable node for load sharing.
4. **Information Policy:** The information policy is responsible for deciding when information about the states of other nodes in the system should be collected, where it should be collected from and what information should be collected. Most information policies are
   - Demand driven
   - Periodic
   - State change driven

4.10 STABILITY — TWO VIEWS OF STABILITY ARE

(i) **The Queuing Theoretic Perspective:** When long term arrival rate of work to a system is greater than the rate at which the system can perform work, the CPU queues grow without bound. Such a system is termed unstable.

Example: Load distributing algorithm performing excessive message exchange to collect state information. A load distributing algorithm is said to be effective under a given set of conditions, if it improves the performance relative to that of a system not using load distributing.

(ii) **Algorithmic Perspective:** If an algorithm perform fruitless actions indefinitely with finite probability the algorithm is said to be unstable, Example- Pr4ocessor thrashing. The transfer of a task to a receiver may increase the receivers queue length to the point of overhead necessitating the transfer of that task to yet another node. This process may respect indefinitely. In this case, a task is more from one node to another in search of a lightly loaded node without ever receiving services.

4.11 PERFORMANCE COMPARISONS

The average service demands for tasks is assumed to be one time unit and task inter arrival times and service demands are independently exponentially distributed. The system load is assumed to be homogenous i. e. all nodes have the same long term task arrival rate. The procedure for selecting a suitable load sharing algòrithm is –

(i) If the system under consideration never attain high load, sender initiated algorithm will give an improved average response over no load sharing at all.

(ii) Stable scheduling algorithm is recommended for systems that can reach high loads.

(iii) For systems that experience wide range of load fluctuations, the stable symmetrically initiated scheduling algorithm is recommended.

(iv) For a system that experience wide fluctuations in load and has a high lost for the migration of partly executed tasks, stable sender initiated algorithms are recommended.

(v) For a system that experiences heterogeneous work arrival, adaptive stable algorithm are preferable.

4.12 TASK MIGRATION

Task migration refers to the transfer of a task that has already begin execution to a new location and continuing its execution there to migrate a partially executed task to a new location, the tasks state should be made available at the new location. The general steps involved in task migration are—

(i) Task Transfer: the transfer of tasks state to the new machine.

(ii) Unfreeze: this task is installed at the new machine and is put in the ready queue. So that it can continue executing.

4.13 ISSUES IN TASK MIGRATION

In the design of a task migration mechanism, several issues play on important role in determining the efficiency of the mechanism. These issues include—

- State transfer
- Location transparency
- Structure/organization

1. **State transfer:** There are two issues to be considered in state transfer.

   (i) The cost to support remote execution, which includes delays due to freezing task.

   (ii) Residual dependencies which refer to the amount of resources a former host of a preempted or migrated task continue, to dedicate to service requests from migrated task.

2. **Location transparency:** In distributed systems, that supports task migration, it is essential that location transparency be supported. i.e. task migration should hide the location of tasks just as a distributed file systems hides the location of files. Location transparency in principle requires that names be independent of their locations.

3. Structure of migration mechanism:

- Whether to separate policy making modules from mechanism modules.
- Deciding whether the policy and mechanism should reside.
- Policy modules decide whether a task transfer should occur.

4.14 FAULT TOLERANCE

The ability of a system to respond gracefully to an unexpected hardware or software failure. There are many levels of fault tolerance, the lowest being the ability to continue operation in the event of a power failure. Many fault-tolerant computer systems *mirror* all operations — that is, every operation is performed on two or more duplicate systems, so if one fails the other can take over.

Fault-tolerant describes a computer system or component designed so that, in the event that a component fails, a backup component or procedure can immediately take its place with no loss of service. Fault tolerance can be provided with software, or embedded in hardware, or provided by some combination.

In the software implementation, the operating system provides an interface that allows a programmer to "checkpoint" critical data at pre-determined points within a transaction. In the hardware implementation (for example, with Stratus and its VOS operating system), the programmer does not need to be aware of the fault-tolerant capabilities of the machine.

At a hardware level, fault tolerance is achieved by duplexing each hardware component. Disks are mirrored. Multiple processors are "lock-stepped" together and their outputs are compared for correctness. When an anomaly occurs, the faulty component is determined and taken out of service, but the machine continues to function as usual.

To avoid disruption due to failure and to improve availability, systems are designed to be fault tolerant. A system can be designed to be fault tolerant in two ways

(i) A system may mask failures or a system may exhibits a well defined failure behavior in the event of failure. When a system is designed to mask failures, it continues performs its specified function in the event of a failure.

(ii) A system designed for well defined behavior may/may not perform the specified function in the event of a failure; however it can facilitate actions suitable for recovery.

One key approach to tolerate failures is redundancy. In this approach , a system may employ a multiple number of processes, a multiple number of hardware components, multiple copies of data etc each with independents failures modes. Since a fault tolerant system must behave in a specified manner in the event of a failure, it is important to study the implications of contains types of failures.

Process Death

When a process die, it is important that the resources allocated to that process are recouped, otherwise they may be permanently lost. If the server machine is fails, it is necessary that client machine be informed so that the client process, waiting for a reply can be unblocked to take suitable action. Likewise, if a client process dies than server process is informed that the client processes no longer exist.

Machine Failure

In the case of a machine failure, all the processes running at machine will die. As far as the behavior of a client process or a server process is concerned, there is not much difference in their behavior in the event of a machine failure or process death.

Network Failures

A communication link failure can partition a network into subnets, making it impossible for a machine to communicate with another machine in a different subnet. A process can not really tell the difference between the machine failure or the network failures.

4.15 FAULT-TOLERANT SYSTEM

Fault-tolerance or **graceful degradation** is the property that enables a system (often computer-based) to continue operating properly in the event of the failure of (or one or more faults within) some of its components. If its operating quality decreases at all, the decrease is proportional to the severity of the failure, as compared to a naïvely-designed system in which even a small failure can cause total breakdown. Fault-tolerance is particularly sought-after in high-availability or life-critical systems.

Fault-tolerance is not just a property of individual machines; it may also characterise the rules by which they interact. For example, the Transmission Control Protocol (TCP) is designed to allow reliable two-way communication in a packet-switched network, even in the presence of communications links which are imperfect or overloaded. It does this by requiring the endpoints of the communication to *expect* packet loss, duplication, reordering and corruption, so that these conditions do not damage data integrity, and only reduce throughput by a proportional amount.

Data formats may also be designed to degrade gracefully. HTML for example, is designed to be forward compatible, allowing new HTML entities to be ignored by Web browsers which do not understand them without causing the document to be unusable.

Recovery from errors in fault-tolerant systems can be characterised as either **roll-forward** or **roll-back**. When the system detects that it has made an error, roll-forward recovery takes the system state at that time and corrects it, to be able to move forward. Roll-back recovery reverts the system state back to some earlier, correct version, for example using checkpointing, and moves forward from there. Roll-back recovery requires that the operations between the checkpoint and the detected erroneous state can be made idempotent. Some systems make use of both roll-forward and roll-back recovery for different errors or different parts of one error.

Within the scope of an *individual* system, fault-tolerance can be achieved by anticipating exceptional conditions and building the system to cope with them, and, in general, aiming for self-stabilization so that the system converges towards an error-free state. However, if the consequences of a system failure are catastrophic, or the cost of making it sufficiently reliable is very high, a better solution may be to use some form of duplication. In any case, if the consequence of a system failure is catastrophic, the system must be able to use reversion to fall back to a safe mode. This is similar to roll-back recovery but can be a human action if humans are present in the loop.

4.16 FAULT TOLERANCE REQUIREMENTS

The basic characteristics of fault tolerance require:

1. No single point of failure
2. No single point of repair
3. Fault isolation to the failing component
4. Fault containment to prevent propagation of the failure
5. Availability of reversion modes

In addition, fault tolerant systems are characterized in terms of both planned service outages and unplanned service outages. These are usually measured at the application level and not just at a hardware level. The figure of merit is called availability and is expressed as a percentage. A five system would therefore statistically provide 99.999% availability.

Fault-tolerant systems are typically based on the concept of redundancy.

4.17 FAULT-TOLERANCE BY REPLICATION

Spare components addresses the first fundamental characteristic of fault-tolerance in three ways:

- Replication: Providing multiple identical instances of the same system or subsystem, directing tasks or requests to all of them in parallel, and choosing the correct result on the basis of a quorum;
- Redundancy: Providing multiple identical instances of the same system and switching to one of the remaining instances in case of a failure.
- Diversity: Providing multiple different implementations of the same specification, and using them like replicated systems to cope with errors in a specific implementation.

All implementations of RAID, redundant array of independent disks, except RAID 0 are examples of a fault-tolerant storage device that uses data redundancy.

A lockstep fault-tolerant machine uses replicated elements operating in parallel. At any time, all the replications of each element should be in the same state. The same inputs are provided to each replication, and the same outputs are expected. The outputs of the replications are compared using a voting circuit. A machine with two replications of each element is termed Dual Modular Redundant (DMR). The voting circuit can then only detect a mismatch and recovery relies on other methods. A machine with three replications of each element is termed Triple Modular Redundancy (TMR). The voting circuit can determine which replication is in error when a two-to-one vote is observed. In this case, the voting circuit can output the correct result, and discard the erroneous version. After this, the internal state of the erroneous replication is assumed to be different from that of the other two, and the voting circuit can switch to a DMR mode. This model can be applied to any larger number of replications.

Lockstep fault tolerant machines are most easily made fully synchronous, with each gate of each replication making the same state transition on the same edge of the clock, and the clocks to the replications being exactly in phase. However, it is possible to build lockstep systems without this requirement.

Bringing the replications into synchrony requires making their internal stored states the same. They can be started from a fixed initial state, such as the reset state. Alternatively, the internal state of one replica can be copied to another replica.

One variant of DMR is **pair-and-spare**. Two replicated elements operate in lockstep as a pair, with a voting circuit that detects any mismatch between their operations and outputs a signal indicating that there is an error. Another pair operates exactly the same way. A final circuit selects the output of the pair that does not proclaim that it is in error. Pair-and-spare requires four replicas rather than the three of TMR, but has been used commercially.

No single point of repair

If a system experiences a failure, it must continue to operate without interruption during the repair process.

Fault isolation to the failing component

When a failure occurs, the system must be able to isolate the failure to the offending component. This requires the addition of dedicated failure detection mechanisms that exist only for the purpose of fault isolation.

Recovery from a fault condition requires classifying the fault or failing component. The National Institute of Standards and Technology NIST categorizes faults based on Locality, Cause, Duration and Effect.

Fault containment

Some failure mechanisms can cause a system to fail by propagating the failure to the rest of the system. An example of this kind of failure is the "Rogue transmitter" which can swamp legitimate communication in a system and cause overall system failure. Mechanisms that isolate a rogue transmitter or failing component to protect the system are required.

4.18 BYZANTINE FAULT TOLERANCE

Byzantine fault tolerance is a sub-field of error tolerance research inspired by the **Byzantine Generals' Problem**, which is a generalized version of the Two Generals' Problem.

The object of Byzantine fault tolerance is to be able to defend against a *Byzantine failure*, in which a component of some system not only behaves erroneously, but also fails to behave consistently when interacting with multiple other components. Correctly functioning components of a Byzantine fault tolerant system will be able to reach the same group decisions assuming there are not too many Byzantine faulty components.

4.18.1 Byzantine Failures

A **Byzantine fault** is an arbitrary fault that occurs during the execution of an algorithm by a distributed system. It encompasses those faults that are commonly referred to as "crash failures" and "send and omission failures". When a Byzantine failure has occurred, the system may respond in any unpredictable way, unless it is designed to have Byzantine fault tolerance.

These arbitrary failures may be loosely categorized as follows:

- a failure to take another step in the algorithm, also known as a crash failure;
- a failure to correctly execute a step of the algorithm; and
- arbitrary execution of a step other than the one indicated by the algorithm.

For example, if the output of one function is the input of another, then small round-off errors in the first function can produce much larger errors in the second. If the second function were fed into a third, the problem could grow even larger, until the values produced are worthless. Another example is in compiling source code. One minor syntaxtical error early on in the code can produce large numbers of perceived errors later, as the parser of the compiler gets out-of-phase with the lexical and syntactic information in the source program.

Steps are taken by processes, the logical abstractions that represent the execution path of the algorithms. A faulty process is one that at some point exhibits one of the above failures. A process that is not faulty is correct.

The Byzantine failure assumption models real-world environments in which computers and networks may behave in unexpected ways due to hardware failures, network congestion and disconnection, as well as malicious attacks. Byzantine failure-tolerant algorithms must cope with such failures and still satisfy the specifications of the problems they are designed to solve. Such algorithms are commonly characterized by their resilience t, the number of faulty processes with which an algorithm can cope.

Many classic agreement problems, such as the Byzantine Generals' Problem, have no solution unless $t < n / 3$, where n is the number of processes in the system.

The Two Generals' Problem is a specific case which assumes that processes are reliable but communication between processes is not reliable.

The consensus (computer science) problem is another case which assumes that processes never send incorrect messages, but any process may crash (stop sending messages) at any time.

4.18.2 Origin

Byzantine refers to the Byzantine Generals' Problem, an agreement problem in which generals of the Byzantine Empire's army must decide unanimously whether to attack some enemy army. The problem is complicated by the geographic separation of the generals, who must communicate by sending messengers to each other, and by the presence of traitors amongst the generals. These traitors can act arbitrarily in order to achieve the following aims: trick some generals into attacking; force a decision that is not consistent with the generals' desires, e.g. forcing an attack when no general wished to attack; or confusing some generals to the point that they are unable to make up their minds. If the traitors succeed in any of these goals, any resulting attack is doomed, as only a concerted effort can result in victory.

Byzantine fault tolerance can be achieved if the loyal (non-faulty) generals have a unanimous agreement on their strategy. Note that if the source general is correct, all loyal generals must agree upon that value. Otherwise, the choice of strategy agreed upon is irrelevant.

4.18.3 Solutions

Several solutions were originally described by Lamport, Shostak, and Pease in 1982. They began by noting that the Generals' Problem can be reduced to solving a "Commander and Lieutenants" problem where Loyal Lieutenants must all act in unison and that their action must correspond to what the Commander ordered in the case that the Commander is Loyal. Roughly speaking, the Generals vote by treating each others' orders as votes.

- One solution considers scenarios in which messages may be forged, but which will be *Byzantine-fault-tolerant* as long as the number of traitorous generals does not equal or exceed one third. The impossibility of dealing with one-third or more traitors ultimately reduces to proving that the 1 Commander + 2 Lieutenants problem cannot be solved if the Commander is traitorous. The reason is, if we have three commanders, A, B, and C, and A is the traitor: when A tells B to attack and C to retreat, and B and C send messages to each other, forwarding A's message, neither B nor C can figure out who is the traitor, since it isn't necessarily A - the other commander could have forged the message purportedly from A. It can be shown that if n is the number of generals in total, and t is the number of traitors in that n, then there are solutions to the problem only when n is greater than or equal to $3t + 1$.
- A second solution requires unforgeable signatures (in modern computer systems, this may be achieved in practice using public-key cryptography), but maintains Byzantine fault tolerance in the presence of an arbitrary number of traitorous generals.
- Also presented is a variation on the first two solutions allowing Byzantine-fault-tolerant behavior in some situations where not all generals can communicate directly with each other.

4.19 INTRUSION TOLERANCE

Intrusion tolerance is a Fault-tolerant design approach to defending information systems against malicious attack. Abandoning the conventional aim of preventing all intrusions, intrusion tolerance instead calls for triggering mechanisms that prevent intrusions from leading to a system security failure.

Projects in this area include the MAFTIA project (Malicious- and Accidental-Fault Tolerance for Internet Applications), which developed concepts and prototyped architectures, and the OASIS program, which implemented several intrusion-tolerant system.

4.20 FAULT-TOLERANT DESIGN

In engineering, **fault-tolerant design**, also known as **fail-safe design**, is a design that enables a system to continue operation, possibly at a reduced level (also known as graceful degradation), rather than failing completely, when some part of the system fails. The term is most commonly used to describe computer-based systems designed to continue more or less fully operational with, perhaps, a reduction in throughput or an increase in response time in the event of some partial failure. That is, the system as a whole is not stopped due to problems either in the hardware or the software. An example in another field is a motor vehicle designed so it will continue to be drivable if one of the tires is punctured. A structure is able to retain its integrity in the presence of damage due to causes such as fatigue, corrosion, manufacturing flaws, or impact.

Components

If each component, in turn, can continue to function when one of its subcomponents fails, this will allow the total system to continue to operate, as well. Using a passenger vehicle as an example, a car can have "run-flat" tires, which each contain a solid rubber core, allowing them to be used even if a tire is punctured. The punctured "run-flat" tire may be used for a limited time at a reduced speed.

Redundancy

This means having backup components which automatically "kick in" should one component fail. For example, large cargo trucks can lose a tire without any major consequences. They have so many tires that no one tire is critical (with the exception of the front tires, which are used to steer).

When to use

Providing fault-tolerant design for every component is normally not an option. In such cases the following criteria may be used to determine which components should be fault-tolerant:

- **How critical is the component?** In a car, the radio is not critical, so this component has less need for fault-tolerance.
- **How likely is the component to fail?** Some components, like the drive shaft in a car, are not likely to fail, so no fault-tolerance is needed.
- **How expensive is it to make the component fault-tolerant?** Requiring a redundant car engine, for example, would likely be too expensive both economically and in terms of weight and space, to be considered.

An example of a component that passes all the tests is a car's occupant restraint system. While we do not normally think of the *primary* occupant restraint system, it is gravity. If the vehicle rolls over or undergoes severe g-forces, then this primary method of occupant restraint may fail.

Restraining the occupants during such an accident is absolutely critical to safety, so we pass the first test. Accidents causing occupant ejection were quite common before seat belts, so we pass the second test. The cost of a redundant restraint method like seat belts is quite low, both economically and in terms or weight and space, so we pass the third test. Therefore, adding seat belts to all vehicles is an excellent idea. Other "supplemental restraint systems", such as airbags, are more expensive and so pass that test by a smaller margin.

Examples

Hardware fault-tolerance sometimes requires that broken parts can be swapped out with new ones while the system is still operational (in computing known as *hot swapping*). Such a system implemented with a single backup is known as **single point tolerant**, and represents the vast majority of fault-tolerant systems. In such systems the mean time between failures should be long enough for the operators to have time to fix the broken devices before the backup also fails. It helps if the time between failures is as long as possible, but this is not specifically required in a fault-tolerant system.

Fault-tolerance is notably successful in computer applications. Tandem Computers built their entire business on such machines, which used single point tolerance to create their **NonStop** systems with uptimes measured in years. Fail-safe architectures may encompass also the computer software, for example by process replication.

Disadvantages

Fault-tolerant design's advantages are obvious, while many of its disadvantages are also:

- **Interference with fault detection in the same component.** To continue the above passenger vehicle example, it may not be obvious to the driver when a tire has been punctured, with either of the fault-tolerant systems. This is usually handled with a separate "automated fault detection system". In the case of the tire, an air pressure monitor detects the loss of pressure and notifies the driver. The alternative is a "manual fault detection system", such as manually inspecting all tires at each stop.
- **Interference with fault detection in another component.** Another variation of this problem is when fault-tolerance in one component prevents fault detection in a different component. For example, if component B performs some operation based on the output from component A, then fault-tolerance in B can hide a problem with A. If component B is later changed (to a less fault-tolerant design) the system may fail suddenly, making it appear that the new component B is the problem. Only after the system has been carefully scrutinized will it become clear that the root problem is actually with component A.
- **Reduction of priority of fault correction.** Even if the operator is aware of the fault, having a fault-tolerant system is likely to reduce the importance of repairing the fault. If the faults are not corrected, this will eventually lead to system failure, when the fault-tolerant component fails completely or when all redundant components have also failed.
- **Test difficulty.** For certain critical fault-tolerant systems, such as a nuclear reactor, there is no easy way to verify that the backup components are functional. The most infamous example

of this is Chernobyl, where operators tested the emergency backup cooling by disabling primary and secondary cooling. The backup failed, resulting in a core meltdown and massive release of radiation.

- **Cost.** Both fault-tolerant components and redundant components tend to increase cost. This can be a purely economic cost or can include other measures, such as weight. Manned spaceships, for example, have so many redundant and fault-tolerant components that their weight is increased dramatically over unmanned systems, which don't require the same level of safety.
- **Inferior components.** A fault-tolerant design may allow for the use of inferior components, which would have otherwise made the system inoperable. While this practice has the potential to mitigate the cost increase, use of multiple inferior components may lower the reliability of the system to a level equal to, or even worse than, a comparable non-fault-tolerant system.

There is a difference between fault-tolerance and fault-tolerance systems that rarely have problems. For instance, the Western Electric crossbar systems had failure rates of two hours per forty years, and therefore were highly *fault resistant*. But when a fault did occur they still stopped operating completely, and therefore were not *fault-tolerant*.

4.21 FAULT-TOLERANT COMPUTER SYSTEMS

Fault-tolerant computer systems are systems designed around the concepts of fault tolerance. In essence, they have to be able to keep working to a level of satisfaction in the presence of faults.

Types of fault tolerance

Most fault-tolerant computer systems are designed to be able to handle several possible failures, including hardware-related faults such as hard disk failures, input or output device failures, or other temporary or permanent failures; software bugs and errors; interface errors between the hardware and software, including driver failures; operator errors, such as erroneous keystrokes, bad command sequences, or installing unexpected software; and physical damage or other flaws introduced to the system from an outside source.

Hardware fault-tolerance is the most common application of these systems, designed to prevent failures due to hardware components. Typically, components have multiple backups and are separated into smaller "segments" that act to contain a fault, and extra redundancy is built into all physical connectors, power supplies, fans, etc. There are special software and instrumentation packages designed to detect failures, such as fault masking, which is a way to ignore faults by seamlessly preparing a backup component to execute something as soon as the instruction is sent, using a sort of voting protocol where if the main and backups don't give the same results, the flawed output is ignored.

Software fault-tolerance is based more around nullifying programming errors using real-time redundancy, or static "emergency" subprograms to fill in for programs that crash. There are many ways to conduct such fault-regulation, depending on the application and the available hardware.

History

The first known fault-tolerant computer was SAPO, built in 1951 in Czechoslovakia by Antonin Svoboda. Its basic design was magnetic drums connected via relays, with a voting method of memory error detection. Several other machines were developed along this line, mostly for military use. Eventually, they separated into three distinct categories: machines that would last a long time without any maintenance, such as the ones used on NASA space probes and satellites; computers that were very dependable but required constant monitoring, such as those used to monitor and control nuclear power plants or supercollider experiments; and finally, computers with a high amount of runtime which would be under heavy use, such as many of the supercomputers used by insurance companies for their probability monitoring.

Most of the development in the so called LLNM (Long Life, No Maintenance) computing was done by NASA during the 1960's in preparation for Project Apollo and other research aspects. NASA's first machine went into a space observatory, and their second attempt, the JSTAR computer, was used in Voyager. This computer had a backup of memory arrays to use memory recovery methods and thus it was called the JPL Self-Testing-And-Repairing computer. It could detect its own errors and fix them or bring up redundant modules as needed. The computer is still working today.

Hyper-dependable computers were pioneered mostly by aircraft manufacturers, nuclear power companies, and the railroad industry in the USA. These needed computers with massive amounts of uptime that would fail gracefully enough with a fault to allow continued operation, while relying on the fact that the computer output would be constantly monitored by humans to detect faults. Again, IBM developed the first computer of this kind for NASA for guidance of Saturn V rockets, but later on BNSF, Unisys, and General Electric built their own.

In general, the early efforts at fault-tolerant designs were focused mainly on internal diagnosis, where a fault would indicate something was failing and a worker could replace it. SAPO, for instance, had a method by which faulty memory drums would emit a noise before failure. Later efforts showed that, to be fully effective, the system had to be self-repairing and diagnosing — isolating a fault and then implementing a redundant backup while alerting a need for repair. This is known as N-model redundancy, where faults cause automatic fail safes and a warning to the operator, and it is still the most common form of level one fault-tolerant design in use today.

Voting was another initial method, as discussed above, with multiple redundant backups operating constantly and checking each other's results, with the outcome that if, for example, four components reported an answer of 5 and one component reported an answer of 6, the other four would "vote" that the fifth component was faulty and have it taken out of service. This is called M out of N majority voting.

Historically, motion has always been to move further from N-model and more to M out of N due to the fact that the complexity of systems and the difficulty of ensuring the transitive state from fault-negative to fault-positive did not disrupt operations.

Fault tolerance verification and validation

The most important requirement of design in a fault tolerant computer system is making sure it actually meets its requirements for reliability. This is done by using various failure models to simulate various failures, and analyzing how well the system reacts. These statistical models are very complex, involving probability curves and specific fault rates, latency curves, error rates, and the like. The most commonly used models are HARP, SAVE, and SHARPE in the USA, and SURF or LASS in Europe.

Fault tolerance research

Research into the kinds of tolerances needed for critical systems involves a large amount of interdisciplinary work. The more complex the system, the more carefully all possible interactions have to be considered and prepared for. Considering the importance of high-value systems in transport, utilities and the military, the field of topics that touch on research is very wide: it can include such obvious subjects as software modeling and reliability, or hardware design, to arcane elements such as stochastic models, graph theory, formal or exclusionary logic, parallel processing, remote data transmission, and more.

4.22 SUMMARY

- In distributed file system, common files can be shared by all autonomous computers.
- In DFS, files can be stored at any machine and computation can be performed at any machine.
- Binding together different file name space to form a single hierarchical structured name space is known as mounting.
- Caching is employed in DFS to reduce delays in accessing of data.
- Encryption is used for enforcing security in distributed system.
- Bulk transfers reduce file access overhead through obtaining a multiple number of blocks with a single seek.
- Hints are cased to remove cache consistency problem.
- The shared memory model provides a virtual address space that is shared among all nodes in a distributed system.
- A memory is coherent if the value returned by a read operation is always the value that the programmer expected.
- Preemptive task transfers involve the transfers of tasks that are partially executed.
- Non preemptive task transfer involves the transfer of tasks that have not begun execution and hence do not require transfer of task state.
- The transfer policy decides whether the node is a sender or receiver for a remote task.
- A selection policy selects a task for transfer.
- The responsibility of a location policy is to find suitable nodes to share load.
- The information policy is responsible for deciding when information about the status of other nodes, in the system should be collected.
- Task migration refers to the transfer of a task that has already begun execution to a new location and continuing its execution there.
- To avoid disruption dues to failures and to improve availability, the systems are designed to be fault tolerant.

4.23 REVIEW QUESTIONS

1. Explain distributed file system and mechanism of building distributed file system.
2. Explain design issues of distributed file systems.
3. Discuss distributed shared memory concept and algorithm for implementing distributed shared memory.
4. Write short notes on
   (i) Memory coherence
   (ii) Name resolution
   (iii) Bulk data transfer
   (iv) Hints
   (v) Caching
5. Differentiate weak consistency with release consistency.
6. Explain coherence protocols.
7. What do you mean by distributed scheduling?
8. Discuss the issues in local distributing.
9. Explain the components of local distributing algorithms.
10. Explain stability.
11. Discuss performance comparisons and task migration.
12. Explain fault tolerance.

CHAPTER 5

Distributed Object and Remote Invocation

5.1 COMMUNICATION BETWEEN DISTRIBUTED OBJECT

Object that can receive remote method invocations are called remote object and they implement a remote interface.

Distributed object communication realizes communication between distributed objects in the distributed computing environment.

The main role is to interconnect objects residing in non-local memory space and allowing them to perform remote calls and exchange data. The widely used approach on how to implement the communication channel is realized by using stubs and skeletons. They are generated objects whose structure and behavior depends on chosen communication protocol, but in general provide additional functionality that ensures reliable communication over the network.

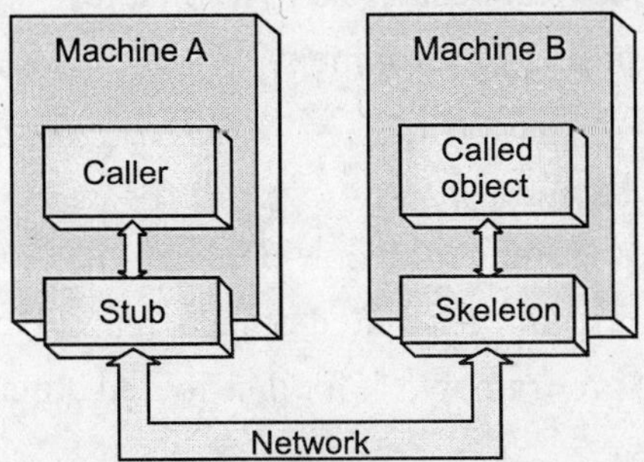

When a caller wants to perform remote call on the called object, it delegates requests to its stub which initiates communication with the remote skeleton. Consequently, the stub passes caller arguments over the network to the server skeleton. The skeleton then passes received data to the called object, waits for a response and returns back the result to the client stub. Note, there is no direct communication between the caller and the called object.

In more details, the communication consists of several steps:

1. caller calls a local procedure implemented by the stub
2. stub marshalls call type and input arguments into a request message
3. client stub sends the message over the network to the server and blocks the current execution thread
4. server skeleton receives the request message from the network
5. skeleton unpacks call type from the request message and looks up the procedure on the called object
6. skeleton unmarshalls procedure arguments
7. skeleton executes the procedure on the called object
8. called object performs a computation and returns the result
9. skeleton packs the output arguments into a response message
10. skeleton sends the message over the network back to the client
11. client stub receives the response message from the network
12. stub unpacks output arguments from the message
13. stub passes output arguments to the caller, releases execution thread and caller then continues in execution

The advantage of this architecture is that neither the caller nor the called object has to implement network related logic. This functionality, that ensures reliable communication channel over the network, has been moved to the stub and the skeleton layer.

Protocols using stub/skeleton approach

- RPC - Remote Procedure Call
- CORBA - Common Object Request Broker Architecture
- DCE - Distributed Computing Environment
- RMI - Remote Method Invocation
- .NET Remoting - .NET Remoting
- DCOM - Distributed Component Object Model
- DDObjects is a framework for distributed objects using Borland Delphi.
- Distributed Ruby (DRb) is a framework for distributed objects using the Ruby programming language.

5.2 DISTRIBUTED OBJECT

Distributed object system may adopt the client-server architecture. In this case, object is managed by servers and their clients invoke their methods using remote method invocation. In RMI, the clients request to invoke a method of an object is sent in a message to the server managing the object. The invocation is carried out by executing a method of the object at the server and the result is returned to the client in another message.

Having client and servers object in different processes enforces encapsulation, that is, the state of an object can be accessed only by the method of the object, which means that it is not possible for unauthorized method to act on the state. However, the data of an object is allow object to provide method for protecting themselves against incorrect accesses.

5.3 DISTRIBUTED OBJECT MODEL

Each process contains a collection of objects, some of which can receive both local and remote invocation, whereas the other object can receive only local invocations. Method invocation between object in different processes, whether in the same computer or not, are known as Remote Method Invocation. While Method invocation between object in the same process are local method invocation. The two fundamental concepts are at the heart of distributed object model-

(i) **Remote object Reference:** A Remote object Reference is an identifier that can be used throughout a distributed system to refer to a particular unique remote object. The remote object to receive a remote method invocation is specified as a remote object reference and remote object reference may be passed as arguments and result of remote method invocations.

(ii) **Remote Interfaces:** The class of a remote object implements the methods of its remote interface. Object in other processes can invoke only the method that belongs to its remote interface. The CORBA system provides an interface definition language (IDL), which is used for defining remote interfaces.

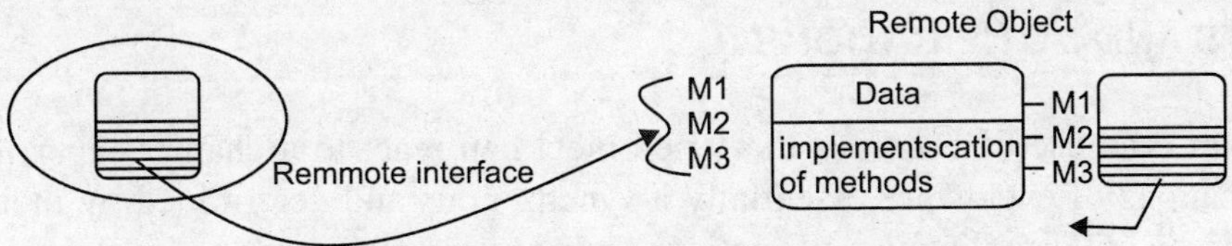

Fig.5.1 A Remote Object and its Remote interface

5.4 REMOTE PROCEDURE CALLS (RPC)

A remote procedure call is very similar to a remote method invocation in another program running in a server process. Server may be clients of other server to allow chains of RPCs. Remote procedure calls are the application through which the servers which are available at the remote servers in the form of some subroutines and procedures are called at the certain work station through which the request is made. For example, in yahoo web site compose box while using graphical user interface, some forts can be called at the client work station even that forts are not available at the work station. Here certain RPCs are used in the coordinated network operating can be available at the work station.

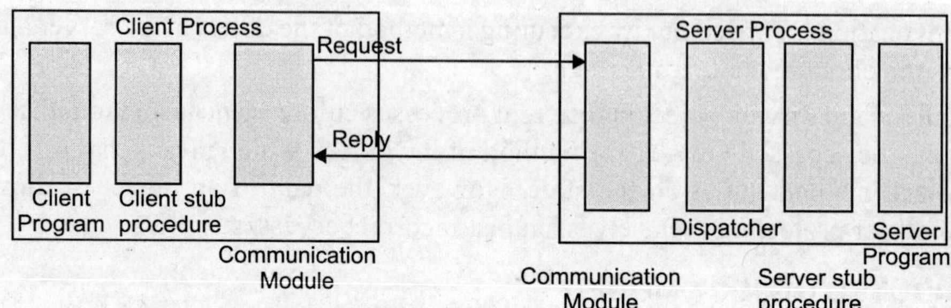

Fig. 5.2 Role of client and server soub procedure in RPC.

The client that accesses a service includes one stub procedure for each procedure in the service interface. The role of a stub procedure is similar to that of a proxy. It behaves like a local procedure to the client, but instead of executing the call, it marshals the procedure identifier and the arguments in tom a request message, which it sends via its communication module to the server. When the reply message arrives it unmarhals the results.

The server process contains a dispatcher together with one server stub procedure and one service procedure for each procedure in the service interface. The dispatcher selects one of the server stub procedures according to the procedure identifier in the request message. A server stub procedure is like a skeleton method in that it unmarshals the arguments in the request message, calls the corresponding services procedure and marshals the return value for the reply message the service procedure implements the procedures in the service interface.

The client and server stub procedure and the dispatcher can be generated by an interface compiler from the interface definition of the service.

5.5 EVENTS AND NOTIFICATIONS

The idea behind the use of events is that one object can react to a change occurring in another object notifications of events are essentially a synchronous and determined by their receives, In particular in interactive application, the actions that the user performs on objects, for examples, by manipulating a button with the mouse or entering text in a text box via the keyboard are seen as events that cause changes in the application. The objects that are responsible for displaying a view of the current state are notified whenever the state changes.

Distributed event –based systems extended the web event model by allowing multiple objects at different locations to be notified of events taking place at an object. They use the publish – subscribe paradigm, in which an object that generates events publishes the type of events that in will make available for observation by other objects.

Objects that represent events are called notifications. Notification may be stored, sent in messages queried and applied in a variety of orders to different things. When a publisher experiences an event, subscribers that expressed an interest in that type of event will receive notifications. Subscribing to a particular type of event is also called registering interest in that type of event. Event and notifications can be used in a wide variety of different applications. For examples, to communicate a shape added to a drawing, a modification to a document, the fact that a person has entered or left a room, Or that a piece of equipment or an electronically tagged book is at a new location. Distributed event based system have two main characteristics—

Heterogeneous: When event notifications are used as a means of communication between distributed as a means of communication between distributed objects, components in a distributed system that were not designed to interoperate can be made to work together. All That is required is that event – generating objects publish the types of events and provide an interface for receiving notifications.

Asynchronous: Notification are sent asynchronously by event – generating objects to all the objects that have subscribed to them to prevent publishes needing to synchronous with subscribers— publisher and subscribers need to be decoupled.

Event types: an event source can generate events of one of more different types. Each event has attributes that specify information about that event, such as the name or identifier of the objects that generates it, the operation, its parameters and the time.

Types and attributes are used both in subscribing to events and, in notifications when subscribing to an event, the type of event is specified, sometimes modified with a criterion as to the values of the attributes, whenever an event of that type occurs that matches the attributes, the interested parties will be notified.

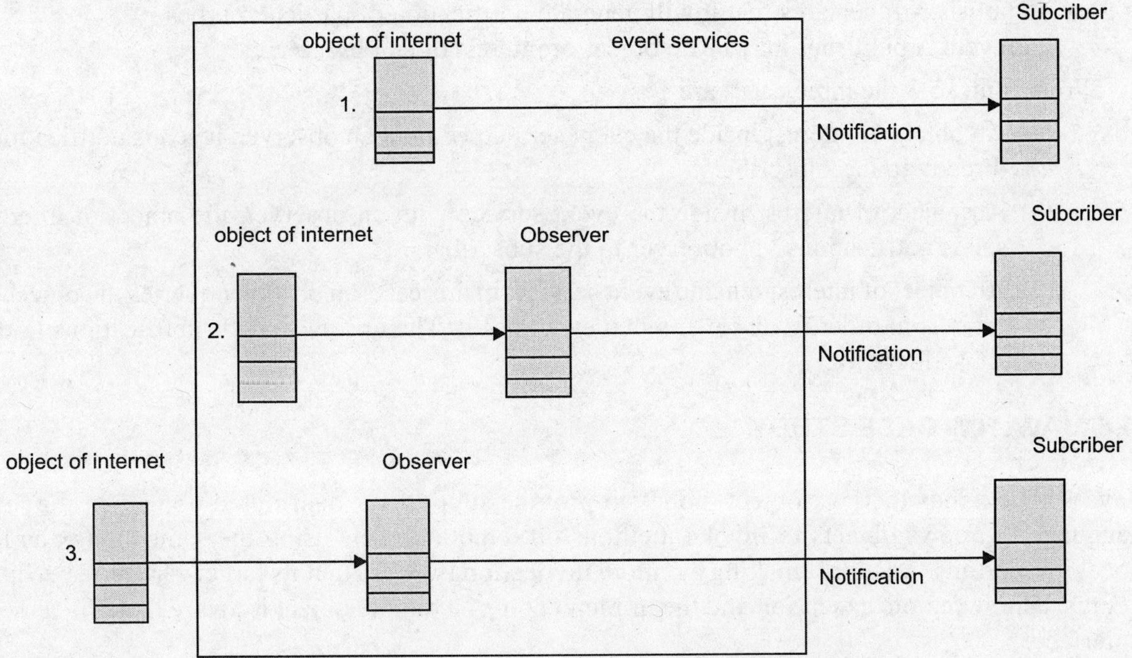

Fig. 5.3 Architecture for distributed event notification

The architecture is designed to decouple the publishers from the subscribers, allowing publishes to be developed independently of their subscribers and as far as possible limiting the work imposed on publishes by subscribers. The main component is an event service that maintains a database of published events and of subscribers interests. Events at an object of interests are published at the event service. Subscribers inform the event service about the type of events they are interested in. When an event occurs at an object of interest a notification is sent to the subscribers to that type of event.

The roles of the participating objects are as follows:

(i) The object of interest- this is an object that experience changes of state, as a result of its operations being invoked. Its changes of state might be of interest to other object the object of interest is considered as part of the event service if it transmits notifications.

(ii) Event- An event occurs at an object of interest as the result of the completion of a method execution.

(iii) Notification- A notification is an object that contain information about an event it contains type of event its attributes.

(iv) Subscriber- A subscriber is an object that has subscribed to same type of events in another object. It receives notifications about such events.

(v) Observer objects- The main purpose of an observer is to decouple an object of interest from its subscribers.

(vi) Publisher- It declares that it will generate notification of particular types ofevent.A publisher may be an object of interest or an observer.

From figure 5.3 the three cases are

(a) An object of interest inside the event service without an observer, it sends notifications directly to the subscribers.

(b) An object of interest inside the event service with an observer, the object of interest sends notifications via observer to the subscribers.

(c) An object of interest outside event service, in this case, an observer queries the object of interest in order to discover when event occur. The observer sends notifications to the subscribers.

5.6 JAVA RMI CASE STUDY

Java RMI extends the java object modes to provide support for distributed objects in the java language. It allows objects to invoke methods on remote objects using the same syntax as for local invocations. An object making a remote invocation is aware that its target is remote because it must handle remote exception and the implementer of a remote object is aware that it is remote interface.

5.6.1 An Overview of RMI Applications

RMI applications are often comprised of two separate programs: a server and a client. A typical server application creates some remote objects, makes references to them accessible, and waits for clients to invoke methods on these remote objects. A typical client application gets a remote reference to one or more remote objects in the server and then invokes methods on them. RMI provides the mechanism by which the server and the client communicate and pass information back and forth. Such an application is sometimes referred to as a *distributed object application*. Distributed object applications need to

- **Locate remote objects:** Applications can use one of two mechanisms to obtain references to remote objects. An application can register its remote objects with RMI's simple naming facility, the rmiregistry, or the application can pass and return remote object references as part of its normal operation.
- **Communicate with remote objects:** Details of communication between remote objects are handled by RMI; to the programmer, remote communication looks like a standard Java method invocation.
- **Load class byte codes for objects that are passed around:** Because RMI allows a caller to pass objects to remote objects, RMI provides the necessary mechanisms for loading an object's code, as well as for transmitting its data.

The following illustration depicts an RMI distributed application that uses the registry to obtain a reference to a remote object. The server calls the registry to associate (or bind) a name with a remote object. The client looks up the remote object by its name in the server's registry and then invokes a method on it. The illustration also shows that the RMI system uses an existing Web server to load class byte codes, from server to client and from client to server, for objects when needed.

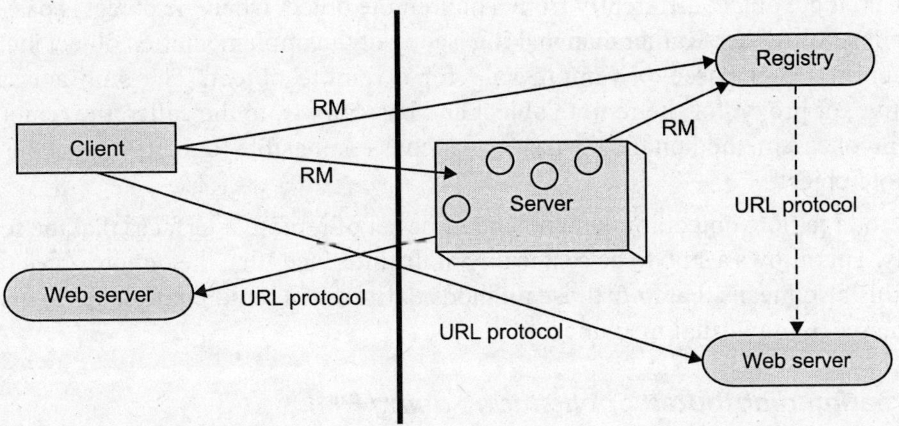

This lesson contains the following sections:

- Advantages of Dynamic Code Loading
- Remote Interfaces, Objects, and Methods
- Creating Distributed Applications Using RMI
- Building a Generic Compute Engine

5.6.1.1 Advantages of dynamic code loading

One of the central and unique features of RMI is its ability to download the *byte codes* (or simply *code*) of an object's class if the class is not defined in the receiver's virtual machine. The types and the behavior of an object, previously available only in a single virtual machine, can be transmitted to another, possibly remote, virtual machine. RMI passes objects by their true type, so the behavior of those objects is not changed when they are sent to another virtual machine. This allows new types to be introduced into a remote virtual machine, thus extending the behavior of an application dynamically. The compute engine example in this chapter uses RMI's capability to introduce new behavior to a distributed program.

5.6.1.2 Remote interfaces, objects, and methods

Like any other application, a distributed application built using Java RMI is made up of interfaces and classes. The interfaces define methods, and the classes implement the methods defined in the interfaces and, perhaps, define additional methods as well. In a distributed application some of the implementations are assumed to reside in different virtual machines. Objects that have methods that can be called across virtual machines are *remote objects*.

An object becomes remote by implementing a *remote interface*, which has the following characteristics.

- A remote interface extends the interface java.rmi.Remote.
- Each method of the interface declares java.rmi.RemoteException in its throws clause, in addition to any application-specific exceptions.

RMI treats a remote object differently from a nonremote object when the object is passed from one virtual machine to another. Rather than making a copy of the implementation object in the receiving virtual machine, RMI passes a remote *stub* for a remote object. The stub acts as the local representative, or proxy, for the remote object and basically *is*, to the caller, the remote reference. The caller invokes a method on the local stub, which is responsible for carrying out the method call on the remote object.

A stub for a remote object implements the same set of remote interfaces that the remote object implements. This allows a stub to be cast to any of the interfaces that the remote object implements. However, this also means that *only* those methods defined in a remote interface are available to be called in the receiving virtual machine.

5.6.1.3 Creating distributed applications using RMI

When you use RMI to develop a distributed application, you follow these general steps.

1. Design and implement the components of your distributed application.
2. Compile sources and generate stubs.
3. Make classes network accessible.
4. Start the application.

5.6.1.4 Design and implement the application components

First, decide on your application architecture and determine which components are local objects and which ones should be remotely accessible. This step includes:

- Defining the remote interfaces: A remote interface specifies the methods that can be invoked remotely by a client. Clients program to remote interfaces, not to the implementation classes of those interfaces. Part of the design of such interfaces is the determination of any local objects that will be used as parameters and return values for these methods; if any of these interfaces or classes do not yet exist, you need to define them as well.
- Implementing the remote objects: Remote objects must implement one or more remote interfaces. The remote object class may include implementations of other interfaces (either local or remote) and other methods (which are available only locally). If any local classes are to be used as parameters or return values to any of these methods, they must be implemented as well.
- Implementing the clients: Clients that use remote objects can be implemented at any time after the remote interfaces are defined, including after the remote objects have been deployed.

5.6.2 Compile Sources and Generate Stubs

This is a two-step process. In the first step you use the javac compiler to compile the source files, which contain the implementation of the remote interfaces and implementations, the server classes, and the client classes. In the second step you use the rmic compiler to create stubs for the remote objects. RMI uses a remote object's stub class as a proxy in clients so that clients can communicate with a particular remote object.

5.6.3 Make Classes Network Accessible

In this step you make everything—the class files associated with the remote interfaces, stubs, and other classes that need to be downloaded to clients—accessible via a Web server.

5.6.4 Start the Application

Starting the application includes running the RMI remote object registry, the server, and the client.

The rest of this lesson walks through the steps to create a compute engine.

5.6.5 Building a Generic Compute Engine

This trail focuses on a simple yet powerful distributed application called a compute engine. The compute engine, a remote object in the server, takes tasks from clients, runs them, and returns any results. The tasks are run on the machine where the server is running. This sort of distributed application could allow a number of client machines to make use of a particularly powerful machine or one that has specialized hardware.

The novel aspect of the compute engine is that the tasks it runs do not need to be defined when the compute engine is written. New kinds of tasks can be created at any time and then given to the compute engine to be run. All that is required of a task is that its class implement a particular interface. Such a task can be submitted to the compute engine and run, even if the class that defines that task was written long after the compute engine was written and started. The code needed to accomplish the task can be downloaded by the RMI system to the compute engine, and then the engine runs the task, using the resources on the machine on which the compute engine is running.

The ability to perform arbitrary tasks is enabled by the dynamic nature of the Java platform, which is extended to the network by RMI. RMI dynamically loads the task code into the compute engine's Java virtual machine and runs the task without prior knowledge of the class that implements the task. An application like this, which has the ability to download code dynamically, is often called a behavior-based application. Such applications usually require full agent-enabled infrastructures. With RMI such applications are part of the basic mechanisms for distributed computing on the Java plat Writing an RMI Server

The computer engine server accepts tasks from clients, runs the tasks, and returns any results. The server is comprised of an interface and a class. The interface provides the definition for the methods that can be called from the client. Essentially the interface defines the client's view of the remote object. The class provides the implementation.

Designing a remote interface

This section shows you the Compute interface, which provides the connection between the client and the server. You will also learn about the RMI API, which supports this communication.

Implementing a remote interface

This section explores the class that implements the Compute interface, thereby implementing a remote object. This class also provides the rest of the code that makes up the server program: a main method that creates an instance of the remote object, registers it with the naming facility, and sets up a security manager.

5.6.6 Designing a remote interface

At the heart of the compute engine is a protocol that allows jobs to be submitted to the compute engine, the compute engine to run those jobs, and the results of the job to be returned to the client. This protocol is expressed in interfaces supported by the compute engine and by the objects that are submitted to the compute engine, as shown in the following figure.

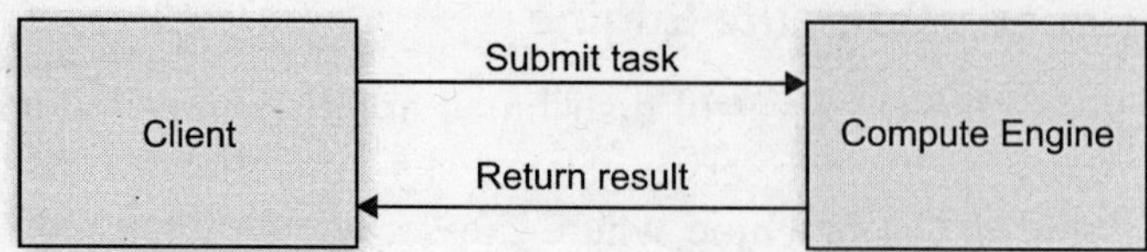

Each of the interfaces contains a single method. The compute engine's interface, Compute, allows jobs to be submitted to the engine; the client interface, Task, defines how the compute engine executes a submitted task.

The compute.Compute interface defines the remotely accessible part—the compute engine itself. Here is the remote interface with its single method:

```
package compute;
    import java.rmi.Remote;
    import java.rmi.RemoteException;

    public interface Compute extends Remote {
     Object executeTask(Task t) throws RemoteException;
    }
```

By extending the interface java.rmi.Remote, this interface marks itself as one whose methods can be called from any virtual machine. Any object that implements this interface becomes a remote object.

As a member of a remote interface, the executeTask method is a remote method. Therefore the method must be defined as being capable of throwing a java.rmi.RemoteException. This exception is thrown by the RMI system during a remote method call to indicate that either a communication failure or a protocol error has occurred. A RemoteException is a checked exception, so any code making a call to a remote method needs to handle this exception by either catching it or declaring it in its throws clause.

The second interface needed for the compute engine defines the type Task. This type is used as the argument to the executeTask method in the Compute interface. The compute.Task interface defines the interface between the compute engine and the work that it needs to do, providing the way to start the work.

```
    package compute;

    import java.io.Serializable;

    public interface Task extends Serializable {
     Object execute();
    }
```

The Task interface defines a single method, execute, which returns an Object, has no parameters, and throws no exceptions. Since the interface does not extend Remote, the method in this interface doesn't need to list java.rmi.RemoteException in its throws clause.

The return value for the Compute's executeTask and Task's execute methods is declared to be of type Object. This means that any task that wants to return a value of one of the primitive types, such as an int or a float, needs to create an instance of the equivalent wrapper class for that type, such as an Integer or a Float, and return that object instead.

Note that the Task interface extends the java.io.Serializable interface. RMI uses the object serialization mechanism to transport objects by value between Java virtual machines. Implementing

Serializable marks the class as being capable of conversion into a self-describing byte stream that can be used to reconstruct an exact copy of the serialized object when the object is read back from the stream.

Different kinds of tasks can be run by a Compute object as long as they are implementations of the Task type. The classes that implement this interface can contain any data needed for the computation of the task and any other methods needed for the computation.

Here is how RMI makes this simple compute engine possible. Since RMI can assume that the Task objects are written in the Java programming language, implementations of the Task object that were previously unknown to the compute engine are downloaded by RMI into the compute engine's virtual machine as needed. This allows clients of the compute engine to define new kinds of tasks to be run on the server machine without needing the code to be explicitly installed on that machine. In addition, because the executeTask method returns a java.lang.Object, any type of object can be passed as a return value in the remote call.

The compute engine, implemented by the ComputeEngine class, implements the Compute interface, allowing different tasks to be submitted to it by calls to its executeTask method. These tasks are run using the task's implementation of the execute method. The compute engine reports results to the caller through its return value: an Object.

5.6.7 Implementing a Remote Interface

Let's turn now to the task of implementing a class for the compute engine. In general the implementation class of a remote interface should at least

- Declare the remote interfaces being implemented
- Define the constructor for the remote object
- Provide an implementation for each remote method in the remote interfaces

The server needs to create and to install the remote objects. This setup procedure can be encapsulated in a main method in the remote object implementation class itself, or it can be included in another class entirely. The setup procedure should

- Create and install a security manager
- Create one or more instances of a remote object
- Register at least one of the remote objects with the RMI remote object registry (or another naming service such as one that uses JNDI), for bootstrapping purposes

The complete implementation of the compute engine follows. The engine.ComputeEngine class implements the remote interface Compute and also includes the main method for setting up the compute engine.

```
package engine;

    import java.rmi.Remote;
    import java.rmi.RemoteException;
```

```
public interface Compute extends Remote {
  Object executeTask(Task t) throws RemoteException;
}


  super();
 }

 public Object executeTask(Task t) {
  return t.execute();
 }

 public static void main(String[] args) {
  if (System.getSecurityManager() == null) {
     System.setSecurityManager(new RMISecurityManager());
    }
    String name = "//host/Compute";
    try {
      Compute engine = new ComputeEngine();
      Naming.rebind(name, engine);
      System.out.println("ComputeEngine bound");
    } catch (Exception e) {
      System.err.println("ComputeEngine exception: " +
                                    e.getMessage());
      e.printStackTrace();
    }
  }
}
```

Now let's take a closer look at each of the components of the compute engine implementation.

5.6.8 Declare the Remote Interfaces Being Implemented

The implementation class for the compute engine is declared as public class ComputeEngine extends UnicastRemote Object implements Compute

This declaration states that the class implements the Compute remote interface (and there fore defines a remote object) and extends the class java.rmi.server.Unicast Remote Object.

Unicast Remote Object is a convenience class, defined in the RMI public API, that can be used as a superclass for remote object implementations. The superclass Unicast Remote Object supplies implementations for a number of java.lang.Object methods (equals, hashCode, toString) so that they are defined appropriately for remote objects. UnicastRemoteObjectalso includes constructors and static methods used to *export* a remote object, that is, make the remote object available to receive incoming calls from clients.

A remote object implementation does not have to extend UnicastRemoteObject, but any implementation that does not must supply appropriate implementations of the java.lang.Object methods. Furthermore, a remote object implementation must make an explicit call to one of UnicastRemoteObject's exportObject methods to make the RMI runtime aware of the remote object so that the object can accept incoming calls. By extending UnicastRemoteObject, the ComputeEngine class can be used to create a simple remote object that supports unicast (point-to-point) remote communication and that uses RMI's default sockets-based transport for communication.

If you choose to extend a remote object from any class other than Unicast-RemoteObject or, alternatively, extend from the new JDK 1.2 class java.rmi.activation.Activatable (used to construct remote objects that can execute on demand), you need to export the remote object by calling either the UnicastRemoteObject.exportObject or Activatable.exportObject method explicitly from your class's constructor.

The compute engine example defines a remote object class that implements only a single remote interface and no other interfaces. The ComputeEngine class also contains some methods that can be called only locally. The first of these is a constructor for ComputeEngine objects; the second is a main method that is used to create a ComputeEngine and make it available to clients.

5.6.9 Define the Constructor

The ComputeEngine class has a single constructor that takes no arguments. The code for the constructor is

```
public ComputeEngine() throws RemoteException {
    super();
}
```

This constructor simply calls the superclass constructor, which is the no-argument constructor of the UnicastRemoteObject class. Although the superclass constructor gets called even if omitted from the ComputeEngine constructor, we include it for clarity.

During construction, a UnicastRemoteObject is *exported*, meaning that it is available to accept incoming requests by listening for incoming calls from clients on an anonymous port.

Note: In JDK 1.2 you may indicate the specific port that a remote object uses to accept requests.

The no-argument constructor for the superclass, UnicastRemoteObject, declares the exception RemoteException in its throws clause, so the Compute-Engine constructor must also declare that it can throw RemoteException. A RemoteException can occur during construction if the attempt to export the object fails—due to, for example, communication resources being unavailable or the appropriate stub class not being found.

5.6.10 Provide Implementations for Each Remote Method

The class for a remote object provides implementations for each of the remote methods specified in the remote interfaces. The Compute interface contains a single remote method, executeTask, which is implemented as follows:

```
public Object executeTask(Task t) {
    return t.execute();
}
```

This method implements the protocol between the ComputeEngine and its clients. Clients provide the ComputeEngine with a Task object, which has an implementation of the task's execute method. The ComputeEngine executes the Task and returns the result of the task's execute method directly to the caller.

The executeTask method does not need to know anything more about the result of the execute method than that it is at least an Object. The caller presumably knows more about the precise type of the Object returned and can cast the result to the appropriate type.

5.6.11 Passing Objects in RMI

Arguments to or return values from remote methods can be of almost any type, including local objects, remote objects, and primitive types. More precisely, any entity of any type can be passed to or from a remote method as long as the entity is an instance of a type that is a primitive data type, a remote object, or a *serializable* object, which means that it implements the interface java.io.Serializable.

A few object types do not meet any of these criteria and thus cannot be passed to or returned from a remote method. Most of these objects, such as a file descriptor, encapsulate information that makes sense only within a single address space. Many of the core classes, including those in the packages java.lang and java.util, implement the Serializable interface.

The rules governing how arguments and return values are passed are as follows.

- Remote objects are essentially passed by reference. A *remote object reference* is a stub, which is a client-side proxy that implements the complete set of remote interfaces that the remote object implements.
- Local objects are passed by copy, using object serialization. By default all fields are copied, except those that are marked static or transient. Default serialization behavior can be overridden on a class-by-class basis.

Passing an object by reference (as is done with remote objects) means that any changes made to the state of the object by remote method calls are reflected in the original remote object. When passing a remote object, only those interfaces that are remote interfaces are available to the receiver; any methods defined in the implementation class or defined in non remote interfaces implemented by the class are not available to that receiver.

For example, if you were to pass a reference to an instance of the Compute Engine class, the receiver would have access only to the compute engine's execute Task method. That receiver would not see either the Compute Engine constructor or its main method or any of the methods in java.lang.Object.

In remote method calls objects—parameters, return values, and exceptions—that are not remote objects are passed by value. This means that a copy of the object is created in the receiving virtual machine. Any changes to this object's state at the receiver are reflected only in the receiver's copy, not in the original instance.

5.6.12 Implement the Server's Main Method

The most involved method of the ComputeEngine implementation is the main method. The main method is used to start the ComputeEngine and therefore needs to do the necessary initialization and housekeeping to prepare the server for accepting calls from clients. This method is not a remote method, which means that it cannot be called from a different virtual machine. Since the main method is declared static, the method is not associated with an object at all but rather with the class ComputeEngine.

5.6.13 Create and Instal a Security Manager

The first thing that the main method does is to create and to instal a security manager, which protects access to system resources from untrusted downloaded code running within the virtual machine. The security manager determines whether downloaded code has access to the local file system or can perform any other privileged operations.

All programs using RMI must install a security manager, or RMI will not download classes (other than from the local class path) for objects received as parameters, return values, or exceptions in remote method calls. This restriction ensures that the operations performed by downloaded code go through a set of security checks.

The ComputeEngine uses a security manager supplied as part of the RMI system, the RMISecurityManager. This security manager enforces a similar security policy as the typical security manager for applets; that is to say, it is very conservative as to what access it allows. An RMI application could define and use another SecurityManager class that gave more liberal access to system resources or, in JDK 1.2, use a policy file that grants more permissions.

Here's the code that creates and installs the security manager:

```
if (System.getSecurityManager() == null) {
    System.setSecurityManager(new RMISecurityManager());
}
```

5.6.14 Make the Remote Object Available to Clients

Next, the main method creates an instance of the ComputeEngine. This is done with the statement

```
Compute engine = new ComputeEngine();
```

As mentioned, this constructor calls the UnicastRemoteObject superclass constructor, which in turn exports the newly created object to the RMI runtime. Once the export step is complete, the

ComputeEngine remote object is ready to accept incoming calls from clients on an anonymous port, one chosen by RMI or the underlying operating system. Note that the type of the variable engine is Compute, not ComputeEngine. This declaration emphasizes that the interface available to clients is the Compute interface and its methods, not the Compute-Engine class and its methods.

Before a caller can invoke a method on a remote object, that caller must first obtain a reference to the remote object. This can be done in the same way that any other object reference is obtained in a program, such as getting it as part of the return value of a method or as part of a data structure that contains such a reference.

The system provides a particular remote object, the RMI registry, for finding references to remote objects. The RMI registry is a simple remote object name service that allows remote clients to get a reference to a remote object by name. The registry is typically used only to locate the first remote object an RMI client needs to use. That first remote object then provides support for finding other objects.

The java.rmi.Naming interface is used as a front-end API for binding, or registering, and looking up remote objects in the registry. Once a remote object is registered with the RMI registry on the local host, callers on any host can look up the remote object by name, obtain its reference, and then invoke remote methods on the object. The registry may be shared by all servers running on a host, or an individual server process may create and use its own registry, if desired.

The ComputeEngine class creates a name for the object with the statement

```
String name = "//host/Compute";
```

This name includes the host name, host, on which the registry (and remote object) is being run and a name, Compute, that identifies the remote object in the registry. The code then needs to add the name to the RMI registry running on the server. This is done later (within the try block) with the statement

```
Naming.rebind(name, engine);
```

Calling the rebind method makes a remote call to the RMI registry on the local host. This call can result in a RemoteException being generated, so the exception needs to be handled. The ComputeEngine class handles the exception within the try/catch block. If the exception is not handled in this way, RemoteException would have to be added to the throws clause (currently nonexistent) of the main method.

Note the following about the arguments to the call to Naming.rebind.

- The first parameter is a URL-formatted java.lang.String representing the location and the name of the remote object. You will need to change the value of host to be the name, or IP address, of your server machine. If the host is omitted from the URL, the host defaults to the local host. Also, you don't need to specify a protocol in the URL. For example, supplying Compute as the name in the Naming.rebind call is allowed. Optionally a port number may be supplied in the URL; for example, the name //host:1234/objectname is legal. If the port is omitted, it defaults to 1099. You must specify the port number only if a server creates a registry on a port other than the default 1099. The default port is useful in that it provides a well-known place to look for the remote objects that offer services on a particular host.

- The RMI runtime substitutes a reference to the stub for the remote object reference specified by the argument. Remote implementation objects, such as instances of ComputeEngine, never leave the VM where they are created, so when a client performs a lookup in a server's remote object registry, a reference to the stub is returned. As discussed earlier, remote objects in such cases are passed by reference rather than by value.
- Note that for security reasons, an application can bind, unbind, or rebind remote object references only with a registry running on the same host. This restriction prevents a remote client from removing or overwriting any of the entries in a server's registry. A lookup, however, can be requested from any host, local or remote.

Once the server has registered with the local RMI registry, it prints out a message indicating that it's ready to start handling calls and then the main method exits. It is not necessary to have a thread wait to keep the server alive. As long as there is a reference to the ComputeEngine object in another virtual machine, local or remote, the ComputeEngine object will not be shut down, or garbage collected. Because the program binds a reference to the ComputeEngine in the registry, it is reachable from a remote client, the registry itself! The RMI system takes care of keeping the ComputeEngine's process up. The ComputeEngine is available to accept calls and won't be reclaimed until its binding is removed from the registry, *and* no remote clients hold a remote reference to the ComputeEngine object.

The final piece of code in the ComputeEngine.main method deals with handling any exception that might arise. The only exception that could be thrown in the code is a RemoteException, thrown either by the constructor of the ComputeEngine class or by the call to the RMI registry to bind the object to the name Compute. In either case the program can't do much more than exit after printing an error message. In some distributed applications it is possible to recover from the failure to make a remote call. For example, the application could choose another server and continue operation.

5.6.15 Compiling the Example Programs

In a real-world scenario in which a service like the compute engine is deployed, a developer would likely create a JAR (Java ARchive) file that contains the Compute and Task interfaces for server classes to implement and client program to use. Next, a developer, perhaps the same developer of the interface JAR file, would write an implementation of the Compute interface and deploy that service on a machine available to clients. Developers of client programs can use the Compute and the Task interfaces, contained in the JAR file, and independently develop a task and client program that uses a Compute service.

In this section you learn how to set up the JAR file, server classes, and client classes. You will see that the client's Pi class will be downloaded to the server at runtime. Also, the Compute Engines remote stub will be downloaded from the server to the client at runtime.

The example separates the interfaces, remote object implementation, and client code into three packages:

- compute (Compute and Task interfaces)
- engine (Compute Engine implementation class and its stub)
- client (ComputePi client code and Pi task implementation)

Let's first build the interface JAR file to provide to server and client developers.

5.6.16 Build a JAR File of Interface Classes

First, you need to compile the interface source files in the compute package and then build a JAR file that contains their class files. Let's suppose a user, waldo, has written these particular interfaces and has placed the source files in c:\home\waldo\src\compute (on UNIX:/home/waldo/src/compute). Given these paths, you can use the following commands to compile the interfaces and create the JAR file.

Microsoft Windows:

```
cd c:\home\waldo\src
javac compute\Compute.java
javac compute\Task.java
jar cvf compute.jar compute\*.class
```

UNIX:

```
cd /home/waldo/src
javac compute/Compute.java
javac compute/Task.java
jar cvf compute.jar compute/*.class
```

The jar command displays the following output (due to the -v option):

```
added manifest
adding: compute/Compute.class (in=281) (out=196)
        (deflated 30%)
adding: compute/Task.class (in=200) (out=164)
        (deflated 18%)
```

Now you can distribute the compute.jar file to developers of server and client applications so that they can make use of the interfaces.

When you build either server or client-side classes with the javac and rmic compilers, you generally need to specify where the resulting class files should reside so that they are network accessible. In this example this location is, for UNIX, /home/user/public_html/classes, because some web servers allow accessing a user's public_html directory via an HTTP URL constructed as http://host/~user/. If your web server does not support this convention, you could use a file URL instead. The file URLs take the form file:/home/user/public_html/classes/ on UNIX or, on the Microsoft Windows platform, file:/c:/home/user/public_html/classes/. You may also select another type of URL, as appropriate.

The network accessibility of the class files allows the RMI runtime to download code when needed. Rather than defining its own protocol for code downloading, RMI uses URL protocols supported by the Java platform (for example, HTTP) to download code. Note that a full, heavyweight web server is not needed to accomplish this downloading of class files.

5.6.17 Build the Server Classes

The engine package contains only one server-side implementation class, Com-puteEngine, the remote object implementation of the Compute interface. Since ComputeEngine is an implementation of a remote interface, you need to generate a stub for the remote object so that clients can contact the remote object.

Let's say that ann, the developer of the ComputeEngine class, has placed ComputeEngine.java in the c:\home\ann\src\engine directory and is deploying the class files for clients to use in a subdirectory of her public_html directory, c:\home\ann\public_html\classes (on UNIX that would be /home/ann/public_html/classes, accessible via some web servers as http://host/~ann/classes/).

Now let's assume that the compute.jar file is located in the directory c:\home\ann \public_html\classes. To compile the ComputeEngine class, your class path must include the compute.jar file and the source directory itself.

Note: Normally we recommend that you set the class path on the command line, using the -classpath option. However, for several compounding reasons this example uses the CLASSPATH environment variable, because both javac and rmic require a class path and the -classpath option is treated differently in JDK 1.1 and JDK 1.2. For detailed information on CLASSPATH refer to:

Solaris:

http://java.sun.com/products/jdk/1.2/docs/tooldocs/solaris/classpath.html

Microsoft Windows:

http://java.sun.com/products/jdk/1.2/docs/tooldocs/win32/classpath.html

We recommend that you do not set CLASSPATH in a login or startup file and that you remember to unset it when you're finished working with this example.

Here's how to set the CLASSPATH environment variable

Microsoft Windows:

```
set CLASSPATH=c:\home\ann\src;c:\home\ann\public_html\classes\compute.jar
```

UNIX:

```
setenv CLASSPATH /home/ann/src:/home/ann/public_html/classes/compute.jar
```

Now you compile the ComputeEngine.java source file, generate a stub for the ComputeEngine class, and make that stub network accessible. To create stub (and optionally skeleton files), run the rmic compiler on the fully qualified class names of the remote object implementations that must be found in the class path. The rmic command takes one or more class names as input and produces as output class files of the form ClassName_Stub.class and ClassName_Skel.class. A skeleton file will not be generated if you run rmic with the -v1.2 option. This option should be used only if all of your clients will be running JDK 1.2 or compatible versions.

Microsoft Windows:

```
cd c:\home\ann\src
javac engine\ComputeEngine.java
```

```
rmic -d . engine.ComputeEngine
mkdir c:\home\ann\public_html\classes\engine
cp engine\ComputeEngine_*.class
   c:\home\ann\public_html\classes\engine
```

UNIX:

```
cd /home/ann/src
javac engine/ComputeEngine.java
rmic -d . engine.ComputeEngine
mkdir /home/ann/public_html/classes/engine
cp engine/ComputeEngine_*.class
   /home/ann/public_html/classes/engine
```

The -d option tells the rmic compiler to place the generated class files, ComputeEngine_Stub.class and ComputeEngine_Skel.class, in the directory c:\home\ann\src\engine. You also need to make the stubs and the skeletons network accessible, so you must copy the stub and the skeleton class to the area: public_html\classes.

Since the ComputeEngine's stub implements the Compute interface, which refers to the Task interface, you need to make these two interface class files network accessible along with the stub. So the final step is to unpack the compute.jar file in the directory c:\home\ann\public_html\classes to make the Compute and the Task interfaces available for downloading.

Microsoft Windows:

```
cd c:\home\ann\public_html\classes
jar xvf compute.jar
```

UNIX:

```
cd /home/ann/public_html/classes
```

jar xvf compute.jar

```
The jar command displays the following output:
created: META-INF/
extracted: META-INF/MANIFEST.MF
extracted: compute/Compute.class
extracted: compute/Task.class
```

Now the compute engine is ready to deploy. You could do that now or wait until after you have built the client. While we are on a building spree, let's build the client-side program next.

5.6.18 Build the Client Classes

Let's assume that user jones has created the client code in the directory c:\home\jones\src\client and will deploy the Pi class, so that it can be downloaded to the compute engine, in the network-accessible directoryc:\home\jones\public_html\classes, also available via some web servers as http:/

/host/~jones/classes/. The two client-side classes are contained in the files Pi.java and ComputePi.java in the client subdirectory.

In order to build the client code, you need the compute.jar file that contains the Compute and the Task interfaces that the client uses. Let's say that the compute.jar file is located in c:\home\jones\public_html\classes. The client classes can be built as follows:

Microsoft Windows:

```
set CLASSPATH=c:\home\jones\src;c:\home\jones\public_html\classes\compute.jar
cd c:\home\jones\src
javac client\ComputePi.java
javac -d c:\home\jones\public_html\classes client\Pi.java
```

UNIX:

```
setenv CLASSPATH /home/jones/src:/home/jones/public_html/classes/compute.jar
cd /home/jones/src
javac client/ComputePi.java
javac -d /home/jones/public_html/classes client/Pi.java
```

Only the Pi class needs to be placed in the directory public_html\classes\client. (The client directory is created by javac if it does not exist.) The reason is that only the Pi class needs to be available for downloading to the compute engine's virtual machine. Now you can run the server and then the client.

5.6.19 Compiling the Example Programs

In a real-world scenario in which a service like the compute engine is deployed, a developer would likely create a JAR (Java ARchive) file that contains the Compute and Task interfaces for server classes to implement and client program to use. Next, a developer, perhaps the same developer of the interface JAR file, would write an implementation of the Compute interface and deploy that service on a machine available to clients. Developers of client programs can use the Compute and the Task interfaces, contained in the JAR file, and independently develop a task and client program that uses a Compute service.

In this section you learn how to set up the JAR file, server classes, and client classes. You will see that the client's Pi class will be downloaded to the server at runtime. Also, the ComputeEngine's remote stub will be downloaded from the server to the client at runtime.

The example separates the interfaces, remote object implementation, and client code into three packages:

- compute (Compute and Task interfaces)
- engine (ComputeEngine implementation class and its stub)
- client (ComputePi client code and Pi task implementation)

Let's first build the interface JAR file to provide to server and client developers.

5.6.20 Build a JAR File of Interface Classes

First, you need to compile the interface source files in the compute package and then build a JAR file that contains their class files. Let's suppose a user, waldo, has written these particular interfaces and has placed the source files in c:\home\waldo\src\compute (on UNIX:/home/waldo/src/compute). Given these paths, you can use the following commands to compile the interfaces and create the JAR file.

Microsoft Windows:

```
cd c:\home\waldo\src
javac compute\Compute.java
javac compute\Task.java
jar cvf compute.jar compute\*.class
```

UNIX:

```
cd /home/waldo/src
javac compute/Compute.java
javac compute/Task.java
jar cvf compute.jar compute/*.class
```

The jar command displays the following output (due to the -v option):

```
added manifest
adding: compute/Compute.class (in=281) (out=196)
        (deflated 30%)
adding: compute/Task.class (in=200) (out=164)
        (deflated 18%)
```

Now you can distribute the compute.jar file to developers of server and client applications so that they can make use of the interfaces.

When you build either server- or client-side classes with the javac and rmic compilers, you generally need to specify where the resulting class files should reside so that they are network accessible. In this example this location is, for UNIX, /home/user/public_html/classes, because some web servers allow accessing a user's public_html directory via an HTTP URL constructed as http://host/~user/. If your web server does not support this convention, you could use a file URL instead. The file URLs take the form file:/home/user/public_html/classes/ on UNIX or, on the Microsoft Windows platform, file:/c:/home/user/public_html/classes/. You may also select another type of URL, as appropriate.

The network accessibility of the class files allows the RMI runtime to download code when needed. Rather than defining its own protocol for code downloading, RMI uses URL protocols supported by the Java platform (for example, HTTP) to download code. Note that a full, heavyweight web server is not needed to accomplish this downloading of class files. In fact, a simple HTTP server that provides all of the functionality needed to make classes available for downloading in RMI via HTTP can be found at ftp://ftp.javasoft.com/pub/jdk1.1/rmi/class-server.zip.

5.6.21 Build the Server Classes

The engine package contains only one server-side implementation class, Com-puteEngine, the remote object implementation of the Compute interface. Since ComputeEngine is an implementation of a remote interface, you need to generate a stub for the remote object so that clients can contact the remote object.

Let's say that ann, the developer of the ComputeEngine class, has placed ComputeEngine.java in the c:\home\ann\src\engine directory and is deploying the class files for clients to use in a subdirectory of her public_html directory, c:\home\ann\public_html\classes (on UNIX that would be /home/ann/public_html/classes, accessible via some web servers as http://host/~ann/classes/).

Now let's assume that the compute.jar file is located in the directory c:\home\ ann\ public_html\classes. To compile the ComputeEngine class, your class path must include the compute.jar file and the source directory itself.

Note: Normally we recommend that you set the class path on the command line, using the -classpath option. However, for several compounding reasons this example uses the CLASSPATH environment variable, because both javac and rmic require a class path and the -classpath option is treated differently in JDK 1.1 and JDK 1.2. For detailed information on CLASSPATH refer to:

Solaris:

http://java.sun.com/products/jdk/1.2/docs/tooldocs/solaris/classpath.html

Microsoft Windows:

http://java.sun.com/products/jdk/1.2/docs/tooldocs/win32/classpath.html

We recommend that you do not set CLASSPATH in a login or startup file and that you remember to unset it when you're finished working with this example.

Here's how to set the CLASSPATH environment variable

Microsoft Windows:

```
set CLASSPATH=c:\home\ann\src;c:\home\ann\public_html\classes\compute.jar
```

UNIX:

```
setenv CLASSPATH /home/ann/src:/home/ann/public_html/classes/compute.jar
```

Now you compile the ComputeEngine.java source file, generate a stub for the ComputeEngine class, and make that stub network accessible. To create stub (and optionally skeleton files), run the rmic compiler on the fully qualified class names of the remote object implementations that must be found in the class path. The rmic command takes one or more class names as input and produces as output class files of the form ClassName_Stub.class and ClassName_Skel.class. A skeleton file will not be generated if you run rmic with the -v1.2 option. This option should be used only if all of your clients will be running JDK 1.2 or compatible versions.

Microsoft Windows:

```
cd c:\home\ann\src
javac engine\ComputeEngine.java
```

```
rmic -d . engine.ComputeEngine
mkdir c:\home\ann\public_html\classes\engine
cp engine\ComputeEngine_*.class
   c:\home\ann\public_html\classes\engine
```

UNIX:

```
cd /home/ann/src
javac engine/ComputeEngine.java
rmic -d . engine.ComputeEngine
mkdir /home/ann/public_html/classes/engine
cp engine/ComputeEngine_*.class
   /home/ann/public_html/classes/engine
```

The -d option tells the rmic compiler to place the generated class files, ComputeEngine_Stub.class and ComputeEngine_Skel.class, in the directory c:\home\ann\src\engine. You also need to make the stubs and the skeletons network accessible, so you must copy the stub and the skeleton class to the area: public_html\classes.

Since the ComputeEngine's stub implements the Compute interface, which refers to the Task interface, you need to make these two interface class files network accessible along with the stub. So the final step is to unpack the compute.jar file in the directory c:\home\ann\public_html\classes to make the Compute and the Task interfaces available for downloading.

Microsoft Windows:

```
cd c:\home\ann\public_html\classes
jar xvf compute.jar
```

UNIX:

```
cd /home/ann/public_html/classes
jar xvf compute.jar
```

The jar command displays the following output:

```
created: META-INF/
extracted: META-INF/MANIFEST.MF
extracted: compute/Compute.class
extracted: compute/Task.class
```

Now the compute engine is ready to deploy. You could do that now or wait until after you have built the client. While we are on a building spree, let's build the client-side program next.

5.6.22 Build the Client Classes

Let's assume that user jones has created the client code in the directory c:\home\jones\src\client and will deploy the Pi class, so that it can be downloaded to the compute engine, in the network-accessible directoryc:\home\jones\public_html\classes, also available via some web servers as http://host/~jones/classes/. The two client-side classes are contained in the files Pi.java and ComputePi.java in the client subdirectory.

In order to build the client code, you need the compute.jar file that contains the Compute and the Task interfaces that the client uses. Let's say that the compute.jar file is located in c:\home\jones\public_html\classes. The client classes can be built as follows:

Microsoft Windows:

```
set CLASSPATH=c:\home\jones\src;c:\home\jones\public_html\classes\compute.jar
cd c:\home\jones\src
javac client\ComputePi.java
javac -d c:\home\jones\public_html\classes client\Pi.java
```

UNIX:

```
setenv CLASSPATH /home/jones/src:/home/jones/public_html/classes/compute.jar
cd /home/jones/src
javac client/ComputePi.java
javac -d /home/jones/public_html/classes client/Pi.java
```

Only the Pi class needs to be placed in the directory public_html\classes\client. (The client directory is created by javac if it does not exist.) The reason is that only the Pi class needs to be available for downloading to the compute engine's virtual machine. Now you can run the server and then the client.

5.7 RUNNING THE EXAMPLE PROGRAMS

5.7.1 A Note About Security

The JDK 1.2 security model is more sophisticated than the model used for JDK 1.1. JDK 1.2 contains enhancements for finer-grained security and requires code to be granted specific permissions to be allowed to perform certain operations.

In JDK 1.1 code in the class path is trusted and can perform any operation; downloaded code is governed by the rules of the installed security manager. If you run this example in JDK 1.2, you need to specify a policy file when you run your server and client. Here is a general policy file that allows downloaded code, from any code base, to do two things:

- Connect to or accept connections on unprivileged ports (ports greater than 1024) on any host
- Connect to port 80 (the port for HTTP)

Here is the code for the general policy file:

```
grant {
    permission java.net.SocketPermission "*:1024-65535",
```

```
        "connect,accept";
    permission java.net.SocketPermission "*:80", "connect";
};
```

If you make your code available for downloading via HTTP URLs, you should use the preceding policy file when you run this example. However, if you use file URLs instead, you can use the following policy file. Note that in Windows-style file names, the backslash character needs to be represented by two backslash characters in the policy file.

```
grant {
    permission java.net.SocketPermission "*:1024-65535",
        "connect,accept";
    permission java.io.FilePermission
        "c:\\home\\ann\\public_html\\classes\\-", "read";
    permission java.io.FilePermission
        "c:\\home\\jones\\public_html\\classes\\-", "read";
};
```

This example assumes that the policy file is called java.policy and that it contains the appropriate permissions. If you run this example on JDK 1.1, you will not need to use a policy file, since the RMISecurityManager provides all of the protection you need.

5.7.2 Start the Server

Before starting the compute engine, you need to start RMI's registry, using the rmiregistry command. As discussed earlier, the RMI registry is a simple server-side bootstrap naming facility that allows remote clients to get a reference to a remote object. Note that before you start the rmiregistry, you must make sure that the shell or window in which you will run rmiregistry either has no CLASSPATH environment variable set or has a CLASSPATH environment variable that does not include the path to any classes, including the stubs for your remote object implementation classes, that you want downloaded to clients of your remote objects.

If you *do* start the rmiregistry and it *can* find your stub classes in CLASSPATH, it will not remember that the loaded stub class can be loaded from your server's code base, specified by the java.rmi.server.codebase property when you started up your server application. Therefore, the rmiregistry will not convey to clients the true code base associated with the stub class and, consequently, your clients will not be able to locate and to load the stub class or other server-side classes.

To start the registry on the server, execute the rmiregistry command. This command produces no output and is typically run in the background. For this example, we will start the registry on the host zaphod.

Microsoft Windows (use javaw if start is not available):

```
unset CLASSPATH
start rmiregistry
```

UNIX:

```
unsetenv CLASSPATH
rmiregistry &
```

By default, the registry runs on port 1099. To start the registry on a different port, specify the port number on the command line. Do not forget to unset your CLASSPATH.

Microsoft Windows:

```
start rmiregistry 2001
```

UNIX:

```
rmiregistry 2001 &
```

Once the registry is started, you can start the server. First, you need to make sure that both the compute.jar file and the remote object implementation class (since that is what you are starting) are in your class path.

Microsoft Windows:

```
set CLASSPATH=c:\home\ann\src;c:\home\ann\public_html\classes\compute.jar
```

UNIX;

```
setenv CLASSPATH /home/ann/src:/home/ann/public_html/classes/compute.jar
```

When you start the compute engine, you need to specify, using the java.rmi.server.codebase property, where the server's classes will be made available. In this example the server-side classes to be made available for downloading are the ComputeEngine's stub and the Compute and the Task interfaces, available in ann's public_html\classes directory. Here, we start the compute engine server on the host zaphod, the same host where we started the registry.

Microsoft Windows:

```
java -Djava.rmi.server.codebase=file:/c:\home\ann\public_html\classes/
    -Djava.rmi.server.hostname=zaphod.east.sun.com
    -Djava.security.policy=java.policy
        engine.ComputeEngine
```

UNIX:

```
java -Djava.rmi.server.codebase=http://zaphod/~ann/classes/
    -Djava.rmi.server.hostname=zaphod.east.sun.com
    -Djava.security.policy=java.policy
        engine.ComputeEngine
```

The preceding java command defines several properties.

- The java.rmi.server.codebase property specifies the location, a code base URL, of classes originating *from* this server so that class information for objects sent to other virtual machines will include the location of the class so that a receiver can load it. If the code base specifies a directory (as opposed to a JAR file), you must include the trailing slash in the code base URL.

- The java.rmi.server.hostname property indicates the fully qualified host name of your server. In some networked environments a fully qualified host name is not obtainable by using the Java APIs. RMI makes a best-effort attempt to obtain the fully qualified host name. If one cannot be determined, it will fall back and use the IP address. To ensure that RMI will use a host name that is usable from potential clients, you may want to set the java.rmi.server.hostname property as a safety measure.
- The java.security.policy property is used to specify the policy file that contains the permissions you intend to grant specific code bases.

The Compute Engine's stub class is dynamically loaded into a client's virtual machine only when the class is not already available locally *and* the java.rmi.server.codebas e property has been set properly, to the network-accessible location of the stub class, when the *server* is started. Once such a stub is loaded, it will not need to be reloaded for additional references to Com-puteEngine's objects.

5.7.3 Start the Client

Once the registry and the engine are running, you can start the client, specifying

- The location where the client serves up its classes (the Pi class), using the java.rmi.server.codebase property
- As command line arguments the host name of the server—so that the client knows where to locate the Compute remote object—and the number of decimal places to use in the π calculation
- The java.security.policy property, used to specify the policy file that contains the permissions you intend to grant specific code bases

First, set the CLASSPATH to see jones's client and the JAR file containing the interfaces. Then start the client on another host (one named ford, for example) as follows:

Microsoft Windows:

```
set CLASSPATH c:\home\jones\src;c:\home\jones\public_html\classes\compute.jar
java -Djava.rmi.server.codebase=file:/c:\home\jones\public_html\classes/
 -Djava.security.policy=java.policy
client.ComputePi zaphod.east.sun.com 20
```

UNIX:

```
setenv CLASSPATH /home/jones/src:/home/jones/public_html/classes/compute.jar
java -Djava.rmi.server.codebase=http://ford/~jones/classes/
-Djava.security.policy=java.policy
 client.ComputePi zaphod.east.sun.com 20
```

Note that the class path is set on the command line so that the interpreter can find jones's client and the JAR file containing the interfaces.

After starting the client, you should see the following output on your display:

3.14159265358979323846

The following figure illustrates where the rmiregistry, the ComputeEngine server, and the ComputePi client obtain classes during program execution.

When the ComputeEngine server binds its remote object reference in the registry, the registry downloads the ComputeEngine_Stub, as well as the Compute and the Task interfaces on which the stub class depends. These classes are downloaded from the ComputeEngine's web server or file system, as the case may be.

The ComputePi client loads the ComputeEngine_Stub, also from the Compute-Engine's web server, as a result of the Naming.lookup call. Since the ComputePi client has both the Compute and the Task interfaces available in its class path, those classes are loaded from the class path, not the remote location.

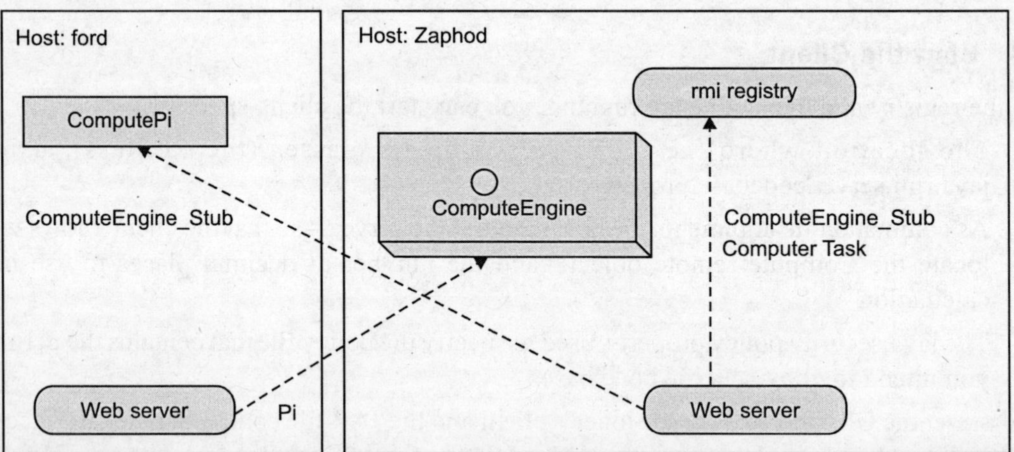

Finally, the Pi class is loaded into the ComputeEngine's virtual machine when the Pi object is passed in the executeTask remote call to the ComputeEngine object. The Pi class is loaded from the client's web server.

5.8 SUMMARY

- Object that can receive remote method invocation are called remote objects.
- Distributed system may adopt the client-server architecture.
- In distributed object model, each process contains a collection of objects
- In remote procedure calls services that are available at remote servers in the term of subroutine are called at contain work station.
- A remote object reference is an identifier that can be used in distributed system.
- The class of a remote object implements the remote interface.
- Notifications are sent asynchronously by event- generating object to all the objects.

- An event source can generate events of one or more different types.
- Types and distributes both are used in subscribing to events.
- A notification contains information about the type of events and its attributes.
- A subscriber is an object that has subscribed to some types of events in another object.

5.9 REVIEW QUESTION

1. Explain the distributed object and give use of communication between objects.
2. Discuss the distributed object model, its advantages and limitations.
3. Explain remote procedure calls and the basic use of remote procedure calls.
4. Discuss the form events and notifications and what role played by notification in generation of events.
5. Explain different types of events notification.
6. What is difference between local; object and remote objects and the also discuss the limitations of local objects.
7. Explain remote object and remote object reference and remote interface role in remote object interface.
8. Explain the role of client and server stub procedure in remote procedure calls.
9. Explain architecture for distributed event notification.
10. Explain remote method invocation (RMI)

CHAPTER 6

Security

Security is the degree of protection against danger, loss, and criminals.Security has to be compared and contrasted with other related concepts: Safety, continuity, reliability. The key difference between security and reliability is that security must take into account the actions of people attempting to cause destruction. The main goal of security is to restrict access to information and resources to those principles that are authorized to have access.

6.1 WHAT IS SECURITY

Different people mean different things when they talk about security, so it is probably good to start by setting some basic definitions. Some people talk about security in terms of computer viruses or hackers making a denial-of-service attack over the Internet. Others refer to privacy and encryption or authentication and authorization. Securing systems requires addressing all these areas. The elements of security fall under four headings:

There are some de facto security standards today, such as the Generic Security Service Application Program Interface (GSS-API), for interfacing programs to security services. Other standards include numerous encryption algorithms such as DES and RSA for message encryption and MD5 and SHA hashing algorithms for the creation of digital "fingerprints."

Authentication

- Is someone who he or she says he or she is?
- Is some object (such as a program) what it says it is?
- Does a message come from where it says it comes from?
- Can someone deny something he or she did (non repudiation)?

Authorization

- What is a specific person or group of people allowed to do?
- What is a specific program allowed to do?

Encryption

- Who is allowed to see what information?

System Protection

This heading groups all protection against system damage. This includes virus protection, firewalls and proxies, protection against denial-of-service attacks, and steps taken to minimize accidental system failures. This protection can be partially addressed by applying authentication, authorization, and encryption techniques. A number of other facilities, such as virus-detection and removal software and virus-resistant systems environments help with this.

Today, there are point solutions that cover all these areas, but there are few provisions for building a complete security architecture. For example, current Secure Socket Layer (SSL) implementations provide Internet server authentication and encryption but not user authentication, although the latest SSL standards (now in version 3.0) address this. Various Kerberos-based private key mechanisms provide all three capabilities, but they are only viable when up to a few thousand user keys need to be administered.

There are some de facto security standards today, such as the Generic Security Service Application Program Interface (GSS-API), for interfacing programs to security services. Other standards include numerous encryption algorithms such as DES and RSA for message encryption and MD5 and SHA hashing algorithms for the creation of digital "fingerprints."

6.1.1 Technology Matters, But Other Things Matter More

When discussing security, many people get excited over encryption key lengths and other technical encryption matters. Though these may be important, they are not where the real danger lies. There are two basic rules of security. One is that there is no such thing as perfect security. Security is always a trade-off between cost and difficulty of use on one side and risk on the other. Technology can increase or decrease the risks for a given cost, but compromises always have to be made. It is a crucial element of security management to be able to evaluate the risks and balance them against the cost and difficulty of use.

The second basic rule is that the biggest security exposures will always be in people's behavior. No amount of technology can make a system secure if people do not behave securely. Therefore a successful technical solution must encourage secure behavior and be able to detect insecure behavior.

One of the biggest problems in security is caused by the proliferation of secure systems. I personally access probably hundreds of sites both internally and on the Internet, many of which require passwords to access. This presents a dilemma. Do I use a different password for each site and risk forgetting them or writing them down? Or do I reuse a small number of passwords and risk giving away a password for one Web site I use to another?

If passwords are reused, they become highly vulnerable. For example, one way to collect such passwords would be to open a valuable but free Web site and make it password-protected. Then the site could be made to require frequently changed passwords and it could conveniently "forget" your password from time to time to encourage you to try out other passwords. Such a site could probably collect many passwords that could be used elsewhere. This is why physical token- and biometric-based authentication and single sign-on are important; they help reduce the security exposure from people's behavior.

One of the biggest problems in security is caused by the proliferation of secure systems. I personally access probably hundreds of sites both internally and on the Internet, many of which require passwords to access. This presents a dilemma. Do I use a different password for each site and risk forgetting them or writing them down? Or do I reuse a small number of passwords and risk giving away a password for one Web site I use to another?

If passwords are reused, they become highly vulnerable. For example, one way to collect such passwords would be to open a valuable but free Web site and make it password-protected. Then the site could be made to require frequently changed passwords and it could conveniently "forget" your password from time to time to encourage you to try out other passwords. Such a site could probably collect many passwords that could be used elsewhere. This is why physical token- and biometric-based authentication and single sign-on are important; they help reduce the security exposure from people's behavior.

6.1.2 Specific Problem Areas

In the world of distributed systems, there are a number of specific areas where there is a clear need for more secure facilities than are generally used today. These include:

- The ability to restrict access to Web pages
- The ability to secure distributed objects, especially CORBA/IIOP communications
- Single sign-on in an Internet/intranet/ extranet environment to let users identify themselves only once to gain access to many systems
- The ability of systems (and not just users) to identify themselves to other systems in a distributed environment
- The ability to provide secure communications between companies (as on an extranet)
- The ability to coordinate many security systems, for example, synchronization of Web security with operating system security and database security
- Secure access to legacy applications in a distributed environment.

6.1.3 Distributed Architectures

Today, most of the parts of such an architecture can be secured, but it requires several different products. For simple client-to-Web server encryption, SSL is generally used. User authentication generally just uses simple password-checking software running on the Web server. The security of the business-rules layer is usually vendor-specific. For example, Tuxedo version 6.3 has built-in by Intel to establish standard security architecture. It consists primarily of a Common Security Services Manager, which sits between the applications and a set of add-in modules that provide cryptographic services, certificates, trust policies, and so on. CDSA may prove to be significant security architecture for all parts of a distributed system, but it's early yet. (CDSA version 1.2 was released on March 17, 1997.) It is not entirely clear that there is a need for a common security interface layer as opposed to a standard security API, such as GSS-API, with the applications interfacing directly to the security services.

6.1.4 Security Architectures

Securing a distributed environment will always require a combination of physical security and logical security (authentication, authorization, and encryption). Providing adequate security also goes beyond technical matters to security protocols and human behavior. All the physical and logical security in the world won't help you if some authorized person gives the information away. Technical security must always be part of a complete security system that incorporates proven protocols and manual procedures.

It is often forgotten that logical security only works if certain parts of the system are physically sensor is not physically secured or if its output is not encrypted. Similarly, even though messages do not need to be physically secured, the private keys must be. Right now there are only three generally available ways to do this. One is to secure the hardware containing the keys in a physically secure environment, such as a data center or even just a locked room. Another option is to secure individual computers physically by hardening them. For example, in some high-security environments, computers are built inside safes. A much more cost-effective method is to secure physically just the keys and the encryption engine. Today, solutions are available that use tamper-resistant PCMCIA Cards or Smart Cards to secure the keys and the encryption engine. The European cellular phone industry uses Smart Cards for security with its Global System for Mobile Communications (GSM) system.

It is important to note that it is not enough to secure the keys physically. The encryption engine also must be secured along with the keys; otherwise the keys can be intercepted between the "key safe" and the encryption engine.

6.1.5 Security Protocols

There are a vast number of security protocols to protect against various scenarios, including eavesdropping, man-in-the-middle attacks, repudiation, and message alteration. Here I will concentrate on mechanisms for authentication, authorization, and encryption.

Private key encryption requires much less computing power than public key techniques and is usually faster, but it requires a shared secret that must be distributed in some other manner (out of band). For a small number of users, keys can be physically distributed using, for example, secure printing techniques. Often private keys are distributed using a public key technique.

Kerberos is a private key encryption approach developed at the Massachusetts Institute of Technology. It is based upon a central (possibly replicated) security server that is trusted by everyone. Commercial implementations are available from such companies as Cyber Safe Corp. Every user has his or her own private key that is shared only with the security server. This setup keeps you from having private keys for each user/server pair. The Kerberos protocol involves the issuing of tickets that grant a user access to a machine. To avoid interception of the tickets, Kerberos uses encrypted time stamps and an expiry time on each ticket. The default for Kerberos is to reject time stamps more than five minutes off. This gives up to five minutes for a ticket to arrive at the server after leaving the client machine. Unfortunately this requires that the clocks on all the client and server machines be accurately synchronized, which can be difficult when there are many users or when the users are in different time zones, which requires special techniques. Kerberos is quite a useful approach for securing server-to-server communications within a business, and you can use it to provide single sign-on at the expense of complex key management.

Public key techniques are currently fashionable. The most popular of these use the RSA algorithm, although other algorithms, such as elliptic curve algorithms, are promising. Public key algorithms are very compute-intensive compared to private key algorithms, so they are often used only for key exchange, after which private key techniques are used for message encryption. SSL key exchange is based upon the RSA algorithm. Key management is simplified with public keys. The most common approach is to have a small number of trusted key distribution centers, which hold the public part of the public/private keys for all the parties that wish to communicate. Then each party only needs to retrieve the public keys for the other party to communicate securely. The private keys never leave their owners.

Other techniques and algorithms include Diffie-Hellman, which uses a public key technique to negotiate a generated private key, rather than having one party generate the private key and send it to the other. The standard Diffie-Hellman protocol is vulnerable to man in the middle attacks, but this can be addressed by signing the messages digitally. Another technique is to use hash functions such as MD5 and SHA to ensure that messages are not altered in transit.

Most attention in the commercial world has been directed to securing messages. This is understandable in a distributed environment, especially given the open nature of the Internet. One area that has had very limited attention is securing databases. Most commercial implementations use simple password protection for access with no encryption and no single sign-on. Also, most database security routines with commercial DBMS are stand-alone and cannot integrate easily with other security mechanisms. This is somewhat surprising because the vulnerability of information is a factor of how long an intruder has to work with it. Messages are short-lived, but data in databases can be around for many years. Today, assuming that steps have been taken to secure the transaction messages, the easiest way to do damage or act fraudulently would be to access the relatively unprotected databases and alter the data. DBMS vendors do have secure-database capabilities, usually directed to military use, but it is rare for commercial databases to be encrypted or protected using public key techniques. I think this will become an area of increasing interest as the problem is recognized. Some companies, such as Protegrity Inc., are beginning to appear in this space. These vendors' products generally encrypt and decrypt data externally to the DBMS on a selective basis.

Probably the biggest problem in securing distributed systems is the integration of disparate security systems. Your Web site may use SSL, your mainframe may use ACF2 password protection, and your internal servers may use Kerberos. There is no general solution to this problem today, although there are some proprietary solutions from vendors such as IBM (under the company's

Secure Way security product umbrella) that cover a wide range of environments. Standards such as GSSAPI and CDSA are starting to address this problem. In the meantime most commercial shops are having to buy several point solutions and integrate them for themselves. There are companies such as Concept 5 that are taking primarily a services approach to addressing this space.

6.1.6 Securing Inter/Intra/Extranet Applications

The Internet is perceived as a hostile place, and as such it is a great proving ground for intranet and extranet security. If security technology works on the Internet, it will work anywhere. Right now, the emphasis on the Internet is providing secure financial transactions. The state of the art requires very careful coding of applications, firewalls, and Secure Sockets Layer- (SSL) capable servers and browsers. SSL is a flexible protocol that supports various encryption algorithms, including RSA and DES. Unfortunately, it only addresses the securing of HTTP traffic today, namely regular Web pages. This is not currently a problem because most Internet transactions are forms-based and as such, use HTML/HTTP. With the introduction of CORBA/IIOP as an Internet transaction protocol, there is another channel to secure. At this time IIOP is in the clear (unencrypted), but secure IIOP is planned. This will be critical to the use of IIOP for transactions over the Internet.

SSL, as used in the standard versions of the popular browsers, only provides server authentication based on public key technology and not public key-based user authentication. Although the software to have password protection for certain Web pages is available on many Web servers, the software uses passwords stored on the server, making them vulnerable to interception if someone uses the same password on many sites.

SSL— though effective in the United States where RSA using more than 512 bits and 128-bit DES algorithms can be used— only secures the connection between the Web browser and the Web server. This is sufficient if the Web pages are stored on the server and the server is secure. Increasingly, in a distributed environment, Web servers are not the source of data but provide access to legacy systems and databases located on other machines. With firewalls, this communication between the Web server and the source systems is isolated from the Internet and is less vulnerable to outside interference. On the other hand, employees behind the firewall with inside knowledge are a major source of fraud, so protection needs to be end-to-end. The key is to secure the middleware, especially in server-to-server communications.

6.1.7 Securing Middleware

Beyond physical security and the provision of dedicated connections between machines, the simplest ý but probably least flexible and most expensive ý way to secure middleware communications is to use hardware. Assuming the servers are in a secure environment, encryption boxes, such as the Sun Screen products from Sun Microsystems Inc., can be used to communicate securely over public connections. This could be an intranet or even the Internet. This approach provides solid point-to-point security. The more flexible approach is to secure the middleware communications at a software level. This is potentially more vulnerable than the hardware approach, but it is cheaper and more flexible when new connections are needed. The potential extra vulnerability is a result of the software running on relatively insecure operating systems environments such as commercial Unix implementations or Windows NT. These environments can be made secure, but it requires significant skill to do so. Most middleware products, such as MQSeries from IBM, provide security exits onto which private or public key encryption can be built. Some, such as Tuxedo 6.3 and DCE, have built-in security facilities. Most shops choose their middleware products with little consideration of their security capabilities, so it is often a matter of retrofitting security.

6.1.8 Authentication and Single Sign-on

Public key mechanisms (such as RSA) are good for authenticating software and hardware elements of a distributed system. So long as the private key of the private/public key pair is physically secure, the identity of the hardware or application can be assured. To be truly secure, the private key has to be physically secured and packaged with the encryption engine so that it never leaves the physically secure environment. Today there are PCMCIA- and Smart Card-based hardware encryption devices that provide such capabilities, available from companies such as Information Resource Engineering Inc. (IRE), Maz Technologies, Chrysalis-ITS Inc., and the partnership of Hewlett-Packard Inc., Informix Software Inc., and Gemplus. It is likely that in the future, there will CPU chips with published public keys and built-in private keys and encryption engines. Short of someone hacking into the chip with an electron microscope, they will be secure. Authentication is a little less certain when the private key is held in software. In this case the keys can potentially be revealed to a hacker. Security becomes dependent on operating system security.

The problem of authenticating people is much more difficult. Passwords, which are just secrets shared between the authenticator and authenticated, can become a big management dilemma. Earlier, I demonstrated the basic problem of having many passwords that need to be kept secret. The use of public/private key pairs can greatly simplify the key maintenance problem by reducing many private key pairs to a single private/public key pair. This approach has two problems. First, people do not have a cryptographic engine in their heads. This means that the private key has to be entered into a cryptographic engine for it to be used for authentication. The key becomes vulnerable to interception at this point. The second problem with this approach is that private keys are long and meaningless, making them very difficult to remember. The answer is to use tokens or biometrics or both.

Tokens, such as the Smart Cards mentioned earlier, make authentication a matter of possessing of something physical and unique. One great advantage of token-based security is that it becomes relatively easy to know if you are vulnerable. The card must be missing because it can’t be copied without great difficulty. Pure token-based security does leave open a window of opportunity if the token is lost or stolen. Supplementing the token with a password can address this shortcoming. Ideally, the password should be entered directly into the token (some have keypads) for maximum security, but in most cases entering the password into the card-reading device is adequate if you are sure of the integrity of the card reader. There are, however, tales of passwords being intercepted using dummy card readers.

Biometric techniques are even better, so long as the biometric sensor is secure and encrypts its output. My favorite is the iris scan technique, although this technology is only just becoming commercially viable. Unlike retinal scan, iris scan is no intrusive. The front of the eyes is scanned from a distance of a foot or so using a high-definition camera. Current research indicates that the iris is a significantly better biometric than fingerprints, thus offering a substantially lower number of false accepts and rejects. With biometrics, there is no need for a user to remember or enter a password that can potentially be intercepted. The cost of biometrics is starting to come down to an acceptable level for normal commercial applications.

6.1.9 Managing Security

As mentioned earlier, technical security alone cannot provide appropriate security at an acceptable cost. Before implementing technical solutions, you must resolve two areas of security management. One involves managing the risk during the design and implementation stage, and the other involves managing the risk during operations.

Risk assessment for security architecture is technically complicated, especially in a distributed environment where many products and protocols may be used. Two questions need to be asked. One is: What is the worst-case scenario, and is that acceptable to the business? The second is: Is the security approach cost-effective? It is almost certain that except for very large organizations, the skills to ask these questions will not be available within an organization. Even if they are, the danger of making a mistake is such that I would recommend the use of an external security consultancy, at least to verify any internal findings.

Technical security does not work unless it is supported by appropriate processes, the right control structure, and educated attitudes toward security. Operational security addresses these issues. As many organizations have well-established security operations departments.

One observation I would like to make concerns the way most organizations require users to change passwords frequently, say every 30 days, and not reuse passwords for a long time. This is an example of a procedure that, theoretically improves security but actually reduces security. The theory is that the vulnerability of a password to discovery is proportional to the length of time available to discover it. Although this is technically true, in practice it doesn't work that way. If token-based security is not used and someone wants your password, this person would probably have it in less than a day by "shoulder surfing" or by intercepting keystrokes. Even if the password has to be broken by brute force, this can usually be achieved in most cases in a matter of hours by variations on a dictionary attack. (A dictionary attack is a brute force attack in which all valid words in a language are tried out for validity. Attackers may also try common variations on the words, such as adding numbers.) This is especially true when the passwords are changed often because people tend to make them easy to remember, following themes such as children's names, favorite hobbies, or computer terms, and tend to reuse passwords from other systems. If a password can be broken in a day, how much value is added by changing it every 30 days? If the passwords are forced to be effectively random, then they will end up being written down and be much more open to discovery.

My preference is token-based security for situations in which security is critical. If not, I prefer truly random keys changed infrequently, maybe yearly, or when it is thought that the password may have been compromised. This approach gives a little more exposure to "shoulder surfing," but with care, it should improve overall security and usability. This example illustrates the importance of operational security procedures.

6.1.10 The State of the Art

Today, securing distributed systems requires a combination of several different types of products. SSL provides link encryption for the Internet and some authentication. Products based on Kerberos or RSA technology can be used to secure the middleware environment, albeit with some integration effort. Some middleware products, such as Tuxedo, provide built-in security facilities, and some Net-based applications, such as Lotus Notes, also provide security facilities. Standards are beginning to emerge for at least securing the messaging part of distributed systems, with secure IIOP being one of the more important areas.

Authentication capabilities, especially single sign-on, are limited today. It may be some time before there is widespread availability of single sign-on authentication implemented on the server side to cover many environments. In the short term, the most promising approach is the use of Smart Card or PC Card technology to give the appearance of single sign-on by holding many keys.

Distributed systems security is an exciting and important area. Providing rock-solid security for the Inter/intra/extranet is essential for it to reach its enormous potential. Hopefully, we can look forward to a brave new secure world on the Net.

Figure 6.1 An example of the three/four-tier architecture.

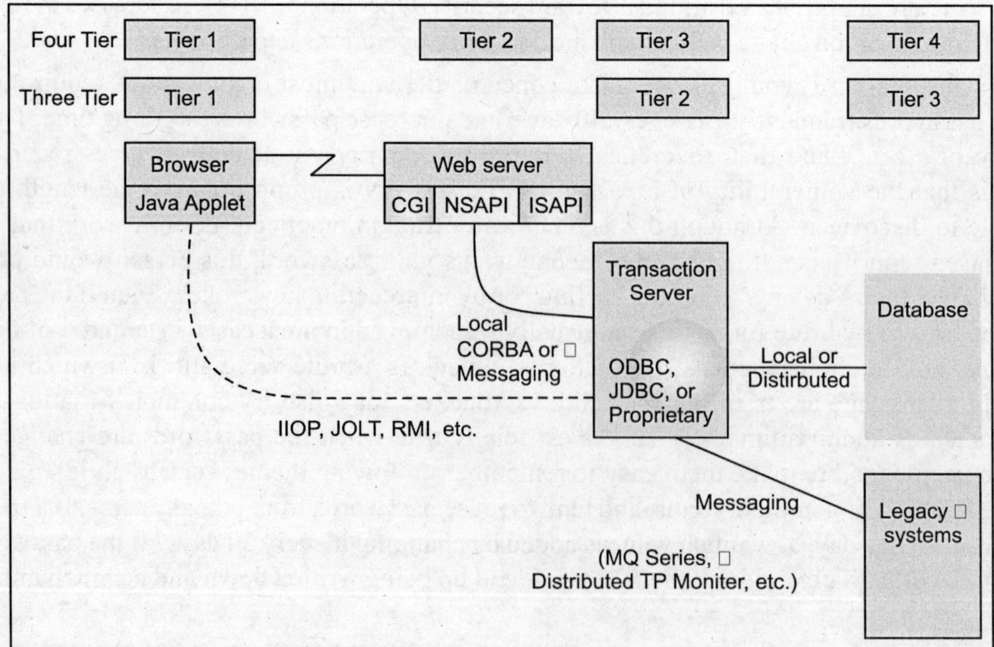

Fig. 6.1

6.2 OVERVIEW OF SECURITY TECHNIQUES

The purpose of security techniques is to introduce the reader to some of the more important techniques and mechanisms for securing distributed system and applications. The main security techniques are:

6.2.1 Cryptography

The art of devising ciphers is known as cryptography. Encryption is the process of encoding a message in such a way as to hide its contents. Modern cryptography includes several secure algorithms for encrypting and decrypting messages. They are all based on the use of secrets called keys. A cryptographic key is a parameter used in an encryption algorithm in such a way that the encryption can not be reversed without knowledge of the key. Cryptography plays three major roles in the implementation of secure systems

- Privacy
- Authentication
- Integrity

The two main cryptography algorithms are private key algorithms and public key encryption.

6.2.2 Access control

In object oriented distributed system there may be many types of objects to which access control must be applied, and the decisions are often application specific. For example, Vikas may be allowed only one cash withdrawal from his bank account per day, while Munesh is allowed three. Access control decisions are usually left to the application- level code, but generic support is provided for much of the machinery that supports the decisions. This includes the authentication of principals, the singing and authentication of request and the management of credentials and access right data.

6.2.3 Credentials

Credentials are a set of evidence provided by a principal when requesting access to a resource. In the sampled case, a certificate from a relevant authority stating the principals identify is sufficient and this would be used to check the principals permissions I an access control list. This is often all that is required or provided, but the concept can be generalized to deal with many more subtle requirements.

It is not convenient to require uses to interact with the system and authenticate themselves each time their authority is required to perform an operation on a protected resource. Instead, the notion that a credentials speaks for a principals is introduced. Thus a users public key process receiving a request authenticated with users private key can assume that the request was issued by that user.

6.2.4 Firewall

Firewalls protect intranets, performing filtering actions on incoming and outgoing communications. Firewalls produce a wall communication environment in which all external communication is intercepted. Messages are forwarded to the intended local recipient only for communications that are explicitly authorized.

Access to internal networks may be controlled by firewalls, but access to public services on the internet is unauthorized because their purpose is to other services to a wide range of users. The use of firewalls offers no protection against attacks from inside an organization on and it is crude in its control of external access. There is a need for finer grained security mechanism; enabling individual users to share information with selected others without compromising privacy and integrity.

Firewalls are not particularly effective against denial of service attacks such as the one based on IP spoofing. The problem is that the flood of messages generated by such attacks overwhelms any single point of defense such as a firewall.

6.3 CRYPTOGRAPHIC ALGORITHMS

A message is encrypted by the sender applying some rule to transform the plaintext message to a cipher text. The recipient must know the inverse rule in order to transform the cipher text into the original plaintext. The encryption transformation is defined with two parts a function E and a key K. The resulting encrypted message is written {M}k

$$E(k, m) = \{M\}\, k$$

The encryption function E defines an algorithm that transforms data items in plaintext into encrypted data items by combining them with the key and transposing them in a manner that is heavily dependent on the value of the key. Decryption is carried out using an inverse function D, which also takes a key as a parameter. For secret key encryption, the key used for decryption is the same as that used for encryption—

$$D(k, E(K, m)) = M$$

Because of its symmetrical use of keys, secret key cryptography is often referred to as symmetric cryptography whereas public key cryptography is referred to as asymmetric cryptography because the keys used for encryption and decryption are different.

6.3.1 Symmetric (secret key) Algorithms

In secret key algorithms, when secret key is allied on plaintext, we get the encrypted text i.e. cipher text at the sender side when receiver gets cipher text it again applies secret key to get original plain text. A principle disadvantages on any type of secret key structure is that all sites, of the common keys. Some administrative and logistic problems arise in the distribution of keys.

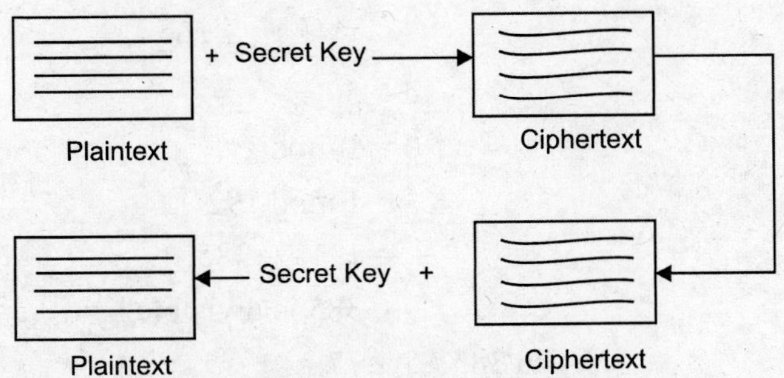

Fig. 6.2 Secret key algorithms

6.3.2 Asymmetric (public key) Algorithms

A public key encryption system can be viewed as a series of public and private keys that locks data when they are transmitted and unlock when they are received. The sender locates the recipients public key in a directory and uses it to encrypt a message. The message is sent in encrypted from over the internet. When the encrypted message arrives the recipient uses his private key to decrypted the data and read the message.

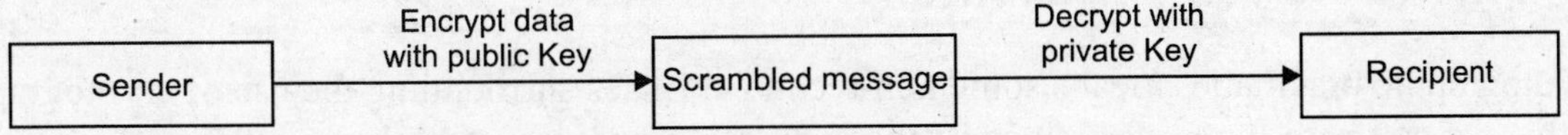

Fig. 6.3 Public key algorithms

In public key algorithms, the encryption keys can be known to everyone only decryption keys are kept secret. To find a key pair e, d the Rivest, samir and Addman (RSA) algorithms are used. In that :

- Choose two large prime number P and Q (each greater than 10^100) and term

$$N = P * Q$$
$$Z = (P-1) * (Q-1)$$

- For d choose any number that is relatively prime with 2 (that is, such that d has no common factors with 2)
- To find e solve the equation

$$E * d = 1 \bmod 2$$

Example: Let $P = 13 \quad Q = 17$

Solution:

$$N = P * Q$$
$$= 13 * 17 = 221$$
$$Z = (P-1) * (Q-1)$$

= 12 * 16 = 192

d = 5

e * d = 1 mod 2

= 1 mod 192

= 1, 193, 385..........

385 is divisible by d

d 385 / 5 =77

6.3.3 Hybrid Cryptographic Algorithms

Public key cryptography is convenient for electronic commerce because there is no need for a secure key distribution mechanism. But the processing costs of public key cryptography are too high for the encryption of medium sized messages normally encountered in electronic commerce. The solution adopted in most large scale distributed systems is to use a hybrid encryption scheme in which public key cryptography is used to authenticate the secret keys, which are used for all subsequent communication. In SSL implementation hybrid cryptographic protocol is used.

6.4 CRYPTOGRAPHY PRAGMATICS

Cryptographic pragmatics means some non-technical issues surrounding the use of cryptography. In this we compare the performance of the encryption and secure hash algorithms. Basically in cryptography pragmatics we concentrate on the performance of cryptographic algorithms and application of the cryptography.

1. **Performance of cryptographic algorithms:** The performances of cryptographic algorithms are studied on basis of key size, extrapolated speed and PRB optimized. The tables for different cryptographic algorithms are:

Algorithms bytes/sec.)	Keys size (Bits)	Extrapolated speed (kb bytes /sec.)	PRB optimized (k b)
TEA	128	700	--------
DES	56	350	7746
Triple-DES	112	120	2842
IDEA	128	700	4469
RSA	512	7	--------
RSA	2048	1	--------
MDS	128	1740	62425
SHA	160	750	25162

2. **Applications of cryptography and political obstacles:** The emergence of cryptographic software was strongly resisted by the US Government. The resistance had two sources, the US National Security Agency (NSA) which was thought to have a police to restrict the

strength of cryptography available to other nations to a level at which the NSA could decrypt any secret communication for military intelligence purposes and the US Federal Bureau of Investigation (FBI) which aimed to ensure that its agents could have privileged access to the cryptographic keys used by all private organizations and individual in the US for law enforcement was classified as a munitions in the united states and was subject to stringent export restrictions. Other countries, especially allies of the USA, applied similar, or in some cases even more stringent restrictions. The problem was compounded by the general ignorance among politicians and general public as to what cryptographic software was and its protection non-military applications.

The export restriction may have hindered the growth of electronic commerce, but they were not particularly elective in preventing the spread of cryptographic expertise or in keeping cryptographic software out of hands, of uses, in other countries, since many programmers inside and outside the USA were eager and able to implements and distribute cryptographic code.

Pretty Good Privacy (PGP) has been developed and distributed with the aim of enabling all computers users to enjoy the level of privacy and integrity afforded by the use of public key cryptography in their communications. PGP generates and manages public and secret keys on behalf of a user. It uses RSA public key encryption for authentication and to transmit secret key to the intended communication partner and its uses IDEA to encrypt all mail messages and other documents.

6.5 DIGITAL SIGNATURE

In case of business transaction, authentication refers to the use of digital signature, which play a function for digital documents similar to that played by hand written signature for printed documents. The signature is an un forgeable piece of data asserting that a named person wrote or otherwise agreed to the document to which the signature is attached.

Unlike encryption, digital signatures are a recent development, the need for which has arisen with the proliferation of e-commerce. The recipient, as well as a third party can variety that the document did indeed originate from the person whose signature is attached and the document has not been altered since it was signed.

Digital signature is ' a digital code that can be attached to an electronically transmitted message to uniquely identify its contents and the sender A secure digital signature system thus consists of two parts:

(i) A method of signing a document such that forgery is infeasible.

(ii) A method of verifying that s signature was actually generated by whomever it represents.

A document with a digital signature can be considerably more resistant to forgery than a hand written one, but the word 'original has little meaning with reference to digital documents. If a secret key is used to encrypt the document, only principals that share the secret key can verify the signature, but if public key cryptography is used, than the signer uses her private key and anyone who has the corresponding public key can verify the signature. This is a better analogue for conventional signatures and meets a wider range of user needs. The verification of signature on whether differently dependency on whether secret key or public key cryptography is used to produce the signature.

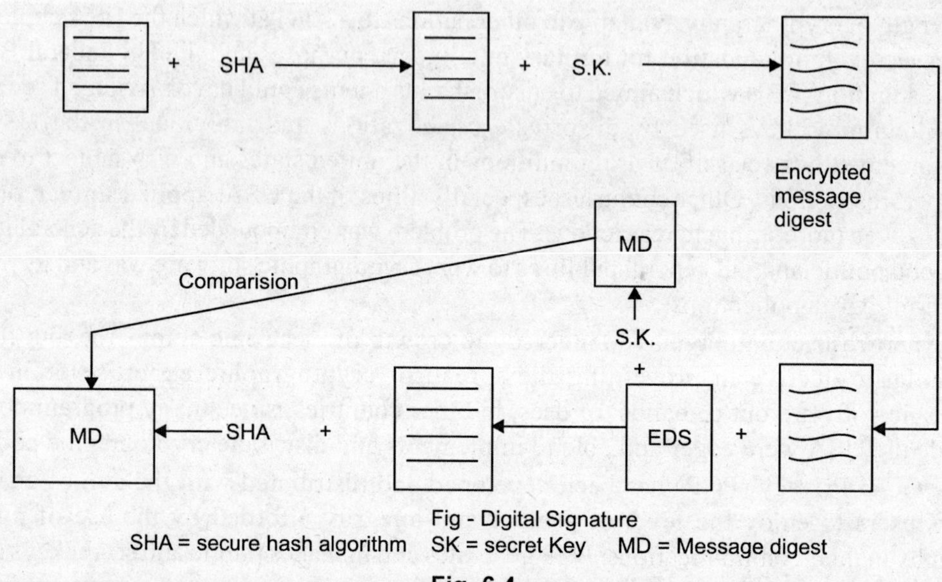

Fig. 6.4

6.5.1 Digital Signature with Public key

Public key cryptography is particularly well adopted for the generation of digital signature because it is relatively simple and does not require any communication between the recipient of a signed document and the signer or any third party.

The method for A to sign a message M and B to verify it is as follows:

(i) A generates a key pair Kpub and Kpriv and publishes the public keys Kpub by placing it in a well- known location.

(ii) A computes the digest of M, H(M) using an agreed secure has function H and encrypts it using the private key Kpriv to produce the signature

$$S = \{ H(M) \} K\ priv$$

(iii) A sends the signed message

$$[M]k = M, S \text{ to } B$$

(iv) B decrypt S using Kpub and compute the digest of M, H(M), if they match signature is valid

6.5.2 Digital Signature with Private Keys

The workings of low cost signing secret key are as follows:

(i) A generates a random key K for signing and distributes it using secure channels to one or more principals, who will need to authenticate message received from A. The principals are frosted not to disclose shared key.

(ii) For any documents M that a wishes to sign, A concatenates M with K, computes digest

$$H = H\ (M + K)$$

(iii) The receiver B, concatenates the secret key K with received document M and computes digest

$$h = H\,(H + K)$$

The signature is verified if h = h, there is no technical reason why a secret key encryption algorithms should not be used to encrypt a digital signature, but in order to verify, such signature the key must be disclosed, and this cause same problems:

(i) The signer must arrange for the receiver to receive the secret key used for signing securely.

(ii) It may be necessary to verify a signature in several contexts and at a different time.

(iii) The signing is undesirable because it weakens the security of signatures made with that key—a signature could be forged by a holder of the key who is not the owner of it.

For these reasons, the public key method for generating and verifying signatures offers the most convenient solution in most situations.

6.6 CASE STUDIES: NEEDHAM – SCHROEDER, KERBEROS, SSL & MILLICENT

The authentication protocols originally published by Needham and Schroeder are at the heart of many security techniques. There are two applications – level security protocol that are important for electronic commerce. The first application level case study deals with secure sockets layer (SSL) protocol. This was designed specially to meet the need for secure electronic transactions. It is now supported by most web browsers and servers and is employed in most of the commercial transactions that take place via the web. The second application level case study deals with Millicent protocol to meet the need for a payment method for micro transactions.

6.6.1 The Needham – Schroeder Protocol

Needham–Schroeder set out a protocol based on use of public keys for authentication and key distribution that does not depend upon the existence of secure keys servers and is hence more suitable for use in networks with much independent management domains, Such as internet- Needham – Schroeder proposed a solution to authentication and key distribution based on an authentication server that supplies secret keys to clients. The job of the authentication server is to provide a secure way for pair of processes to obtain shared keys. It must communicate with its clients using encrypted messages.

In this model, a process acting on behalf of a principal A that wishes to initiate secure communication with process acting on behalf of a principal B can obtain a key for the purpose. The protocol is described for two arbitrary processes A and B, in client server systems A is likely to be a client initiating a sequence of requests to some server B. The key is supplied to A in two forms, one that A can use to encrypt messages that it sends to B and one that it can transmit security to B.

The authentication server S maintains a table containing a name and a secret key for each principal known to the system. The secret key used only to authenticate client processes to the authentication server and to transmit messages securely between client and authentication server. It is never disclosed to third parties and it is transmitted across the network at most once, when it is generated.

The protocol is based on the generation and transmission of tickets by the authentication server. A ticket is an encrypted message containing a secret key for use in communication between A and B. There is a weakness in this protocol in that B has no reason to believe that message is fresh. An intruder who manages to obtain the key kAB and make a copy of the ticket.

6.6.2 Kerberos

Kerberos was developed at MIT in 1980 to provide a range of authentication and security facilities for use in the campus computing networks at MIT and other intranets. Kerberos deals with three kinds of security objects:

(i) **Tickets:** A token issued to a client by Kerberos ticket – generating service for presentation to a particular server, verifying that the sender has recently been authenticated by Kerberos. Tickets include an expiry time and a newly generated session key for use by the client and server.

(ii) **Authentication:** A token constructed by a client nd sent to server to prove the identity of user and the currency of any communication with a server. An authenticator can be used only once. It contains clients name and a timestamp and is encrypted in the appropriate session key.

(iii) **Session Key:** A secret key randomly generated by Kerberos and issued to a client for use when communicating with a particular server. Encryption is not mandatory for all communication with servers. The session key is used for encrypting communication with those servers that demand it and for encrypting all authentications.

A Kerberos server is known as key distribution centre (KDC). Each KDC offer an authentication service (AS) and a ticket granting service (TGS). When a user logs in to a work station, the login program sends the users name to the Kerberos authentication service. If user is known to it replies with a session key and a nonce encrypted in the users password and a ticket for the TGS. The login program then attempts to decrypt the session key and nonce using the password that user typed in response to the password prompt. If the password is correct, the login program obtains the session keys and nonce.

Whenever a program running on a workstation needs to access a new service, it requests a ticket for the service from the ticket granting service. Kerberos is implemented as a server that runs on a secure machine. A set of applications and services, the DES encryption algorithms is used, but this is implemented as a separate module that can be easily replaced.

The security of Kerberos depends on limited session life times— the period of validity of TGS tickets is generally limited to a few hours. The period must be chosen to be long enough to avoid inconvenient interruption of service but short enough to ensure that users who have been de-registered or download do not continue to use the resources for more than a short period.

6.6.3 Secure Socket layer (SSL)

The Netscape communication has proposed a protocol for providing data security layered between high level application protocols and TCP/IP. This security protocol called secure socket layer that provides data encryption, server authentication, message integrity and optional client authentication for a TCP/IP connection.

Electronic commerce applications
Secure - hypertext transfer protocol (S - http)
TCP - based application protocol (HTTP, SMTP, NNTP)
secure socket layer (SSL)
Internet protocol (IP)

Fig. 6.5 Web security Protocol

SSL provides a security handshake to initiate the TCP/IP connection. Its only role is to encrypt and decrypt message streams. This protocol fully encrypts all the information in both HTTP request and HTTP response, including the URC the client is requesting, any submitted from contents, any HTTP access authorization information and all the data returned from the server to the client. SSL provides encryption that creates a secure channel to prevent third parties on the network from being able to temper with and read messages being exchanged between the client and server and authentication that use a digital signature to verify the legitimacy of the server.

The SSL protocol is implemented at the host station instead of server. The client request from server, the server sends its digital certification to client including public key and digital signature.

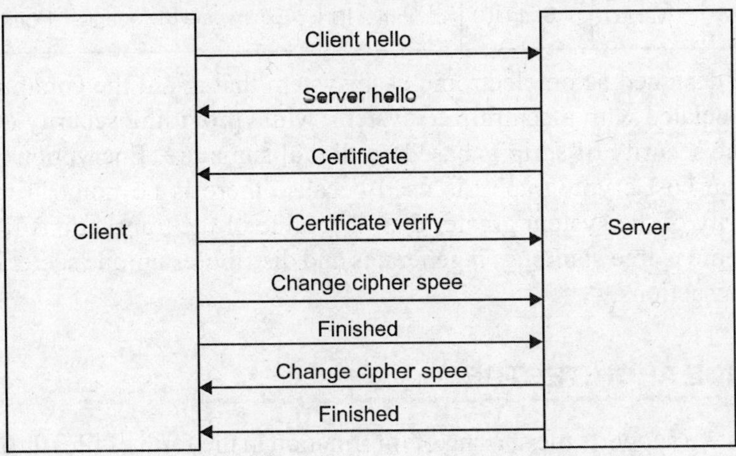

Fig. 6.6 SSL handshake protocol

When client verify digital certification is going on, the server select best algorithm based on client request. The client generate secret key with the help of secret key of client + public key of server, all generated keys are different and sent to server. Now server opens this using session key all should taken through session key.

6.6.4 Millicent Protocol

A secure internet payment system is required that is cost effective and convenient for the purchase of low prices services and access to electronic resources at prices in the range 0.1 – 100 cents.

The problem of using credit cards for small transactions is the high transaction cost. In case of customers maintain accounts with vendors transaction costs are low but initial overhead tends to discourage casual transactions. Again in case of digital case the problem of double spending arises i.e. a consequence of the fact that the holder of a digital token can make any number of undetectable copies.

The Millicent project has developed a scheme for the secure distribution and use of scrip – a specialized form of digital cash that is designed for use in low–value transactions. The scrip is designed to offer following procedures:

(i) It has value only at a specific vendor.

(ii) It can be spent only once.

(iii) It is tamper resistant and hard to counterfeit.

(iv) It can be spent only by its rightful owner.

(v) It can be produced and validated efficiently.

The scrip–vendor specific money introduced by Millicent is represented by digital tokens with following formats:

Vendor	Value	Scrip ID	customer ID	Expiry date	Properties	Certificate

Millicent was designed as on electronic cash system that avoid the communication overhead and the delays associated with a centralized system, while providing security adequate to prevent fraudulent use. The security of scrip is based on digital signature. Encryption is used for secrecy where necessary ùù cost cryptography is used because there is no point in making the cost of breaking the security of the system greater than the value of the transactions for which it is used. The Millicent scheme is free standing; it generates and distributes unique secret keys for use by the parties to scrip transactions.

6.7 FILE SERVICE ARCHITECTURE

Distributed file system supports the sharing of information in the form of files throughout an intranet. A well designed file service provides access to files stored at a server with performance and reliability similar to and in some cases better than file stored on local disks.

File system are responsible for the organization, storage, retrieval, naming, sharing and protection of files. Files contain both data and structure. Files systems are designed to store and manage large numbers of files with facilities for creating naming and deleting files. The scope for open, configurable systems is enhanced if the file service is structured as three components- a flat file service, a directory service and a client module. The flat file service and a directory services each export an interface for use by client programs and their RPC interfaces taken together provide a comprehensive set of operations for access to file. The client module provides a single programming interface with operations on files similar to those founds in conventional file systems.

(i) **Flat File Services:** The flat file service is concerned with implementing operations on the contents of files. Unique file identifiers are used to refer to files in all requests for flat file services operations. The division of responsibilities between between the flat file services and directory services is based upon the use of unique file identifiers (UFIDs). When the flat file service receives a request to create a file, it generates a new UFID for it and returns to requestor.

(ii) **Directory Service:** The directory services provide a mapping between text names for files and their UFID. Clients may obtain the UFID of a file by quoting its text name to directory service. The directory service provides the functions needed to generate directories, to add new file names to directories and to obtain UFID from directories. It is a client of flat file services, its directory file are stored in flat file services.

(iii) **Client Module:** A client module runs in each client computer, integrating and extending the operations of flat file services and directory file services 0under a single application programming interface that is available to user level programs in client computers. The client module also holds information about the network locations of the flat file services and directory services.

6.8 SUN NETWORK FILE SYSTEMS

All implementations of Network File System (NFS) SUPPORTS THE NETWORK PROTOCALS –A set of remote procedure calls that provides the means for clients to perform operations on a remote file store. The NFS Protocols is operating systems independent but was originally developed for use in networks of UNIX systems. The NFS client and server modules communicate using remote procedure calling. Suns RPC system was developed for use in NFS. It can be configured to use either UDP or TCP and the NFS protocols in compatible with both.

NFS provides access transparency, user programs can issue file operations for local or remote file without distinction. The integration is achieved by a virtual file system module, which has been added to the UNIX kernel to distinguish between local and remote files and to translate between the UNIX independent file identifiers normally used in UNIX and other file systems.

The file identifiers used in NFS are called file handles. Files handles is opaque to clients and contains whatever information the server needs to distinguish an individuals file. File handles are passed from server to client in the result of lookup, create and mkdir operations find from client to server in the argument lists of all server operations.

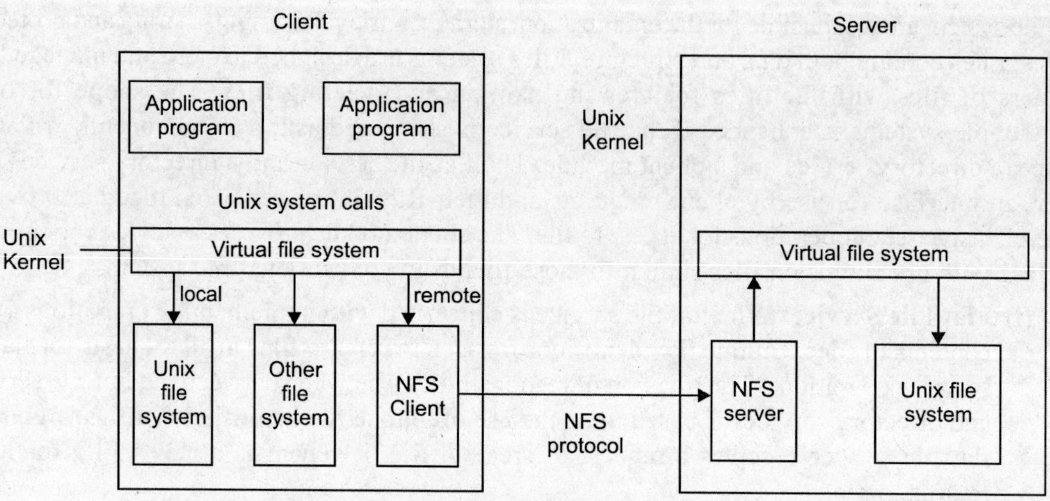

Fig. 6.7 NFS Achitecture

The NFS client module plays the role described for client module in our architectural models, supplying an interface suitable for use by conventional application programs. It is integrated with kernel and not supplied as a library for loading into client processes so that-

- Users programs can access files via UNIX system call without recompilation or reloading.
- Single client module servers all of the user level processes, with a shared cache of recently used blocks.
- The encryption key used to authenticate user IDs passed to the server can be retained in the kernel, preventing impersonation by user- level clients.

6.9 THE ANDREW FILE SYSTEMS

Like NFS, AFS provides transparent access to remote shared files for UNIX programs running on workstations. Access to AFS files is via the normal UNIX file primitives, enabling existing UNIX programs to access AFS files without modification or recompilation. AFS is compatible with NFS, AFS servers hold, 'local UNIX files but the filling system in the servers in NFS- based, so files are refereed by NFS- style file.

AFS differs from NFS in its design and implementation. AFS is designed to perform well with larger numbers of active users than others distributed file systems. The key strategy for achieving scalability is the caching of whole files in client nodes. AFS has two unusual design characteristics

(i) The entire contents of directories and files are transmitted to client computers by AFS servers.

(ii) Once a copy of a file is transmitted to client computer, it is stored in a cache on local disk. The cache is permanent, surviving reboots of the client computer.

The operations of AFS are:

1. When a user process in a client computer issues an open system call for a file in the shared file space and there is not a current copy of the file in the local cache, the server holding the file is located and is sent a request for a copy of the file.
2. The copy is stored in the local UNIX file system in the client computer, the copy is then opened and the resulting UNIX file descriptor is returned to the client.
3. Subsequent read, write and other operations on the file by processes in the client computers are applied to the local copy.
4. When the processes in the client issues a close system calls, if the local copy has been updated its contents are sent back to the server. The server updates the file contents and the timestamps on the file. The copy on the clients local disk is returned in case it is needed.

AFS is implemented as two software components that exist as UNIX processes called vice and Venus. Vice is the name given to the server software that runs as a user level UNIX programs in each server computers and Venus is a user level process that runs in each client computer and corresponds to the client module in our abstract model.

The file available to user processes running on workstations is either local or shared. Local files are handles as normal UNIX files. They are stored on a workstations disk and are available only to local user process. Shared files are stored on servers and copies of them are cached on the local disks of workstations. Local files are used only for temporary files and processes that are essential for workstation start ups.

AFS transfers files between client and servers in 64 Kb chunks. The use of such a large packet size is an important aid to performance, minimizing the effects of network latency. The partial file caching facility is also provided in AFS. The primary goal of AFS is scalability, so its performance with large numbers of users is of particular interest.

6.10 RECENT ADVANCE

Some recent effort by sun and other NFS developers have been directed at making NFS servers more accessible and useful in wide area networks. The state less server architecture of NFS brought great advantages in robustness and case of implementation for NFS.

NFS project certainly indicate that it is possible to achieve one copy update semantics without substantial loss of performance. The server sets an upper bound on the time for which a client may bold a lease on an open file, if the client wishes to continue beyond that time, it must renew lease. Callback are used in a similar manner to request client to flush their caches when a write request occurs, but if the client does not reply ,the server simply waits until their lease expire before responding to new write request.

In AFS, callbacks are generated only when the server receives a close operation for a file that has been updated. In order to update a file a client must obtain a write token from the server, specifying a range of bytes n the file that the client is permitted to update. When a write token is requested, client holding copies of the same file for reading receive revocation callbacks. Tokens of other types are used to achieve consistency for cached file attributes and other metadata. All tokens have an associated lifetime, and client must renew them after their lifetime has expired. The availability of high performance switched networks have prompted several efforts to provide persistent storage systems that distribute file data in a highly scalable and fault tolerant manner among many nodes on an intranet, separating the responsibilities the metadata and servicing client request.

Recent advances have employed data striping across multiple disks and log – structured writing to further improves performance and scalability. Current state of the art distributed file systems are highly scalable, provide, good performance across both local and wide area networks, maintain one – copy file update semantics, and tolerate and recover from failure. Future requirements include support for mobile users with disconnected operation, and automatic reintegration and quality of service guarantee to meet the need for the persistent storage and delivery of streams of multimedia and other time dependent data.

6.11 SUMMARY

- The art of devising ciphers is known as cryptography.
- The two algorithms private key algorithms and public key algorithms are used in cryptography.
- Firewalls protect intranets, performing filtering actions on incoming and outgoing communication.
- A message is encrypted by the sender applying some rule to transforms the plaintext message to a cipher text.
- The digital signature is used for authentication in business transformations.
- The digital signature is a digital lode that can be attached to an electronically transmitted message to uniquely identify its contents and sender.
- Secure socket layer provides a security handshake to initiate the TCP/IP connection.
- Distributed file systems supports the sharing of information in the form of files throughout an intranet.
- Recent advances have employed data striping across multiple disks.

6.12 REVIEW QUESTIONS

(i) Explain about various types of security techniques.

(ii) Explain cryptographic pragmatics & various cryptographic algorithms.

(iii) Discuss the security feature of digital signature and role of digital certification.(

(iv) Explain various types of file service architecture.

(v) Differentiate features of sun network file system and Andrew file system.

(vi) Outline methods by which a client module could emulate the UNIX file system interface using our model file service.

(vii) Why should UFIDs, be unique across all possible file systems? How is uniqueness for UFIDs ensured?

(viii) What data must the NFS client module hold on behalf of each user level process?

(ix) Outline the client module for NFS on behalf of open() and read() system calls?

(x) Explain why the RPC interface to early implementations of NFS is potentially insecure?

(xi) Explain how does NFS Automounter help to improve the performance and scalability of NFS?

(xii) How does AFS deal with the risk that callback messages may be lost?

CHAPTER 7

Transaction and Concurrency Control

The goal of transaction is to ensure that all the objects managed by a server remains in a Consistent state when they are accessed by multiple transactions and in the presence of Server crashes, the server must guarantee that either the entire transaction is carried out and the result recorded in permanent storage or in case that one or more of them crashes.

7.1 DATABASE TRANSACTION

A **database transaction** comprises a unit of work performed within a database management system (or similar system) against a database, and treated in a coherent and reliable way independent of other transactions. Transactions in a database environment have two main purposes:

1. To provide reliable units of work that allow correct recovery from failures and keep a database consistent even in cases of system failure, when execution stops (completely or partially) and many operations upon a database remain uncompleted, with unclear status.
2. To provide isolation between programs accessing a database concurrently. Without isolation the programs' outcomes are typically erroneous.

A database transaction, by definition, must be atomic, consistent, isolated and durable. Database practitioners often refer to these properties of database transactions using the acronym ACID.

Transactions provide an "all-or-nothing" proposition, stating that each work-unit performed in a database must either complete in its entirety or have no effect whatsoever. Further, the system must isolate each transaction from other transactions, results must conform to existing constraints in the database, and transactions that complete successfully must get written to durable storage.

7.1.1 Purpose

Databases and other data stores which treat the integrity of data as paramount often include the ability to handle transactions to maintain the integrity of data. A single transaction consists of one or more independent units of work, each reading and/or writing information to a database or other data store. When this happens it is often important to ensure that all such processing leaves the database or data store in a consistent state.

Examples from double-entry accounting systems often illustrate the concept of transactions. In double-entry accounting every debit requires the recording of an associated credit. If one writes a check for Rs 100 to buy groceries, a transactional double-entry accounting system must record the following two entries to cover the single transaction:

1. Debit Rs 100 to Groceries Expense Account
2. Credit Rs 100 to Checking Account

A transactional system would make both entries — or both entries would fail. By treating the recording of multiple entries as an atomic transactional unit of work the system maintains the integrity of the data recorded. In other words, nobody ends up with a situation in which a debit is recorded but no associated credit is recorded, or vice versa.

7.1.2 Transactional Databases

Most modern relational database management systems fall into the category of databases that support transactions: **transactional databases**. In a database system a transaction might consist of one or more data-manipulation statements and queries, each reading and/or writing information in the database. Users of database systems consider consistency and integrity of data as highly important. A simple transaction is usually issued to the database system in a language like SQL wrapped in a transaction, using a pattern similar to the following:

1. Begin the transaction
2. Execute several data manipulations and queries
3. If no errors occur then commit the transaction and end it
4. If errors occur then rollback the transaction and end it

If no errors occurred during the execution of the transaction then the system commits the transaction. A transaction commit operation applies all data manipulations within the scope of the transaction and persists the results to the database. If an error occurs during the transaction, or if the user specifies a rollback operation, the data manipulations within the transaction are not persisted to the database. In no case can a partial transaction be committed to the database since that would leave the database in an inconsistent state.

Internally, multi-user databases store and process transactions, often by using a transaction ID or XID.

7.1.3 In SQL

A START TRANSACTION statement in SQL or, on some systems, any statement that will modify data, starts a **transaction** within a relational database management system (RDBMS).

The result of any work done after this point will remain invisible to other database-users until the system processes a COMMIT statement. A ROLLBACK statement can also occur, which will undo any work performed since the START TRANSACTION command. Both COMMIT and ROLLBACK will end the transaction: another START TRANSACTION will need to be issued to start a new one. Some database systems allow the synonyms BEGIN, BEGIN WORK and BEGIN TRANSACTION, and may have other options available.

7.2 WHAT IS A TRANSACTION?

A *transaction* is a set of related actions. A *global transaction* is a set of related actions that span multiple programs and resource managers. In this topic, whenever we use the term transaction, we are referring to a global transaction.

A simple example of a transaction is a withdrawal from a bank account, which can be described as a set of actions that changes the state of an account balance (by reducing it). For this transaction, the system must execute a procedure that consists of three operations.

Procedure for Any Transaction	Procedure for Bank Withdrawal Example
1. Verify the activity to be performed.	1. Verify that a withdrawal will be made.
2. Perform the work of the transaction account.	2. Withdraw a specified amount from the account.
3. Create a permanent record of the completed work.	3. Update the record of the balance of the record.

These steps are performed by a discrete software module created expressly for the purpose of executing this transaction. The module must also include or use code that launches and ends the transaction. If the code sections that launch and end the transaction are not part of the main transaction software module, then they are usually packaged together in a separate module.

A *transaction coordinator* is a software module that executes the logic to manage a transaction among all participating resources.

7.3 WHAT ARE THE ACID PROPERTIES

In some situations clients requires a sequence of separate request to a server to be atomic in the sense that

1. They are free from interferences by operations on behalf of other concurrent clients.
2. Either all the operations must be completed successfully or they must have no effect at all in the case of server crashes.

Transactions originate from database management system. In the context a transaction is execution of a program that excesses a database. Transactions were introduced to distributed system execution of a sequence of clients request for the total operation. A transaction consists of execution of sequence of client requests. Transactions can be provided as a part of middleware. A transaction appears to be a recoverable object and it appears to be atomic. It is often called an atomic transaction. appears to be a recoverable object and it appears to be atomic. It is often called an atomic transaction. The acid properties of transaction are:

1 **Atomicity:** A transaction must be all or nothing
2. **Consistencty:** a transaction takes the system from one consistent state to another state
3. **Isolation:** each transaction must be performed without the interference of other transactions
4. **Durability:** After a transaction is completed successfully its entire object are saved in permanent storage.

When a transaction such as a bank withdrawal is performed, it is imperative that all its constituent operations either succeed or fail together. Consider the problems that can occur if one operation in a transaction succeeds while another operation in the same transaction fails: a bank that allows a customer to withdraw money without recording the reduced balance in an updated account record will not stay in business for long!

A transaction that adheres to the rule that all constituent operations either succeed or fail is characterized by *atomicity*. The BEA Tuxedo system requires all transactions to be characterized by atomicity and three related attributes: *consistency*, *isolation*, and *durability*. These four attributes are known collectively as the *ACID properties* of transactions performed within the BEA Tuxedo system.

ACID Properties of BEA Tuxedo Transactions

This Property...	Means That ...
Atomicity	A transaction is a discrete unit of work: all constituent operations must either succeed or fail. These operations may include queuing messages, updating databases, and displaying the results of a transaction on a screen.
Consistency	A transaction must either (a) leave the system in a correct state or (b) abort. If a transaction cannot achieve a stable state, it must return to its initial state.
Isolation	The behavior of a transaction is not affected by other transactions being executed simultaneously. A transaction must serialize all access to shared resources and guarantee that concurrent programs do not corrupt each other's operations.
Durability	The effects of a committed transaction are permanent. Even if the system fails, the changes resulting from a transaction are permanent and durable.

How a Transaction Succeeds or Fails

If . . .	Then . . .
Any operation within the transaction fails for any reason	The transaction *aborts*, that is, it terminates abruptly. The transaction *rolls back*, that is, it undoes its own work and restores the state of the enterprise For example, after an attempt to withdraw money from a bank account fails and is rolled back, the bank account contains the same amount of money it contained before the transaction, and the record of the account balance shows the same amount that it showed before the transaction.
All operations within the transaction succeed	The client *commits* the transaction. In other words, it formally signals that it is ready to terminate and the effects of the transaction should be preserved: the order database is updated permanently and the order sent to the shipping department is kept as a permanent record in that department's queue.

Whether a transaction succeeds or fails depends on the requirements of atomicity.

7.4 BENEFITS OF USING TRANSACTIONS

The BEA Tuxedo system, including its communication APIs and protocols, is designed to support the use of transactions. The BEA Tuxedo communication calls, which make it easy to create transactions, are indispensable tools for writing distributed applications.

By using transactions you can:

- Create distributed applications easily
- Commit the effects of your communications as a single unit
- Quickly manage potential problems that may occur in a distributed environment, such as machine, program, or network failures
- Undo work, when errors occur, in a simple, programmatic way

7.5 EXAMPLE OF A GLOBAL TRANSACTION

An e-retailer uses a service called CUST_ORDER. When a customer places an order through the company's Web site, the CUST_ORDER service performs two operations:

- It updates the company's database of orders.
- It sends the new order to the shipping department, where it is put on a queue, awaiting fulfillment.

The company wants to be sure that the CUST_ORDER service adheres to the principle of atomicity: whenever CUST_ORDER is executed, both the database update and the enqueueing of the customer request on the shipping department queue must be completed successfully. To make sure that the CUST_ORDER service always handles customer orders with atomicity, the client that invokes CUST_ORDER associates its request with a *global transaction*.

To associate a service with a global transaction, a client:

1. Calls tpbegin() to begin the transaction
2. Issues a service request
3. Calls tpcommit() to end the transaction

As part of a global transaction, the operation is performed as a single unit of work. When the CUST_ORDER service is invoked, the server is propagated with the client's transaction. The two resulting operations, accessing the order database and enquiring the order to the shipping queue, become part of the client's transaction.

If either operation fails for any reason, whether due to a system error or an application error, the work of the transaction is undone or *rolled back*. In other words, the transaction is returned to its initial state.

If both operations succeed, however, the client *commits* the transaction. In other words, it formally signals that the effects of the transaction should be made permanent: the order database is updated permanently and the order sent to the shipping department is kept in that department's queue.

7.5.1 What Is the BEA Tuxedo Transaction Manager (TM)?

A *resource manager* (RM) is a data repository, such as a database management system or the Application Queuing Manager, with tools for accessing the data. The BEA Tuxedo system uses one or more RMs to maintain the state of an application. For example, bank records in which account balances are maintained are kept in an RM. When the state of the application changes through a service that allows a customer to withdraw money from an account, the new balance in the account is recorded in the appropriate RM.

The BEA Tuxedo system helps you manage transactions involving resource managers that support the XA interface. To coordinate all the operations performed and all the modules affected by a transaction, the BEA Tuxedo system plays the role of the Transaction Manager (TM).

The TM coordinates global transactions involving system-wide resources. Local resource managers (RMs) are responsible for individual resources. The Transaction Manager Server (TMS) begins, commits, and aborts transactions involving multiple resources. The application code uses the normal embedded SQL interface to the RM to perform reads and updates. The TMS uses the XA interface to the RM to perform the work of a global transaction.

The following table summarizes the actions taken by the Transaction Manager on behalf of each transaction.

Actions Performed by the Transaction Manager When...	The Transaction Manager...
The application launches a trnsaction	Assigns a global transaction identifier (GTRID) to the transaction.
Other processes communicate with the process that launched the transact ion	Tracks those communication partners.
The RM is accessed as part of the work of the transaction	Passes the appropriate GTRID to the RM so the RM can monitor which database records are being accessed for the transaction.
The application signals that a transaction is to be committed	Performs a two-phase commit protocol. Specifically, it: (a) contacts communication partners during Phase 1, (b) logs the successful outcome of Phase 1, and (c) contacts partners in Phase 2.
The application indicates that the transaction is to be aborted	Executes a rollback procedure.
A failure occurs	Executes a recovery procedure.

7.5.2 How the System Tracks Distributed Transaction Processing

BEA Tuxedo transactions can be used in a distributed architecture: a local machine involved in a transaction can communicate with a remote machine which may, in turn, communicate with another remote machine. The work of transactions executed in this type of arrangement is referred to as *distributed transaction processing*.

Because the system must constantly maintain enough information about a transaction to be able to roll it back (that is, to restore it to its initial state) at any moment, tracking distributed transaction processing (DTP) can be a complex task. To perform this task successfully, the BEA Tuxedo system stores tracking information about all the participants in a transaction in a dedicated file called a *transaction log*, or TLOG. The following diagram shows an application in which two Transaction Managers (TMs) are being used. Both TMs record tracking data in the same TLOG.

7.6 TRANSACTION MANAGEMENT

Before committing a transaction, the TM must repeatedly answer the question of whether to proceed. If necessary, the TM makes the decision to roll back.

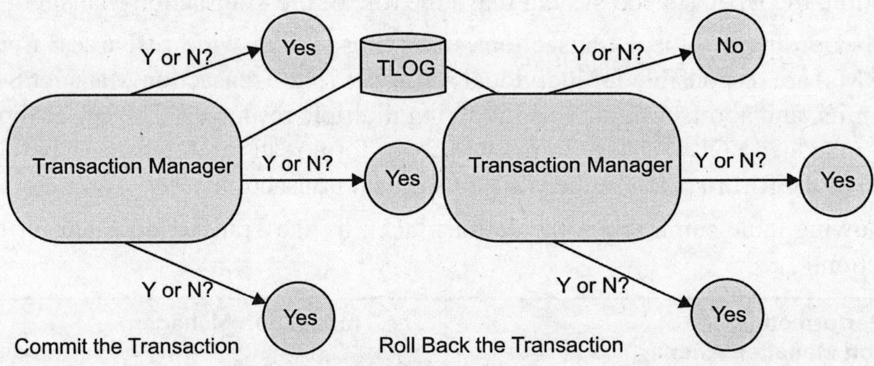

Fig. 7.1

7.6.1 How the System Uses Global Transaction Identifiers (GTRIDs) for Tracking

The BEA Tuxedo system tracks the flow of all transactions being executed within a distributed system, including those being executed concurrently. When it is time to commit a transaction, the coordinator must know which RMs have participated in the transaction and, therefore, needs to be able to distinguish among transactions. For this reason the BEA Tuxedo system assigns a *global transaction identifier* or GTRID to each transaction.

The BEA Tuxedo system communicates with any RM accessed by an application through the XA interface. The RMs track transactions by assigning local transaction identifiers, and map global identifiers to local identifiers.

7.6.2 How the System Uses a Transaction Log (TLOG) for Tracking

A global transaction is recorded in the transaction log (TLOG) only when it is in the process of being committed. At the end of the first phase of a two-phase commit protocol, the TLOG records the reply from the global transaction participants. The existence of a TLOG record indicates that a global transaction should be committed; no TLOG records are written for transactions that are to be rolled back.

In the first "pre-commit" phase, each resource manager must commit to performing the transaction request. If all parties commit, transaction management performs the second phase: it commits and completes the transaction. If either task fails because of an application or system failure, both tasks fail and the work performed is undone or "rolled back" to its initial state.

The TMS that coordinates global transactions uses the TLOG file. Each machine should have its own TLOG. If you are using the Domains component in your application, keep in mind that the Domains gateway performs the functions of the TMS in Domains groups. However, Domains uses its own transaction log containing information similar to that recorded in the TLOG, in addition to Domains-specific information.

7.6.3 How the System Uses a Two-Phase Commit to Commit Transactions

A *two-phase commit* is an algorithm used to ensure the integrity of a committing transaction. To understand how this algorithm works, consider the following sample scenario. A group of six friends wants to rent a house for a one-week vacation. No member of the group can afford to pay more than one sixth of the rent; if any of the six cannot participate, then the house cannot be rented.

1. In Phase 1 of this project, the organizer of the vacation contacts each person to verify availability and collect a sixth of the rent. If the organizer learns that even one person cannot participate, she contacts every member of the group, individually, to notify him or her that the house cannot be rented. If, however, each member of the group confirms availability and pays one sixth of the rent, the Phase 1 concludes successfully.
2. In Phase 2 of the project, the organizer notifies each member of the group that the vacation will take place as planned.

A two-phase transaction commit works in much the same way as the vacation planning project.

1. In Phase 1, the transaction coordinator contacts potential participants in the transaction. The participants all agree to make the results of the transaction permanent, but do not do so immediately. The participants log information to disk to ensure they can complete Phase 2. If all the participants agree to commit, the coordinator logs that agreement and the outcome is decided. The recording of this agreement in the log ends Phase 1.
2. In Phase 2, the coordinator informs each participant of the decision, and they permanently update their resources.

7.6.4 How the System Handles Transaction Infection

Any application module called by another module to participate in a transaction is said to be *transactional infected.* Once an application module is infected, the BEA Tuxedo system tracks all participants to determine which of them should be involved in the two-phase commit. The following figure shows how the system tracks participants.

Transactional Infection

In the preceding figure, Client 1 begins the transaction and calls three services: A, B, and C. because they have been called into the transaction, Services A, B, and C is transactional infected. All work performed by servers A, B, and C is part of the transaction begun by Client 1. All work is performed as one unit; either it is performed together and is successful, or it fails and is rolled back by calling tpabort. If the transaction fails, it returns to its initial state and its effects of the transaction on resource managers are undone. (Resource managers that are not transactional aware and those that are accessed from outside the transaction cannot be rolled back.)

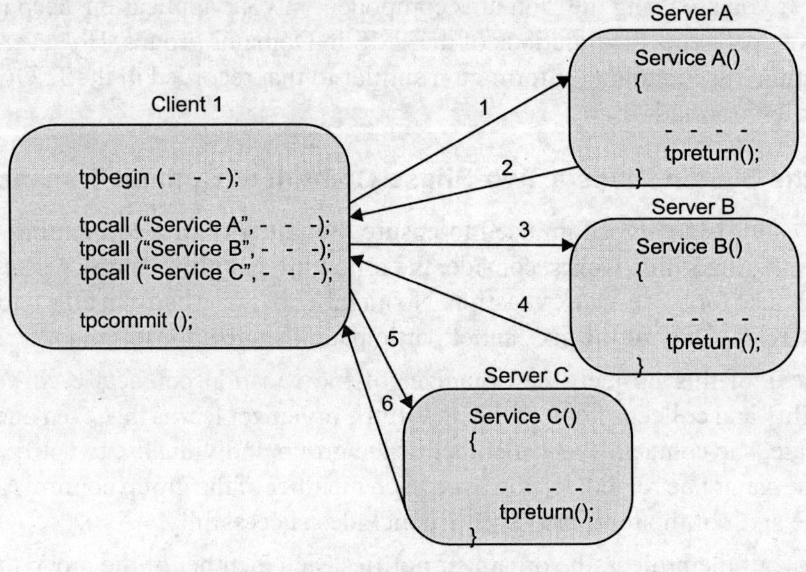

Fig. 7.2

7.6.5 How the ATMI Protects a Transaction's Integrity before a Two-Phase Commit

All work performed by each resource involved in a transaction must be completed before a two-phase commit is begun. The ATMI ensures that all the work of the transaction is stopped when it is time for the two-phase commit protocol to begin.

The following step-by-step description of a transaction shows how the ATMI stops a transaction process before a two-phase commit.

1. Client_1 initiates (with tpbegin()) a transaction.
2. Client_1 invokes (with tpcall()) Service_A, which:
   (a) Is *infected* with the transaction
   (b) Executes its operations
   (c) Calls tpreturn()
   (d) Completes its work for the transaction
3. Client_1 invokes (with tpcall()) Service_B, which:
   (a) Is *infected* with the transaction
   (b) Executes its operations

   (c) Calls tpreturn()
   (d) Completes its work for the transaction
4. Client_1 invokes (with tpcall()) Service_C, which:
   (a) Is *infected* with the transaction
   (b) Executes its operations
   (c) Calls tpreturn()
   (d) Completes its work for the transaction
5. Client_1 initiates (with tpcommit()) the commitment process.

If, during the transaction, an invoked service is performing another service, or is involved in an open conversation, the ATMI tracks that activity and prevents the application from proceeding to the commitment process until the activity is complete.

The ATMI guarantees that the transaction is committed only if all invoked services have performed their transaction work successfully. When all work has been performed successfully, the Transaction Manager informs the resource managers that all updates made during the transaction are permanent.

7.7 CONCURRENCY CONTROL

Concurrency Control refers to the problem of returning correct results for concurrent transactions in a database. If two people are simultaneously trying to use their joint bank account, then the Database Management System must ensure that the results of the operation will lead to a predictable state, and that the system will behave as if the two transactions happened sequentially. Common techniques to ensure proper execution are mutexes, semaphores, and critical sections, as well as overarching concepts of Transactions and Read/Write Dependences.

7.7.1 Concurrency Control in Databases

Concurrency control in database management systems (DBMS) ensures that database transactions are performed concurrently without the concurrency violating the data integrity of a database. Executed transactions should follow the ACID rules, as described below. The DBMS must guarantee that only serializable (unless Serializability is intentionally relaxed), recoverable schedules are generated. It also guarantees that no effect of committed transactions is lost, and no effect of aborted (rolled back) transactions remains in the related database.

7.7.2 Concurrency Control Mechanism

The main categories of concurrency control mechanisms are:

- **Optimistic:** Delay the synchronization for a transaction until its end without blocking (read, write) operations, and then abort transactions that violate desired synchronization rules.
- **Pessimistic:** Block operations of transaction that would cause violation of synchronization rules.

Many methods for concurrency control exist. Major methods, which have each many variants, include:

- Two phase locking
- Conflict (serializability, precedence) graph checking
- Timestamp ordering
- Commitment ordering
- Multiversion concurrency control
- Index concurrency control (for synchronizing indexes)

Almost all implemented concurrency control mechanisms, typically quite efficient, guarantee schedules that are conflict serializable, unless relaxed forms of serializability are allowed (depending on application) for better performance.

7.7.3 Concurrency Control in Operating Systems

Operating systems, especially real-time operating systems, need to maintain the illusion that many tasks are all running at the same time. Such multitasking is fairly simple when all tasks are independent from each other. However, when several tasks try to use the same resource, or when tasks try to share information, it can lead to confusion and inconsistency. The task of concurrent computing is to solve that problem. Some solutions involve "locks" similar to the locks used in databases, but they risk causing problems of their own such as deadlock. Other solutions are lock-free and wait-free algorithms.

7.7.4 Multiversion Concurrency Control

Multiversion concurrency control (abbreviated **MCC** or **MVCC**), in the database field of computer science, is a concurrency control method commonly used by database management systems to provide concurrent access to the database. MVCC provides each user connected to the database with a "snapshot" of the database for that person to work with. Any changes made will not be seen by other users of the database until the transaction has been committed.

7.7.5 Global Concurrency Control

Global concurrency control typically pertains to the concurrency control of a system comprising several components, each with its own concurrency control. Global concurrency control is the concurrency control of the system as a whole.

In many cases a system may be distributed over a communication network. In this case we deal with distributed concurrency control of the system, and the two terms sometimes intersect. However, distributed concurrency control typically relates to a case where the distributed system's components do not have each concurrency control of its own, but rather are involved with a concurrency control mechanism that spans several components in order to operate. For example, as typical in a distributed database.

In database systems and transaction processing global concurrency control relates to the concurrency control of a multidatabase system (for example, a Federated database). It deals with the properties of the global schedule, which is the unified schedule of the multidatabase system, comprising all the individual schedules of the database systems and possibly other transactional objects in the system. A major goal for global concurrency control is global serializability. The problem of achieving global serializability in a heterogeneous environment had been open for many years, until an effective solution based on Commitment ordering has been proposed (see Global serializability). Global concurrency control deals also with relaxed forms of global serializability which compromise global serializability (and in many applications also correctness). While local (to a database system) relaxed serializability methods compromise serializability for performance gain (utilized when the application allows), it is unclear that the various proposed relaxed global serializability methods provide any performance gain over commitment ordering, which guarantees global serializability.

7.7.6 Distributed Concurrency Control

Distributed concurrency control relates to the concurrency control of a system distributed over a computer network. In database systems and transaction processing distributed concurrency control relates primarily to the concurrency control of a distributed database. It also relates to the concurrency control in a multidatabase environment (federated database. A major goal for distributed concurrency control is serializability (or global serializability for multidatabase systems). Distributed concurrency control poses special challenges beyond centralized one, primarily due to communication and computer latency. It often requires special techniques, like distributed lock manager over fast computer networks with low latency, like switched fabric (e.g., InfiniBand).

The most common distributed concurrency control technique is strong strict two-phase locking, which is also a common centralized concurrency control technique. SS2PL provides both the serializability, strictness, and commitment ordering properties. Strictness, a special case of recoverability, is utilized for effective recovery from failure, and commitment ordering allows participating in a general solution for global serializability. For large-scale distribution and complex transactions, distributed locking's typical heavy performance penalty (due to delays, latency) can be saved by using the atomic commitment protocol, which is needed in a distributed database (e.g., 2PC, or a simpler one in a reliable system), together with some local commitment ordering instead of distributed locking, to achieve global serializability in the entire system (this comprises a distributed serializability protocol). All the commitment ordering theoretical results are applicable whenever atomic commitment is utilized over partitioned, distributed data. Such technique can be utilized also for a large-scale parallel database, where a single large database, residing on many nodes and using a distributed lock manager, is replaced with a (homogeneous) multidatabase, comprising many relatively small databases (loosely defined; any process that supports transactions and participates in atomic commitment complies), fitting each into a single node, and using commitment ordering together with some appropriate atomic commitment protocol (without using a distributed lock manager).

7.8 NESTED TRANSACTIONS

Nested transactions extent the above transaction model by allowing transactions to be composed of other transactions. Thus several transactions can be separate of within a transaction, allowing transactions to be regarded as modules that can be composed as required. The outer most transaction in a set of nested transactions is called the top level transaction and other than the top level transactions are called sub transactions.

A transaction appears to atomic to its parent with respect to transaction fail our and with respect to concurrent access. Sub transactions at the same level such as t1 and t2 can run concurrently but their access to common object is serialized. Each transaction can fail independently of its parent and all of the other sub transactions. When a sub transaction aborts the parent transaction can choose alternate transaction to complete the task.

Nested transactions have the following main advantages

- Sub transactions at one level can run concurrently with the other transactions at the same level in the hierarchy. This can allow additional concurrency in the transaction. When transactions run in different server they can run in parallel.
- Sub transactions can commit or abort independently .in comparison with single transaction a set of nested transaction are potentially more robust.

Rule for Commitment: The rules for commitment at nested transactions are rather subtle.

1. A transaction may commit or abort only if its child transaction is completed.
2. When a sub transaction completes it makes an independent decision either to commit provisionally or to abort. its decision to abort is final.
3. When a parent is aborted all its sub transactions is aborted.
4. When a sub transaction aborts its parent decides weather to abort or not.
5. If the top level transaction commit then all the other transactions that have provisionally committed can commit too, provided that none of their ancestors has aborted.

7.9 LOCKS

Transactions must be scheduled so that their effect on stored data is serially equivalent. A server can achieve serially equivalent transactions by serializing access to objects. A simple example of serializing mechanism is to use exclusive locks. In this locking scheme the server attempts to lock any object that is about to be used by any operation of a client transaction. If a client request access to a object that is already locked due to another client transaction the request is suspended and the client must wait until the object is unlocked.

When a transaction t is about to use an account b, it is locked for t, subsequently when another transaction u about to use account b it is still locked for t and transaction u waits. When transaction t is committed b unlock the transaction and u is resumed the use of lock on b affectively serializes the access of b.

Transaction t	transaction u
Open transaction	Open Transaction
Lock b	wait for t
Lock a	Lock b
Close transaction	Lock c
Unlock a, b	Close transaction
	Unlock b, c

Serial equivalence requires that all the transactions accesses to a particular object be serialized with respect to access by other transactions .the first phase of each transaction is growing phase during which new logs are required. In the second phase locks are released. Two types of locks are used…

1. read locks
2. write locks

Before the transaction read operation is performed, a read lock should be sent on the object and before the transaction write operation is performed a write lock should be send on the object. Whenever it is impossible to set a lock immediately the transaction must wait until it is possible to do so. A client request is never rejected.

As pairs of read operation from different transactions do not conflict, an attempt is set to read lock on the object with a read lock is always successful. All the transactions reading the same object share the read lock, for this reason read lock are sometimes called shared locks

The operation conflict rule says….

1. If an operation t is already performed a read operation on a particular object then a concurrent ransaction u must not u must not write the object until t commits or aborts
2. If transaction t is already performed an operation on a particular object then transaction u must not read or write the object until t commits or aborts.

For one object		lock required	
		Read	write
Lock alredy set	none	o.k.	o.k
	read	o.k.	wait
	write	wait	wait

Fig. 7.3 locks compatibility

7.9.1 Use of Locks in Strict Two Phase Locking

1. When an operation access an object with a transaction,
   (i) If the object is not already locked it is locked and operation proceeds.
   (ii) If other object has a conflicting lock set by another transaction the transaction must wait until it is unlocked.
   (iii) If the object has a non conflicting lock set by another transaction, the lock is shared and the operation proceeds.

(iv) If the object is already been locked in the same transaction, the lock will be prompted if necessary and the operation proceeds.

2. When a transaction is committed or aborted the server unlocks all objects which are locked for the transaction.

7.9.2 Locking Rules for Nested Transactions

The aim of locking scheme for nested transaction is to serialize the object so that

1. Each set of nested transaction is a single entity that must be prevented from observing the partial effect on any other set of nested transaction.
2. Each transaction within a set of nested transaction must be prevented from observing the partial effect on any transaction in the set .the first rule is enforced by arranging that every lock that is acquired by a successful sub transaction is inherited by its parent when it completes

Inherited locks are also inherited by ancestors.

The second rule is enforced as follows:

1. Parent transaction is not allowed to run concurrently with there child transaction. If the parent transaction has a lock on any object, it retains the lock during the time that the child transaction is executing. This means that the child transaction is acquired the lock from its parent for its duration.
2. Sub transaction at the same level are allowed to run concurrently , so that they access the same object, the locking scheme must serialize their access

The following rule describes locks acquisition are release

1. For a transaction to acquire a read lo ck on the object no there active transaction should have a write lock on the object and its only retain ness on the read and write lock on the object are its ancestors
2. For a transaction to acquire a write lo ck on the object no there active transaction should have a write or read lock on the object and its only retain ness on the read and write lock on the object are its ancestors
3. When a transaction commit its locks is inherited by its parent allowing the parent to retain the lock in the same mode as a child
4. When a sub transaction aborts its locks are discarded. If the parent already retain the lock it continues to do so.

7.10 OPTIMISTIC CONCURRENCY CONTROL

The drawbacks of locking are …

- Locks maintenance represents an overhead.
- Use of locks can result in deadlocks

- To avoid cascading aborts locks cannot be released until the end of transaction this may reduce significantly the potential for concurrency

In the optimistic concurrency control proposed by Kung and Robinson, Transaction s are allowed to proceed as there are no possibility to conflict with other until the client completes its task and issue a close transaction request .when a conflict arises some transaction is generally aborted and will need to be restarted by the client.

When a transaction is aborted it is generally be restarted by the client program. But in schemes that rely on aborting and restarting transactions there is no guarantee that which transaction will pass the validation. The presentation of transaction ever been able to commit is called starvation. Occurrence of starvation is likely to be rare but a server that uses optimistic concurrent control must ensure that a client doesnt have his transaction aborted repeatedly. Kung and Robinson suggest that when a server detects such a transaction it should be given exclusive access by a critical section protection by a semaphore.

7.11 TIMESTAMP ORDERING

Each transaction is assigned a unique timestamp value when it starts. The timestamp defines its position in the time sequence of the transaction .requests from transaction can be totally ordered according to their timestamp. The basic timestamp ordering rule is based on operation conflicts and it is very simple. a transaction request to write an object is valid only if that object was last read and written by earlier transaction request to read an object is valid only if that objects was last written by an earlier transaction.

The timestamp ordering rule is refined to ensure that each transaction accesses a consistent set of versions of the objects. The write operations may be performed after the close transaction operation has returned. With out making the client wait, but the client must wait when read operations need to wait for earlier transactions to finish. The time stamps are assigned from servers clocks.

The write operations are recorded in tentative versions of objects and are invisible to other transactions until a close transaction request is issued and the transaction is committed. The write time stamp of the committed object is earlier than that of any of its tentative versions and the set of read time stamps can be represented by its maximum members.

Whenever a transactions write operation as an object is accepted, the server creates a new tentative version of the objects with write time stamp set to the transaction time stamp. Transactions read operation is directed to the version with the maximum write time stamp less than the transaction time stamp. Whenever a transactions read operation on an object is accepted, the timestamp of the transaction is added to its set of read timestamp. When a transaction is committed, the value of the tentative versions becomes the value of the objects and the timestamp of the tentative versions becomes the timestamps of the corresponding objects.

7.11.1 Multi Version Timestamp Ordering

The multi version time stamp ordering is introduced by Reed in 1983, in this a list of old committed versions as a well as tentative version is kept for each object. This list represents the history of the values of the objects. The benefit of using multi versions is that read operations that arrive too late need not be rejected.

Each version has a read timestamp recording the largest timestamp of any transaction that has read from it in addition to write time stamp. Whenever a write operation is accepted, it is directed to a tentative version with the write timestamp of the transaction. Whenever a read operation is carried out it is directed to the versions with the largest write timestamp less than the transaction time stamp. If the transaction time stamp is larger than the read timestamp of the version being used, the read timestamp of the version is set to the transaction timestamp. In multi version timestamp ordering, read operations are always permitted, although they have to wait for earlier transaction to complete and there is no conflict between write operation of the different transaction, because each transactions writes its own committed versions of the objects it accesses.

7.12 COMPARISON OF METHODS FOR CONCURRENCY CONTROL

The three methods to controlling the concurrent access to shared data are

(i) Strict two phase locking

(ii) Optimistic methods

(iii) Timestamp ordering

The timestamp ordering methods is similar to two phases locking in that both use pessimistic approaches in which conflicts between transactions are detected as each object is accessed. The timestamp decides serialization statically while two phases decides serialization dynamically. Timestamp ordering is better than strict two phases locking for read only transaction while two phase locking is better when the operations in transactions are predominantly updates.

Timestamp ordering aborts the transaction immediately, whereas locking makes transaction wait. When the optimistic concurrency control is used, all transactions are allowed to proceed, but some of them are aborted when they attempt to commit. This results in relatively efficient operation when there are few conflicts, but a substantial amount of work may have to be repeated when a transaction is aborted.

7.13 SUMMARY

- The goal of transaction is to ensure that all the objects managed by a server remains in a Consistent state when they are accessed by multiple transactions and in the presence of Server crashes, the server must guarantee that either the entire transaction is carried out and the result recorded in permanent storage or in case that one or more of them crashes.
- A **database transaction** comprises a unit of work performed within a database management system (or similar system) against a database, and treated in a coherent and reliable way independent of other transactions.
- A *transaction* is a set of related actions. A *global transaction* is a set of related actions that span multiple programs and resource managers. In this topic, whenever we use the term transaction, we are referring to a global transaction.

- Concurrency Control refers to the problem of returning correct results for concurrent transactions in a database.
- Concurrency control in database management systems (DBMS) ensures that database transactions are performed concurrently without the concurrency violating the data integrity of a database.
- **Multiversion concurrency control** (abbreviated **MCC** or **MVCC**), in the database field of computer science, is a concurrency control method commonly used by database management systems to provide concurrent access to the database.
- **Global concurrency control** typically pertains to the concurrency control of a system comprising several components, each with its own concurrency control. Global concurrency control is the concurrency control of the system as a whole.
- **Distributed concurrency control** relates to the concurrency control of a system distributed over a computer network. In database systems and transaction processing distributed concurrency control relates primarily to the concurrency control of a distributed database.
- Nested transactions extent the above transaction model by allowing transactions to be composed of other transactions
- Transactions must be scheduled so that their effect on stored data is serially equivalent. A server can achieve serially equivalent transactions by serializing access to objects.
- Each transaction is assigned a unique timestamp value when it starts. The timestamp defines its position in the time sequence of the transaction .requests from transaction can be totally ordered according to their timestamp.

7.14 REVIEW QUESTION

1. What do you mean by database transaction?
2. What do you mean by transaction and compare it with the nested transactions.
3. Define locks and use of locks in strict two phase locking.
4. Define locking status rules for nested transactions.
5. Define optimistic concurrency control and compare it with timestamp ordering.
6. Differentiate timestamp ordering with multi version timestamp ordering.
7. Explain distributed transactions and differentiate flat and nested distributed transactions.
8. Explain comparison of methods for concurrency control.
9. Discuss atomic commit protocol and two phases commits protocols.
10. Write short notes on the following
    (i) Multi version concurrency control
    (ii) Global concurrency control
    (iii) Distributed concurrency control

CHAPTER 8

Distributed Transactions

8.1 INTRODUCTION

In distributed transactions accesses objects are managed by multiple servers, when a distributed transaction comes to an end, the atomicity property of transaction requires that either all of the servers involved commit the transaction or all of them abort the transaction.

To achieve this, one of the servers takes on a coordinator role, which involves ensuring the same outcomes at all of the servers. The manner in which the coordinator achieves this depends on the protocols chosen. A protocol known as the "two phase commit protocol" is most commonly used. This protocol allows the servers to communicate with one another to reach a joint decision as to whether to commit or abort.

Each server apply local concurrency control its own objects, which ensures that transactions are serialized locally. Distributed transactions must me serialized globally. The method of achieving this varies whether locking, timestamp ordering or optimistic concurrency control is in use.

In some cases, the transaction may be serialized at the individual servers, but at the same time a cycle of dependencies between the different servers may occur and distributed deadlock arise. Transaction recovery is concerned with ensuring that all the objects involved in transactions are recoverable, it guarantee that the values of the objects reflects all the changes made by committed transactions and none of those made by aborted ones.

8.2 FLAT AND NESTED DISTRIBUTED TRANSACTIONS

A client transaction becomes distributed if it involves operations in several different servers.Two types of distributed transactions are-

- Flat distributed transaction
- Nested distributed transaction

In a flat transaction, a client makes request to more than one server. A flat client transaction completes each of its requests before going to the next one.Therefore, each transaction accesses servers objects sequentially, when servers use locking, a transaction can only be waiting for one objects at a time.

From figure, transaction T is a flat transaction that involves operations on objects in servers X, Y, Z.In a nested transaction, the top level transaction can open sub transactions And each sub transactions can open further sub transactions down to any depth of nesting. From figure 7.3 client's transaction T opens two sub transactions T1 and T2, which accesses objects at servers X and Y. the sub transactions T1 and T2 open further sub transactions T11,T12,T21and T22., which accesses objects at servers M,N and P. In nested case, sub transactions at the same level, can run concurrently, so T1 and T2 are concurrent and they invoke objects in different servers, they can run in parallel.

Servers that execute requests as part of a distributed transaction need to be able to communicate with one another to coordinate their actions when the transaction commits. The coordinator that opened the transaction becomes the coordinator for distributed transaction and at the end is responsible for committing or aborting it.

During the progress of transaction, the coordinator records a list of references, to the participants and each participants records a references to the coordinator. The coordinator records new participants in its participant list. the fact that the coordinator knows all the participants and each participants knows the coordinator will enable them to collect the information that will be need at commit time.

8.3 ATOMIC COMMIT PROTOCOLS

The atomicity of transactions requires that when a distributed transaction comes to an end, either all of the operations are carried out or none of them. In case of distributed transaction, the client has requested the operations at more than one server. A transaction comes to an end when the client requests that a transaction be committed or aborted.

In one phase atomic commit protocol, coordinator communicates for commit or abort request to all of the participants in the transaction and keep on repeating request until all of them have acknowledged that they had carried it out. The two phase commit protocol is allow any participants to abort its parts of a transaction, due to the requirement for atomicity, if one part of a transaction is aborted, then the whole transaction must also be aborted. In first phase of the protocol, each participants votes for the transaction to be committed or aborted. Once a participant has voted to commit a transaction, it is not allowed to abort it.

In the second phase of protocol, every participant in the transactions carries out the joint decision. If any one participant votes to abort, then decision must be to abort the transaction. If all the participants votes to commit, then decision is to commit the transaction. Commit protocols are designed to work in an asynchronous system in which servers may crash and messages may be lost. The two phase commit protocol is an example of a protocol for reaching a consensus.

8.3.1 Two Phase Commit Protocol

During the progress of transaction there is no communication between the coordinator and participants apart from participants informing the coordinator when they join the transaction. In the first phase of the two phase commit protocol the coordinators asks to each participants if they are prepared to commit and each participants votes for the transaction to be committed or aborted. Once a participant has voted to commit a transaction, it is not allowed to abort it. In the second phase of protocol, every participant in the transactions carries out the joint decision. If any one participant votes to abort, then decision must be to abort the transaction. If all the participants votes to commit, then decision is to commit the transaction.

The two phase commit protocol consists of a voting phase and a completion phase. The exchange of information between the coordinator and participants can fail when one of the servers crashes or when messages lost.

Phase 1: Voting Phase

- The coordinator sends can commit? Requests to each participant in the transactions.
- When the participants receive can commit? Request it replies with the its votes (YES\NO) to the coordinator, before passing voting YES, it prepares to commit by saving objects in permanent storage, if vote NO the participants abort immediately.

Phase 2: Completion Phase

- The coordinator collects votes, if there are no failures. Find all votes are YES, the coordinator decides to commit otherwise abort the transaction.
- Participants that votes YES are waiting for a do commit or do abort request from coordinator. When participants receive one of these messages it acts accordingly.

8.4 CONCURRENCY CONTROL IN DISTRIBUTED TRANSACTIONS

Each server manages a set of objects and is responsible for ensuring that they remain consistent when accesses by concurrent transactions. Therefore, each server is responsible for applying concurrency control to its own objects. The members of a collection of servers of distributed transactions are jointly responsible for ensuring that they are performed in a serially equivalent manner.

8.5 LOCKING

In a distributed transaction, the locks on objects are hold locally. The local lock manager decides whether to grant a lock or make the requesting transaction wait. However, it can not release any locks until it knows that the transaction has been committed or aborted at all the servers involved in the transactions.

When locking is used for concurrency control, the objects remain locked and are unavailable for other transactions during the atomic commit protocol, although an aborted transaction releases its locks after phase 1 of the protocol. As a lock manager in different servers set their locks independently of one another, it is possible that different servers may impose different ordering on transactions. These different ordering can lead to cyclic dependencies between transactions and a distributed deadlock situation arises. When a deadlock is detected, a transaction is aborted to resolve the deadlock. In this case, the coordinator will be informed and will abort the transaction at the participants involved in the transaction.

8.6 TIMESTAMP ORDERING CONCURRENCY CONTROL

In a single server transaction, the coordinator issues a unique timestamp to each transaction when it starts. In distributed transactions, we require that each coordinator issue globally unique timestamps. A globally unique transaction timestamp is issued to the client by first coordinator accesses by a transaction. The transaction timestamp is passed to the coordinator at each server whose objects perform an operation in the transaction.

The servers of distributed transactions are jointly responsible for ensuring that they are performed in a serially equivalent manner. To achieve the same ordering at all the servers, the coordinator must agree as to the ordering of their timestamps. The same ordering of transactions can be achieved at all the servers even if their local locks are not synchronized.

When timestamps ordering is used for concurrency control, conflicts are resolved as each operation is performed. If the resolution of a conflict requires a transaction to be aborted, the coordinator will be informed and it will abort the transaction at all the participants. Therefore, any transaction that reaches the client request to commit should always be able to commit. Therefore a participant in the two phase commit protocol will normally agree to commit. The only situation in which a participant will not agree to commit is if it had crashed during the transaction.

8.7 OPTIMISTIC CONCURRENCY CONTROL

In optimistic concurrency control, each transaction is validated before it is allowed to commit. Transaction numbers are assigned at the start of validation and transactions are serialized according to the order of the transaction number. A distributed transaction is validated by a collection of independent servers, each of which validated transactions that access its own objects. The validations at all of the servers take place during the first phase of two-phase commit protocol.

8.8 DISTRIBUTED DEADLOCKS

Deadlocks can arise when a single server when locking is used for concurrency control. Servers must prevent or detect and resolve deadlocks with deadlock detection schemes; a transaction is aborted only when it is involved. Most deadlock detection schemes operate by finding cycles in t5he transaction wait for graph. As the global wait for graph is held in part by each of the several servers involved, communication between these servers is required to find cycles in the graph.

A simple solution is to use centralized deadlock detection, in which one server takes on the role of global deadlock detector but it is not good idea because it depends on a single server to carry it out. It suffers from poor availability, lack of fault tolerance and no ability to scale. In addition, cost of frequent transaction for local wait for graph is high. If global graph is collected less frequently, deadlocks may take longer to be detected.

8.8.1 Phantom Deadlocks

A deadlock that is ‘detected but is not really a deadlock is called a Phantom Deadlock. In distributed deadlock detection, information about wait for relationships between transactions is transmitted from one server to another. If there is a deadlock, the necessary information will eventually be collected in one place and a cycle will be detected. In mean while there is a chance that one of the transactions that holds a lock will released it, in which case the deadlock will no longer exist.

A phantom deadlock could be detected, if a waiting transaction in a deadlock cycle aborts during the deadlock detection procedure.

8.8.2 Edge Chasing

Edge chasing or path pushing is used in distributed deadlock detection. In this, the global wait for graph is not constructed, but each of the servers involved has knowledge about some of its edges. The servers attempt to find cycles by forwarding messages called probes, which follows the edges of the graph throughout the distributed system. A probe message consisting of transactions wait for relationship representing a path in the global wait for graph. Edge chasing has three steps—

- **Initiation:** The server initiates to detect deadlock.
- **Detection:** Detection consists of receiving probes and deciding whether deadlock has occurred and forward probes.
- **Resolution:** When a cycle detected. A transaction in the cycle is aborted to break deadlock.

8.9 TRANSACTION RECOVERY

Recovery is concerned with ensuring that a servers objects are durable and that the service provides failure atomicity. Failure atomicity requires that effects of transactions are atomic even when the server crashes.

When a server is running it kept all of its objects in its volatile memory and records its committed objects in a recovery file or files. Therefore recovery consists of restoring the server with latest committed versions of its objects from permanent storage. The recovery manager dealt with two requirements durability and failure atomicity. The task of recovery manager is—

- To save objects in permanent storage.
- To restore the servers object after crash.
- To recognize the recovery file to improve the performance of recovery.
- To reclaim storage space.

To deal with recovery of a server that can be involved in distributed transactions, further information in addition to the values of the object is stored in the recovery file. Each object in recovery file is associated with a particular transaction by saving the data.

8.9.1 Logging

The logging techniques records transaction status entries, intentions list and object all in same log file. The order of entries in log reflects the order in which transactions have prepared, committed or aborted at server. During normal operation of a server, its recovery manager is called whenever a transaction prepares to commit, commits or aborts a transaction. When the server is prepared to commit a transaction the recovery manager appends the entire object in its intention list to the recovery file. When a transaction is eventually committed or aborted, the recovery manager appends the corresponding status of the transaction to its recovery file.

8.9.2 Shadow Versions

The shadow version use a map to locate versions of the servers objects in a file called a version store. The map associates the identifiers of their current versions in the version store. The versions written by each transaction are shadow of the previous committed versions.

When a transaction is prepared to commit, any of the objects changed by the transaction are appended to the version store, leaving corresponding committed version unchanged. These new as yet tentative versions are called shadow versions. When a transaction commits, a new map is made by copying old map and entering the position of shadow versions. To complete the commit process, the new map is replaces old map.

To store objects when a server is replaced after a crash, its recovery manager reads the map and uses the information in the map to locate the objects in the version store. The shadow versions method provides faster recovery than logging because the positions of current committed objects are recorded in the map, whereas recovery from a log requires searching throughout the log for objects.

Shadow versions on their own are not sufficient for a server that handles distributed transactions. The transaction status entries and intentions lists are saved in a file called transaction status file. Each intentions list represents the part of the map that will be altered by a transaction when it commits. The use of transaction status items and intentions lists in the recovery file is essential for a server that is intended to participate in distributed transaction.

8.9.3 Recovery from Two Phases Commit Protocol

In phase 1, when coordinator is prepared to commit, its recovery manager adds a coordinator entry to its recovery file. Before participants votes yes, it must have already prepared to commit. When it votes yes, its recovery manger records a participants entry and when votes No, it adds abort transaction status to its recovery file.

In phase 2, of the protocol, the recovery manager of the coordinator adds either a committed or aborted transaction status to its recovery file, according to the decision. This must be a forced write. Recovery manager of the participants adds a commit or abort transaction status to their recovery file according to messages received from coordinator. When a coordinator has received a confirmation from all of its participants, its recovery manager adds a done transaction status to its recovery file-this need not to be forced. The done status entry is not part of the protocol but is used when the recovery file is recognized.

8.10 SUMMARY

- A distributed transaction is any transaction whose activity involved in several different servers.

- A nested transactions structure may be used to allow additional concurrency and independent committing by the servers in a distributed transaction.
- Transactions must be scheduled so that their effect on stored data is serially equivalent. A server can achieve serially equivalent transactions by serializing access to objects .a simple example of serializing mechanism is to use exclusive locks
- Each transaction within a set of nested transaction must be prevented from observing the partial effect on any transaction in the set .the first rule is enforced by arranging that every lock that is acquired by a successful sub transaction is inherited by its parent when it completes
- The timestamp ordering rule is refined to ensure that each transaction accesses a consistent set of versions of the objects. The write operations may be performed after the close transaction operation has returned. With out making the client wait, but the client must wait when read operations need to wait for earlier transactions to finish. The time stamps are assigned from servers clocks.
- The multiversion time stamp ordering is introduced by Reed in 1983, in this a list of old committed versions as a well as tentative version is kept for each object. This list represents the history of the values of the objects. The benefit of using multiversions is that read operations that arrive too late need not be rejected.
- Timestamp ordering aborts the transaction immediately, whereas locking makes transaction wait. When the optimistic concurrency control is used, all transactions are allowed to proceed, but some of them are aborted when they attempt to commit.
- Each server manages a set of objects and is responsible for ensuring that they remain consistent when accesses by concurrent transactions. Therefore, each server is responsible for applying concurrency control to its own objects.
- In distributed transactions accesses objects are managed by multiple servers, when an distributed transaction comes to an end, the atomicity property of transaction requires that either all of the servers involved commit the transaction or all of them abort the transaction.
- The atomicity of transactions requires that when a distributed transaction comes to an end, either all of the operations are carried out or none of them. In case of distributed transaction, the client has requested the operations at more than one server. A transaction comes to an end when the client requests that a transaction be committed or aborted.
- During the progress of transaction, there is no communication between the coordinator and participants apart from participants informing the coordinator when they join the transaction. In the first phase of the two phase commit protocol the coordinators asks to each participants if they are prepared to commit and each participants votes for the transaction to be committed or aborted. Once a participant has voted to commit a transaction, it is not allowed to abort it.
- A deadlock that is 'detected but is not really a deadlock is called a Phantom Deadlock. A phantom deadlock could be detected, if a waiting transaction in a deadlock cycle aborts during the deadlock detection procedure.
- The logging techniques records transaction status entries, intentions list and object all in

same log file. The order of entries in log reflects the order in which transactions have prepared, committed or aborted at server.

- Recovery is concerned with ensuring that a servers objects are durable and that the service provides failure atomicity. Failure atomicity requires that effects of transactions are atomic even when the server crashes.
- The shadow version use a map to locate versions of the servers objects in a file called a version store. The map associates the identifiers of their current versions in the version store. The versions written by each transaction are shadow of the previous committed versions.

In phase 1, when coordinator is prepared to commit, its recovery manager adds a coordinator entry to its recovery file.

In phase 2, of the protocol, the recovery manager of the coordinator adds either a committed or aborted transaction status to its recovery file, according to the decision. This must be a forced write. Recovery manager of the participants adds a commit or abort transaction status to their recovery file according to messages received from coordinator.

8.11 REVIEW QUESTIONS

1. What do you mean by transaction and compare it with the nested transactions.
2. Define locks and use of locks in strict two phase locking.
3. Define locking status rules for nested transactions.
4. Define optimistic concurrency control and compare it with timestamp ordering.
5. Differentiate timestamp ordering with multiversion timestamp ordering.
6. Explain distributed transactions and differentiate flat and nested distributed transactions.
7. Explain comparison of methods for concurrency control.
8. Discuss atomic commit protocol and two phases commits protocols.
9. Explain different methods for concurrency control in distributed transactions.
10. Explain distributed deadlock and methods of edge chasing for detecting and resolution of distributed deadlock.
11. Discuss the conditions of phantom deadlocks.
12. What do you mean by phantom deadlock and how it occurs in distributed system and its disadvantages?
13. Discuss transaction recovery and different methods of transaction recovery.
14. Explain how the two-phase commit protocol for nested transactions ensure that if the top level transactions commits, all the right descendants are committed or aborted.
15. Consider edge chasing algorithms and give examples to show that it could detect phantom deadlock.

CHAPTER 9

Replication

To provide high availability and fault tolerance replication is used in distributed system. High availability is of increasing interest with the tendency towards mobile computing and consequently disconnected operation. Fault tolerance is an abiding Concern for service provided in safety article and other system.

9.1 REPLICATION

The replication is "the maintenance of copies of date at multiple computers. Replication is a key to the effectiveness of distributed systems in that it provides enhanced performance, high availability and fault tolerance high. For example the catching of resources from web server from web browser and web proxy server is a form of replication, since the data held in cache and at servers are replicas of one another.

Replication is a technique for enhancing a service. The motivations for replication are to improve a service is performance, to increase its availability, or to it fault tolerant. When data are replicated the replication transparency is required i.e. clients should not normally have to aware that multiple copies of data exist. The consistency of data is another requirement.

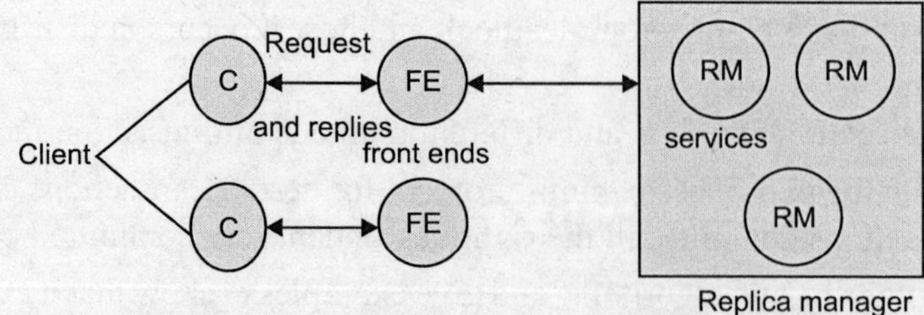

Fig.9.1 Architecture model for the management of replicated data

9.2 SYSTEM MODEL GROUP COMMUNICATION

The data consists of collection of terms thats called objects. But each such logical objects is implemented by a collection of physical copies called replicas. The system model provide for managing replicas and describe group communication.

The model involves replicas hells by distinct replicas managers, which are the components that contain the replicas on a given computer and perform operations upon them directly. This general model may be applied in a client – server environment, in which case replicas manager is a server.

The set of replicas managers may be static or dynamic. In a dynamic system, new replicas managers may appear, this is not allowed in a static system. In a dynamic system, replicas managers may crash and they are then deemed to have left system, but in static system, replicas managers do not crash, but they may cease operating for an infinite period. The group communication is also known as multicast communication because process group are destination of multicast messages. Groups are useful for managing replicated data and in other system where process corporate to wards a condition good receiving and processing the same set of multicast messages.

A full implementation of group communication in cop rates a group member slip service to manage the dynamic member ship of groups, in addition to multicast communication. Multicast and group member ship management are strongly interrelated." The group communication service has to manage chances in the group" member ship white multi cards take place constantly.

A group Member ship service has focus Main task, they are –

- Providing an inter face for group member ship changes.
- Implementing a failure detector.
- Notifying members of group member ship changes.
- Performing group address expansion.

A full group member ship service maintains group views, which are lists of the current group members,identified by their unique process identifiers, the list of ordered according to the sequence in which the members joined group. Anew group view is generated when process are added or executed.

The membership service exclude process from group evens through it may not have crashed.because a communication failure may have made the process unreachable write it continues to execute normally the effect of exclusion is that no massage will be delivered to that process hence forth. A false suspicion of a process and consequent exclusion o f the process from group may reduce groups effectiveness.

9.3 FAULT –TOLERANT SERVICE

For fault tolerant service we provide a service that is correct despite up to process failure, by replicating data and functionality at replica manager s. for the sake of simplicity,we assume that communication remains reliable and that no positions occur. Each replica managers is assumed to behave according to the specification at the semantics of the objects it managers, when they have no crashed.

For example, a bank account specification would include an assurance that fund transferred between accounts can never disappear, and that only deposits and withdrawals affect the balance at any particular account.

9.3.1 Passive (Primary–Backup) Replication

In passive model of replication for fault tolerance there is at any one time a single primary replica manager and one or more secondary replica managers backup or salvers. In pare form of model front ends communicate only with primary replica managers to obtain service. The primary replica manager executes operations and sends copies of updated data to backups. If primary fails one of backup is promoted to act as the primary.

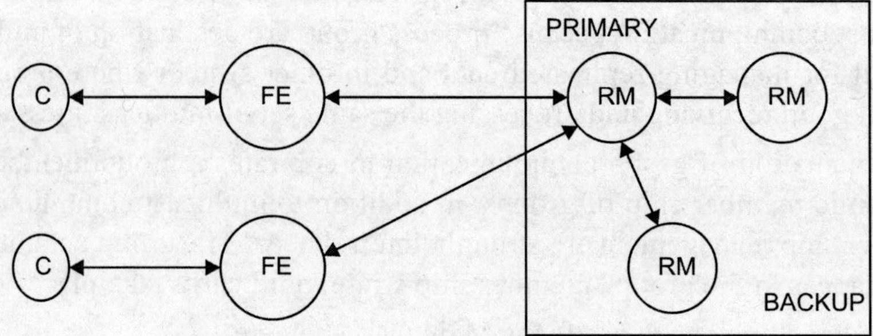

Fig. 9.2 Passive Model for fault Tolrance

9.3.2 Active Replication

In active mode of replication for fault tolerance, the replica managers are state machines that play equivalent roles and are organized as a group. Front ends multicast their requests to the group of replica managers and the entire replica manager process the request independently but identically and reply. If any replica manager crashes, then this have no impact upon the performance of service, since the remaining replica managers continue to responds in a normal way.

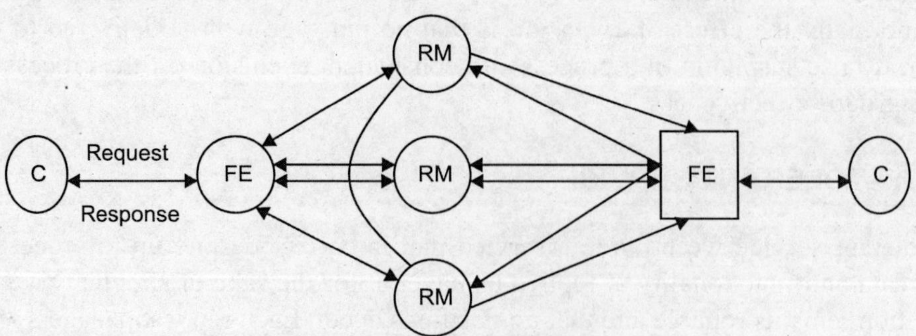

Fig. 9.3 Active Replication

9.4 HIGHLY AVAILABLE SERVICES

To make services highly available, by applying replication techniques is on giving clients access to the services with reasonable response times- for as much of time as possible, even if some results do not confirm to sequential consistency.

In fault tolerance systems updates are transmitted to the replica manager in an eager fashion i.e. all correct replica managers receives the updates as soon as possible and they reach collective agreement before passing control back to the client. The systems that provide highly available services are:

- Gossip
- Bayou
- Coda

Gossip architecture

A framework for implementing highly available services by replicating data close to the points where groups of clients need it the name reflects the fact that replica managers exchange 'gossip messages periodically in order to convey the updated they have each received from clients. A gossip services provides two basic types of operation- queries are used only operations and update modify but do not read the state.

The system makes two guarantees, one that each client obtains a consistent service over time and other relaxed consistency between replicas. In terms of basic replication model, a Gossip service processes queries and update operations as follows

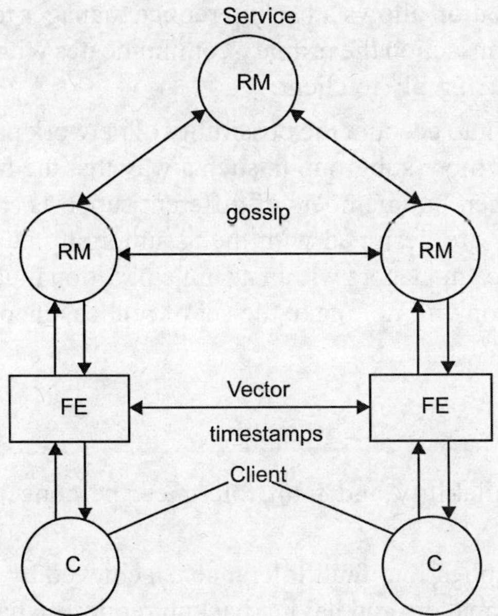

Fig. 9.4 Fronted propogate their timestamps whenever client communicate directly

1. The front end request only single replica manager and if it fails then they try to more others if the normal manager is heavily loaded.
2. If the request is an updated then replica manager replies as it received updates.
3. Receiving updates from other replica managers in gossip message, no other coordination between replica managers is involved.
4. The replica manager executes the request.
5. The replica managers update one another by exchanging gossip messages which contain the most recent updates they have received.

9.5 TRANSACTIONS WITH REPLICATED DATA

The effect of transactions performed by client on replicated objects should be the same if they had been performed one at a time on a single set of objects. This property is called one-copy serializability.

Each replica manager provides concurrency control and recovery of its own objects. Recovery is complicated by the fact that a failed replica manager is a member of a collection and that the other members continue to provide service during that time it is unavailable. When a replica manager recovers from failure, it uses information obtained from the other replica managers to restore its objects to their current values, taking into account all the changes that have occurred during time it was unavailable.

The replica managers that receives a request to perform an operation on a particular object is responsible for getting the cooperation of other replica managers in the group that have copies of that objects. In primary copy replication, all client requests are directed to a single primary replica manager. This form of replication allows a backup replica manager to take over consistently if the primary fails. To commit a transaction the primary communicates with the backup replica managers and then, in the eager approach reply to client.

Replication need to take into account the possibility of network partitions. It separates group of replica managers into two or more subgroup in such a way that the members of one subgroup can communicate with one another, but members of different supports can not communicate with one another. Replication scheme are designed with the assumption that partitions will eventually be repaired. Therefore the replica managers within a single partition must ensure that any request that they execute during a partition will not make the set of replicas inconsistent when the partition is repaired.

9.6 SUMMARY

- To achieve high availability and fault tolerance the concept of replication are used in distributed system.
- In primary backup replication, fault tolerance is achieved by directly all request through a distinguish replica managers and having backup replica manager take over if this fails.
- In active replication all replica managers processes request independently.

- Group communication is in both replications.
- Replica manager exchange updates with one another when they become reconnected.
- Replication takes into account for the possibility of partition.
- Each replica manager is assumed to behave according to a specification of the semantics of the object it manages.
- Replication need to take into account the possibility of network partitions. It separates group of replica managers into two or more subgroup in such a way that the members of one subgroup can communicate with one another, but members of different supports can not communicate with one another.
- Replication scheme are designed with the assumption that partitions will eventually be repaired.
- To achieve highly available service giving clients access to the service with reasonable response time.
- Each client obtains a consistent service over time.
- Relaxed consistency between replicas.
- To support relaxed consistency the gossip architecture supports casual update ordering.

9.7 REVIEW QUESTIONS

1. Explain system models and concept of group communication.
2. Explain why making some replica managers read- only may improve the performance of a gossip system.
3. Explain the difference between linearizability and sequential consistency and why the latter is more practical to implement.
4. What is the consistency issue raised by state transfer.
5. Explain fault tolerance services and highly available services.
6. Discuss the transactions with replicated data.
7. Explain gossip architecture.

CHAPTER 10

Communication Protocol

10.1 INTRODUCTION TO COMMUNICATION PROTOCOL

The OSI (open system interconnection) protocol suite is a group of standards for protocols that have been standardized into a logical structure for network operations.

Structure of network operations

The structure contains seven layers that are commonly to as OSI model. The seven layer of OSI model from highest to lowest are – Application, Presentation, Session, Transport, Network, Data link and Physical.

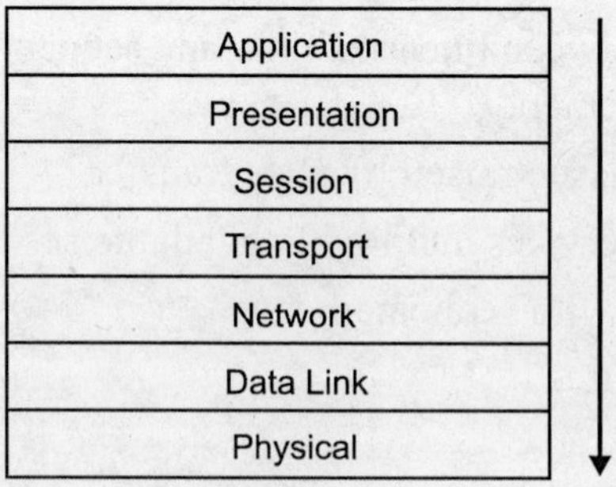

Application
Presentation
Session
Transport
Network
Data Link
Physical

Fig. 10.1

1. **Physical Layer:** The bottom layer of OSI stack is concerned only with moving bits of data onto and off the network medium.
2. **Data Link Layer:** The data li0nk layer handles many issues for communicating on a simple network. This layer takes the frames generated by the upper layers and takes apart for transmission. When receiving message from the network, it reassembles this information back into frames to send to upper layers.

3. **Network Layer:** The network layer is one of most complex and important ones. The network layer manages addressing and delivering packets on a complex internet work. Internet works are joined by devices known as routs, which utilize routing tables and routing algorithms to determine how tom send data from one network to another.
4. **Transport Layer:** The transport layer work hard to ensure reliable delivery of data to its destinations. The transport layer also interacts with the network layer.
5. **Session Layer:** The session layer manages dialogs between computers. It does this by establishing, managing and terminating communications between the two computers.
6. **Presentation Layer:** It is up to the presentation layer to make sure that data sent by the application layer and received by the session layer is in a standard format.
7. **Application Layer:** The application layer provides a consistent, neutral interface to network such as a word processor.

To do so the protocol maintains state information, recording which data has already been sent, which data has been certified to be received and so on. For two entities to successfully communicate, they must ' speak the same language. What is communicated, when it is communicated, and how it is communicated must confirm. The communication protocols are used for reliable exchange of data between two sites. So the main function of these protocols is reliable data transmission. The reliable data transmission includes the

(i) Repeated sending of messages that are lost.

(ii) Rejecting or correcting messages that are garbled.

(iii) Discarding duplicate messages.

To some mutually acceptable set of conventions between involved.The set, of Conventions are referred as communication protocol, which may be defined as a set of rules governing the exchange of data between two entities.

The key elements of the protocols are:

(i) Syntax: Includes such things as data format, coding and single format.

(ii) Semantics: Includes control information for co-ordination and error handing.

(iii) Timing: Includes speed, matching and sequencing.

10.2 BALANCED SLIDING WINDOW PROTOCOL

This protocol is used for exchange of information between stations that are directly connected through a line.

Let us see how this protocol works. Assume A and B are sites connected via full duplex link. If site B allocates buffer space for n frames, means A is allowed to send n frames without waiting for any acknowledgement. To keep track of which frames have been acknowledged and how many frames have been sent, each is labeled with a sequence number. B acknowledges a frame by sending on acknowledgement that includes the sequence number of next frame expected. This acknowledgement also announces that B is prepared to receive next n frames beginning with number specified.

As the sequence number occupies a field in frame,. It is clearly of bounded size. Assume if 3 bit sequence number is used, then frames may be numbered from 0 to 7. The Sliding Window Protocol is described below

At the Senders end

- A sliding window may have maximum 2^n frames (n is bits sequence number)
- The frames in window indicate that they are to be sent
- As the frame is sent, that frame is executed from window, thus window shrikes.
- As the acknowledgement is received, the window grows maximum limits from the sequence number specified in acknowledgement.

At the Receivers end

- The frames in the window at receiver end denote that receiver is ready to receive those frames.
- As soon as frame is received, that frame is excluded from window thus window shrinks.
- When the receiver sends the acknowledgement, the windows grow up to the maximum possible size from the sequence number specified in acknowledgement.

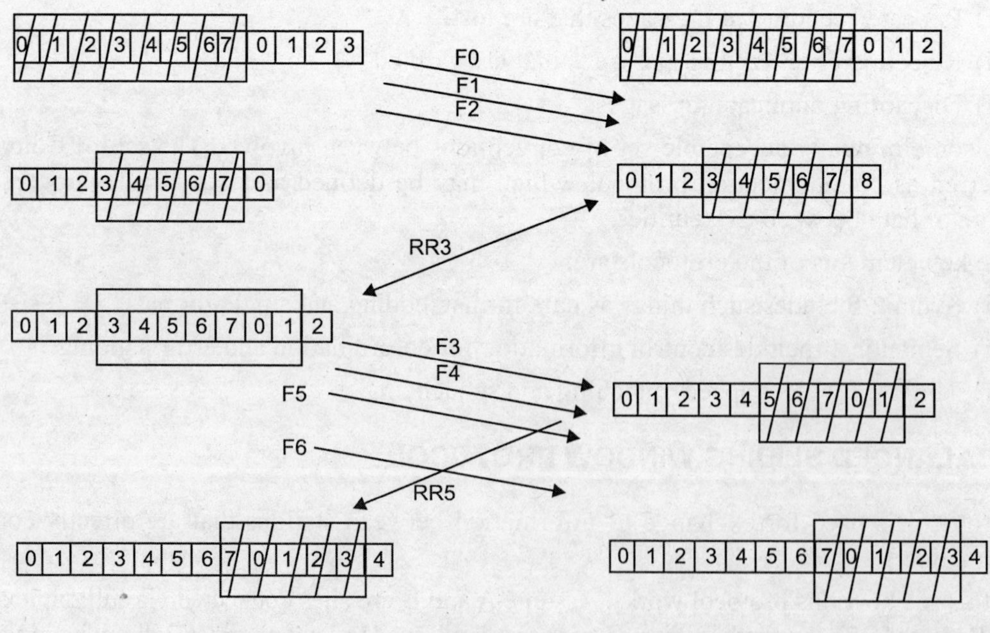

Fig. 10.2

Note: An acknowledgment messages RR3 (ready to receive 3) indicate 'I have received all frames up through frame number 2 and am ready to receive frame number 3; in fact I am ready o receive seven frames beginning with frame number 3.

10.3 ROUTING ALGORITHMS

A site in general is not generally connected directly to every site in distributed system. A site can send packets of information directly to a subset of sites called neighbors. Routing is the term used to describe the decision procedures by which a site selects one or more of its neighbors to forward a packet on its way to on ultimate destination. The objective in designing a routing algorithm is to guarantee a decision procedure to this function and guarantee delivery of each packet.

For the routing decisions each site must maintain the information about the topology of networks. Such information is maintained in routing tables. So the routing algorithms must ensures the following:

Table computation

The routing tables must be computed when network is initialized and must be brought up to date if topology of network changes.

Packet forwarding

When a packet is to be sent through network, it must be forwarded using routing tables.

Objectives of good routing algorithms

Correctness: The algorithms must deliver every packet offered to network, to its ultimate destination.

Efficiency: The algorithm must send packets through 'good paths. The path that suffers. The complexity of routing algorithms should be as less as possible. The aspect of complexity includes

- How fast the routing decisions can be made?
- How fast a packet can be made ready for transmission?
- How much storage space the routing table takes?

Robustness

Robust means storage and not likely to fail in a situation. The robustness of routing algorithm means in the case of topological changes, the algorithm updates the routing tables in order to perform in modified network.

Adaptive ness

The algorithm balances the load of channels and nodes by adopting the tables in order to avoid paths through channels or nodes with high load and preferring the channels or nodes with currently light load.

Fairness: The algorithm must provide services to every user in same degree.

Criteria for optimal routing algorithm

As we know that network is represented as a graph, where the nodes of the graph are the nodes of the network, and there is an edge between two nodes if they are neighbors (i.e. they have a communication channels between them). The optimality of an algorithm depends on what is 'best path in the graph, there are several notions of what is 'best, each with its own class of routing algorithms.

1. **Minimum Hop:** The cost of using a path is measured as the number of hopes (traversed channels or steps from node to node) of the path. A minimum hop routing algorithm uses a path with the smallest possible number of hopes.
2. **Smallest Path:** Each channel is statically assigned a (non-negative) weight and the cost of a path is measured as the sum of the weights of the channels in the path. A shortest part algorithm uses a path with lowest possible cost.
3. **Minimum Delay:** Each channel is dynamically assigned a weight depending on the traffic on the channels A minimum delay algorithm repeatedly revises the tables in such a way with a (near) minimal total delay are always chosen.

10.4 DESTINATION BASED ROUTING

The routing decisions made when forwarding a packet is usually based only on destination of packet and is independent of the original sender of packet. A path from a source to destination is called optimal if there exists no path between them with lower cost.

Note: the optimal path is not always unique, there may exist different path with same minimal costs.

Pre requisites for destination based routing

(i) The cost of sending a packet via a path is actual utilization of path. The cost of using a path is being denoted here as a function of path C®.

(ii) The cost of concatenation of two paths equals to the sum of the costs of concatenated paths.

C(U1,U2,U3,——Uk) = C(U1,U2,U3,———Ui)+C(Ui,———Uk)n

Note: the cost of forwarding a packet along a path P is computed by considering the distance, bandwidth, average traffic, communication costs, measured delay etc.

The destination based routing uses the optimality principal – which is as follows:

Optimality principle

If a node J is an optimal path from node I to K, then optimal path from J to K also falls along same route.

Proof

Let r1 be the part of that optimal path and connects the I to J. Let the rest of that optimal path is r2, which connects J to K. If a path better than r2 exist from J to K, it must be concatenated with r, to improve the optimal path from I to J and that is contradicting statement so r1r2 is optimal.

Thus by using optimality principal, in the destination based routing, the optimal path from all sources to the destination are searched a, which results in a tree rooted at destination. Such a tree is called optimal sink tree. Consider the following network:

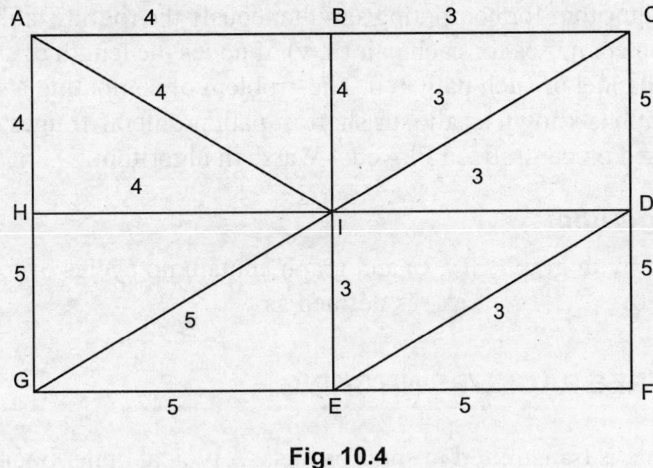

Fig. 10.4

If the destination is B the optical sink tree will be as:

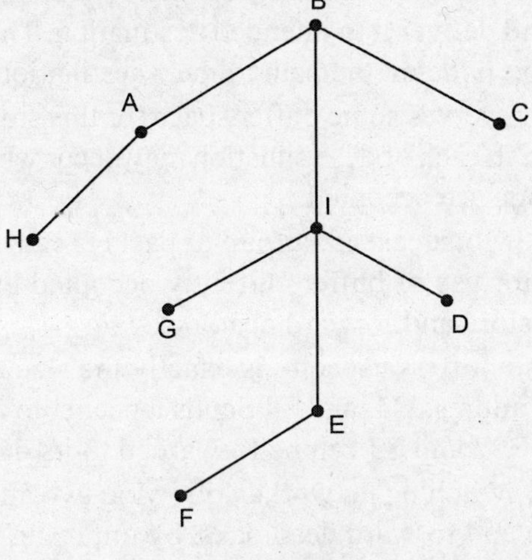

Fig. 10.5

The existence of optical sink tree implies that it is no compromise to optimality, if following packet forwarding mechanism is used. (When packet with destination D was received)

If d = 4

Then deliver the packet locally

Else send packet to table_lookupu (d)

Here table_lookupu (d) returns the of u in sink tree.

10.5 ALL PAIR SHORTEST PATH PROBLEM (APSP)

Toueg introduced an algorithm for computing simultaneously the routing tables for all the nodes in network. The algorithm computes for each pair (u, v) of nodes the length of shortest path from u to v and stores the first channel of such path in u. The problem of computing a shortest path between any two nodes of a graph is known as all pair shortest path problem. Touges distributed algorithm for this problem is based on centralized Floyed – Warshall algorithm.

Floyed warshall algorithm

Yet Wuv => weight of uv in graph G(v, e) and graph contain no cycles of total negative weights. The weight of both <u0.................ck> is defined as

10.6 DEADLOCK FREE PACKET SWITCHING

In packet switching data is transmitted in short packets. A typical upper bound on packet length is 1000 bytes. If a source has longer message to send, the message is broken into a series of packets. Each packet contains a portion of users data plus some control information. The control information, at a minimum, includes the information that the network requires in order to be able to route the packet through the network and deliver it to intended destination. This packet is stored at each node before being forwarded to next node on the path to their destination.

Each node of the network reserves some buffer space for this store and forward purpose. As the amount of buffer space is finite in each node, a situation may occur where no packet can be forwarded because all buffers in next node are occupied.

The situation becomes the worst case if a group of packets can never reach to their destination because they all are waiting for use of buffer currently occupied by another packet in the group. Such a situation is known as store and forward deadlock.

In above example suppose buffers capacity is exactly the size of one packet. If S1 has sent a packet to S2 with destination address S4, and S4 Sends a packet to S3 with destination S1 none of the packets stored in buffer of S2 and S3 can be forwarded to its destination.

So in the design of packet switching networks, following two approaches are introduced which avoids the possibility of store and forward deadlocks, by imposing restrictions on a packet can be generated or forwarded.

1. Structured Approach
2. Unstructured Approach

Structured approach

In this approach buffer graph is constructed. A buffer graph BG(B,E) is a directed graph on the buffers of network such that:

- BG is acyclic.
- B=(b1,b2,b3————bn) where b1,b2 — are the buffers in nodes of network.
- If b1,b2,b3————bn is a path in BG, then if Ui is the node where buffer bi resides then U0,U1,U2,——— Un is a sequence of node such that for each i<n either U0,U1,U2,——— UnÝ E OR Ui=Ui+1
- Let p be a packet in the node u with destination v. a buffer b is suitable for p if there is a path in BG from b to a buffer c in v. such a path is designed as guranteed path.

Structured solution is implemented as follows:

(i) The generation is packet p in u is allowed if and only if the buffer fb(p) is free. if the packet is generated it is placed in this buffer.

(ii) The forwarding a packet p from a buffer in u to a buffer w is allowed only if nb(p) is free. If the forwarding takes place p is placed in nb(p,b).

Unstructured approach

unlike to structured solution this solution do not prescribe in which buffer a packet must be placed and uses simple local information such as hop count or the number of occupied buffers in a node. This solution is implemented by forward count and backward count controllers.

Forward count controllers

Forward count controllers accepts a packet if the node contains more free buffers than packet has hops to go i.e. the controller accepts a packet p in node u if and only if sp<fu Where sp: number of hops the packet has to make to its destination.

fu: number of free buffers in u

Backward count controllers

This controller accepts a packet on the basis of number of steps a packet has already made. This controller accepts a packet p in node u if and only if

Tp>k-fu

Where tp: number of hops the packet has made from its source.

K: total number of hops

Fu: number of free buffers in u.

10.7 WAVE AND TRAVERSAL ALGORITHMS

Computer network are the natural application field of distributed algorithms. Distributed algorithms are designed for an interconnected collection of autonomous processes (or processes), cooperating to solve given problems:

In the design of distributed algorithms, very general problems appear frequently as sub tasks,. these elementary subtasks include:

(a) Broadcasting of information.

(b) Achieving global synchronization.

(c) Executing distributed computation (each process holds a part of input).

(d) Mutual exclusion etc.

Wave algorithms (sometimes referred to as total algorithms) are widely used as the basis to solve many network control problems. "A wave algorithms is a distributed algorithms where the participation of all the processes in network is required before a particular event, called a decision, is taken".

Definition of wave algorithms

Consider a computation C (Each computation is collection of events partially ordered by casual precedence relation á)

- Set of all process is denoted by P.
- The number of events in computation denoted as !C!.
- The subsets of events of computation C that occur in process p in denoted as Cp.

A wave algorithm is a distributed algorithm that satisfies the following three requirements:

Termination: each computation is finite

Decision: each computation contains at least one decide events.

Dependence: in each computation, each decides event is casually preceded by an event in each process.

A wave algorithm exchanges a finite number of messages and then makes a decision, which depends casually on some event in each process.

In the computation some processes are known as initiators also known as starters and some known as non initiators also known as followers.

- A process is initiators if it starts the execution of its local algorithms spontaneously. The first event of initiators is send event.
- Non initiator is involved in algorithms only when a message of algorithms arrives and triggers the execution of process algorithms. The first event of non initiators is receiving event.

Variety of wave algorithms

The variety of wave algorithms exists because algorithms may differ in many respects. The list of aspects in which wave algorithms differ from each other is given below:

Centralization: An algorithm is called centralized

If there must be exactly one initiators in each computation. These algorithms are also called single source algorithms.

Decentralized

An algorithm is called decentralized if the algorithms can be started spontaneously by an arbitrary subset of processes. These algorithms are also known as multiple source algorithms.

Topology

An algorithms may be designed for a specific topology such as ring, tree etc.

Classification of wave algorithms

Wave algorithms include token circulation (TC) and propagation of information with feedback (PIF).

- The purpose of TC scheme is to implement a token circulation scheme where the token, initiated by a process referred as root is passed through every process in network, is returned to root.
- The PIF scheme can be informally described as follows: root initiates a wave by broadcasting a message m. the wave terminates when all processes have acknowledged to root, the receipt of m.

Note: the TC and PIF schemes are useful when broadcasting of messages is required. Wave and traversal algorithms are also useful for synchronization. Consider the following scenario:

General wave algorithms

1. Ring algorithms
2. Tree algorithms
3. Echo algorithms
4. Polling algorithms
5. Phase algorithms
6. Finns algorithms

1. **Ring algorithms:** This is the centralized approach and uses the TC scheme. This is wave algorithms for ring network.

   The initiators sends message <tok> (called token) along the cycle, each process passes it on and when it returns to the initiators the initiators decides.

   For the initiators:

   Begin:

   Send <tok> to nextp.

   Receive <tok>

   Decide

   End.

```
For the non - initiators:
Begin:
Receive <tok>
Send <tok> to nextp.
End.
```

2. **Tree algorithms:** This is the decentralized approach because it can also be used in arbitrary network if spanning tree is available, and uses the TC scheme. This is wave algorithms for tree network.

   It is assumed that all leaves of tree initiates the algorithms. Each process sends exactly one message. if a process has received a message via each of its incident channels excepts one, the process sends a message via remaining channel, if a process has received a message via all of its channels it decides.

```
Boolean recp{q} for each qÝ neigh p
(initialized with false means p has not received message from q)
begin
 while#{q: rec p {q} is false }>1
begin
receive <tok> from q:
rec p{q}=true.
End
(now there is one q0 with rec p{q0}=false}
send <tok> to q0.
Receive <tok> from q0.
Rec p{q0}=true
Decide
(inform other proceses of decision)
 for all qÝ neigh p
send <tok> to q.
end.
```

3. **Echo algorithms:** This is the centralized approach for network of arbitrary topology. This is wave algorithms that use the propagation of information with feedback scheme (PIF).

   In this algorithms, the initiators sends message <tok> (called token)to the its neighbors, a non initiators forwards message to all its neighbors except one from which message is received and makes the process from which it has received the message, its father. When a process has no neighbor except its father, it sends echo messages immediately. When non-initiator has received echo message from all its neighbors it sends echo massage to its father. When initiator has received echo message from all its neighbors it decides.

```
int rec p(counts number of received messages)
process father p
For initiator
begin
        for all q ª Neigh p
         send < tok > to q
        while rec p < # Neigh p
         begin
                receive < tok >; rec p =. rec p + 1
         end
        decide
end
For non- initiator
begin
        receive < tok > from neighbor q;
        father p = q
        rec p = rec p + 1
        for all q ª Neigh p : q.# father p
         send < tok > to q
        while rec p < # Neigh p
         begin
                receive < tok >
                rec p = rec p + 1
         end
        send < tok > to father P
end
```

4. **Polling Algorithm:** This algorithm is used in star network in which initiator is in center. The initiator asks each neighbor to reply with messages and decides after receipt of all messages.

```
Int rec p
For initiator
Begin
Forall qîNeigh p
Send <tok> to q
While rec p<k%Neigh p
Begin
Receive <tok>
```

```
Rec p=rec p+
End
Decide:
End
For non initiator
Begin
Receive <tok> from q
Send <tok> to q
End.
```

5. **Phase Algorithms:** It is a decentralized algorithm for network of arbitrary topology. This can be used as wave algorithms for directed networks. The algorithms require that the process know the diameter D of the network. The algorithm is also correct if the process uses instead of D, a constant D larger than the network diameter. Thus in order to apply this algorithms it is not necessary that diameter is known exactly, it suffers if the upper bound (i.e. n–1) on the network diameter is known.

   As it can be used in arbitrary directed networks where channels can carry messages in one direction only, the neighbors of node p are:

   In neighbors: process that can send messages to p.

   Out neighbors: process to which p can send messages.

   In the phase algorithms each process sends exactly D messages to each out-neighbor. Only after I messages have been received from each in-neighbors,(i+1)th messages is sent to each out neighbors.

6. **Finns Algorithms:** This is another wave algorithm that can be used in arbitrary directed networks. It does not requires the diameter of the network to be known in advance, but relies on the availability of the unique identifiers for the processes. Set of processes identities are exchanged in messages, which causes the bit complexity of the algorithms to be rather high.

Process P maintains two set of process identities:

Incp: is the set of processes q such that an event in q precedes the most recent event in p.

Nincp: is the set of processes q such that for all neighbors r of q, an event in r precedes the most recent event in p.

This relation is maintained as follows:

Initially Incp = {p}

And Nincp = ϕ

Process p sends messages, including Incp and Nincp, each time one of them has increased. when p receives a message, including an Inc Set and Ninc Set, these received identities are inserted into ps version of these sets. When the p has received from all in-neighbors p is inserted into Nincp. When the two sets become equal p decides.

10.8 ELECTION ALGORITHMS

An algorithm for choosing a unique process to play a particular role is called election algorithms. For example, in a variant of client server algorithms for mutual exclusion or deadlock detection one server or coordinator is chosen by all processes. An election algorithm is needed to choose which of the process will play the role of the coordinator; it is essential that all the processes agree on same choice. Afterwards, if a process that plays the role of coordinator wishes to retire, then another election is required to choose a replacement.

The process of election is understood as follows:

- A leader is often needed in distributed systems- as coordinator or controllers.
- We need to elect a leader on startup and when current leader fails
- Assumption- every process knows ID of all the other processes
- Condition- Operational process with ID wins
  - All operational process should be informed of a new leader
  - Recovering process can find current leader.

Following two algorithms may be used for election process:

1. Bully Algorithm
2. Ring Algorithm

Bully algorithm

This algorithm was devised by Garcia-Molina. In this algorithm election is initiated by any process (P) which notices that coordinator is no longer responding. Concurrent multiple elections are possible.

Algorithm

- P sends ELECTION messages to all process with higher ID
- If no one responds, P wins and becomes coordinator
- Sends out COORDINATOR messages to all other processes

  If one of higher-ups answers, it takes over. P is done.

The performance of the Bully Algorithm can be analyzed as:

Best case: Process with highest ID (among operational ones) starts election

- ELECTION message = 1
- COORDINATOR announcements = N – 1

Worst case: process with lowest ID starts election

- N– 1 ELECTION messages + N –1 Acknowledgements = 2(N – 1)
- Machine 2 starts ELECTION = 2(N–2)
- Machine N–1 = 2
- Coordinator announcements = N–1
- TOTAL: O(N 2)

Ring Algorithms

The ring algorithms works as follows

Assumptions

- Processes are physically or logically ordered and construct a ring.
- Each process knows its successor (and all others).

Algorithms

- Initiator send election message with its ID to its successor, if successor is down, it skips over to the next node in the ring.
- When election message is received
- If it contains the receivers ID, decides who wins election and convert it to coordinator message and send them to its successor and if not, put its own ID and send over to its successor.

Variations of ring algorithms

- Putting all IDs in election message is not desirable; keep only max ID among the processes which have been seen so far.
- How can it be known that all live processes have been checked?, receivers ID is found in the election message.
- How to absorb unnecessary message from concurrent elections? Identify another election
- See RCV_ID<ID while it is currently participating another election (why?) then, when concurrent election is redundant remove, it.

10.9 SUMMARY

- The OSI (open system interconnection) protocol suite is a group of standards for protocols that have been standardized into a logical structure for network operations.
- The communication protocols are used for reliable exchange of data between two sites. So the main function of these protocols is reliable data transmission.
- Sliding window Protocol is used for exchange of information between stations that are directly connected through a line.
- Routing is the term used to describe the decision procedures by which a site selects one or more of its neighbors to forward a packet on its way to on ultimate destination. The objective in designing a routing algorithm is to guarantee a decision procedure to this function and guarantee delivery of each packet.
- The routing decisions made when forwarding a packet is usually based only on destination of packet and is independent of the original sender of packet. A path from a source to destination is called optimal if there exists no path between them with lower cost.

- The control information, at a minimum, includes the information that the network requires in order to be able to route the packet through the network and deliver it to intended destination. This packet is stored at each node before being forwarded to next node on the path to their destination.
- Computer network are the natural application field of distributed algorithms. Distributed algorithms are designed for an interconnected collection of autonomous processes (or processes), cooperating to solve given problems:
- An algorithm for choosing a unique process to play a particular role is called election algorithms. For example, in a variant of client server algorithms for mutual exclusion or deadlock detection one server or coordinator is chosen by all processes. An election algorithm is needed to choose which of the process will play the role of the coordinator; it is essential that all the processes agree on same choice.

10.10 REVIEW QUESTIONS

1. What do you mean by communication protocol, explain the protocol suite of OSI.
2. Discuss the functionality of balanced sliding window protocol.
3. Explain the purpose of routing and objectives of good routing algorithms.
4. Explain destination based routing.
5. Explain the all pairs shortest path problem with examples.
6. Discuss the functionality of deadlock free packet switching and explain the role of store and forward techniques.
7. Write the definitions of wave algorithms and explain different types of wave algorithms.
8. Differentiate wave and traversal algorithms.
9. Explain election algorithms.
10. Differentiate the bully election algorithms and ring election algorithms.

CHAPTER 11

Corba and Rmi

11.1 INTRODUCTION TO JAVA RMI

The Java Remote Method Invocation (RMI) system allows an object running in one Java Virtual Machine (VM) to invoke methods on an object running in another Java VM. RMI provides for remote communication between programs written in the Java programming language.

11.1.1 An Overview of RMI Applications

RMI applications are often comprised of two separate programs: a server and a client. A typical server application creates some remote objects, makes references to them accessible, and waits for clients to invoke methods on these remote objects. A typical client application gets a remote reference to one or more remote objects in the server and then invokes methods on them. RMI provides the mechanism by which the server and the client communicate and pass information back and forth. Such an application is sometimes referred to as a *distributed object application*.

Distributed object applications need to

- *Locate remote objects*: Applications can use one of two mechanisms to obtain references to remote objects. An application can register its remote objects with RMI's simple naming facility, the rmiregistry, or the application can pass and return remote object references as part of its normal operation.
- *Communicate with remote objects*: Details of communication between remote objects are handled by RMI; to the programmer, remote communication looks like a standard Java method invocation.
- *Load class bytecodes for objects that are passed around*: Because RMI allows a caller to pass objects to remote objects, RMI provides the necessary mechanisms for loading an object's code, as well as for transmitting its data.

The following illustration depicts an RMI distributed application that uses the registry to obtain a reference to a remote object. The server calls the registry to associate (or bind) a name with a remote object. The client looks up the remote object by its name in the server's registry and then invokes a method on it. The illustration also shows that the RMI system uses an existing Web server to load class bytecodes, from server to client and from client to server, for objects when needed.

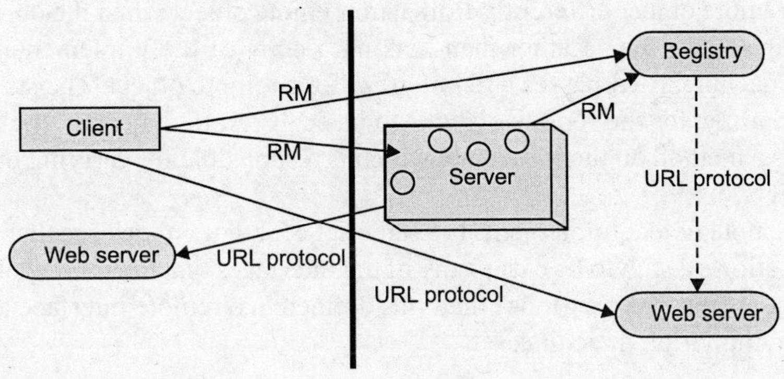

Fig. 11.1

This lesson contains the following sections:

- Advantages of Dynamic Code Loading
- Remote Interfaces, Objects, and Methods
- Creating Distributed Applications Using RMI
- Building a Generic Compute Engine

11.1.2 Advantages of Dynamic Code Loading

One of the central and unique features of RMI is its ability to download the *bytecodes* (or simply *code*) of an object's class if the class is not defined in the receiver's virtual machine. The types and the behavior of an object, previously available only in a single virtual machine, can be transmitted to another, possibly remote, virtual machine. RMI passes objects by their true type, so the behavior of those objects is not changed when they are sent to another virtual machine. This allows new types to be introduced into a remote virtual machine, thus extending the behavior of an application dynamically.The compute engine example in this chapter uses RMI's capability to introduce new behavior to a distributed program.

11.1.3 Remote Interfaces, Objects, and Methods

Like any other application, a distributed application built using Java RMI is made up of interfaces and classes. The interfaces define methods, and the classes implement the methods defined in the interfaces and, perhaps, define additional methods as well. In a distributed application some of the implementations are assumed to reside in different virtual machines. Objects that have methods that can be called across virtual machines are *remote objects*.

An object becomes remote by implementing a *remote interface*, which has the following characteristics.

- A remote interface extends the interface java.rmi.Remote.
- Each method of the interface declares java.rmi.RemoteException in its throws clause, in addition to any application-specific exceptions.

RMI treats a remote object differently from a nonremote object when the object is passed from one virtual machine to another. Rather than making a copy of the implementation object in the receiving virtual machine, RMI passes a remote *stub* for a remote object. The stub acts as the local representative, or proxy, for the remote object and basically *is*, to the caller, the remote reference. The caller invokes a method on the local stub, which is responsible for carrying out the method call on the remote object.

A stub for a remote object implements the same set of remote interfaces that the remote object implements. This allows a stub to be cast to any of the interfaces that the remote object implements. However, this also means that *only* those methods defined in a remote interface are available to be called in the receiving virtual machine.

11.1.4 Creating Distributed Applications Using RMI

When you use RMI to develop a distributed application, you follow these general steps.

1. Design and implement the components of your distributed application.
2. Compile sources and generate stubs.
3. Make classes network accessible.
4. Start the application.

11.1.5 Design and Implement the Application Components

First, decide on your application architecture and determine which components are local objects and which ones should be remotely accessible. This step includes:

- **Defining the remote interfaces:** A remote interface specifies the methods that can be invoked remotely by a client. Clients program to remote interfaces, not to the implementation classes of those interfaces. Part of the design of such interfaces is the determination of any local objects that will be used as parameters and return values for these methods; if any of these interfaces or classes do not yet exist, you need to define them as well.
- **Implementing the remote objects:** Remote objects must implement one or more remote interfaces. The remote object class may include implementations of other interfaces (either local or remote) and other methods (which are available only locally). If any local classes are to be used as parameters or return values to any of these methods, they must be implemented as well.
- **Implementing the clients:** Clients that use remote objects can be implemented at any time after the remote interfaces are defined, including after the remote objects have been deployed.

11.1.6 Compile Sources and Generate Stubs

This is a two-step process. In the first step you use the javac compiler to compile the source files, which contain the implementation of the remote interfaces and implementations, the server classes, and the client classes. In the second step you use the rmic compiler to create stubs for the remote objects. RMI uses a remote object's stub class as a proxy in clients so that clients can communicate with a particular remote object.

11.1.7 Make Classes Network Accessible

In this step you make everything—the class files associated with the remote interfaces, stubs, and other classes that need to be downloaded to clients—accessible via a Web server.

11.1.8 Start the Application

Starting the application includes running the RMI remote object registry, the server, and the client.

The rest of this lesson walks through the steps to create a compute engine.

11.1.9 Building a Generic Compute Engine

This trail focuses on a simple yet powerful distributed application called a compute engine. The compute engine, a remote object in the server, takes tasks from clients, runs them, and returns any results. The tasks are run on the machine where the server is running. This sort of distributed application could allow a number of client machines to make use of a particularly powerful machine or one that has specialized hardware.

The novel aspect of the compute engine is that the tasks it runs do not need to be defined when the compute engine is written. New kinds of tasks can be created at any time and then given to the compute engine to be run. All that is required of a task is that its class implement a particular interface. Such a task can be submitted to the compute engine and run, even if the class that defines that task was written long after the compute engine was written and started. The code needed to accomplish the task can be downloaded by the RMI system to the compute engine, and then the engine runs the task, using the resources on the machine on which the compute engine is running.

The ability to perform arbitrary tasks is enabled by the dynamic nature of the Java platform, which is extended to the network by RMI. RMI dynamically loads the task code into the compute engine's Java virtual machine and runs the task without prior knowledge of the class that implements the task. An application like this, which has the ability to download code dynamically, is often called a behavior-based application. Such applications usually require full agent-enabled infrastructures. With RMI such applications are part of the basic mechanisms for distributed computing on the Java platform.

11.2 WRITING AN RMI SERVER

The compute engine server accepts tasks from clients, runs the tasks, and returns any results. The server is comprised of an interface and a class. The interface provides the definition for the methods that can be called from the client. Essentially the interface defines the client's view of the remote object. The class provides the implementation.

11.3 DESIGNING A REMOTE INTERFACE

At the heart of the compute engine is a protocol that allows jobs to be submitted to the compute engine, the compute engine to run those jobs, and the results of the job to be returned to the client. This protocol is expressed in interfaces supported by the compute engine and by the objects that are submitted to the compute engine, as shown in the following figure.

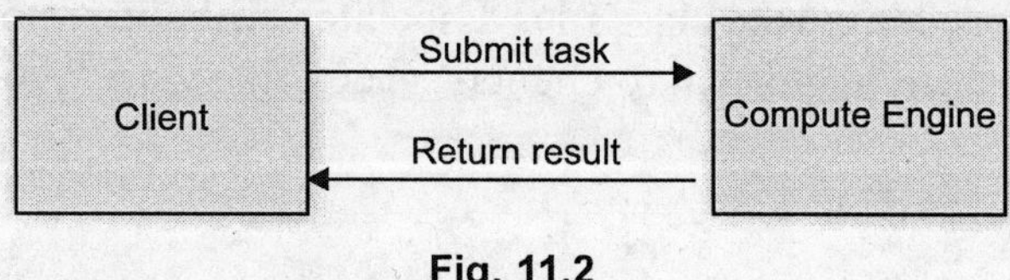

Fig. 11.2

Each of the interfaces contains a single method. The compute engine's interface, Compute, allows jobs to be submitted to the engine; the client interface, Task, defines how the compute engine executes a submitted task.

The compute.Compute interface defines the remotely accessible part—the compute engine itself. Here is the remote interface with its single method:

```
package compute;

import java.rmi.Remote;
import java.rmi.RemoteException;

public interface Compute extends Remote {
 Object executeTask(Task t) throws RemoteException;
}
```

By extending the interface java.rmi.Remote, this interface marks itself as one whose methods can be called from any virtual machine. Any object that implements this interface becomes a remote object.

As a member of a remote interface, the executeTask method is a remote method. Therefore the method must be defined as being capable of throwing a java.rmi.RemoteException. This exception is thrown by the RMI system during a remote method call to indicate that either a communication failure or a protocol error has occurred. A RemoteException is a checked exception, so any code making a call to a remote method needs to handle this exception by either catching it or declaring it in its throws clause.

The second interface needed for the compute engine defines the type Task. This type is used as the argument to the executeTask method in the Compute interface. The compute.Task interface defines the interface between the compute engine and the work that it needs to do, providing the way to start the work.

```
package compute;
import java.io.Serializable;
```

```
public interface Task extends Serializable {
 Object execute();
}
```

The Task interface defines a single method, execute, which returns an Object, has no parameters, and throws no exceptions. Since the interface does not extend Remote, the method in this interface doesn't need to list java.rmi.RemoteException in its throws clause.

The return value for the Compute's executeTask and Task's execute methods is declared to be of type Object. This means that any task that wants to return a value of one of the primitive types, such as an int or a float, needs to create an instance of the equivalent wrapper class for that type, such as an Integer or a Float, and return that object instead.

Note that the Task interface extends the java.io.Serializable interface. RMI uses the object serialization mechanism to transport objects by value between Java virtual machines. Implementing Serializable marks the class as being capable of conversion into a self-describing byte stream that can be used to reconstruct an exact copy of the serialized object when the object is read back from the stream.

Different kinds of tasks can be run by a Compute object as long as they are implementations of the Task type. The classes that implement this interface can contain any data needed for the computation of the task and any other methods needed for the computation.

Here is how RMI makes this simple compute engine possible. Since RMI can assume that the Task objects are written in the Java programming language, implementations of the Task object that were previously unknown to the compute engine are downloaded by RMI into the compute engine's virtual machine as needed. This allows clients of the compute engine to define new kinds of tasks to be run on the server machine without needing the code to be explicitly installed on that machine. In addition, because the executeTask method returns a java.lang.Object, any type of object can be passed as a return value in the remote call.

The compute engine, implemented by the ComputeEngine class, implements the Compute interface, allowing different tasks to be submitted to it by calls to its executeTask method. These tasks are run using the task's implementation of the execute method. The compute engine reports results to the caller through its return value: an Object.

11.4 IMPLEMENTING A REMOTE INTERFACE

In general the implementation class of a remote interface should at least

- Declare the remote interfaces being implemented
- Define the constructor for the remote object
- Provide an implementation for each remote method in the remote interfaces

The server needs to create and to install the remote objects. This setup procedure can be encapsulated in a main method in the remote object implementation class itself, or it can be included in another class entirely. The setup procedure should

- Create and install a security manager
- Create one or more instances of a remote object
- Register at least one of the remote objects with the RMI remote object registry (or another naming service such as one that uses JNDI), for bootstrapping purposes

The complete implementation of the compute engine follows. The engine.ComputeEngine class implements the remote interface Compute and also includes the main method for setting up the compute engine.

```
package engine;

import java.rmi.*;
import java.rmi.server.*;
import compute.*;

public class ComputeEngine extends UnicastRemoteObject
implements Compute
{
public ComputeEngine() throws RemoteException {
super();
}

public Object executeTask(Task t) {
return t.execute();
}

public static void main(String[] args) {
if (System.getSecurityManager() == null) {
System.setSecurityManager(new RMISecurityManager());
}
String name = "//host/Compute";
try {
Compute engine = new ComputeEngine();
Naming.rebind(name, engine);
System.out.println("ComputeEngine bound");
} catch (Exception e) {
System.err.println("ComputeEngine exception: " +
                        e.getMessage());
e.printStackTrace();
```

```
        }
      }
    }
```

Now let's take a closer look at each of the components of the compute engine implementation.

11.4.1 Declare the Remote Interfaces Being Implemented

The implementation class for the compute engine is declared as public class ComputeEngine extends Unicast Remote Objectimplements Compute

This declaration states that the class implements the Compute remote interface (and therefore defines a remote object) and extends the class java.rmi.server.UnicastRemoteObject.

UnicastRemoteObject is a convenience class, defined in the RMI public API, that can be used as a superclass for remote object implementations. The superclass UnicastRemoteObject supplies implementations for a number of java.lang.Object methods (equals, hashCode, toString) so that they are defined appropriately for remote objects. UnicastRemoteObjectalso includes constructors and static methods used to *export* a remote object, that is, make the remote object available to receive incoming calls from clients.

A remote object implementation does not have to extend UnicastRemoteObject, but any implementation that does not must supply appropriate implementations of the java.lang.Object methods. Furthermore, a remote object implementation must make an explicit call to one of UnicastRemoteObject's exportObject methods to make the RMI runtime aware of the remote object so that the object can accept incoming calls. By extending UnicastRemoteObject, the ComputeEngine class can be used to create a simple remote object that supports unicast (point-to-point) remote communication and that uses RMI's default sockets-based transport for communication.

If you choose to extend a remote object from any class other than Unicast-RemoteObject or, alternatively, extend from the new JDK 1.2 class java.rmi.activation.Activatable (used to construct remote objects that can execute on demand), you need to export the remote object by calling either the UnicastRemoteObject.exportObject or Activatable.exportObject method explicitly from your class's constructor (or another initialization method, as appropriate).

The compute engine example defines a remote object class that implements only a single remote interface and no other interfaces. The ComputeEngine class also contains some methods that can be called only locally. The first of these is a constructor for ComputeEngine objects; the second is a main method that is used to create a ComputeEngine and make it available to clients.

11.4.2 Define the Constructor

The ComputeEngine class has a single constructor that takes no arguments. The code for the constructor is

```
public ComputeEngine() throws RemoteException {
super();
}
```

This constructor simply calls the superclass constructor, which is the no-argument constructor of the UnicastRemoteObject class. Although the superclass constructor gets called even if omitted from the ComputeEngine constructor, we include it for clarity.

During construction, a UnicastRemoteObject is *exported*, meaning that it is available to accept incoming requests by listening for incoming calls from clients on an anonymous port.

Note: In JDK 1.2 you may indicate the specific port that a remote object uses to accept requests.

The no-argument constructor for the superclass, UnicastRemoteObject, declares the exception RemoteException in its throws clause, so the Compute-Engine constructor must also declare that it can throw RemoteException. A RemoteException can occur during construction if the attempt to export the object fails—due to, for example, communication resources being unavailable or the appropriate stub class not being found.

11.4.3 Provide Implementations for Each Remote Method

The class for a remote object provides implementations for each of the remote methods specified in the remote interfaces. The Compute interface contains a single remote method, executeTask, which is implemented as follows:

```
public Object executeTask(Task t) {
 return t.execute();
}
```

This method implements the protocol between the ComputeEngine and its clients. Clients provide the ComputeEngine with a Task object, which has an implementation of the task's execute method. The ComputeEngine executes the Task and returns the result of the task's execute method directly to the caller.

The executeTask method does not need to know anything more about the result of the execute method than that it is at least an Object. The caller presumably knows more about the precise type of the Object returned and can cast the result to the appropriate type.

11.4.4 Passing Objects in RMI

Arguments to or return values from remote methods can be of almost any type, including local objects, remote objects, and primitive types. More precisely, any entity of any type can be passed to or from a remote method as long as the entity is an instance of a type that is a primitive data type, a remote object, or a *serializable* object, which means that it implements the interface java.io.Serializable.

A few object types do not meet any of these criteria and thus cannot be passed to or returned from a remote method. Most of these objects, such as a file descriptor, encapsulate information that makes sense only within a single address space. Many of the core classes, including those in the packages java.lang and java.util, implement the Serializable interface.

The rules governing how arguments and return values are passed are as follows.

- Remote objects are essentially passed by reference. A *remote object reference* is a stub, which is a client-side proxy that implements the complete set of remote interfaces that the remote object implements.
- Local objects are passed by copy, using object serialization. By default all fields are copied, except those that are marked static or transient. Default serialization behavior can be overridden on a class-by-class basis.

Passing an object by reference (as is done with remote objects) means that any changes made to the state of the object by remote method calls are reflected in the original remote object. When passing a remote object, only those interfaces that are remote interfaces are available to the receiver; any methods defined in the implementation class or defined in nonremote interfaces implemented by the class are not available to that receiver.

For example, if you were to pass a reference to an instance of the ComputeEngine class, the receiver would have access only to the compute engine's executeTask method. That receiver would not see either the ComputeEngine constructor or its main method or any of the methods in java.lang.Object.

In remote method calls objects—parameters, return values, and exceptions—that are not remote objects are passed by value. This means that a copy of the object is created in the receiving virtual machine. Any changes to this object's state at the receiver are reflected only in the receiver's copy, not in the original instance.

11.4.5 Implement the Server's main Method

The most involved method of the ComputeEngine implementation is the main method. The main method is used to start the ComputeEngine and therefore needs to do the necessary initialization and housekeeping to prepare the server for accepting calls from clients. This method is not a remote method, which means that it cannot be called from a different virtual machine. Since the main method is declared static, the method is not associated with an object at all but rather with the class ComputeEngine.

11.4.6 Create and Install a Security Manager

The first thing that the main method does is to create and to install a security manager, which protects access to system resources from untrusted downloaded code running within the virtual machine. The security manager determines whether downloaded code has access to the local file system or can perform any other privileged operations.

All programs using RMI must install a security manager, or RMI will not download classes (other than from the local class path) for objects received as parameters, return values, or exceptions in remote method calls. This restriction ensures that the operations performed by downloaded code go through a set of security checks.

The ComputeEngine uses a security manager supplied as part of the RMI system, the RMISecurityManager. This security manager enforces a similar security policy as the typical security manager for applets; that is to say, it is very conservative as to what access it allows. An RMI application could define and use another SecurityManager class that gave more liberal access to system resources or, in JDK 1.2, use a policy file that grants more permissions.

Here's the code that creates and installs the security manager:

```
if (System.getSecurityManager() == null) {
 System.setSecurityManager(new RMISecurityManager());
}
```

11.4.7 Make the Remote Object Available to Clients

Next, the main method creates an instance of the ComputeEngine. This is done with the statement

```
Compute engine = new ComputeEngine();
```

As mentioned, this constructor calls the UnicastRemoteObject superclass constructor, which in turn exports the newly created object to the RMI runtime. Once the export step is complete, the ComputeEngine remote object is ready to accept incoming calls from clients on an anonymous port, one chosen by RMI or the underlying operating system. Note that the type of the variable engine is Compute, not ComputeEngine. This declaration emphasizes that the interface available to clients is the Compute interface and its methods, not the Compute-Engine class and its methods.

Before a caller can invoke a method on a remote object, that caller must first obtain a reference to the remote object. This can be done in the same way that any other object reference is obtained in a program, such as getting it as part of the return value of a method or as part of a data structure that contains such a reference.

The system provides a particular remote object, the RMI registry, for finding references to remote objects. The RMI registry is a simple remote object name service that allows remote clients to get a reference to a remote object by name. The registry is typically used only to locate the first remote object an RMI client needs to use. That first remote object then provides support for finding other objects.

The java.rmi.Naming interface is used as a front-end API for binding, or registering, and looking up remote objects in the registry. Once a remote object is registered with the RMI registry on the local host, callers on any host can look up the remote object by name, obtain its reference, and then invoke remote methods on the object. The registry may be shared by all servers running on a host, or an individual server process may create and use its own registry, if desired.

The ComputeEngine class creates a name for the object with the statement

```
String name = "//host/Compute";
```

This name includes the host name, host, on which the registry (and remote object) is being run and a name, Compute, that identifies the remote object in the registry. The code then needs to add the name to the RMI registry running on the server. This is done later (within the try block) with the statement

```
Naming.rebind(name, engine);
```

Calling the rebind method makes a remote call to the RMI registry on the local host. This call can result in a RemoteException being generated, so the exception needs to be handled. The ComputeEngine class handles the exception within the try/catch block. If the exception is not handled in this way, RemoteException would have to be added to the throws clause (currently nonexistent) of the main method.

Note the following about the arguments to the call to Naming.rebind.

- The first parameter is a URL-formatted java.lang.String representing the location and the name of the remote object. You will need to change the value of host to be the name, or IP address, of your server machine. If the host is omitted from the URL, the host defaults to the local host. Also, you don't need to specify a protocol in the URL. For example, supplying Compute as the name in the Naming.rebind call is allowed. Optionally a port number may be supplied in the URL; for example, the name //host:1234/objectname is legal. If the port is omitted, it defaults to 1099. You must specify the port number only if a server creates a registry on a port other than the default 1099. The default port is useful in that it provides a well-known place to look for the remote objects that offer services on a particular host.
- The RMI runtime substitutes a reference to the stub for the remote object reference specified by the argument. Remote implementation objects, such as instances of ComputeEngine, never leave the VM where they are created, so when a client performs a lookup in a server's remote object registry, a reference to the stub is returned. As discussed earlier, remote objects in such cases are passed by reference rather than by value.
- Note that for security reasons, an application can bind, unbind, or rebind remote object references only with a registry running on the same host. This restriction prevents a remote client from removing or overwriting any of the entries in a server's registry. A lookup, however, can be requested from any host, local or remote.

Once the server has registered with the local RMI registry, it prints out a message indicating that it's ready to start handling calls and then the main method exits. It is not necessary to have a thread wait to keep the server alive. As long as there is a reference to the ComputeEngine object in another virtual machine, local or remote, the ComputeEngine object will not be shut down, or garbage collected. Because the program binds a reference to the ComputeEngine in the registry, it is reachable from a remote client, the registry itself! The RMI system takes care of keeping the ComputeEngine's process up. The ComputeEngine is available to accept calls and won't be reclaimed until its binding is removed from the registry, *and* no remote clients hold a remote reference to the ComputeEngine object.

The final piece of code in the ComputeEngine.main method deals with handling any exception that might arise. The only exception that could be thrown in the code is a RemoteException, thrown either by the constructor of the ComputeEngine class or by the call to the RMI registry to bind the object to the name Compute. In either case the program can't do much more than exit after printing an error message. In some distributed applications it is possible to recover from the failure to make a remote call. For example, the application could choose another server and continue operation.

11.5 CREATING A CLIENT PROGRAM

The compute engine is a pretty simple program: it runs tasks that are handed to it. The clients for the compute engine are more complex. A client needs to call the compute engine, but it also has to define the task to be performed by the compute engine.

Two separate classes make up the client in our example. The first class, ComputePi, looks up and calls a Compute object. The second class, Pi, implements the Task interface and defines the work to be done by the compute engine. The job of the Pi class is to compute the value of to some number of decimal places.

As you recall, the nonremote Task interface is defined as follows:

```
package compute;
public interface Task extends java.io.Serializable {
 Object execute();
}
```

The Task interface extends java.io.Serializable so that an object that implements the interface can be serialized by the RMI runtime and sent to a remote virtual machine as part of a remote method invocation. We could have chosen to have our implementation classes implement both the Task interface and the Serializable interface and gotten the same effect. However, the whole purpose of the Task interface is to allow implementations of that interface to be passed to a Compute object, so having a class that implements the Task interface that does not also implement the Serializable interface doesn't make sense. Therefore we associate the two interfaces explicitly in the type system, ensuring that all Task objects are serializable.

The code that calls a Compute object's methods must obtain a reference to that object, create a Task object, and then request that the task be executed. The definition of the task Pi is shown later. A Pi object is constructed with a single argument, the desired precision of the result. The result of the task execution is a java.math.BigDecimal representing calculated to the specified precision.

The client class client.ComputePi is as follows.

```
package client;
import java.rmi.*;
import java.math.*;
import compute.*;
public class ComputePi {
public static void main(String args[]) {
if (System.getSecurityManager() == null) {
System.setSecurityManager(new RMISecurityManager());
 }
 try {
 String name = "//" + args[0] + "/Compute";
```

```
Compute comp = (Compute) Naming.lookup(name);
Pi task = new Pi(Integer.parseInt(args[1]));
BigDecimal pi = (BigDecimal) (comp.executeTask(task));
System.out.println(pi);
} catch (Exception e) {
System.err.println("ComputePi exception: "+
e.getMessage());
e.printStackTrace();
    }
  }
}
```

Like the ComputeEngine server, the client begins by installing a security manager. This is necessary because RMI could be downloading code to the client. In this example the ComputeEngine's stub is downloaded to the client. Any time code is downloaded by RMI, a security manager must be present. As with the server, the client uses the security manager provided by the RMI system for this purpose.

After installing a security manager, the client constructs a name used to look up a Compute remote object. The value of the first command line argument, args[0], is the name of the remote host on which the Compute object runs. The client uses the Naming.lookup method to look up the remote object by name in the remote host's registry. When doing the name lookup, the code creates a URL that specifies the host where the compute server is running. The name passed in the Naming.lookup call has the same URL syntax as the name passed in the Naming.rebind call, which was discussed earlier.

Next, the client creates a new Pi object, passing to the Pi constructor the second command line argument, args[1], which indicates the number of decimal places to use in the calculation. Finally, the client invokes the executeTask method of the Compute remote object. The object passed into the executeTask call returns an object of type java.math.BigDecimal, so the program casts the result to that type and stores the return value in the variable result. Then, the program prints out the result. The following figure depicts the flow of messages among the ComputePi client, the rmiregistry, and the ComputeEngine.

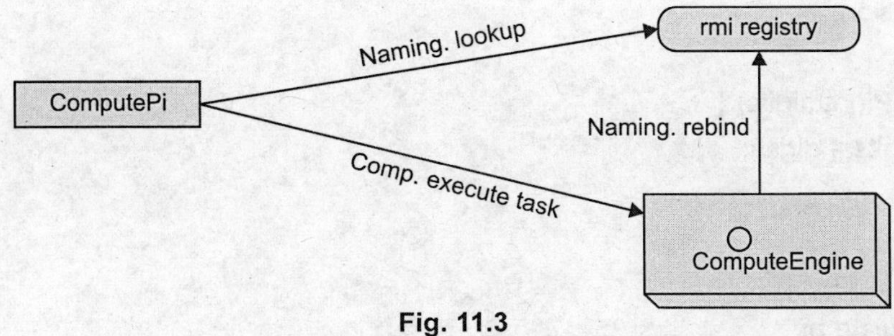

Fig. 11.3

Finally, let's look at the reason for all of this in the first place: the Pi class. This class implements the Task interface and computes the value of to a specified number of decimal places. For this example the actual algorithm is unimportant except, of course, for the accuracy of the computation. All that is important is that the computation is numerically rather expensive and thus the sort of thing that you would want to have occur on a more capable server.

Here is the code for the class client.Pi, which implements Task.

```
package client;

import compute.*;
import java.math.*;

public class Pi implements Task {

/** constants used in pi computation */
private static final BigDecimal ZERO =
BigDecimal.valueOf(0);
private static final BigDecimal ONE =
BigDecimal.valueOf(1);
private static final BigDecimal FOUR =
BigDecimal.valueOf(4);

/** rounding mode to use during pi computation */
private static final int roundingMode =
BigDecimal.ROUND_HALF_EVEN;

/** digits of precision after the decimal point */
private int digits;

/**
* Construct a task to calculate pi to the specified
* precision.
*/
public Pi(int digits) {
this.digits = digits;
}

/**
* Calculate pi.
```

```
*/
public Object execute() {
return computePi(digits);
}
/**
* Compute the value of pi to the specified number of
* digits after the decimal point. The value is
* computed using Machin's formula:
*
* pi/4 = 4*arctan(1/5) - arctan(1/239)
*
* and a power series expansion of arctan(x) to
* sufficient precision.
*/
public static BigDecimal computePi(int digits) {
int scale = digits + 5;
BigDecimal arctan1_5 = arctan(5, scale);
BigDecimal arctan1_239 = arctan(239, scale);
BigDecimal pi = arctan1_5.multiply(FOUR).subtract(
arctan1_239).multiply(FOUR);
return pi.setScale(digits,
BigDecimal.ROUND_HALF_UP);
}
/**
* Compute the value, in radians, of the arctangent of
* the inverse of the supplied integer to the speficied
* number of digits after the decimal point. The value
* is computed using the power series expansion for the
* arc tangent:
*
* arctan(x) = x - (x^3)/3 + (x^5)/5 - (x^7)/7 +
* (x^9)/9...
*/
public static BigDecimal arctan(int inverseX,
int scale)
{
BigDecimal result, numer, term;
```

```
BigDecimal invX = BigDecimal.valueOf(inverseX);
BigDecimal invX2 =
BigDecimal.valueOf(inverseX * inverseX);

numer = ONE.divide(invX, scale, roundingMode);

result = numer;
int i = 1;
do {
numer =
numer.divide(invX2, scale, roundingMode);
int denom = 2 * i + 1;
term =
numer.divide(BigDecimal.valueOf(denom),
scale, roundingMode);
if ((i % 2) != 0) {
result = result.subtract(term);
} else {
result = result.add(term);
}
i++;
} while (term.compareTo(ZERO) != 0);
return result;
    }
}
```

The most interesting feature of this example is that the Compute object never needs Pi's class definition until a Pi object is passed in as an argument to the executeTask method. At that point the code for the class is loaded by RMI into the Compute object's virtual machine, the execute method is called, and the task's code is executed. The resulting Object, which in the case of the Pi task is a java.math.BigDecimal object, is handed back to the calling client, where it is used to print out the result of the calculation.

The fact that the supplied Task object computes the value of Pi is irrelevant to the ComputeEngine object. You could also implement a task that, for example, generated a random prime number by using a probabilistic algorithm. That would also be numerically intensive and therefore a candidate for being shipped over to the ComputeEngine, but it would involve very different code. This code could also be downloaded when the Task object was passed to a Compute object. In just the way that the algorithm for computing Pi is brought in when needed, the code that generates the random prime would be brought in when needed. The Compute object knows only that each object it receives implements the execute method; it does not know, and does not need to know, what the implementation does.

11.6 COMPILING AND RUNNING THE EXAMPLE

11.7 COMPILING THE EXAMPLE PROGRAMS

In a real-world scenario in which a service like the compute engine is deployed, a developer would likely create a JAR (Java ARchive) file that contains the Compute and Task interfaces for server classes to implement and client program to use. Next, a developer, perhaps the same developer of the interface JAR file, would write an implementation of the Compute interface and deploy that service on a machine available to clients. Developers of client programs can use the Compute and the Task interfaces, contained in the JAR file, and independently develop a task and client program that uses a Compute service.

In this section you learn how to set up the JAR file, server classes, and client classes. You will see that the client's Pi class will be downloaded to the server at runtime. Also, the ComputeEngine's remote stub will be downloaded from the server to the client at runtime.

The example separates the interfaces, remote object implementation, and client code into three packages:

- compute (Compute and Task interfaces)
- engine (ComputeEngine implementation class and its stub)
- client (ComputePi client code and Pi task implementation)

Let's first build the interface JAR file to provide to server and client developers.

11.7.1 Build a JAR File of Interface Classes

First, you need to compile the interface source files in the compute package and then build a JAR file that contains their class files. Let's suppose a user, waldo, has written these particular interfaces and has placed the source files in c:\home\waldo\src\compute (on UNIX:/home/waldo/src/compute). Given these paths, you can use the following commands to compile the interfaces and create the JAR file.

Microsoft Windows:

```
cd c:\home\waldo\src
javac compute\Compute.java
javac compute\Task.java
jar cvf compute.jar compute\*.class
```

UNIX:

```
cd /home/waldo/src
javac compute/Compute.java
```

```
javac compute/Task.java
jar cvf compute.jar compute/*.class
```

```
The jar command displays the following output (due to the -v option):
added manifest
adding: compute/Compute.class (in=281) (out=196)
        (deflated 30%)
adding: compute/Task.class (in=200) (out=164)
        (deflated 18%)
```

Now you can distribute the compute.jar file to developers of server and client applications so that they can make use of the interfaces.

When you build either server- or client-side classes with the javac and rmic compilers, you generally need to specify where the resulting class files should reside so that they are network accessible. In this example this location is, for UNIX, /home/user/public_html/classes, because some web servers allow accessing a user's public_html directory via an HTTP URL constructed as http://host/~user/. If your web server does not support this convention, you could use a file URL instead. The file URLs take the form file:/home/user/public_html/classes/ on UNIX or, on the Microsoft Windows platform, file:/c:/home/user/public_html/classes/. You may also select another type of URL, as appropriate.

The network accessibility of the class files allows the RMI runtime to download code when needed. Rather than defining its own protocol for code downloading, RMI uses URL protocols supported by the Java platform (for example, HTTP) to download code. Note that a full, heavyweight web server is not needed to accomplish this downloading of class files.

11.7.2 Build the Server Classes

The engine package contains only one server-side implementation class, Com-puteEngine, the remote object implementation of the Compute interface. Since ComputeEngine is an implementation of a remote interface, you need to generate a stub for the remote object so that clients can contact the remote object.

Let's say that ann, the developer of the ComputeEngine class, has placed ComputeEngine.java in the c:\home\ann\src\engine directory and is deploying the class files for clients to use in a subdirectory of her public_html directory, c:\home\ann\public_html\classes (on UNIX that would be /home/ann/public_html/classes, accessible via some web servers as http://host/~ann/classes/).

Now let's assume that the compute.jar file is located in the directory c:\home\ann\public_html\classes. To compile the ComputeEngine class, your class path must include the compute.jar file and the source directory itself.

Note: Normally we recommend that you set the class path on the command line, using the -classpath option. However, for several compounding reasons this example uses the CLASSPATH environment variable, because both javac and rmic require a class path and the-classpath option is treated differently in JDK 1.1 and JDK 1.2. For detailed information on CLASSPATH refer to:

We recommend that you do not set CLASSPATH in a login or startup file and that you remember to unset it when you're finished working with this example.

Here's how to set the CLASSPATH environment variable

```
Microsoft Windows:
set
CLASSPATH=c:\home\ann\src;c:\home\ann\public_html\classes\compute.jar
UNIX:
setenv CLASSPATH /home/ann/src:/home/ann/public_html/classes/compute.jar
```

Now you compile the ComputeEngine.java source file, generate a stub for the ComputeEngine class, and make that stub network accessible. To create stub (and optionally skeleton files), run the rmic compiler on the fully qualified class names of the remote object implementations that must be found in the class path. The rmic command takes one or more class names as input and produces as output class files of the form ClassName_Stub.class and ClassName_Skel.class. A skeleton file will not be generated if you run rmic with the -v1.2 option. This option should be used only if all of your clients will be running JDK 1.2 or compatible versions.

```
Microsoft Windows:
cd c:\home\ann\src
javac engine\ComputeEngine.java
rmic -d. engine.ComputeEngine
mkdir c:\home\ann\public_html\classes\engine
cp engine\ComputeEngine_*.class
 c:\home\ann\public_html\classes\engine
UNIX:
cd /home/ann/src
javac engine/ComputeEngine.java
rmic -d. engine.ComputeEngine
mkdir /home/ann/public_html/classes/engine
cp engine/ComputeEngine_*.class
 /home/ann/public_html/classes/engine
```

The-d option tells the rmic compiler to place the generated class files, ComputeEngine_Stub.class and ComputeEngine_Skel.class, in the directory c:\home\ann\src\engine. You also need to make the stubs and the skeletons network accessible, so you must copy the stub and the skeleton class to the area: public_html\classes.

Since the ComputeEngine's stub implements the Compute interface, which refers to the Task interface, you need to make these two interface class files network accessible along with the stub. So the final step is to unpack the compute.jar file in the directory c:\home\ann\public_html\classes to make the Compute and the Task interfaces available for downloading.

```
Microsoft Windows:
cd c:\home\ann\public_html\classes
jar xvf compute.jar
UNIX:
cd /home/ann/public_html/classes
jar xvf compute.jar
```

The jar command displays the following output:

```
created: META-INF/
extracted: META-INF/MANIFEST.MF
extracted: compute/Compute.class
extracted: compute/Task.class
```

Now the compute engine is ready to deploy. You could do that now or wait until after you have built the client. While we are on a building spree, let's build the client-side program next.

11.7.3 Build the Client Classes

Let's assume that user jones has created the client code in the directory c:\home\jones\src\client and will deploy the Pi class, so that it can be downloaded to the compute engine, in the network-accessible directoryc:\home\jones\public_html\classes, also available via some web servers as http://host/~jones/classes/. The two client-side classes are contained in the files Pi.java and ComputePi.java in the client subdirectory.

In order to build the client code, you need the compute.jar file that contains the Compute and the Task interfaces that the client uses. Let's say that the compute.jar file is located in c:\home\jones\public_html\classes. The client classes can be built as follows:

```
Microsoft Windows:
set
CLASSPATH=c:\home\jones\src;c:\home\jones\public_html\classes\compute.jar
cd c:\home\jones\src
javac client\ComputePi.java
javac -d c:\home\jones\public_html\classes client\Pi.java
UNIX:
setenv CLASSPATH /home/jones/src:/home/jones/public_html/classes/compute.jar
cd /home/jones/src
javac client/ComputePi.java
javac -d /home/jones/public_html/classes client/Pi.java
```

Only the Pi class needs to be placed in the directory public_html\classes\client. (The client directory is created by javac if it does not exist.) The reason is that only the Pi class needs to be available for downloading to the compute engine's virtual machine. Now you can run the server and then the client.

11.8 RUNNING THE EXAMPLE PROGRAMS

11.8.1 A Note about Security

The JDK 1.2 security model is more sophisticated than the model used for JDK 1.1. JDK 1.2 contains enhancements for finer-grained security and requires code to be granted specific permissions to be allowed to perform certain operations.

In JDK 1.1 code in the class path is trusted and can perform any operation; downloaded code is governed by the rules of the installed security manager. If you run this example in JDK 1.2, you need to specify a policy file when you run your server and client. Here is a general policy file that allows downloaded code, from any code base, to do two things:

- Connect to or accept connections on unprivileged ports (ports greater than 1024) on any host
- Connect to port 80 (the port for HTTP)

Here is the code for the general policy file:

```
grant {
 permission java.net.SocketPermission "*:1024-65535",
 "connect,accept";
 permission java.net.SocketPermission "*:80", "connect";
};
```

If you make your code available for downloading via HTTP URLs, you should use the preceding policy file when you run this example. However, if you use file URLs instead, you can use the following policy file. Note that in Windows-style file names, the backslash character needs to be represented by two backslash characters in the policy file.

```
grant {
 permission java.net.SocketPermission "*:1024-65535",
 "connect,accept";
 permission java.io.FilePermission
 "c:\\home\\ann\\public_html\\classes\\-", "read";
 permission java.io.FilePermission
 "c:\\home\\jones\\public_html\\classes\\-", "read";
};
```

This example assumes that the policy file is called java.policy and that it contains the appropriate permissions. If you run this example on JDK 1.1, you will not need to use a policy file, since the RMISecurityManager provides all of the protection you need.

11.8.2 Start the Server

Before starting the compute engine, you need to start RMI's registry, using the rmiregistry command. As discussed earlier, the RMI registry is a simple server-side bootstrap naming facility that allows remote clients to get a reference to a remote object. Note that before you start the rmiregistry, you must make sure that the shell or window in which you will run rmiregistry either has no CLASSPATH environment variable set or has a CLASSPATH environment variable that does not include the path to any classes, including the stubs for your remote object implementation classes, that you want downloaded to clients of your remote objects.

If you *do* start the rmiregistry and it *can* find your stub classes in CLASSPATH, it will not remember that the loaded stub class can be loaded from your server's code base, specified by the java.rmi.server.codebase property when you started up your server application. Therefore, the rmiregistry will not convey to clients the true code base associated with the stub class and, consequently, your clients will not be able to locate and to load the stub class or other server-side classes.

To start the registry on the server, execute the rmiregistry command. This command produces no output and is typically run in the background. For this example, we will start the registry on the host zaphod.

Microsoft Windows (use javaw if start is not available):

unset CLASSPATH

start rmiregistry

UNIX:

unsetenv CLASSPATH

rmiregistry &

By default, the registry runs on port 1099. To start the registry on a different port, specify the port number on the command line. Do not forget to unset your CLASSPATH.

Microsoft Windows:

start rmiregistry 2001

UNIX:

rmiregistry 2001 &

Once the registry is started, you can start the server. First, you need to make sure that both the compute.jar file and the remote object implementation class (since that is what you are starting) are in your class path.

Microsoft Windows:

set

CLASSPATH=c:\home\ann\src;c:\home\ann\public_html\classes\compute.jar

UNIX:

setenv CLASSPATH /home/ann/src:/home/ann/public_html/classes/compute.jar

When you start the compute engine, you need to specify, using the java.rmi.server.codebase property, where the server's classes will be made available. In this example the server-side classes to be made available for downloading are the ComputeEngine's stub and the Compute and the Task interfaces, available in ann's public_html\classes directory. Here, we start the compute engine server on the host zaphod, the same host where we started the registry.

Microsoft Windows:

```
java -Djava.rmi.server.codebase=file:/c:\home\ann\public_html\classes/
-Djava.rmi.server.hostname=zaphod.east.sun.com
-Djava.security.policy=java.policy
 engine.ComputeEngine
```

UNIX:

```
java -Djava.rmi.server.codebase=http://zaphod/~ann/classes/
 -Djava.rmi.server.hostname=zaphod.east.sun.com
 -Djava.security.policy=java.policy
 engine.ComputeEngine
```

The preceding java command defines several properties.

- The java.rmi.server.codebase property specifies the location, a code base URL, of classes originating *from* this server so that class information for objects sent to other virtual machines will include the location of the class so that a receiver can load it. If the code base specifies a directory (as opposed to a JAR file), you must include the trailing slash in the code base URL.
- The java.rmi.server.hostname property indicates the fully qualified host name of your server. In some networked environments a fully qualified host name is not obtainable by using the Java APIs. RMI makes a best-effort attempt to obtain the fully qualified host name. If one cannot be determined, it will fall back and use the IP address. To ensure that RMI will use a host name that is usable from potential clients, you may want to set the java.rmi.server.hostname property as a safety measure.
- The java.security.policy property is used to specify the policy file that contains the permissions you intend to grant specific code bases.

The ComputeEngine's stub class is dynamically loaded into a client's virtual machine only when the class is not already available locally *and* the java.rmi.server.codebas e property has been set properly, to the network-accessible location of the stub class, when the *server* is started. Once such a stub is loaded, it will not need to be reloaded for additional references to Com-puteEngine's objects.

11.8.3 Start the Client

Once the registry and the engine are running, you can start the client, specifying

- The location where the client serves up its classes (the Pi class), using the java.rmi.server.codebase property
- As command line arguments the host name of the server—so that the client knows where to locate the Compute remote object—and the number of decimal places to use in the calculation
- The java.security.policy property, used to specify the policy file that contains the permissions you intend to grant specific code bases

First, set the CLASSPATH to see jones's client and the JAR file containing the interfaces. Then start the client on another host (one named ford, for example) as follows:

Microsoft Windows:

```
set CLASSPATH c:\home\jones\src;c:\home\jones\public_html\classes\compute.jar
java -Djava.rmi.server.codebase=file:/c:\home\jones\public_html\classes/
 -Djava.security.policy=java.policy
client.ComputePi zaphod.east.sun.com 20
```

UNIX:

```
setenv CLASSPATH /home/jones/src:/home/jones/public_html/classes/compute.jar
java -Djava.rmi.server.codebase=http://ford/~jones/classes/
-Djava.security.policy=java.policy
client.ComputePi zaphod.east.sun.com 20
```

Note that the class path is set on the command line so that the interpreter can find jones's client and the JAR file containing the interfaces.

After starting the client, you should see the following output on your display:

3.14159265358979323846

The following figure illustrates where the rmiregistry, the ComputeEngine server, and the ComputePi client obtain classes during program execution.

When the ComputeEngine server binds its remote object reference in the registry, the registry downloads the ComputeEngine_Stub, as well as the Compute and the Task interfaces on which the stub class depends. These classes are downloaded from the ComputeEngine's web server or file system, as the case may be.

The ComputePi client loads the ComputeEngine_Stub, also from the Compute-Engine's web server, as a result of the Naming.lookup call. Since the ComputePi client has both the Compute and the Task interfaces available in its class path, those classes are loaded from the class path, not the remote location.

Finally, the Pi class is loaded into the ComputeEngine's virtual machine when the Pi object is passed in the executeTask remote call to the ComputeEngine object. The Pi class is loaded from the client's web server.

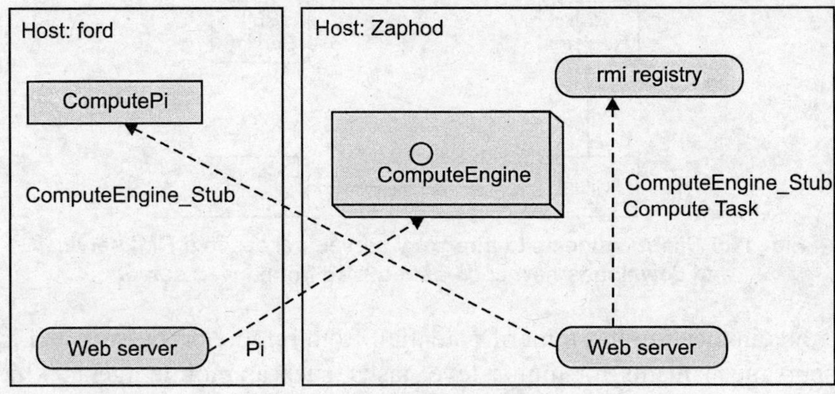

Fig. 11.4

11.9 CORBA CASE STUDY

With the introduction of CORBA support to Java (as of version 1.2), developers now face the question of whether to continue to use remote method invocation (RMI), or make a move to CORBA. The choice is made more difficult if your applications are already written in RMI - considerable effort might have to be made to convert to CORBA. Is it worth the move? This article discusses the pros and cons, and evaluates the potential of these two technologies.

11.10 WHAT IS REMOTE METHOD INVOCATION?

Remote method invocation allows Java developers to invoke object methods, and have them execute on remote Java Virtual Machines (JVMs). Under RMI, entire objects can be passed and returned as parameters, unlike many remote procedure call based mechanisms which require parameters to be either primitive data types, or structures composed of primitive data types. That means that any Java object can be passed as a parameter - even new objects whose class has never been encountered before by the remote virtual machine.

This is an exciting property, because it means that new code can be sent across a network and dynamically loaded at run-time by foreign virtual machines. Java developers have a greater freedom when designing distributed systems, and the ability to send and receive new classes is an incredible advantage. Developers don't have to work within a fixed codebase - they can submit new classes to foreign virtual machines and have them perform different tasks. When working with remote services, RMI clients can access new versions of Java services as they are made available - there's no need to distribute code to all the clients that might wish to connect. While code can be accessed from a local or remote file-system, it can also be accessed via a web server, making distribution easier. RMI also supports a registry, which allows clients to perform lookups for a particular service. The following diagram shows the interaction between different components of an RMI system. Clients that know about a service can look up its location from a registry and access the service. If a new class is required, it can be downloaded from a web server.

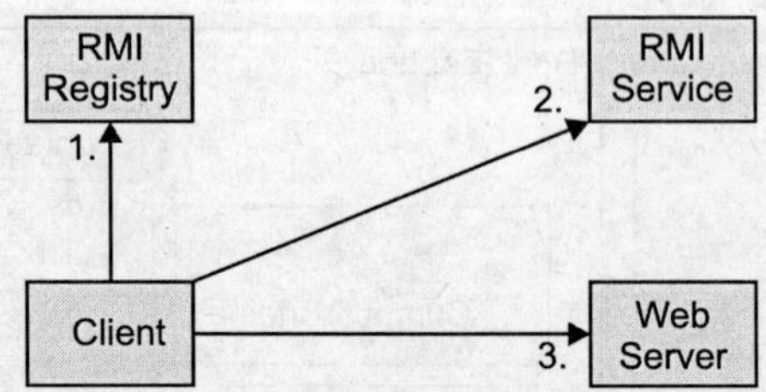

Fig. 11.5 Client connects to a registry server, accesses a RMI service, and downloads new code as required from a web server.

Remote method invocation has a lot of potential, from remote processing and load sharing of CPU's to transport mechanisms for higher level tasks, such as mobile agents which execute on remote machines. Because of the flexibility of remote method invocation, it has become an important tool for Java developers when writing distributed systems. However, there are many legacy systems written in C/C++, Ada, Fortran, Cobol, and other exotic languages. If legacy systems need to interface with your RMI systems, or your RMI systems need to interface with them, problems can occur. RMI is Java specific, and you'll need to write a bridge between older systems. Additionally, if you or your company plans on using other languages in the future, you may also find yourself in a bind because of RMI's tie to Java - one day Java itself may become a legacy platform. Writing interfaces to legacy systems isn't my idea of fun programming.

11.11 WHAT IS CORBA

Common Object Request Broker Architecture (CORBA) is a competing distributed systems technology that offers greater portability than remote method invocation. Unlike RMI, CORBA isn't tied to one language, and as such, can integrate with legacy systems of the past written in older languages, as well as future languages that include support for CORBA. CORBA isn't tied to a single platform (a property shared by RMI), and shows great potential for use in the future. That said, for Java developers, CORBA offers less flexibility, because it doesn't allow executable code to be sent to remote systems.

CORBA services are described by an interface, written in the Interface Definition Language (IDL). IDL mappings to most popular languages are available, and mappings can be written for languages written in the future that require CORBA support. CORBA allows objects to make requests of remote objects (invoking methods), and allows data to be passed between two remote systems. Remote method invocation, on the other hand, allows Java objects to be passed and returned as parameters. This allows new classes to be passed across virtual machines for execution (mobile code). CORBA only allows primitive data types, and structures to be passed - not actual code.

Under communication between CORBA clients and CORBA services, method calls are passed to Object Request Brokers (ORBs). These ORBs communicate via the Internet Inter-ORB Protocol (IIOP). IIOP transactions can take place over TCP streams, or via other protocols (such as HTTP), in the event that a client or server is behind a firewall. The following diagram shows a client and a servant communicating.

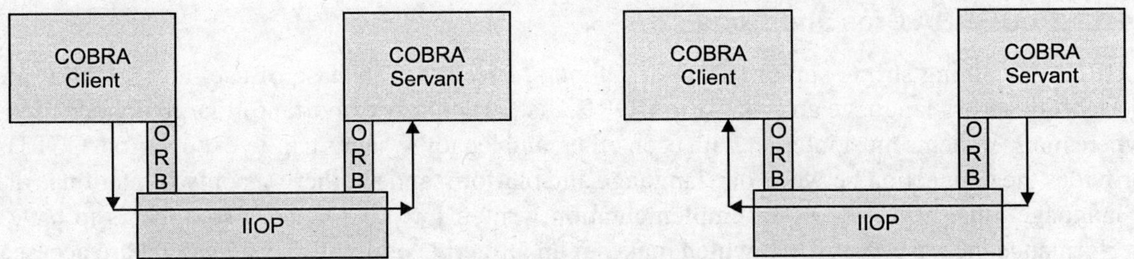

Fig. 11.6 CORBA client sends a request through its local ORB to a remote ORB's servant CORBA servant sends back a response to a remote ORB

11.12 RMI VS CORBA

Comparing RMI and CORBA doesn't reveal an optimum solution - one is not "better" than the other. The properties of these two technologies lend themselves to different situations. A comparison of RMI and CORBA helps to highlight individual strengths and weaknesses, but the applicability of one technology over the other depends largely on the purposes for which it is to be used, the experience of the developers who will design, implement and maintain the distributed system, and whether non-Java systems are intended to access the system now or in the future.

11.12.1 RMI Pros and Cons

Remote method invocation has significant features that CORBA doesn't possess - most notably the ability to send new objects (code and data) across a network, and for foreign virtual machines to seamlessly handle the new objects.Remote method invocation has been available since JDK 1.02, and so many developers are familiar with the way this technology works, and organizations may already have systems using RMI. Its chief limitation, however, is that it is limited to Java Virtual Machines, and cannot interface with other languages.

Remote method invocation	
Pros	**Cons**
Portable across many platforms	Tied only to platforms with Java support
Can introduce new code to foreign JVMs	Security threats with remote code execution, and limitations on functionality enforced by security restrictions
Java developers may already have experience with RMI (available since JDK1.02)	Learning curve for developers that have no RMI experience is comparable with CORBA
Existing systems may already use RMI - the cost and time to convert to a new technology may be prohibitive	Can only operate with Java systems - no support for legacy systems written in C++, Ada, Fortran, Cobol, and others (including future languages).

11.12.2 CORBA Pros and Cons

CORBA is gaining strong support from developers, because of its ease of use, functionality, and portability across language and platform CORBA is particularly important in large organizations, where many systems must interact with each other, and legacy systems can't yet be retired. CORBA provides the connection between one language and platform and another - its only limitation is that a language must have a CORBA implementation written for it. CORBA also appears to have a performance increase over RMI, which makes it an attractive option for systems that are accessed by users who require real-time interaction

Common Object Request Broker Architecture	
Pros	**Cons**
Services can be written in many different languages, executed on many different platforms, and accessed by any language with an interface definition language (IDL) mapping.	Describing services require the use of an interface definition language (IDL) which must be learned. Implementing or using services require an IDL mapping to your required language - writing one for a language that isn't supported would take a large amount of work.
With IDL, the interface is clearly separated from implementation, and developers can create different implementations based on the same interface.	IDL to language mapping tools create code stubs based on the interface - some tools may not integrate new changes with existing code.
CORBA supports primitive data types, and a wide range of data structures, as parameters	CORBA does not support the transfer of objects, or code.
CORBA is ideally suited to use with legacy systems, and to ensure that applications written now will be accessible in the future.	The future is uncertain - if CORBA fails to achieve sufficient adoption by industry, then CORBA implementations become the legacy systems.
CORBA is an easy way to link objects and systems together	Some training is still required, and CORBA specifications are still in a state of flux.
CORBA systems may offer greater performance	Not all classes of applications need real-time performance, and speed may be traded off against ease of use for pure Java systems.

11.13 JAVA AND CORBA

CORBA, for those who haven't heard of it before, stands for Common Object Request Broker Architecture. This architecture allows clients to invoke methods of objects running on remote servers. The idea is nothing new - many developers will have come across similar systems such as RPC (remote procedure call), or Java's own RMI (remote method invocation). The differen ce between these and CORBA is that CORBA is much more interoperable with other platforms - a C++ object running on a Wintel system can communicate with a Java object on a Unix box. Developers don't need to know what language a CORBA service is written in, or even where it is physically located. This makes CORBA systems very versatile - one can change the location of a CORBA object, and then re-register with a nameserver. Clients that look up the service can then find its new location, and then continue to make requests. Java makes it easy to integrate support for CORBA into applications and applets, thanks to the introduction of Java IDL in JDK1.2

11.13.1 Interface Definition Language (IDL)

Developers use the Interface Definition Language (IDL) to describe the interface to a CORBA object. An IDL schema can then be used to generate Java code for the client and server that will use the object. The same IDL schema could be used to generate either a client or server in C++, Ada, or any other language that supports CORBA. You don't write your implementation of a CORBA service in IDL - so you can continue to write in pure Java code if you so wish.

Let's start by taking a look at a sample IDL schema, to give you an idea what I'm talking about. The following schema shows a very simple CORBA service, which allows clients to get and store the name associated with an email address. For the purposes of this example, we won't worry about modifying or deleting an existing user.

```
// Address book system module
module address_book_system
{
 // Specify interface to our address book
 interface address_book
 {
        // Unknown user exception
        exception unknown_user {};

        // User already exists exception
        exception user_exists {};

        // Lookup name from email address
        string name_from_email(in string email)
 raises (unknown_user);

        // Lookup email from full name
        string email_from_name(in string name)
 raises (unknown_user);
        // Record a new name and email
        void record_user(in string name, in string email)
         raises user_exists;
        };
};
```

Listing 1-0 address book.idl

We start by declaring a module for our address book system (modules can be mapped to Java packages). Inside the module, we declare our interfaces and the exceptions they can raise. Since its such as simple system, the methods of the interface will only return a string, but we can create more complex return values if needed. As well as returning values, we accept as input two strings for our record_user method. As you can see, IDL really isn't to hard to pick up.

Once you've written your interface using IDL, you can then begin to write client and servers in the language of the choice. We'll choose Java for now, but there's no reason why the client or the server couldn't be written in another language. Provided you have an interface in IDL format, you could write code that interacts with the object it describes.

11.13.2 From IDL to Java

Converting an IDL schema into Java source code is quite straightforward. Sun provides a free tool, *idltojava*, that creates the source code for you. This tool is currently distributed separately to JDK 1.2, but is freely available for members of the Java Developer Connection.

```
idltojava -fno-cpp AddressBook.idl
```

Based on the name of your IDL schema's module, a package will be generated that contains skeleton source code for your CORBA client and server, as well a second package to cover our two exceptions. The following is a list of the files it creates for us

\address_book_system
_address_bookStub.java
address_book.java
address_bookHolder.java
address_bookHelper.java
address_bookPackage
_address_bookImplBase.java

address_bookPackage
unknown_user.java
unknown_userHelper.java
unknown_userHolder.java
user_exists.java
user_existsHelper.java
user_existsHolder.java

As you can see, there are a lot of files! Fortunately, we only need three to implement a complete CORBA client and server. The first file is a servant, which serves the requests made by clients. The second is a server, which will accept requests, and the third is a standalone application which will issue requests.

11.13.3 Implementing a CORBA Servant

Under CORBA, a servant is responsible for handling service requests. When we ran the idltojava tool, an abstract class was created that handles most of the hard work for us. All we need to do is create an AddressBookServant class, that implements the _address_bookImplBase. It will contain the code for our three methods described in the IDL schema.

```
skip to next section
package address_book_system;
import address_book_system.address_bookPackage.*;

import java.util.Hashtable;
import java.util.Enumeration;
//
//
// AddressBookServant
//
// This servant class is responsible for implementing
// three methods
//
// * String name_from_email ( String email );
// * String email_from_name ( String name );
// * void record_user ( String name, String email );
//
//
class AddressBookServant extends _address_bookImplBase
{
 private Hashtable name2email;

 public AddressBookServant()
 {
          // Create a new hashtable to store name & email
          name2email = new Hashtable();
 }

 // Get the name of this email user
 public String name_from_email ( String email )
 throws unknown_user
 {
```

```
        if (name2email.contains(email))
        {
         // Begin search for that name
         for (Enumeration e = name2email.keys();
    e.hasMoreElements();)
         {
                String name = (String) e.nextElement();
                String e_mail = (String) name2email.get(name);

                // Match on email ?
                if (email.compareTo(e_mail) == 0)
                {
                        return name;
                }
         }
        }

        // User not found - throw unknown user exception
        throw new unknown_user();
}

// Get the email of this person
public String email_from_name ( String name )
throws unknown_user
{
        // If user exists
        if (name2email.containsKey(name))
        {
                // Return email address
                return (String) name2email.get(name);
        }

        // User doesn't exist
        throw new unknown_user();
}

// Add a new user to the system
```

```
public void record_user ( String name, String email )
throws user_exists
{
        // Is the user already listed
        if (name2email.containsKey( name ) ||
         name2email.contains( email ) )
        {
                // If so, throw exception
                throw new user_exists();
        }

        // Add to our hash table
        name2email.put (name, email);
}
}
```

The servant class maintains a list of people's email addresses, and stores this information inside a Hashtable. When the CORBA server receives a request, it will call upon the name_from_email, email_from_name, and record_user methods of the servant to fulfill the request.

11.13.4 Writing a CORBA server

Writing a CORBA server is pretty straightforward. We need to create an ORB (object-request-broker), and register our servant with it. We'll also notify a nameserver of our ORB, so that CORBA clients can access our address book. Once we've registered, CORBA clients will be able to look for our interface, and send requests through our ORB to the servant object.

```
package address_book_system;
import org.omg.CORBA.*;
import org.omg.CosNaming.*;
import org.omg.CosNaming.NamingContextPackage.*;
//
//
// AddressBookServer
//
// This server is responsible for creating an object
// request broker (ORB), and registering an AddressBookServant
// with a naming service
//
//
```

```
public class AddressBookServer
{
 public static void main(String args[])
 {
        try
        {
                // Create a new object request broker
                ORB orb = ORB.init(args, null);

                // Create a new address book...
                AddressBookServant servant = new AddressBookServant();

                //... and connect it to our orb
                orb.connect(servant);

                // Object Request Broker Initialised
                System.out.println ("Address book ORB initialised");

                // Obtain reference for our nameservice
                org.omg.CORBA.Object object =
                orb.resolve_initial_references('NameService');

                // Since we have only an object reference, we must
                // cast it to a NamingContext. We use a helper
                // class for this purpose
                NamingContext namingContext =
                NamingContextHelper.narrow(object);

                // Add a new naming component for our interface
                NameComponent list[] =
                { new NameComponent("address_book", "") };

                // Now notify naming service of our new interface
                namingContext.rebind(list, servant);

                // Wait for clients
                for (;;){}
```

```
        }
        catch (Exception e)
        {
              System.err.println ("ORB Error - "+ e);
              e.printStackTrace(System.out);
              System.exit(0);
        }
    }
}
```

11.13.5 Writing a CORBA client

Now that we have a finished server, we need to write a client to show that the server works. Our client is very simple. It looks up our AddressBook service through a naming service, and then sends requests in response to commands made by the user. The client also traps exceptions thrown by the AddressBook service, in the event that a user's details doesn't exist or that a duplicate is being inserted into the system.

```
package address_book_system;
import address_book_system.address_bookPackage.*;

import org.omg.CORBA.*;
import org.omg.CosNaming.*;
import java.io.*;

//
//
// AddressBookClient
//
// This client demonstrates the AddressBook server and servant.
// A menu is presented to the user, allow he or she to add
// users, and look up their names & email addresses
//
//
public class AddressBookClient
{
 public static void main(String args[]) throws IOException
 {
```

```
try
        {
        // Create an object request broker
        ORB orb = ORB.init(args, null);

        // Obtain object reference for name service...
org.omg.CORBA.Object object =
orb.resolve_initial_references('NameService');

//... and narrow it to a NameContext
NamingContext namingContext =
NamingContextHelper.narrow(object);

// Create a name component array
NameComponent nc_array[] =
{ new NameComponent("address_book","") };

// Get an address book object reference...
org.omg.CORBA.Object objectReference =
namingContext.resolve(nc_array);

//... and narrow it to get an address book
address_book AddressBook =
address_bookHelper.narrow(objectReference);

// DataInputStream for system.in
DataInputStream din = new DataInputStream
(System.in);

for (;;)
{
try
{
                // Print menu
System.out.println ("1- Add user');
System.out.println ('2- Look up email');
System.out.println ("3- Look up name');
```

```
System.out.println ("4- Exit");

System.out.print ("Command :");

// Read a line from user
String command = din.readLine();

// Convert to number
Integer num = new Integer (command);
int choice = num.intValue();

// Variables we'll need for service calls
String name;
String email;

switch (choice)
{
case 1:
                System.out.print ("Name:");
                name = din.readLine();
                System.out.print ("Email:");
                email = din.readLine();

                // Call AddressBook service
                AddressBook.record_user(name,email);
                break;

case 2:
                System.out.println ("Name:");
                name = din.readLine();
                // Call AddressBook service
                email = AddressBook.email_from_name(name);
                System.out.println ("Email of "+ name + "is "+ email);
                break;

case 3:
                System.out.println ("Email:");
```

```
                    email = din.readLine();

                // Call AddressBook service
                    name = AddressBook.name_from_email(email);
                    System.out.println ('Name of "+ email + "is "+ name);

                    break;

    case 4:
                    System.exit(0);
    }
    }
                catch (user_exists already_there)
                {
                 System.out.println ('User already exists - cannot be added to address
book');
                }
                catch (unknown_user bad_user)
                {
                 System.out.println ('User doesn't exist');
                }
    }
    }
            catch (Exception e)
            {
    System.err.println ("CORBA error - "+ e);
            }
    }
    }
```

11.13.6 Putting it all Together

Now that we have a CORBA server and a CORBA client, the next step is to have the client connect to the server. If you've already compiled the source code, then you're ready to begin.

1. Start the nameservice that comes with JDK1.2
2. Start the server
3. Start the client

11.13.6.1 Start the nameservice that comes with JDK1.2

If your Java installation directory is in the path, you can type the following from your prompt

```
tnameserv -ORBInitialPort 2000
```

The port parameter is necessary for Unix users who aren't logged it as root. Windows users can omit the parameter. If you do specify a port parameter, make sure you do so for the client and server as well.

11.13.6.2 Start the server

All of the examples are part of the address_book_system package. Some users have reported problems running the examples. Make sure that the current directory is in the classpath, and then go to the directory where you've compiled the examples, or where you've unzipped them. Next, start the server

```
java address_book_system.AddressBookServer
-ORBInitialPort 2000
-ORBInitialHost myhost
```

The port parameter is optional (but needed if you've specified a port for your nameservice). You'll also need to specify the hostname if you run the server on a different machine to the nameservice (omit it if running everything locally).

11.13.6.3 Start the client

You'll need to go to the directory where the examples are stored. Make sure that the nameservice and server are already running, and then start the client

```
java address_book_system.AddressBookClient -ORBInitialPort 2000
-ORBInitialHost myhost
```

The port parameter is optional (but needed if you've specified a port for your nameservice). You'll also need to specify the hostname if you run the client on a different machine to the nameservice (omit it if running everything locally).

11.13.7 Running the client

The client is capable of invoking all the methods defined in our IDL. It can record new users, look up an email address, and look up a name. While the demonstration is relatively simple, it does show how easy it is to write clients that interact with services on remote systems. This demo is a standalone application, but you could just as easily write an applet that implemented the same functionality.

1. Add user
2. Look up email
3. Look up name
4. Exit

Command :1

Name: David Reilly

Email: dodo@fan.net.au

1. Add user
2. Look up email
3. Look up name
4. Exit

Command :2

Name:

David Reilly

Email of David Reilly is dodo@fan.net.au

11.14 SUMMARY

CORBA technology offers developers many benefits over other techniques for distributed computing, but its most compelling is the ease with which developers can create distributed services that are platform independent. Once a service is described by an IDL schema, the developer can choose to implement either client or server (or both) in Java. Being able to use Java is an attractive option, because Java brings platform portability - but its nice to know that one can also connect a C++ module to Java. CORBA allows developers to connect objects together, and developers can still choose the versatility and familiarity of Java.

A further advantage is that CORBA services can be moved throughout the network or intranet. Java 1.2 includes a nameservice, which allows ORBs to register (or bind) their services. This means that services can be moved from system to system as needed, and that clients don't need to be aware of the physical location of the service. CORBA is a powerful technology for distributed computing, and the introduction of support for CORBA in JDK1.2 offers developers greater freedom when they create distributed systems.

Appendix 1

A1.1 INTERNETWORKING BASICS

The OSI model represents the building blocks for internetworks. Understanding the conceptual model helps you understand the complex pieces that make up an internetwork.

A1.1.1 What Is an Internet Work

An internetwork is a collection of individual networks, connected by intermediate networking devices, that functions as a single large network. Internetworking refers to the industry, products, and procedures that meet the challenge of creating and administering internetworks. Figure 12-1 illustrates some different kinds of network technologies that can be interconnected by routers and other networking devices to create an internetwork.

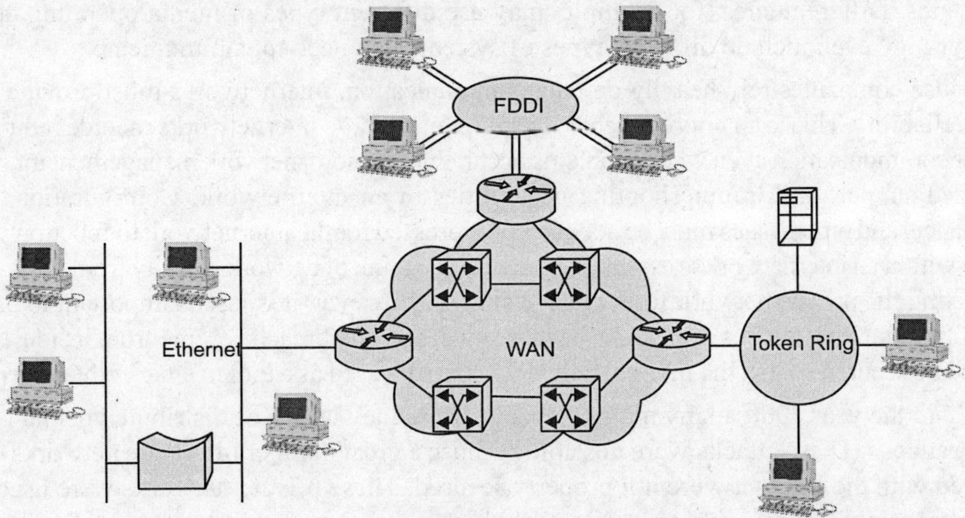

Fig. A1. 1 Different Network Technologies Can Be Connected to Create an Internetwork

A1.1.2 History of Internetworking

The first networks were time-sharing networks that used mainframes and attached terminals. Such environments were implemented by both IBM's Systems Network Architecture (SNA) and Digital's network architecture. Local-area networks (LANs) evolved around the PC revolution. LANs enabled multiple users in a relatively small geographical area to exchange files and messages, as well as access shared resources such as file servers and printers.

Wide-area networks (WANs) interconnect LANs with geographically dispersed users to create connectivity. Some of the technologies used for connecting LANs include T1, T3, ATM, ISDN, ADSL, Frame Relay, radio links, and others. New methods of connecting dispersed LANs are appearing everyday. Today, high-speed LANs and switched internetworks are becoming widely used, largely because they operate at very high speeds and support such high-bandwidth applications as multimedia and videoconferencing.

Internetworking evolved as a solution to three key problems: isolated LANs, duplication of resources, and a lack of network management. Isolated LANs made electronic communication between different offices or departments impossible. Duplication of resources meant that the same hardware and software had to be supplied to each office or department, as did separate support staff. This lack of network management meant that no centralized method of managing and troubleshooting networks existed.

A1.1.3 Internetworking Challenges

Implementing a functional internetwork is no simple task. Many challenges must be faced, especially in the areas of connectivity, reliability, network management, and flexibility. Each area is key in establishing an efficient and effective internetwork.

The challenge when connecting various systems is to support communication among disparate technologies. Different sites, for example, may use different types of media operating at varying speeds, or may even include different types of systems that need to communicate.

Because companies rely heavily on data communication, internetworks must provide a certain level of reliability. This is an unpredictable world, so many large internetworks include redundancy to allow for communication even when problems occur. Furthermore, network management must provide centralized support and troubleshooting capabilities in an internetwork. Configuration, security, performance, and other issues must be adequately addressed for the internetwork to function smoothly. Security within an internetwork is essential. Many people think of network security from the perspective of protecting the private network from outside attacks. However, it is just as important to protect the network from internal attacks, especially because most security breaches come from inside. Networks must also be secured so that the internal network cannot be used as a tool to attack other external sites.

Early in the year 2000, many major web sites were the victims of distributed denial of service (DDOS) attacks. These attacks were possible because a great number of private networks currently connected with the Internet were not properly secured. These private networks were used as tools for the attackers. Because nothing in this world is stagnant, internetworks must be flexible enough to change with new demands.

A1.2 OPEN SYSTEM INTERCONNECTION REFERENCE MODEL

The Open System Interconnection (OSI) reference model describes how information from a software application in one computer moves through a network medium to a software application in another computer. The OSI reference model is a conceptual model composed of seven layers, each specifying particular network functions. The model was developed by the International Organization for Standardization (ISO) in 1984, and it is now considered the primary architectural model for inter computer communications. The OSI model divides the tasks involved with moving information between networked computers into seven smaller, more manageable task groups. A task or group of tasks is then assigned to each of the seven OSI layers. Each layer is reasonably self-contained so that the tasks assigned to each layer can be implemented independently. This enables the solutions offered by one layer to be updated without adversely affecting the other layers. The following list details the seven layers of the Open System Interconnection (OSI) reference model:

- Layer 7—Application
- Layer 6—Presentation
- Layer 5—Session
- Layer 4—Transport
- Layer 3—Network
- Layer 2—Data link
- Layer 1—Physical

Note A handy way to remember the seven layers is the sentence "All people seem to need data processing." The beginning letter of each word corresponds to a layer.

- All—Application layer
- People—Presentation layer
- Seem—Session layer
- To—Transport layer
- Need—Network layer
- Data—Data link layer
- Processing—Physical layer

Fig. A1.2: illustrates the seven-layer OSI reference model.

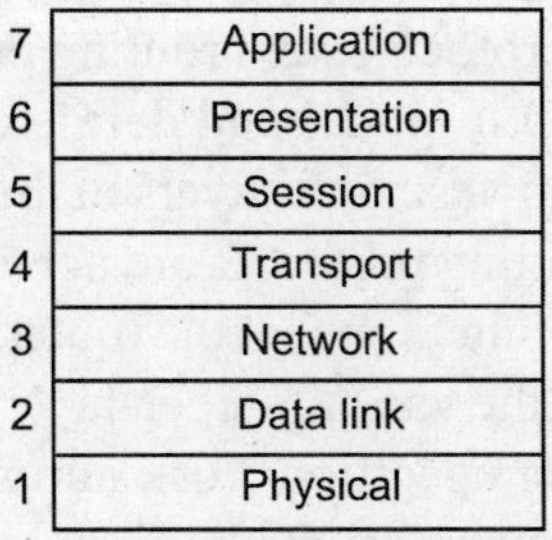

7	Application
6	Presentation
5	Session
4	Transport
3	Network
2	Data link
1	Physical

Fig. A1.2 The OSI Reference Model Contains Seven Independent Layers

A1.2.1 Characteristics of the OSI Layers

The seven layers of the OSI reference model can be divided into two categories: upper layers and lower layers.

The upper layers of the OSI model deal with application issues and generally are implemented only in software. The highest layer, the application layer, is closest to the end user. Both users and application layer processes interact with software applications that contain a communications component. The term upper layer is sometimes used to refer to any layer above another layer in the OSI model.

The lower layers of the OSI model handle data transport issues. The physical layer and the data link layer are implemented in hardware and software. The lowest layer, the physical layer, is closest to the physical network medium (the network cabling, for example) and is responsible for actually placing information on the medium. Figure A1-3 illustrates the division between the upper and lower OSI layers.

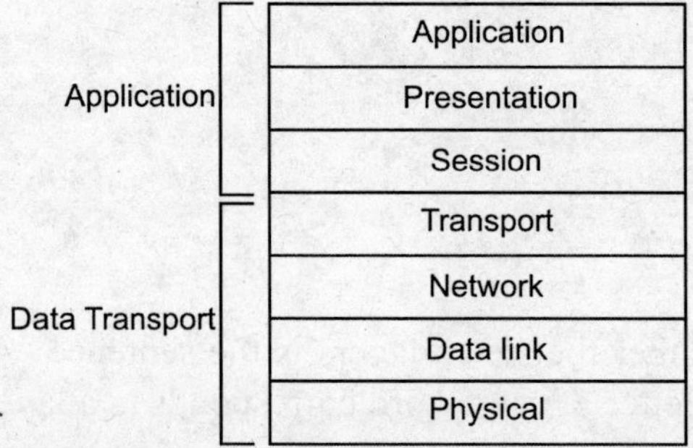

Fig. A1.3 Two Sets of Layers Make Up the OSI Layers

A1.2.2 Protocols

The OSI model provides a conceptual framework for communication between computers, but the model itself is not a method of communication. Actual communication is made possible by using communication protocols. In the context of data networking, a protocol is a formal set of rules and conventions that governs how computers exchange information over a network medium. A protocol implements the functions of one or more of the OSI layers.

A wide variety of communication protocols exist. Some of these protocols include LAN protocols, WAN protocols, network protocols, and routing protocols. LAN protocols operate at the physical and data link layers of the OSI model and define communication over the various LAN media. WAN protocols operate at the lowest three layers of the OSI model and define communication over the various wide-area media. Routing protocols are network layer protocols that are responsible for exchanging information between routers so that the routers can select the proper path for network traffic. Finally, network protocols are the various upper-layer protocols that exist in a given protocol suite. Many protocols rely on others for operation. For example, many routing protocols use network protocols to exchange information between routers. This concept of building upon the layers already in existence is the foundation of the OSI model.

A1.2.3 OSI Model and Communication Between Systems

Information being transferred from a software application in one computer system to a software application in another must pass through the OSI layers. For example, if a software application in System A has information to transmit to a software application in System B, the application program in System A will pass its information to the application layer (Layer 7) of System A. The application layer then passes the information to the presentation layer (Layer 6), which relays the data to the session layer (Layer 5), and so on down to the physical layer (Layer 1). At the physical layer, the information is placed on the physical network medium and is sent across the medium to System B. The physical layer of System B removes the information from the physical medium, and then its physical layer passes the information up to the data link layer (Layer 2), which passes it to the network layer (Layer 3), and so on, until it reaches the application layer (Layer 7) of System B. Finally, the application layer of System B passes the information to the recipient application program to complete the communication process.

A1.2.4 Interaction between OSI Model Layers

A given layer in the OSI model generally communicates with three other OSI layers: the layer directly above it, the layer directly below it, and its peer layer in other networked computer systems. The data link layer in System A, for example, communicates with the network layer of System A, the physical layer of System A, and the data link layer in System B. Figure A1-4 illustrates this example.

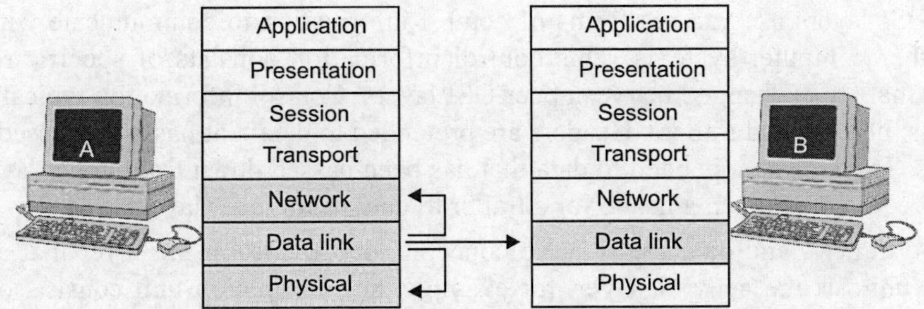

Fig. A1.4 OSI model layers communicate with other layers

A1.2.5 OSI Layer Services

One OSI layer communicates with another layer to make use of the services provided by the second layer. The services provided by adjacent layers help a given OSI layer communicate with its peer layer in other computer systems. Three basic elements are involved in layer services: the service user, the service provider, and the service access point (SAP).

In this context, the service user is the OSI layer that requests services from an adjacent OSI layer. The service provider is the OSI layer that provides services to service users. OSI layers can provide services to multiple service users. The SAP is a conceptual location at which one OSI layer can request the services of another OSI layer. Figure A1-5 illustrates how these three elements interact at the network and data link layers.

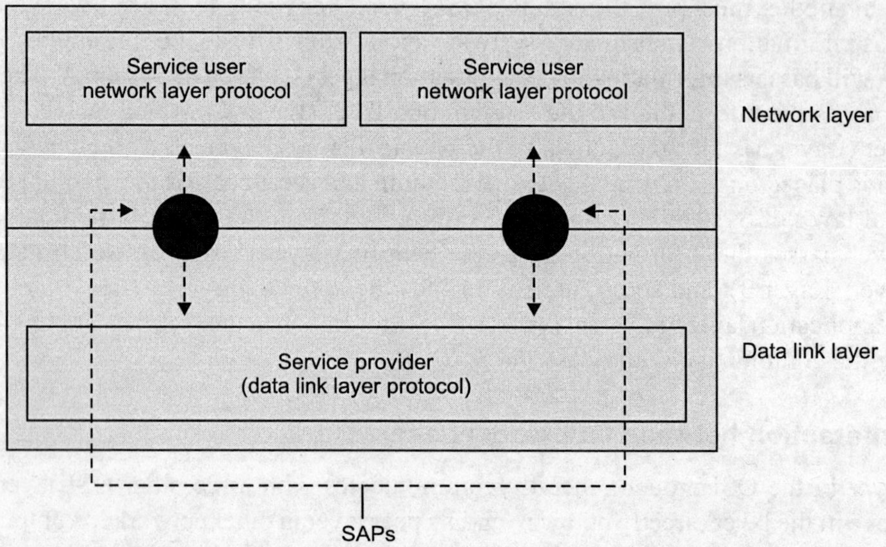

Fig. A1.5 Service users, providers, and SAPs interact at the network and data link layers

A1.2.6 OSI Model Layers and Information Exchange

The seven OSI layers use various forms of control information to communicate with their peer layers in other computer systems. This control information consists of specific requests and instructions that are exchanged between peer OSI layers. Control information typically takes one of two forms: headers and trailers. Headers are pretended to data that has been passed down from upper layers. Trailers are appended to data that has been passed down from upper layers. An OSI layer is not required to attach a header or a trailer to data from upper layers.

Headers, trailers, and data are relative concepts, depending on the layer that analyzes the information unit. At the network layer, for example, an information unit consists of a Layer 3 header and data. At the data link layer, however, all the information passed down by the network layer (the Layer 3 header and the data) is treated as data.

In other words, the data portion of an information unit at a given OSI layer potentially can contain headers, trailers, and data from all the higher layers. This is known as encapsulation. Figure A1-6 shows how the header and data from one layer are encapsulated into the header of the next lowest layer.

A1.2.7 Information Exchange Process

The information exchange process occurs between peer OSI layers. Each layer in the source system adds control information to data, and each layer in the destination system analyzes and removes the control information from that data.

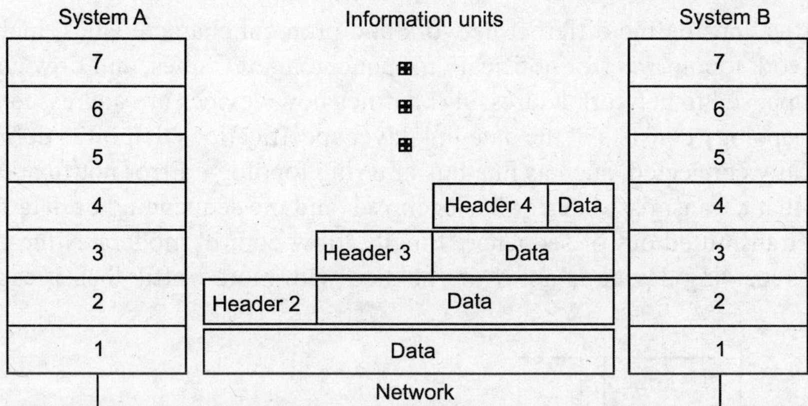

Fig. A1.6 Headers and data can be encapsulated during information exchange

If System A has data from software application to send to System B, the data is passed to the application layer. The application layer in System A then communicates any control information required by the application layer in System B by pretending a header to the data. The resulting information unit (a header and the data) is passed to the presentation layer, which pretends its own header containing control information intended for the presentation layer in System B. The information unit grows in size as each layer pretends its own header (and, in some cases, a trailer) that contains control information to be used by its peer layer in System B. At the physical layer, the entire information unit is placed onto the network medium.

The physical layer in System B receives the information unit and passes it to the data link layer. The data link layer in System B then reads the control information contained in the header pretended by the data link layer in System A. The header is then removed, and the remainder of the information unit is passed to the network layer. Each layer performs the same actions: The layer reads the header from its peer layer, strips it off, and passes the remaining information unit to the next highest layer. After the application layer performs these actions, the data is passed to the recipient software application in System B, in exactly the form in which it was transmitted by the application in System A.

A1.2.8 OSI Model Physical Layer

The physical layer defines the electrical, mechanical, procedural, and functional specifications for activating, maintaining, and deactivating the physical link between communicating network systems. Physical layer specifications define characteristics such as voltage levels, timing of voltage changes, physical data rates, maximum transmission distances, and physical connectors. Physical layer implementations can be categorized as either LAN or WAN specifications. Figure A1-7 illustrates some common LAN and WAN physical layer implementations.

A1.2.9 OSI Model Data Link Layer

The data link layer provides reliable transit of data across a physical network link. Different data link layer specifications define different network and protocol characteristics, including physical addressing, network topology, error notification, sequencing of frames, and flow control. Physical addressing (as opposed to network addressing) defines how devices are addressed at the data link layer. Network topology consists of the data link layer specifications that often define how devices are to be physically connected, such as in a bus or a ring topology. Error notification alerts upper-layer protocols that a transmission error has occurred, and the sequencing of data frames reorders frames that are transmitted out of sequence. Finally, flow control moderates the transmission of data so that the receiving device is not overwhelmed with more traffic than it can handle at one time.

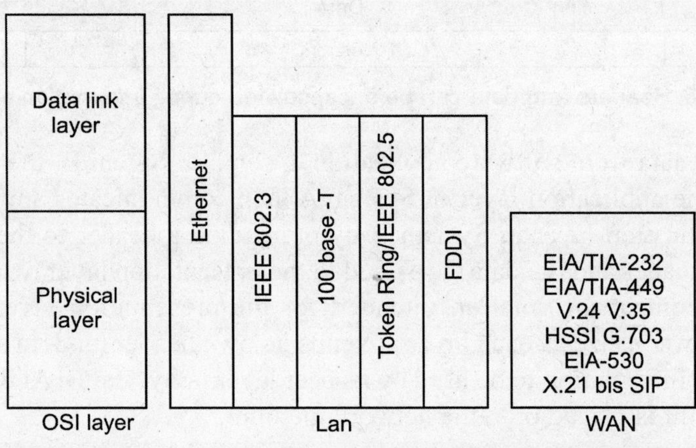

Fig. A1.7 Physical layer implementations can be LAN or WAN specifications

The Institute of Electrical and Electronics Engineers (IEEE) has subdivided the data link layer into two sub layers: Logical Link Control (LLC) and Media Access Control (MAC). Figure A1-8 illustrates the IEEE sub layers of the data link layer.

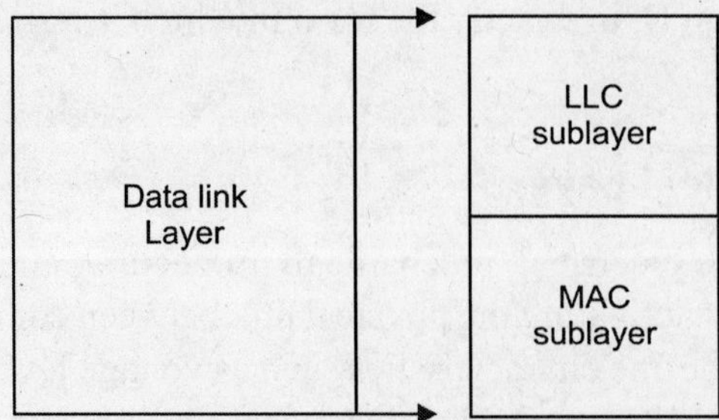

Fig. A1.8 The data link layer contains two sub layers

The Logical Link Control (LLC) sub layer of the data link layer manages communications between devices over a single link of a network. LLC is defined in the IEEE 802.2 specification and supports both connectionless and connection-oriented services used by higher-layer protocols. IEEE 802.2 defines a number of fields in data link layer frames that enable multiple higher-layer protocols to share a single physical data link. The Media Access Control (MAC) sub layer of the data link layer manages protocol access to the physical network medium. The IEEE MAC specification defines MAC addresses, which enable multiple devices to uniquely identify one another at the data link layer.

A1.2.10 OSI Model Network Layer

The network layer defines the network address, which differs from the MAC address. Some network layer implementations, such as the Internet Protocol (IP), define network addresses in a way that route selection can be determined systematically by comparing the source network address with the destination network address and applying the subnet mask. Because this layer defines the logical network layout, routers can use this layer to determine how to forward packets. Because of this, much of the design and configuration work for internetworks happens at Layer 3, the network layer.

A1.2.11 OSI Model Transport Layer

The transport layer accepts data from the session layer and segments the data for transport across the network. Generally, the transport layer is responsible for making sure that the data is delivered error-free and in the proper sequence. Flow control generally occurs at the transport layer.

Flow control manages data transmission between devices so that the transmitting device does not send more data than the receiving device can process. Multiplexing enables data from several applications to be transmitted onto a single physical link. Virtual circuits are established, maintained, and terminated by the transport layer. Error checking involves creating various mechanisms for detecting transmission errors, while error recovery involves acting, such as requesting that data be retransmitted, to resolve any errors that occur. The transport protocols used on the Internet are TCP and UDP.

A1.2.12 OSI Model Session Layer

The session layer establishes, manages, and terminates communication sessions. Communication sessions consist of service requests and service responses that occur between applications located in different network devices. These requests and responses are coordinated by protocols implemented at the session layer. Some examples of session-layer implementations include Zone Information Protocol (ZIP), the AppleTalk protocol that coordinates the name binding process; and Session Control Protocol (SCP), the DECnet Phase IV session layer protocol.

A1.2.13 OSI Model Presentation Layer

The presentation layer provides a variety of coding and conversion functions that are applied to application layer data. These functions ensure that information sent from the application layer of one system would be readable by the application layer of another system. Some examples of presentation layer coding and conversion schemes include common data representation formats, conversion of character representation formats, common data compression schemes, and common data encryption schemes.

Common data representation formats, or the use of standard image, sound, and video formats, enable the interchange of application data between different types of computer systems. Conversion schemes are used to exchange information with systems by using different text and data representations, such as EBCDIC and ASCII. Standard data compression schemes enable data that is compressed at the source device to be properly decompressed at the destination. Standard data encryption schemes enable data encrypted at the source device to be properly deciphered at the destination.

Presentation layer implementations are not typically associated with a particular protocol stack. Some well-known standards for video include QuickTime and Motion Picture Experts Group (MPEG). QuickTime is an Apple Computer specification for video and audio, and MPEG is a standard for video compression and coding. Among the well-known graphic image formats are Graphics Interchange Format (GIF), Joint Photographic Experts Group (JPEG), and Tagged Image File Format (TIFF). GIF is a standard for compressing and coding graphic images. JPEG is another compression and coding standard for graphic images, and TIFF is a standard coding format for graphic images.

A1.2.14 OSI Model Application Layer

The application layer is the OSI layer closest to the end user, which means that both the OSI application layer and the user interact directly with the software application. This layer interacts with software applications that implement a communicating component. Such application programs fall outside the scope of the OSI model. Application layer functions typically include identifying communication partners, determining resource availability, and synchronizing communication.

When identifying communication partners, the application layer determines the identity and availability of communication partners for an application with data to transmit. When determining resource availability, the application layer must decide whether sufficient network resources for the requested communication exist. In synchronizing communication, all communication between applications requires cooperation that is managed by the application layer. Some examples of application layer implementations include Telnet, File Transfer Protocol (FTP), and Simple Mail Transfer Protocol (SMTP).

A1.2.15 Information Formats

The data and control information that is transmitted through internetworks takes a variety of forms. The terms used to refer to these information formats are not used consistently in the internetworking industry but sometimes are used interchangeably. Common information formats include frames, packets, datagrams, segments, messages, cells, and data units.

A frame is an information unit whose source and destination are data link layer entities. A frame is composed of the data link layer header (and possibly a trailer) and upper-layer data. The header and trailer contain control information intended for the data link layer entity in the destination system. Data from upper-layer entities is encapsulated in the data link layer header and trailer. Figure A1-9 illustrates the basic components of a data link layer frame.

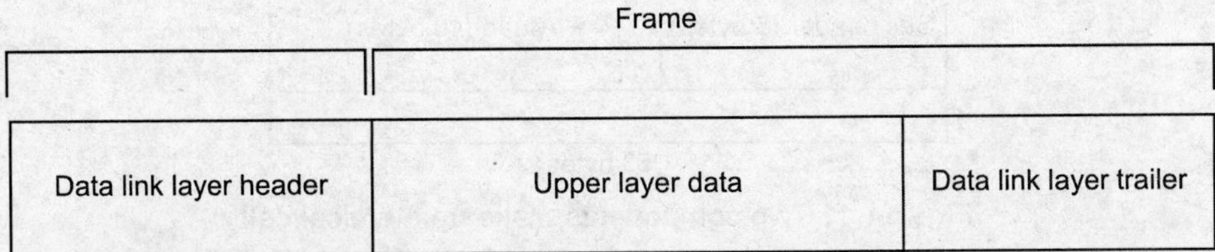

Fig. A1.9 Data from upper-layer entities makes up the data link layer frame

A packet is an information unit whose source and destination are network layer entities. A packet is composed of the network layer header (and possibly a trailer) and upper-layer data. The header and trailer contain control information intended for the network layer entity in the destination system. Data from upper-layer entities is encapsulated in the network layer header and trailer. Figure A1-10 illustrates the basic components of a network layer packet.

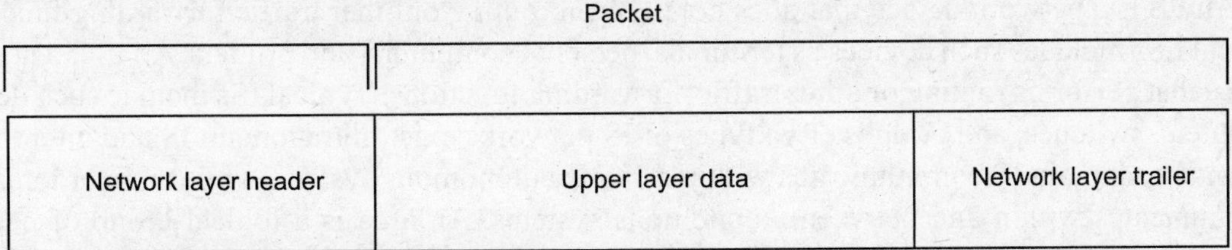

Fig. A1.10 Three basic components make up a network layer packet

The term datagram usually refers to an information unit whose source and destination are network layer entities that use connectionless network service.

The term segment usually refers to an information unit whose source and destination are transport layer entities. A message is an information unit whose source and destination entities exist above the network layer (often at the application layer).

A cell is an information unit of a fixed size whose source and destination are data link layer entities. Cells are used in switched environments, such as Asynchronous Transfer Mode (ATM) and Switched Multi megabit Data Service (SMDS) networks. A cell is composed of the header and payload. The header contains control information intended for the destination data link layer entity and is typically 5 bytes long. The payload contains upper-layer data that is encapsulated in the cell header and is typically 48 bytes long. The length of the header and the payload fields always are the same for each cell. Figure A1-11 depicts the components of a typical cell.

Data unit is a generic term that refers to a variety of information units. Some common data units are service data units (SDUs), protocol data units, and bridge protocol data units (BPDUs). SDUs are information units from upper-layer protocols that define a service request to a lower-layer protocol. PDU is OSI terminology for a packet. BPDUs are used by the spanning-tree algorithm as hello messages.

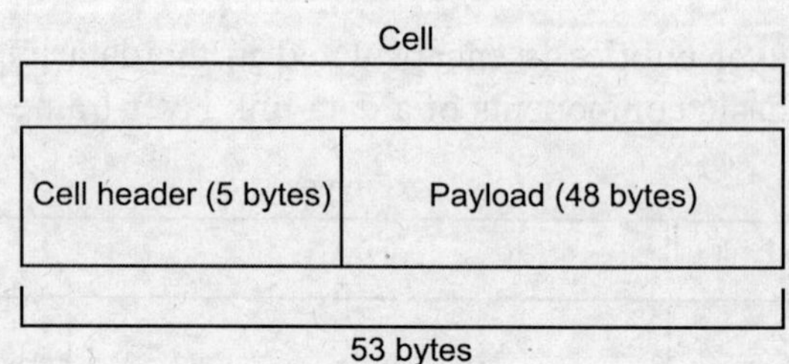

Fig. A1.11 Two components make up a typical cell

A1.3 ISO HIERARCHY OF NETWORKS

Large networks typically are organized as hierarchies. A hierarchical organization provides such advantages as ease of management, flexibility, and a reduction in unnecessary traffic. Thus, the International Organization for Standardization (ISO) has adopted a number of terminology conventions for addressing network entities. Key terms defined in this section include end system (ES), intermediate system (IS), area, and autonomous system (AS).

An ES is a network device that does not perform routing or other traffic forwarding functions. Typical ESs includes such devices as terminals, personal computers, and printers. An IS is a network device that performs routing or other traffic-forwarding functions. Typical ISs include such devices as routers, switches, and bridges. Two types of IS networks exist: intradomain IS and interdomain IS. An intradomain IS communicates within a single autonomous system, while an interdomain IS communicates within and between autonomous systems. An area is a logical group of network segments and their attached devices. Areas are subdivisions of autonomous systems (AS's). An AS is a collection of networks under a common administration that share a common routing strategy. Autonomous systems are subdivided into areas, and an AS is sometimes called a domain. Figure A1-12 illustrates a hierarchical network and its components.

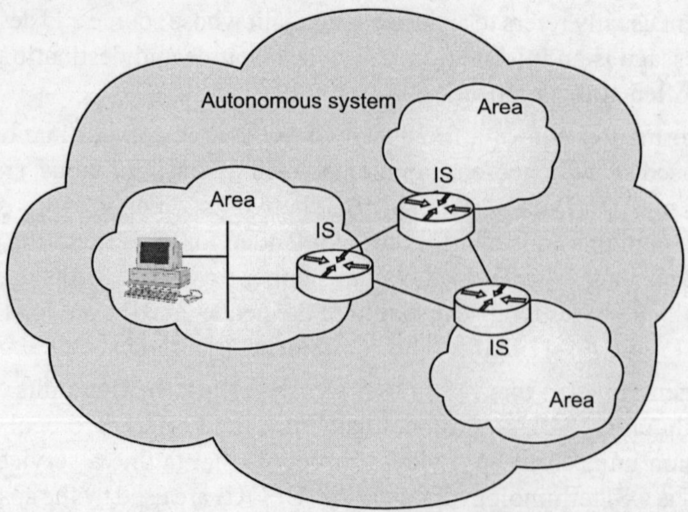

Fig. A1.12 A hierarchical network contains numerous components

A1.4 CONNECTION-ORIENTED AND CONNECTIONLESS NETWORK SERVICES

In general, transport protocols can be characterized as being either connection-oriented or connectionless. Connection-oriented services must first establish a connection with the desired service before passing any data. A connectionless service can send the data without any need to establish a connection first. In general, connection-oriented services provide some level of delivery guarantee, whereas connectionless services do not.

Connection-oriented service involves three phases: connection establishment, data transfer, and connection termination. During connection establishment, the end nodes may reserve resources for the connection. The end nodes also may negotiate and establish certain criteria for the transfer, such as a window size used in TCP connections. This resource reservation is one of the things exploited in some denial of service (DOS) attacks. An attacking system will send many requests for establishing a connection but then will never complete the connection. The attacked computer is then left with resources allocated for many never-completed connections. Then, when an end node tries to complete an actual connection, there are not enough resources for the valid connection.

The data transfer phase occurs when the actual data is transmitted over the connection. During data transfer, most connection-oriented services will monitor for lost packets and handle resending them. The protocol is generally also responsible for putting the packets in the right sequence before passing the data up the protocol stack.

When the transfer of data is complete, the end nodes terminate the connection and release resources reserved for the connection. Connection-oriented network services have more overhead than connectionless ones. Connection-oriented services must negotiate a connection, transfer data, and tear down the connection, whereas a connectionless transfer can simply send the data without the added overhead of creating and tearing down a connection. Each has its place in internetworks.

A1.5 INTERNETWORK ADDRESSING

Internetwork addresses identify devices separately or as members of a group. Addressing schemes vary depending on the protocol family and the OSI layer. Three types of internetwork addresses are commonly used: data link layer addresses, Media Access Control (MAC) addresses, and network layer addresses.

A1.5.1 Data Link Layer Addresses

A data link layer address uniquely identifies each physical network connection of a network device. Data-link addresses sometimes are referred to as physical or hardware addresses. Data-link addresses usually exist within a flat address space and have a pre-established and typically fixed relationship to a specific device.

End systems generally have only one physical network connection and thus have only one data-link address. Routers and other internetworking devices typically have multiple physical network connections and therefore have multiple data-link addresses. Figure 12-13 illustrates how each interface on a device is uniquely identified by a data-link address.

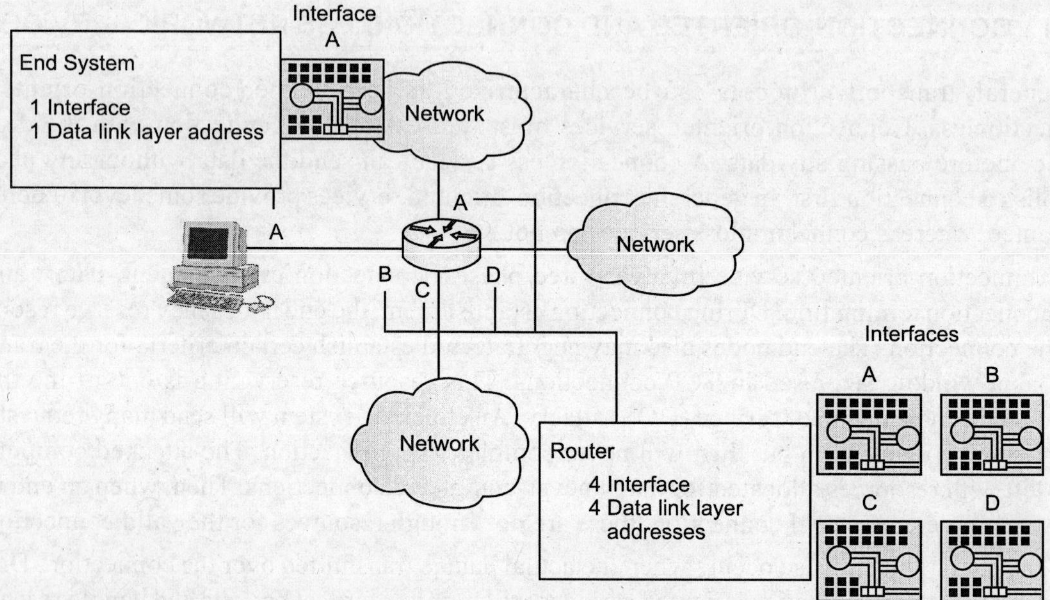

Fig. A1.13 Each interface on a device is uniquely identified by a data-link address.

A1.5.2 MAC Addresses

Media Access Control (MAC) addresses consist of a subset of data link layer addresses. MAC addresses identify network entities in LANs that implement the IEEE MAC addresses of the data link layer. As with most data-link addresses, MAC addresses are unique for each LAN interface. Figure A1-14 illustrates the relationship between MAC addresses, data-link addresses, and the IEEE sub layers of the data link layer.

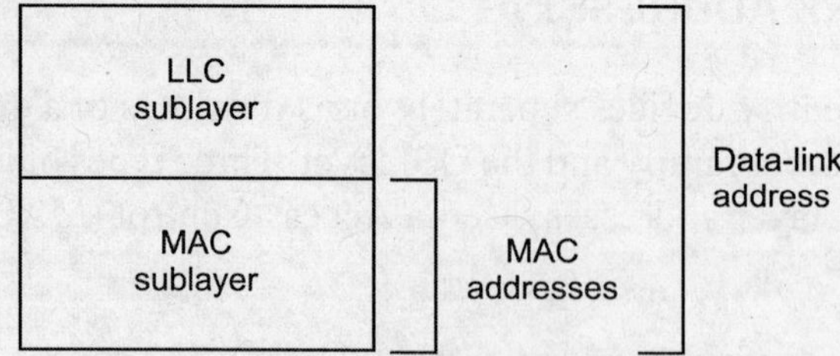

Fig. A1.14 MAC addresses, data-link addresses, and the IEEE sub layers of the data link layer are all related

MAC addresses are 48 bits in length and are expressed as 12 hexadecimal digits. The first 6 hexadecimal digits, which are administered by the IEEE, identify the manufacturer or vendor and thus comprise the Organizationally Unique Identifier (OUI). The last 6 hexadecimal digits comprise the interface serial number, or another value administered by the specific vendor. MAC addresses sometimes are called burned-in addresses (BIAs) because they are burned into read-only memory (ROM) and are copied into random-access memory (RAM) when the interface card initializes. Figure A1-15 illustrates the MAC address format.

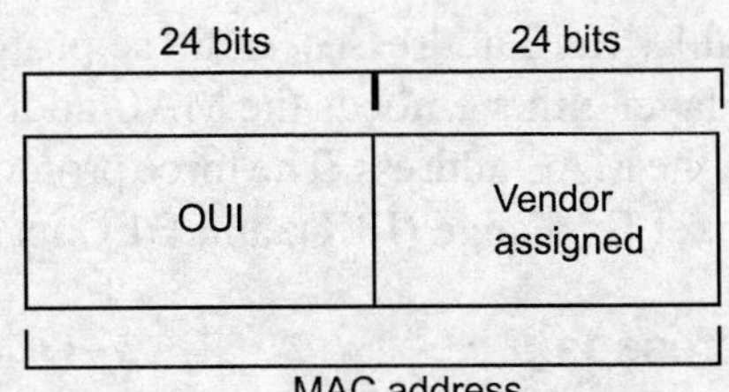

Fig. A1.15 The MAC address contains a unique format of hexadecimal digits

A1.5.3 Mapping Addresses

Because internetworks generally use network addresses to route traffic around the network, there is a need to map network addresses to MAC addresses. When the network layer has determined the destination station's network address, it must forward the information over a physical network using a MAC address. Different protocol suites use different methods to perform this mapping, but the most popular is Address Resolution Protocol (ARP).

Different protocol suites use different methods for determining the MAC address of a device. The following three methods are used most often. Address Resolution Protocol (ARP) maps network addresses to MAC addresses. The Hello protocol enables network devices to learn the MAC addresses of other network devices. MAC addresses either are embedded in the network layer address or are generated by an algorithm.

Address Resolution Protocol (ARP) is the method used in the TCP/IP suite. When a network device needs to send data to another device on the same network, it knows the source and destination network addresses for the data transfer. It must somehow map the destination address to a MAC address before forwarding the data. First, the sending station will check its ARP table to see if it has already discovered this destination station's MAC address. If it has not, it will send a broadcast on the network with the destination station's IP address contained in the broadcast.

Every station on the network receives the broadcast and compares the embedded IP address to its own. Only the station with the matching IP address replies to the sending station with a packet containing the MAC address for the station. The first station then adds this information to its ARP table for future reference and proceeds to transfer the data.

When the destination device lies on a remote network, one beyond a router, the process is the same except that the sending station sends the ARP request for the MAC address of its default gateway. It then forwards the information to that device. The default gateway will then forward the information over whatever networks necessary to deliver the packet to the network on which the destination device resides. The router on the destination device's network then uses ARP to obtain the MAC of the actual destination device and delivers the packet.

The Hello protocol is a network layer protocol that enables network devices to identify one another and indicate that they are still functional. When a new end system powers up, for example, it broadcasts hello messages onto the network. Devices on the network then return hello replies, and hello messages are also sent at specific intervals to indicate that they are still functional. Network devices can learn the MAC addresses of other devices by examining Hello protocol packets.

Three protocols use predictable MAC addresses. In these protocol suites, MAC addresses are predictable because the network layer either embeds the MAC address in the network layer address or uses an algorithm to determine the MAC address. The three protocols are Xerox Network Systems (XNS), Novell Internetwork Packet Exchange (IPX), and DECnet Phase IV.

A1.5.4 Network Layer Addresses

A network layer address identifies an entity at the network layer of the OSI layers. Network addresses usually exist within a hierarchical address space and sometimes are called virtual or logical addresses. The relationship between a network address and a device is logical and unfixed; it typically is based either on physical network characteristics (the device is on a particular network segment) or on groupings that have no physical basis (the device is part of an AppleTalk zone). End systems require one network layer address for each network layer protocol that they support. (This assumes that the device has only one physical network connection.) Routers and other internetworking devices require one network layer address per physical network connection for each network layer protocol supported. For example, a router with three interfaces each running AppleTalk, TCP/IP, and OSI must have three network layer addresses for each interface. The router therefore has nine network layer addresses. Figure A1-16 illustrates how each network interface must be assigned a network address for each protocol supported.

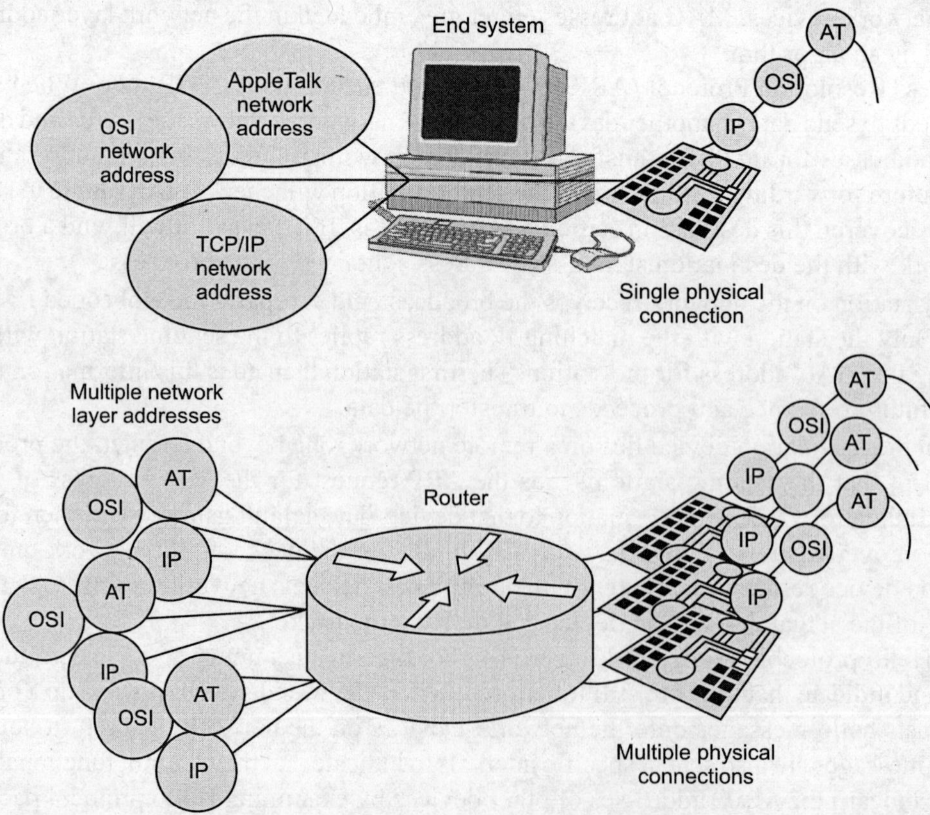

Fig. A1.16 Each network interface must be assigned a network address for each protocol supported

A1.5.5 Hierarchical Versus Flat Address Space

Internet work address space typically takes one of two forms: hierarchical address space or flat address space. A hierarchical address space is organized into numerous subgroups, each successively narrowing an address until it points to a single device (in a manner similar to street addresses). A flat address space is organized into a single group (in a manner similar to U.S. Social Security numbers).

Hierarchical addressing offers certain advantages over flat-addressing schemes. Address sorting and recall is simplified using comparison operations. For example, "Ireland" in a street address eliminates any other country as a possible location. Figure A1-17 illustrates the difference between hierarchical and flat address spaces.

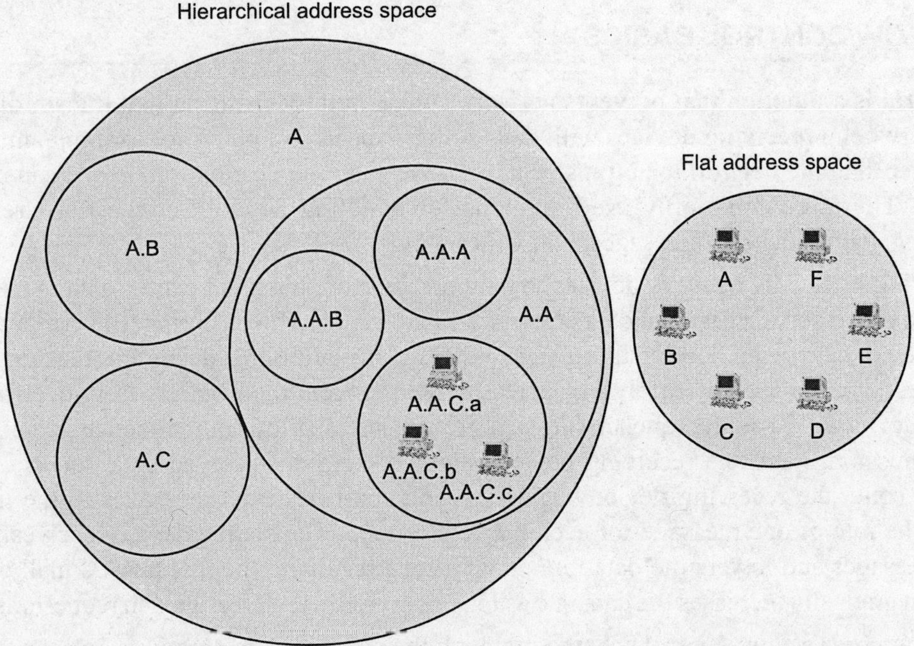

Fig. A1.17 Hierarchical and flat address spaces differ in comparison operations

A1.5.6 Address Assignments

Addresses are assigned to devices as one of two types: static and dynamic. Static addresses are assigned by a network administrator according to a preconceived internetwork addressing plan. A static address does not change until the network administrator manually changes it. Dynamic addresses are obtained by devices when they attach to a network, by means of some protocol-specific process. A device using a dynamic address often has a different address each time that it connects to the network. Some networks use a server to assign addresses. Server-assigned addresses are recycled for reuse as devices disconnect. A device is therefore likely to have a different address each time that it connects to the network.

A1.5.7 Addresses Versus Names

Internetwork devices usually have both a name and an address associated with them. Internetwork names typically are location-independent and remain associated with a device wherever that device moves (for example, from one building to another). Internetwork addresses usually are location-dependent and change when a device is moved (although MAC addresses are an exception to this rule). As with network addresses being mapped to MAC addresses, names are usually mapped to network addresses through some protocol. The Internet uses Domain Name System (DNS) to map the name of a device to its IP address. For example, it's easier for you to remember www.cisco.com instead of some IP address. Therefore, you type www.cisco.com into your browser when you want to access Cisco's web site. Your computer performs a DNS lookup of the IP address for Cisco's web server and then communicates with it using the network address.

A1.6 FLOW CONTROL BASICS

Flow control is a function that prevents network congestion by ensuring that transmitting devices do not overwhelm receiving devices with data. A high-speed computer, for example, may generate traffic faster than the network can transfer it, or faster than the destination device can receive and process it. The three commonly used methods for handling network congestion are buffering, transmitting source-quench messages, and windowing.

Buffering is used by network devices to temporarily store bursts of excess data in memory until they can be processed. Occasional data bursts are easily handled by buffering. Excess data bursts can exhaust memory, however, forcing the device to discard any additional datagrams that arrive. Source-quench messages are used by receiving devices to help prevent their buffers from overflowing. The receiving device sends source-quench messages to request that the source reduce its current rate of data transmission. First, the receiving device begins discarding received data due to overflowing buffers. Second, the receiving device begins sending source-quench messages to the transmitting device at the rate of one message for each packet dropped. The source device receives the source-quench messages and lowers the data rate until it stops receiving the messages. Finally, the source device then gradually increases the data rate as long as no further source-quench requests are received.

Windowing is a flow-control scheme in which the source device requires an acknowledgment from the destination after a certain number of packets have been transmitted. With a window size of 3, the source requires an acknowledgment after sending three packets, as follows. First, the source device sends three packets to the destination device. Then, after receiving the three packets, the destination device sends an acknowledgment to the source. The source receives the acknowledgment and sends three more packets. If the destination does not receive one or more of the packets for some reason, such as overflowing buffers, it does not receive enough packets to send an acknowledgment. The source then retransmits the packets at a reduced transmission rate.

A1.7 ERROR-CHECKING BASICS

Error-checking schemes determine whether transmitted data has become corrupt or otherwise damaged while traveling from the source to the destination. Error checking is implemented at several of the OSI layers. One common error-checking scheme is the cyclic redundancy check (CRC), which detects and discards corrupted data. Error-correction functions (such as data retransmission) are left to higher-layer protocols. A CRC value is generated by a calculation that is performed at the source device. The destination device compares this value to its own calculation to determine whether errors occurred during transmission. First, the source device performs a predetermined set of calculations over the contents of the packet to be sent. Then, the source places the calculated value in the packet and sends the packet to the destination. The destination performs the same predetermined set of calculations over the contents of the packet and then compares its computed value with that contained in the packet. If the values are equal, the packet is considered valid. If the values are unequal, the packet contains errors and is discarded.

A1.8 MULTIPLEXING BASICS

Multiplexing is a process in which multiple data channels are combined into a single data or physical channel at the source. Multiplexing can be implemented at any of the OSI layers. Conversely, demultiplexing is the process of separating multiplexed data channels at the destination. One example of multiplexing is when data from multiple applications is multiplexed into a single lower-layer data packet. Figure A1-18 illustrates this example.

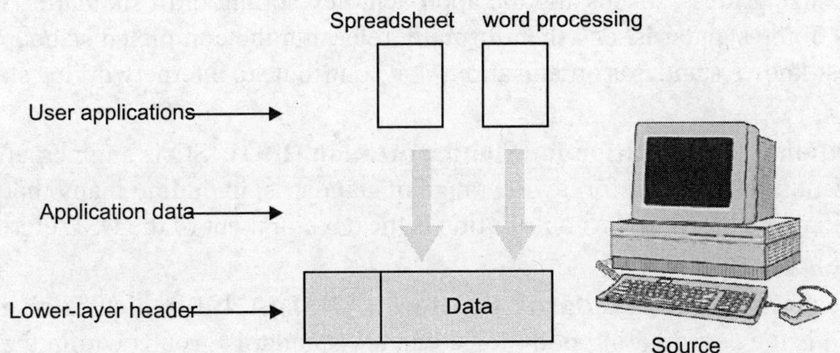

Fig. A1.18 Multiple applications can be multiplexed into a single lower-layer data packet

Another example of multiplexing is when data from multiple devices is combined into a single physical channel (using a device called a multiplexer). Figure A1-19 illustrates this example.

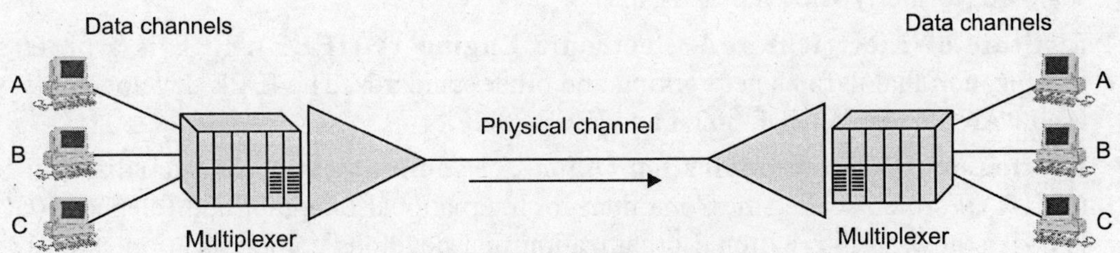

Fig. A1.19 Multiple devices can be multiplexed into a single physical channel

A multiplexer is a physical layer device that combines multiple data streams into one or more output channels at the source. Multiplexers demultiplex the channels into multiple data streams at the remote end and thus maximize the use of the bandwidth of the physical medium by enabling it to be shared by multiple traffic sources.

Some methods used for multiplexing data are time-division multiplexing (TDM), asynchronous time-division multiplexing (ATDM), frequency-division multiplexing (FDM), and statistical multiplexing.

In TDM, information from each data channel is allocated bandwidth based on preassigned time slots, regardless of whether there is data to transmit. In ATDM, information from data channels is allocated bandwidth as needed by using dynamically assigned time slots. In FDM, information from each data channel is allocated bandwidth based on the signal frequency of the traffic. In statistical multiplexing, bandwidth is dynamically allocated to any data channels that have information to transmit.

A1.9 STANDARDS ORGANIZATIONS

A wide variety of organizations contribute to internetworking standards by providing forums for discussion, turning informal discussion into formal specifications, and proliferating specifications after they are standardized. Most standards organizations create formal standards by using specific processes: organizing ideas, discussing the approach, developing draft standards, voting on all or certain aspects of the standards, and then formally releasing the completed standard to the public. Some of the best-known standards organizations that contribute to internetworking standards include these:

- **International Organization for Standardization (ISO):**ISO is an international standards organization responsible for a wide range of standards, including many that are relevant to networking. Its best-known contribution is the development of the OSI reference model and the OSI protocol suite.
- **American National Standards Institute (ANSI):**ANSI, which is also a member of the ISO, is the coordinating body for voluntary standards groups within the United States. ANSI developed the Fiber Distributed Data Interface (FDDI) and other communications standards.
- **Electronic Industries Association (EIA):**EIA specifies electrical transmission standards, including those used in networking. The EIA developed the widely used EIA/TIA-232 standard (formerly known as RS-232).
- **Institute of Electrical and Electronic Engineers (IEEE):**IEEE is a professional organization that defines networking and other standards. The IEEE developed the widely used LAN standards IEEE 802.3 and IEEE 802.5.
- **International Telecommunication Union Telecommunication Standardization Sector (ITU-T) :**Formerly called the Committee for International Telegraph and Telephone (CCITT), ITU-T is now an international organization that develops communication standards. The ITU-T developed X.25 and other communications standards.

- **Internet Activities Board (IAB) :**IAB is a group of internetwork researchers who discuss issues pertinent to the Internet and set Internet policies through decisions and task forces. The IAB designates some Request For Comments (RFC) documents as Internet standards, including Transmission Control Protocol/Internet Protocol (TCP/IP) and the Simple Network Management Protocol (SNMP).
- **Networking and Internetworking:** Networking and Internetworking. Networking and Internetworking

A1.10 INTER-PROCESS COMMUNICATION

A capability supported by some operating systems that allows one process to communicate with another process. The processes can be running on the same computer or on different computers connected through a network. IPC enables one application to control another application, and for several applications to share the same data without interfering with one another. IPC is required in all multiprocessing systems, but it is not generally supported by single-process operating systems such as DOS. OS/2 and MS-Windows support an IPC mechanism called DDE.

Inter-Process Communication (IPC) is a set of techniques for the exchange of data between two or more *threads* in one or more *processes*. Processes may be running on one computer or on two or more computers connected by a *network*. IPC techniques are divided into methods for *message passing*, *synchronization*, *shared memory*, and *remote procedure calls* (RPC). The method of IPC used may vary based on the bandwidth and latency of communication between the threads, and the type of data being communicated. It is widely accepted that IPC can be implemented significantly faster in a *microkernel* environment than in classical *monolithic kernel* systems. IPC may also be referred to as inter-thread communication and inter-application communication.

A1.10.1 Implementations

There are a number of *APIs* which may be used for IPC. A number of platform independent APIs include the following:

- *Anonymous pipes* and *named pipes*
- *Sockets*
- *Distributed Computing Environment* (DCE)
- *Common Object Request Broker Architecture* (CORBA)
- *Message Bus* (MBUS) (specified in *RFC 3259*)
- *XML XML-RPC* or SOAP
- *ZeroC*'s Internet Communications Engine (ICE)

The following are platform specific APIs:

- *Apple Computer*'s *Apple events* (previously known as Interapplication Communications (IAC)).
- *Freedesktop.org*'s *D-Bus*
- *KDE*'s *Desktop Communications Protocol* (DCOP)

- The *Mach kernel*'s *Mach Ports*
- *Microsoft*'s *ActiveX*, *Component Object Model* (COM), *Distributed Component Object Model* (DCOM), *Dynamic Data Exchange* (DDE), *Object Linking and Embedding* (OLE), *anonymous pipes*, *named pipes*, *Local Procedure Call*
- *Novell*'s *SPX*
- *POSIX mmap*, message queues, semaphores, and shared memory
- *RISC OS*'s messages
- *Solaris*'s *Doors*
- *Sun Microsystems*' *RPC*
- *System V*'s message queues, semaphores, and shared memory

A1.10.2 Table of IPC Methods

Method	Provided by (*Operating systems* or other environments)
File	All operating systems
Signal	Most operating systems; some systems, such as Windows, only implement signals in the C run-time library and do not actually provide support for their use as an IPC technique.
Socket	Most operating systems.
Pipe	All POSIX systems.
Named pipe	All POSIX systems
Semaphore	All POSIX systems
Shared memory	All POSIX systems
Message passing (shared nothing)	Used in *MPI* paradigm, *Java RMI*, *CORBA* and others.
Memory map	All *POSIX systems;* may carry *race condition* risk if a temporary file is used. Windows also supports this technique but the APIs used are platform specific.
Message queue	Most *operating systems.*
Mailbox	Some *operating systems*

A1.11 WIDE AREA NETWORK TECHNOLOGIES

A wide area network or WAN, spans a large geographical area, often a country or continent. It contains a collection of machines intended for running user (i.e. application) programs.

In most WANs, the subnet consists of two distinct components

- Transmission Lines
- Switching Element.

Transmission lines (also called circuits, or channel) more bits between machines. The switching elements are specialized computers used to connect two or more transmission lines. When data arrive on an incoming line, the switching element must choose an outgoing line to forward them on.

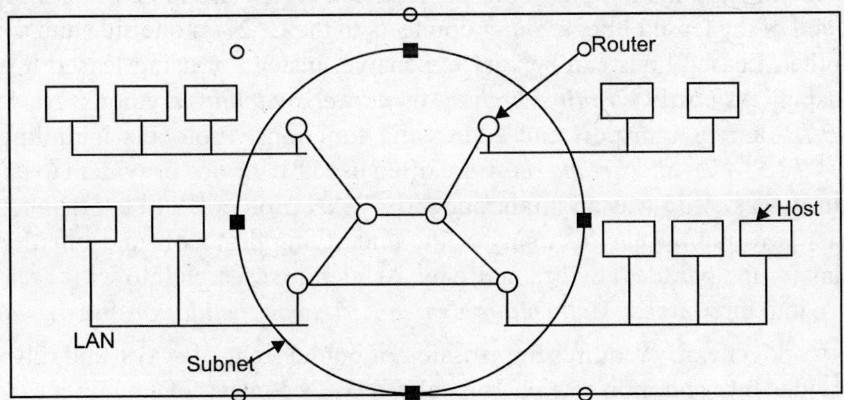

Fig. A1.20 Relation between hosts and subnet

In most WANs, the network contains numerous cables or telephone lines, each one onnecting a pair of routers. If two routers that do not share a cable nevertheless wish to communicate, they must do this in directory, via other routers, when a packet is sent from one router to another via one or more intermediate routers, the packet is received at each inter mediate router in its entirely, stored until the required output line is free, and then forwarded. A subnet using this principle is called a point-to-point, store and forward or packet – switched subnet.

Wide Area Networks typically have irregular topologies. WAN Bandwidth for data communications is a critical issue. In terminal to host N/W, traffic generated by applications could be modeled and the network would then be sized accordingly, enabling effective use of the Bandwidth.

With LAN inter connections and application that enable users to transfer large files (such as through e-mail attachment) and images; this modeling is much harder to perform. In the short term, the chances are even more dramatic as the migration from a host centric environment to a distributed client/server environment prevents the use of any past experience in guessing the actual network requirements.

Network managers must cope with these changes by seeking those technologies that will let them acquire bandwidth cost effectively while allowing flexibility t serve these new applications. WAN services have recently emerged that address this issue by providing the appropriate flexibility inherently required for these applications.

A1.11.1 Wide Area Network

A wide area network or **WAN** is a *computer network* covering a broad geographical area. Contrast with *personal area networks* (PANs), *local area networks* (LANs) or *metropolitan area networks* (MANs) that are usually limited to a room, building or campus. The largest and most well-known example of a WAN is the *Internet*.

WANs are used to connect *local area networks* (LANs) together, so that users and computers in one location can communicate with users and computers in other locations. Many WANs are built for one particular organization and are private. Others, built by *Internet service providers*, provide connections from an organization's LAN to the Internet. WANs are most often built using *leased lines*. At each end of the leased line, a *router* connects to the LAN on one side and a hub within the WAN on the other. Leased lines can be very expensive. Instead of using leased lines, WANs can also be built using less costly *circuit switching* or *packet switching* methods. Network *protocols* including *TCP/IP* deliver transport and addressing functions. Protocols including *Packet over SONET/SDH*, *MPLS*, *ATM* and *Frame relay* are often used by service providers to deliver the links that are used in WANs. *X.25* was an important early WAN protocol, and is often considered to be the "grandfather" of Frame Relay as many of the underlying protocols and functions of *X.25* are still in use today (with upgrades) by Frame Relay. Academic research into wide area networks can be broken down into three areas: *Mathematical models*, *network emulation* and *network simulation*.

Such a network generally requires the crossing of public right-of-ways, and rely at least in part on circuits provided by a common carrier, Typically, a WAN consists of a number of interconnected switching nodes. A transmission from any one device is routed through these internal nodes to the specified destination device. These nodes (including the boundary nodes) are not concerned with the contents of data; rather their purpose is to provide a switching facility that will move the data from node to node until they reach their destination. Performance improvements are sometimes delivered via *WAFS* or *WAN Optimization*.

A1.11.2 WAN connectivity options

Several options are available for WAN connectivity:

Option	Description	Advantages	Disadvan-tage	Bandwidth range	Sample protocols used
Leased line	Point-to-Point connection between two computers	Most secure	Expensive		PPP, HDLC, SDLC
Circuit switching	A dedicated circuit path is created between end points Best example is eialup connections		Call set up		PPP, ISDN
Packet switching	Devices transport packets via a shared single point-to-point or point-to-multipoint link across a carrier internet work. Variable length packts are				X.25 Frame-Relay

	transmitted over Permanent Virtual Circuits (PVC) or Switched Virtual Circuits (SVC)				
Call relay	Similar to packet switching, but uses fixed length cells instead of variable length packets, data is divided into fixed length cells and then transported across virtual circuits	Best for symultaneous use of Voice and data	Overhead can be considerable		ATM

Transmission rate usually range from 1200 bits/second to 6 Mbit/s. Typical communication links used in WANs are telephone lines, microwave links & satellite channels.

A1.11.3 Wide Area Network Technologies Overview

A Wide Area Network (WAN) is a computer network covering multiple distance areas, which may spread across the entire world. WANs often connect multiple smaller networks, such as local area networks (LANs) or metro area networks (MANs). The world's most popular WAN is the Internet. Some segments of the Internet are also WANs in themselves. The key difference between WAN and LAN technologies is scalability C WAN must be able to grow as needed to cover multiple cities, even countries and continents.

A set of switches and routers are interconnected to form a Wide Area Network. The switches can be connected in different topologies such as full mesh and half mesh. A wide area network may be privately owned or rented from a service provider, but the term usually connotes the inclusion of public (shared user) networks.

Both packet switching and circuit switching technologies are used in the WAN. Packet switching allows users to share common carrier resources so that the carrier can make more efficient use of its infrastructure. In a packet switching setup, networks have connections into the carrier's network, and many customers share the carrier's network. The carrier can then create virtual circuits between customers' sites by which packets of data are delivered from one to the other through the network.

Circuit Switching allows data connections to be established when needed and then terminated when communication is complete. This works like a normal telephone line works for voice communication. Integrated Services Digital Network (ISDN) is a good example of circuit switching. When a router has data for a remote site, the switched circuit is initiated with the circuit number of the remote network.

Virtual private network (VPN) is a tecnology widely used in a public switched network (PSTN) to provide private and secured WAN for an organization. VPN uses encryption and other techniques to make it appear that the organisation has a dedicated network, while making use of the shared infrastructure of the WAN.

WAN technologies generally function at the lower three layers of the OSI reference model: the physical layer, the data link layer, and the network layer. Key technologies often found in WANs include SONET, Frame Relay, X.25, ATM and PPP.

- ATM: A dedicated-connection switching technology that organizes digital data into 53-byte cell units. Individually, a cell is processed asynchronously relative to other related cells and is queued before being multiplexed over the transmission path. Speeds on ATM networks can reach 10 Gbps.
- Frame Relay: (FR). A high-speed packet-switched data communications service, similar to X.25. Frame relay is widely used for LAN-to-LAN interconnect services, and is well suited to the bursty demands of LAN environments.
- SONET/SDH: Synchronous Optical Network is an international standard for high speed communication over fiber-optic networks. The SONET establishes Optical Carrier (OC) levels from 51.8 Mbps to 10 Gbps (OC-192) or even higher. Synchronous Digital Hierarchy (SDH) is a European equivalent of SONET.
- X.25: The X.25 protocol allows computers on different public networks to communicate through an intermediary computer at the network layer level.
- PPP: A *point-to-point link* provides a single, pre-established WAN communications path from the customer premises through a carrier network, such as a telephone company, to a remote network. Point-to-point lines are usually leased from a carrier and thus are often called leased lines. For a point-to-point line, the carrier allocates pairs of wire and facility hardware to your line only.

IP can also be considered as a WAN technology in the packet switching environment

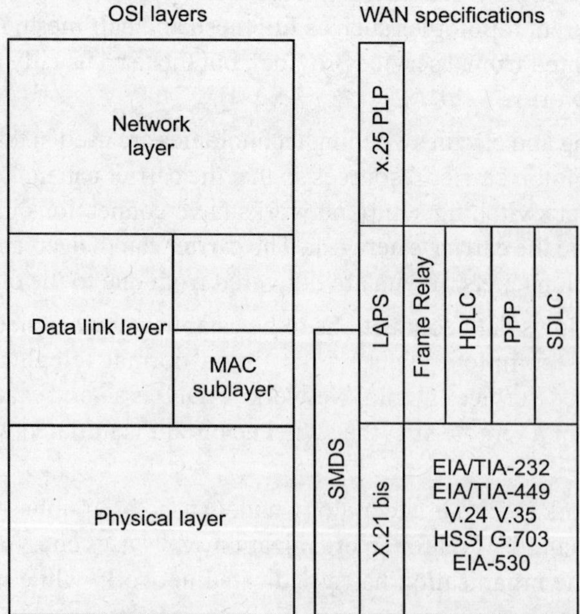

Fig. A1. 21 Wide area network technologies overview

A1.11.4 Wide Area Networks (WAN)

The size of a network is limited due to size and distance constraints. However networks may be connected over a high speed communications link (called a WAN link) to link them together and thus become a WAN. WAN links are usually:

- Dial up connection
- Dedicated connection - It is a permanent full time connection. When a dedicated connection is used, the cable is leased rather than a part of the cable bandwidth and the user has exclusive use.
- Switched network - Several users share the same line or the bandwidth of the line. There are two types of switched networks:
    1. Circuit switching - This is a temporary connection between two points such as dial-up or ISDN.
    2. Packet switching - This is a connection between multiple points. It breaks data down into small packets to be sent across the network. A virtual circuit can improve performance by establishing a set path for data transmission. This will shave some overhead of a packet switching network. A variant of packet switching is called cell-switching where the data is broken into small cells with a fixed length.

A1.11.5 WAN Connection Technologies

- X.25 - This is a set of protocols developed by the CCITT/ITU which specifies how to connect computer devices over an internetwork. These protocols use a great deal of error checking for use over unreliable telephone lines. They establish a virtual communication circuit. It uses a store and forward method which can cause about a half second delay in data reception when two way communications are used. Their speed is about 64Kbps. normally X.25 is used on packed switching PDNs (Public Data Networks). A line must be leased from the LAN to a PDN to connect to an X.25 network. A PAD (packet assembler/disassembler) or an X.25 interface is used on a computer to connect to the X.25 network. CCITT is an abbreviation for International Telegraph and Telephone Consultative Committee. The ITU is the International Telecommunication Union.
- Frame Relay - Error checking is handled by devices at both sides of the connection. Frame relay uses frames of varying length and it operates at the data link layer of the OSI model. A permanent virtual circuit (PVC) is established between two points on the network. Frame relay speed is between 56Kbps and 1.544Mbps. Frame relay networks provide a high-speed connection up to 1.544Mbps using variable-length packet-switching over digital fiber-optic media. Frame relay does not store data and has less error checking than X.25.
- Switched Multi-megabit Data Service (SMDS) - Uses fixed length cell switching and runs at speeds of 1.533 to 45Mbps. It provides no error checking and assumes devices at both ends provide error checking.
- Telephone connections

- Dial up
- Leased lines-These are dedicated analog lines or digital lines. Dedicated digital lines are called digital data service (DDS) lines. A modem is used to connect to analog lines, and a Channel Service Unit/Data Service Unit or Digital Service Unit(CSU/DSU) is used to connect to digital lines. The DSU connects to the LAN and the CSU connects to the line.
- T Carrier lines - Multiplexors are used to allow several channels on one line. The T1 line is basic T Carrier service. The available channels may be used separately for data or voice transmissions or they may be combined for more transmission bandwidth. The 64Kbps data transmission rate is referred to as DS-0 (Digital Signal level 0) and a full T1 line is referred to as DS-1.

Signal	System	Total Kbps	Channels	Number of equivalent T 1 lines
DS–1	T1	1544	24	1
DS–2	T2	6312	96	4
DS–3	T3	44736	672	28
DS–4	T4	274760	4032	3668

- T1 and T3 lines are the most common lines in use today. T1 and T2 lines can use standard copper wire. T3 and T4 lines require fiber-optic cable or other high-speed media. These lines may be leased partially called fractional T1 or fractional T3 which means a customer can lease a certain number of channels on the line. A CSU/DSU and a bridge or router is required to connect to a T1 line.
- Integrated Services Digital Network (ISDN) - Comes in two types and converts analog signals to digital for transmission. It is a dial up service
- Basic Rate ISDN (BRI) - Two 64Kbps B-channels with one 16Kbps D channel. The D-channel is used tor call control and setup.
- Primary Rate ISDN (PRI) - 23 B-channels and one D channel.

  A device resembling a modem (called an ISDN modem) is used to connect to ISDN. The computer and telephone line are plugged into it.
- Switched-56 - A switched line similar to a leased line where customers pay for the time they use the line. Speed is 56Kbps. It is not dedicated and will not work to connect a WAN.
- Asynchronous Transfer Mode (ATM) - May be used over a variety of media with both baseband and broadband systems. It is used for audio, video, and data. It uses fixed length data packets of 53 8 bit bytes called cell switching. 5 bytes contain header information.
- The cell contains path information that the packet is to use. It uses hardware devices to perform the switching of the data. Speeds from 155Mbps to 622 Mbps are achieved. Error checking is done at the receiving device, not by ATM. A permanent virtual connection or circuit (PVC) is established. It may also use a switched virtual circuit (SVC). Service classes:

- Constant bit rate for data.
- Variable bit rate for audio or video.
- Connection less for data.
- Connection oriented for data.

ATM can be embedded in other protocols such as ATM-25, T1, T3, OC-1, OC-3, OC-12, and OC-48. Some ATM technologies include:

- ATM-25 - 25Mbps speed.
- STS-3 - 155Mbps on fiber or category 5 cable.
- STS-12 - 620 Mbps on fiber cable for campus wide network.
- STS-48 - 2.2 Gbps on fiber cable on a MAN.
- STS-192 - 8.8 Gbps on fiber cable on intercity long distance. This is normally used by phone companies.
- Synchronous Optical Network (SONET) - A physical layer standard that defines voice, data, and video delivery methods over fiber optic media. It defines data rates in terms of optical carrier (OC) levels. The transmission rate of OC-1 is 51.8 Mbps. Each level runs at a multiple of the first. The OC-5 data rate is 5 times 51.8 Mbps which is 259 Mbps. SONET also defines synchronous transport signals (STS) for copper media which use the same speed scale of OC levels. STS-3 runs at the same speed of OC-3. Mesh or ring topology is used to support SONET. SONET uses multiplexing. The ITU has incorporated SONET into their Synchronous Digital Hierarchy (SDH) recommendations

A1.11.6 WAN Technology comparisons

Technology	Speed	Characteristics
Switched 56	56 Kbps	Switched line, not dedicated
X.25	64 Kbps	Packet switching, error correction, store and foreward, with round trip delay
Frame Relay	56 Kbps to 1.544 Mbps	Varying length frames with permanent virtual circuit
SMDS	1.533 to 45 Mbps	Fixed cell length with no error checking
T1	1.544 Mbps	24 Multiplexed channels
T3	44.736 Mbps	672 Multiplexed channels
SONET	51.8 Mbps (OC–1)	OC2 is 2 □ OC1, OC3 is 3 □ OC1
ATM	155 Mbps to 622 Mbps	Fixed length packets, works on SONET and T carrier lines. Uses virtual circuits

A1.12 FRAME RELAY

Frame Relay is a service for people, who want an absolute bare – bones connection oriented way to move bits from A to B at reasonable speed and low cost.

Twenty years ago, communication using telephone lines was slow, analog & unreliable and computers were slow and expensive. As a result, complex protocols were required t mask errors and the users computers were too expensive to have them to do this work.

The leased lines (leased telephone lines) are now fast, digital and reliable, and computers are fast and inexpensive. This suggests the use of simple protocols with must of the work being done by the users computers, rather than by the network. Is this environment that frame relay addresses.

Frame Relay can be thought of as a virtual leased line. The customer leases a permanent virtual circuit between two points and then send Frames (i.e. packets) of upto 1600 bytes between them. It is also possible to lease permanent virtual circuits between a given site and multiple other sits, so each frame carries a 10 bit number telling which virtual circuit to use.

Frame Relay Networks are often qualified as virtual private networks. They share a public infrastructure but implement virtual circuits between the senders and the receivers, similar to actual circuits. It is therefore a connection oriented network.

The difference between an actual leased line and a virtual leased line is that with an actual one, the user can send traffic all day long at the maximum speed with a virtual one, data bursts may be sent at full speed, but the long term average usage must be below a predetermined level.

In addition to competition with leased lines, frame relay also competes with X.25 Permanent virtual circuits, excepts that it operates at higher speeds usually 1.5 Mbps. Frame Relay provides a minimal services.

A1.13 SWITCHED MULTI MEGABIT DATA SERVICES (SMDS)

Switched Multi megabit Data Service (SMDS) is a Connectionless, high speed, packet switched data service. SMDS is used to interconnect distribute corporate LANs and WANs through the public Networks, because it is connectionless, SMDS elements, the need for carrier switches to establish a call path between two points of data transmission.

SMDS uses the IEEE 802.6 protocol, which has developed as a Metropolitan- area- network. The IEEE Qo2.6standarel is often described as a cell relay Technology. The IEEE 802.6 pockets called cells have a fixed size of 53 octets, 48 octets for data and 5 octets for the address header.

SMDS access devices pass 53 byte cells to a carrier switch. The switch reads addresses and forwards cells one by one over any available path to the desired endpoint.

Advantage (Benefits)

(i) Reduce the need for precise traffic flow predictions over the entire networks.

(ii) Relies only on connections between fixed locations.

(iii) No need for a pre defined path between devices.

(iv) Data can travel over the least congested routers.

(v) Providing faster transmission

(vi) Increased security.

(vii) Greater flexibility to add or drop network sites.

SMDS defines a three-tiered Architecture:

(i) A switching infrastructure comprising SMDS compatible switches.

(ii) A delivery system made up of T-1 and T-3 circuits called subscriber Network interfaces (SNIs)

(iii) An Access control system for users to connect to the switching infrastructure.

Note: Connecting a LAN to an SMDS Network requires only a router and an SMDS compatible network interface card.

A1.14 ATM IN THE WIDE AREA NETWORK

ATM scheme is widely used for data communication network. ATM Network uses the ATM switch, which receives the requests for data transfer from different computers. The ATM switch facilitates the data Transmission in Asynchronous mode. Various computers are connected to the ATM switch, the ATM switch connects the senders and receivers computers and transfer the packets to destination at a high speed. ATM Network is similar to star Network.

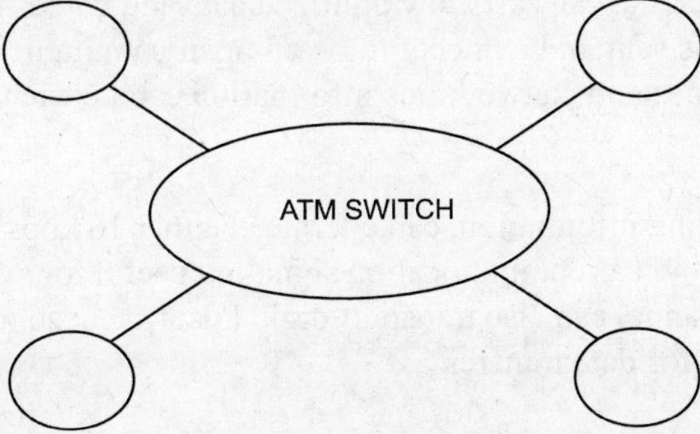

Fig. A1.22 ATM Switch

Note: ATM Network (Switch) is more reliable or suitable for multimedia data transfer, which contains the text audio and video. The speed of communication between the computers and ATM switch is 155 Mbps.

The basic idea behind ATM is to transmit all information in small fixed size packets called cells. The cells are 53 bytes long of which 5 bytes are header and 48 bytes for data. The ATM uses cell switching technology and is also known as cell (switching) relay service.

The cell switching technology has got the following advantages on traditional circuit switching technology-

(i) It is highly flexible and can handle both fixed rate and variable rate traffic equally well.

(ii) At the high speed envisioned, digital switching of cells is easier than using traditional multiplexing techniques.

(iii) For Television distribution broad casting is essential, cell switching can provide this and circuit switching can not.

ATM networks are connection-oriented making call require First sending a message to set up the connection; After that subsequent calls are follow the same path to the destination. Cell delivery is not guaranteed but their order is guaranteed.

The intended speeds for ATM networks are 155 Mbps and 622 Mbps. The speed 155 Mbps are chosen because this is the speed needed to transmit high definition television. ATM appears to be future of high speed networking for several business and technical reasons. ATM has been designed to be independent of the transmission medium.

A1.15 ISDN: INTEGRATED SERVICES DIGITAL NETWORK

ISDN stands for integrated services digital network. It is the forerunner of B-ISDN. ISDN was designed to utilize the pre-existing copper wiring that runs from the telephone exchange. To telephones on the customer premises. ISDN operates by increasing the calling capacity of the existing telephone lines. Three types of ISDN channels are defined B, D and H.

B – Channel

It is a 64 kbps clear channel that can carry any digitized data and voice. A Clear channel means that no signaling information is sent and is meant to be an open communication line. There are two b channels on each ISDN lines and so two kinds information can be exchanged simultaneously.

D – Channel

D- channel used for signaling information, can operate at either 16 kbps for 64 kbps, the D channel can be used for what is known as communication signaling useful for synchronization, monitoring and alarm signals. This channel can also transport digital data at speed upto 9600 bits/second. This channel uses X.25 format for data transfer.

H – Channel

Three H channels all providing higher speed transmission than D channel. The Ho channel operates at 384 kbps and can be used for video conferencing, high speed fax or packet switched data.

Upto four Ho channels can be multiplexed into a single H_1 Channel, which operates at 1.55 Mbps. The H_1 channel is used for high speed data communications or LAN inter connections, The H_2 channel operates at 1.9 Mbps is available only in Europe.

ISDN is used to transmit and receive data at high speeds. ISDN can provide high quality and performance services for remote access to a LAN.

B – ISDN

The B-ISDN stand for broad band integrated service digital network. The main goal of B-ISDN is integration of voice and non-voice (i.e. Audio and Video) data communication services.

A1.16 NETWORK MANAGEMENT

When Applications reside on a single central processor, the issues of network management assume great importance but often can be addressed by attentive operations staff. With the movement of client/server applications, processors may reside away from this attentiveness.

If the data or application logic necessary to run the business resides at a location remote from the glass house central computer room, these resources must be visible to some network managers. The provision of a network control center to manage all resources in a distributed network is the major challenge facing most large organizations today. Many organizations view this issue as the most significant obstacle to successful rollout of client/ server applications.

The key layers in the management system architecture-

(i) Presentation describes the management console environment and the tools used there.

(ii) Reduction refers to distributed intelligence which acts as an intermediary for the network management interface. Reduction enables information to be consolidated and filtered and allowing the presentation service to delegates tasks through the use of an emerging distributed program services such as RPC.

(iii) Gathering of information is done by device agents. These device agents provide detailed diagnostics, detailed statistics and precise control.

There are five key OSI management areas:

- Fault Management
- Performance Management
- Inventory Management
- Accounting Management
- Configuration Management

A1.16.1 What Is Network Management?

Network management means different things to different people. In some cases, it involves a solitary network consultant monitoring network activity with an outdated protocol analyzer. In other cases, network management involves a distributed database, autopolling of network devices, and high-end workstations generating real-time graphical views of network topology changes and traffic. In general, network management is a service that employs a variety of tools, applications, and devices to assist human network managers in monitoring and maintaining networks.

A1.16.2 A Historical Perspective

The early 1980s saw tremendous expansion in the area of network deployment. As companies realized the cost benefits and productivity gains created by network technology, they began to add networks and expand existing networks almost as rapidly as new network technologies and products were introduced. By the mid-1980s, certain companies were experiencing growing pains from deploying many different (and sometimes incompatible) network technologies.

The problems associated with network expansion affect both day-to-day network operation management and strategic network growth planning. Each new network technology requires its own set of experts. In the early 1980s, the staffing requirements alone for managing large, heterogeneous networks created a crisis for many organizations. An urgent need arose for automated network management (including what is typically called network capacity planning) integrated across diverse environments.

A1.16.3 Network Management Architecture

Most network management architectures use the same basic structure and set of relationships. End stations (managed devices), such as computer systems and other network devices, run software that enables them to send alerts when they recognize problems (for example, when one or more user-determined thresholds are exceeded). Upon receiving these alerts, management entities are programmed to react by executing one, several, or a group of actions, including operator notification, event logging, system shutdown, and automatic attempts at system repair.

Management entities also can poll end stations to check the values of certain variables. Polling can be automatic or user-initiated, but agents in the managed devices respond to all polls. Agents are software modules that first compile information about the managed devices in which they reside, then store this information in a management database, and finally provide it (proactively or reactively) to management entities within network management systems (NMSs) via a network management protocol. Well-known network management protocols include the Simple Network Management Protocol (SNMP) and Common Management Information Protocol (CMIP). Management proxies are entities that provide management information on behalf of other entities. Figure A1.4 depicts typical network management architecture.

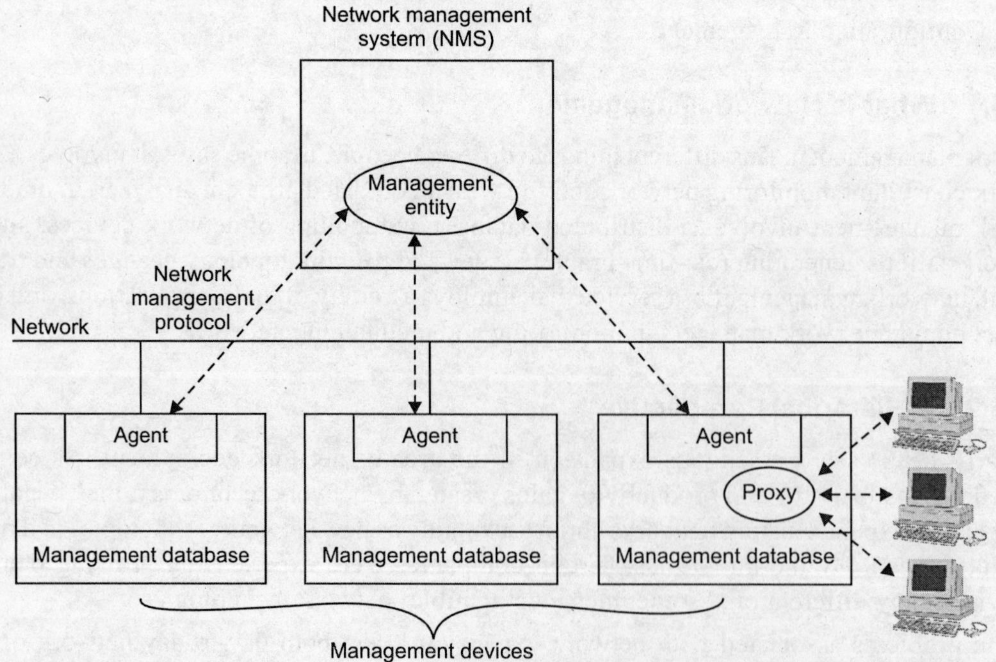

Fig. A1.23 A typical network management architecture maintains many relationships

A1.16.4 ISO Network Management Model

The ISO has contributed a great deal to network standardization. Its network management model is the primary means for understanding the major functions of network management systems. This model consists of five conceptual areas, as discussed in the next sections.

A1.16.5 Performance Management

The goal of performance management is to measure and make available various aspects of network performance so that internetwork performance can be maintained at an acceptable level. Examples of performance variables that might be provided include network throughput, user response times, and line utilization.

Performance management involves three main steps. First, performance data is gathered on variables of interest to network administrators. Second, the data is analyzed to determine normal (baseline) levels. Finally, appropriate performance thresholds are determined for each important variable so that exceeding these thresholds indicates a network problem worthy of attention.

Management entities continually monitor performance variables. When a performance threshold is exceeded, an alert is generated and sent to the network management system.

Each of the steps just described is part of the process to set up a reactive system. When performance becomes unacceptable because of an exceeded user-defined threshold, the system reacts by sending a message. Performance management also permits proactive methods: For example, network simulation can be used to project how network growth will affect performance metrics. Such simulation can alert administrators to impending problems so that counteractive measures can be taken.

A1.16.6 Configuration Management

The goal of configuration management is to monitor network and system configuration information so that the effects on network operation of various versions of hardware and software elements can be tracked and managed.

Each network device has a variety of version information associated with it. An engineering workstation, for example, may be configured as follows:

- Operating system, Version 3.2
- Ethernet interface, Version 5.4
- TCP/IP software, Version 2.0
- NetWare software, Version 4.1
- NFS software, Version 5.1
- Serial communications controller, Version 1.1
- X.25 software, Version 1.0
- SNMP software, Version 3.1

Configuration management subsystems store this information in a database for easy access. When a problem occurs, this database can be searched for clues that may help solve the problem.

A1.16.7 Accounting Management

The goal of accounting management is to measure network utilization parameters so that individual or group uses on the network can be regulated appropriately. Such regulation minimizes network problems (because network resources can be apportioned based on resource capacities) and maximizes the fairness of network access across all users.

As with performance management, the first step toward appropriate accounting management is to measure utilization of all important network resources. Analysis of the results provides insight into current usage patterns, and usage quotas can be set at this point. Some correction, of course, will be required to reach optimal access practices. From this point, ongoing measurement of resource use can yield billing information as well as information used to assess continued fair and optimal resource utilization.

A1.16.8 Fault Management

The goal of fault management is to detect, log, notify users of, and (to the extent possible) automatically fix network problems to keep the network running effectively. Because faults can cause downtime or unacceptable network degradation, fault management is perhaps the most widely implemented of the ISO network management elements.

Fault management involves first determining symptoms and isolating the problem. Then the problem is fixed and the solution is tested on all-important subsystems. Finally, the detection and resolution of the problem is recorded.

A1.16.9 Security Management

The goal of security management is to control access to network resources according to local guidelines so that the network cannot be sabotaged (intentionally or unintentionally) and sensitive information cannot be accessed by those without appropriate authorization. A security management subsystem, for example, can monitor users logging on to a network resource and can refuse access to those who enter inappropriate access codes.

Security management subsystems work by partitioning network resources into authorized and unauthorized areas. For some users, access to any network resource is inappropriate, mostly because such users are usually company outsiders. For other (internal) network users, access to information originating from a particular department is inappropriate. Access to Human Resource files, for example, is inappropriate for most users outside the Human Resources department.

Security management subsystems perform several functions. They identify sensitive network resources (including systems, files, and other entities) and determine mappings between sensitive network resources and user sets. They also monitor access points to sensitive network resources and log inappropriate access to sensitive network resources.

A1.17 TCP/IP PROTOCOL SUITE

The TCP/IP Protocol suite is compassed of following protocols, which are abide with certain services either N/W locally (LAN) or on WAN or with internet. The TCP/IP protocol suite is now being used in many commercial applications. It is particularly evident in inter networking between different LAN environments. TCP/IP is specially designed to handle communications through networks of inter connected networks.

(i) Internet Protocol
(ii) Transport Protocol
(iii) Telnet
(iv) File Transfer Protocol (FTP)
(v) Simple Network Management Protocol (SNMP)
(vi) Network File System Protocol
(vii) Simple Mail Transfer Protocol

A1.17.1 Internet Protocol

Internet protocol represents the network layer and is equivalent to open system inter-connecting internet protocol. A unique network address is assigned to every system whether the system is connected to LAN or WAN. The system interacts with its associated routing protocols and lower level functions such as network to physical address resolution protocol (ARP). Commonly the routing protocol used on LAN or WAN t coordinate the IP is RIP (Routing Internet Protocol).

A1.17.2 Transport Protocol

TCP provides the transport services over IP. It is a connection oriented i.e. a session to be set up between the two parties (two workstation) to provide a service. The major role of transport protocol are transport the services, ensure end t end data transmission. Ordering of data and flow control of the data and also the error recovery. TCP provides the kind of communications the users and programs expect t have in locally connected sessions.

UDP provides connectionless transport services and is used in very specific applications that do not require end to end reliability such as that provided by TCP.

A1.17. 3 Telnet

Telnet is an application which provides some services using TCP. It provides terminal connection services and also supports the terminal to host connection over an internet work. It is measurely composed by client entity and server entity. Client entity provides services to access host and server entity provides services to be access by clients. Every workstation operating systems such as OS/2 and windows can provides telnet server supports using telnet application.

A1.17.4 File Transfer Protocol (FTP)

FTP uses TCP services to provide file transfer services to applications. FTP includes a client and server portions. The server FTP for a session initiation sends the direction to the clients FTP, when request is made from the clients to downloaded certain files from the server. In a similar manner, In reverse order, process will carry on when a file is uploaded from client to server.

A1.17.5 Simple N/W Management Protocol

SNMP provides intelligence and services to effectively manage an internet work. This protocol measurely uses in hubs that preferred to use a technology to monitor and manage the information between two connective workstations.

A1.17.6 Network File System Protocol

The network file system protocol use IP services by server to share the disk space or the files either by the LAN manager network or LAN application. This protocol is useful in the environment in which the servers are running different O.S.

A1.17.7 Simple Mail Transfer Protocol

SMTP user TCP services connections to transfer the text oriented electronic mail among the user on the same host or among host over the network. Most electronic mail system now a days provides some form of SMTP gateway to let user connected globally.

A1.18 SUMMARY

- An internetwork is a collection of individual networks, connected by intermediate networking devices, that functions as a single large network. Internetworking refers to the industry, products, and procedures that meet the challenge of creating and administering internetworks.
- The Open System Interconnection (OSI) reference model describes how information from a software application in one computer moves through a network medium to a software application in another computer.
- The OSI reference model is a conceptual model composed of seven layers, each specifying particular network functions. The model was developed by the International Organization for Standardization (ISO) in 1984, and it is now considered the primary architectural model for inter computer communications.
- The OSI model divides the tasks involved with moving information between networked computers into seven smaller, more manageable task groups.
- Connectivity is the unbiased transport of packets between two end points. This is also the essential definition of "IP" (Internet Protocol).
- **Inter-Process Communication (IPC)** is a set of techniques for the exchange of data between two or more threads in one or more processes. Processes may be running on one computer or on two or more computers connected by a network. IPC techniques are divided into methods for message passing, synchronization, shared memory, and remote procedure calls (RPC).

- A wide area network or WAN, spans a large geographical area, often a country or continent. It contains a collection of machines intended for running user (i.e. application) programs.
- Switched Multimegabit Data Service (SMDS) is a Connectionless, high speed, packet switched data service. SMDS is used to interconnect distribute corporate LANs and WANs through the public Networks, because it is connectionless, SMDS elements, the need for carrier switches to establish a call path between two points of data transmission.
- ATM scheme is widely used for data communication network. ATM Network uses the ATM switch, which receives the requests for data transfer from different computers. The ATM switch facilitates the data Transmission in Asynchronous mode.
- ISDN stands for integrated services digital network. It is the forerunner of B-ISDN. ISDN was designed to utilize the pre-existing copper wiring that runs from the telephone exchange. To telephones on the customer premises.

A1.19 REVIEW QUESTIONS

Q.1. What are the layers of the OSI model?

Ans. Application, presentation, session, transport, network, data link, physical. Remember the sentence "All people seem to need data processing."

Q.2. Which layer determines path selection in an internetwork?

Ans. Layer 3, the network layer.

Q.3. What types of things are defined at the physical layer?

Ans. Voltage levels, time of voltage changes, physical data rates, maximum transmission distances, physical connectors, and type of media.

Q.4. What is one method of mapping network addresses to MAC addresses?

Ans. ARP, Hello, predictable.

Q.5. Which includes more overhead, connection-oriented or connectionless services?

Ans. Connection-oriented.

Q.6. Name the different areas of network management.

Ans. Configuration, accounting, fault, security, and performance.

Q.7. What are the goals of performance management?

Ans. Measure and make available various aspects of network performance so that internetwork performance can be maintained at an acceptable level.

Q.8. What are the goals of configuration management?

Ans. Monitor network and system configuration information so that the effects on network operation of various versions of hardware and software elements can be tracked and managed.

Q.9. What are the goals of accounting management?

Ans. Measure network utilization parameters so that individual or group uses on the network can be regulated appropriately.

Q.9. What are the goals of fault management?

Ans. Detect, log, notify users of, and automatically fix network problems to keep the network running effectively.

Q.10. What are the goals of security management?

Ans. Control access to network resources according to local guidelines so that the network cannot be sabotaged and so that sensitive information cannot be accessed by those without appropriate authorization.

Multiple Choice Question & Answers

1. All of the following are examples of real security and privacy risks EXCEPT:

   A Hackers **B. Spam**
   C. Viruses D. Identity theft

2. A process known as .... is used by large retailers to study trends.

   A. Data mining B. Data selection
   C. POS D. Data conversion

3. .... terminals (formerly known as cash registers) are often connected to complex inventory and sales computer systems.

   A. Data **B. Point-of-sale (POS)**
   C. Sales D. Query

4. A(n)..................... system is a small, wireless handheld computer that scans an itemâ€™s tag and pulls up the current price (and any special offers) as you shop.

   A. PSS B. POS
   C. inventory D. data mining

5. The ability to recover and read deleted or damaged files from a criminalâ€™s computer is an example of a law enforcement specialty called:

   A. Robotics. B. Simulation.
   C. Computer forensics. D. Animation

6. Which of the following is NOT one of the four major data processing functions of a computer?

   A. gathering data B. processing data into information
   C. analyzing the data or information D. storing the data or information

7. .... tags, when placed on an animal, can be used to record and track in a database all of the animalâ€™s movements.

   A. POS **B. RFID**
   C. PPS D. GPS

8. Surgeons can perform delicate operations by manipulating devices through computers insteadof manually. This technology is known as:

A. robotics B. computer forensics.
C. simulation. D. forecasting.

9. Technology no longer protected by copyright, available to everyone, is considered to be:

A. proprietary. B. open.
C. experimental. D. in the public domain.

10. .... is the study of molecules and structures whose size ranges from 1 to 100 nanometers.

A. Nanoscience B. Microelectrodes
C. Computer forensics D. Artificial intelligence

11. .... is the science that attempts to produce machines that display the same type of intelligence that humans do.

A. Nanoscience B. Nanotechnology
C. Simulation **D. Artificial intelligence (AI)**

12. .... is data that has been organized or presented in a meaningful fashion.

A. A process B. Software
C. Storage **D. Information**

13. The name for the way that computers manipulate data into information is called:

A. programming. **B. processing.**
C. storing. D. organizing.

14. Computers gather data, which means that they allow users to.....................data.

A. present **B. input**
C. output D. store

15. After a picture has been taken with a digital camera and processed appropriately, the actual print of the picture is considered:

A. data. **B. output.**
C. input. D. the process.

16. Computers use the .... language to process data.

A. processing B. kilobyte
C. binary D. representational

17. Computers process data into information by working exclusively with:

A. multimedia. B. words.
C. characters. **D. numbers.**

18. In the binary language each letter of the alphabet, each number and each special character is made up of a unique combination of:

A. eight bytes. B. eight kilobytes.
C. eight characters. **D. eight bits.**

19. The term bit is short for:
A. megabyte. B. binary language.
C. binary digit D. binary number.

20. A string of eight 0s and 1s is called a:
A. megabyte. **B. byte.**
C. kilobyte. D. gigabyte.

21. A .... is approximately one billion bytes.
A. kilobyte B. bit
C. gigabyte D. megabyte

22. A .... is approximately a million bytes.
A. gigabyte B. kilobyte
C. megabyte D. terabyte

23. .... is any part of the computer that you can physically touch.
A. Hardware B. A device
C. A peripheral D. An application

24. The components that process data are located in the:
A. input devices. B. output devices.
C. system unit. D. storage component.

25. All of the following are examples of input devices EXCEPT a:
A. scanner. B. mouse.
C. keyboard. **D. printer.**

26. Which of the following is an example of an input device?
A. scanner B. speaker
C. CD D. printer

27. All of the following are examples of storage devices EXCEPT:
A. hard disk drives. **B. printers.**
C. floppy disk drives. D. CD drives.
Answer: B

28. The ...., also called the â€œbrainsâ€• of the computer, is responsible for processing data.
A. motherboard B. memory
C. RAM **D. central processing unit (CPU)**

29. The CPU and memory are located on the:

A. expansion board. **B. motherboard.**
C. storage device. D. output device.

30. Word processing, spreadsheet, and photo-editing are examples of:
A. application software. B. system software.
C. operating system software. D. platform software.

31. .... is a set of computer programs used on a computer to help perform tasks.
A. An instruction **B. Software**
C. Memory D. A processor

32. System software is the set of programs that enables your computerâ€™s hardware devices and .... software to work together.
A. management B. processing
C. utility **D. application**

33. The PC (personal computer) and the Apple Macintosh are examples of two different:
A. platforms. B. applications.
C. programs. D. storage devices.

34. Apple Macintoshes (Macs) and PCs use different .... to process data and different operating systems.
A. languages B. methods
C. CPUs D. storage devices

35. Servers are computers that provide resources to other computers connected to a:
A. network. B. mainframe.
C. supercomputer. D. client.

36. Smaller and less expensive PC-based servers are replacing .... in many businesses.
A. supercomputers B. clients
C. laptops **D. mainframes**

37. .... are specially designed computers that perform complex calculations extremely rapidly.
A. Servers **B. Supercomputers**
C. Laptops D. Mainframes

38. DSL is an example of a(n) .... connection.
A. network B. wireless
C. slow **D. broadband**

39. The difference between people with access to computers and the Internet and those without this access is known as the:
A. digital divide. B. Internet divide.
C. Web divide. D. broadband divide.

40. .... is the science revolving around the use of nanostructures to build devices on an extremely small scale.

A. Nanotechnology B. Micro-technology

C. Computer forensics D. Artificial intelligence

41. Which of the following is the correct order of the four major functions of a computer?

A. Process Ã Output Ã Input Ã Storage B. Input Ã OutputÃ Process Ã Storage

C. Process Ã Storage Ã Input Ã Output **D. Input Ã Process Ã Output Ã Storage**

42. .... bits equal one byte.

A. Eight B. Two

C. One thousand D. One million

43. The binary language consists of..................... digit(s).

A. 8 **B. 2**

C. 1,000 D. 1

44. A byte can hold one .... of data.

A. bit B. binary digit

C. character D. kilobyte

45. .... controls the way in which the computer system functions and provides a means by which users can interact with the computer.

A. The platform **B. The operating system**

C. Application software D. The motherboard

46. The operating system is the most common type of .... software.

A. communication B. application

C. system D. word-processing software

47. .... are specially designed computer chips that reside inside other devices, such as your car or your electronic thermostat.

A. Servers **B. Embedded computers**

C. Robotic computers D. Mainframes

48. The steps and tasks needed to process data, such as responses to questions or clicking an icon, are called:

A. instructions. B. the operating system.

C. application software. D. the system unit.

49. The two broad categories of software are:

A. word processing and spreadsheet. B. transaction and application.

C. Windows and Mac OS. **D. system and application.**

50. The metal or plastic case that holds all the physical parts of the computer is the:

A. system unit. B. CPU.

C. mainframe. D. platform.

Fill in the balnks:

1. Between PCs and Macs, the .... is the platform of choice for graphic design and animation.
2. The .... is the program that manages the hardware of the computer system, including the CPU, memory, storage devices, and input/outputdevices.
3. The type of operating system software you use depends on your computerâ€™s ....
4. ....software helps you carry out tasks, such as typing a document or creating aspreadsheet.
5. ....are the fastest and most expensive computers.
6. A .... is approximately 1,000 bytes.
7. Input devices are used to provide the steps and tasks the computer needs to process data, and these steps and tasks are called ....
8. A computer gathers data, processes it, outputs the data or information, and .... the data or information.
9. The binary language consists of two digits: .... and ....
10. A string of .... 0s and 1s is called a byte.
11. The devices you use to enter data into a computer system are known as ....devicex known as .... devices
12. .... is thc sct of computer instructions or programs that enables the hardware to perform different tasks.
13. When you connect to the ...., your computer is communicating with a server at your Internet service provider (ISP).
14. .... are computers that excel at executing many different computer programs at the same time
15. .... is the application of computer systems and techniques to gather legal evidence.
16. .... is the science that attempts to create machines that will emulate the human thought process.
17. Macintosh computers use the Macintosh operating system (Mac OS), whereas PCs generally run .... as an operating system
18. A process known as..................... tracks trends and allows retailers to respond to consumer buying patterns.
19. Hard disk drives and CD drives are examples of ____________ devices.

20. You would use .... software to create spreadsheets, type documents, and edit photos
21. .... are computers that support hundreds or thousands of users simultaneously.
22. .... is the term given to the act of stealing someoneâ€™s identity and ruining their credit rating
23. Surgeons are using .... to guide robots to perform delicate surgery.
24. Patient .... are life-sized mannequins that have a pulse and a heartbeat and respond to procedures just like humans.

True and False

1. Currently, the performance of tasks by robots is based on preprogrammed algorithms.
2. Data can be a number, a word, a picture, or a sound.
3. Strictly defined, a computer is a data processing device.
4. The discrepancy between the â€œhavesâ€• and â€œhave-notsâ€• with regard to computer technology is commonly referred to as the digital society.
5. One of the benefits of becoming computer fluent is being a savvy computer user and consumer and knowing how to avoid viruses, the programs that pose threats to computer security.
6. Trend-spotting programs, developed for business, have been used to predict criminal activity.
7. Employers do not have the right to monitor e-mail and network traffic on employee systems used at work.
8. Clicking on an icon with the mouse is a form of giving an instruction to the computer.
9. Output devices store instructions or data that the CPU processes.
10. The CPU and memory are located on a special circuit board in the system unit called the motherboard.
11. Nanostructures represent the smallest human-made structures that can be built.
12. The main difference between a supercomputer and a mainframe is that supercomputers are designed to execute a few programs as quickly as possible, whereas mainframes are designed to handle many programs running at the same time (but at a slower pace).
13. Being computer fluent means that you should be able to build a computer yourself.
14. Embedded computers are self-contained computer devices that have their own programming and do not receive input.
15. A Web browser is a special device that is installed in your computer that allows it to communicate with other devices on a network.
16. With a wireless network, it is easier to relocate devices.
17. The most common type of memory that the computer uses to process data is ROM.

Matching:

1. Match the following terms with their approximate size:

(i) Kilobyte	A. one million bytes
(ii) Byte	B. eight bits
(iii) Gigabyte	C. one thousand bytes
(iv) Megabyte	D. one billion bytes
(v) Terabyte	E. one trillion bytes

Answer: C, B, D, A, E

2. Match the following terms with their meanings:

(i) P rinter	A. storage device
(ii) Scanner	B. output device
(iii) RAM	C. input device
(iv) CPU	D. a type of memory
(v) CD drive	E. processor

Answer: B, C, D, E, A

3. Match the following terms with their meanings:

(i) Mainframe	A. the most expensive computers that perform complex calculations extremely rapidly
(ii) Supercomputer	B. a computer that provides resources to other computers connected to a network
(iii) Embedded computer	C. a large, expensive computer that supports hundreds or thousands of users simultaneously
(iv) PDA	D. a self-contained computer device that usually performs preprogrammed functions such as temperaturecontrol
(v) Server	E. a small mobile computing device

Answer:C, A, D, E, B

4. Match the following terms with their meanings:

(i) Software	A. transforming data into information
(ii) Hardware	B. data that has been organized or presented in a meaningful fashion
(iii) Operating system	C. any part of the computer that you can physically touch
(iv) Processing	D. a set of computer programs that enables hardware to perform different tasks

(v) Information	E. the most common type of system software, it controls the way in which the computer system functions

Answer: D, C, E, A, B

5. Match the following terms with their meanings:

(i) System software	A. the set of programs that enables computer hardware devices and application software to work together
(ii) application software	B. the kind of operating system software you will use depends on this
(iii) Platform	C. operating system software generally used on PCs
(iv) Microsoft Windows	D. a set of programs used to accomplish a specific task
(v) Mac OS	E. operating system software used on the Apple Macintosh

Answer: A, D, B, C, E

6. Match the following terms with their meanings:

(i) Data	A. the main circuit board in the system unit
(ii) Memory	B. the representation of a fact or idea (unprocessed information)
(iii) Output	C. processed data or information
(iv) Storage	D. holds instructions or data that the CPU processes
(v) Motherboard	E. data or information that can be accessed again

Answer: B, D, C, E, A

7. Match the following terms with their meanings:

(i) Bit	A. the science revolving around the use of nanostructures to build devices on an extremely small scale
(ii) Binary language	B. the case that contains the system components
(iii) Instructions	C. consists of 0s and 1s
(iv) System unit	D. short for binary digit
(v) Nanotechnology	E. steps and tasks necessary to process data into usableinformation

Answer: D, C, E, B, A

8. Match the following fields to the related computer technology:

(i) Medicine	A. Internet research and virtual tours
(ii) Business	B. data mining
(iii) Law enforcement	C. robotics and simulation
(iv) Education	D. computer forensics
(v) Aarcheology	E. digital recreations of ruins

Multiple Choice Answers

1. Mac	2. operating system	3. platform
4. Application	5. Supercomputers	6. kilobyte
7. Instructions	8. Stores	9. 0 and 1,
10. eight(8),	11. output,	12. software,
13. Internet	14. Mainframes	15. Computer forensics
16. Artificial intelligence (AI)	17. Microsoft Windows	18. Data mining
19. Sttorang,	20. Application,	21. Mainframes,
22. Identity theft	23. computers	24. simulators

True and False

1. True,	2. True	3. True
4. False (digital divide),	5. True	6. True
7. False	8. True	9. False (Memory)
10. True	11. True	12. True
13. False	14. True	15. False (network adapter)
16. True	17. Flase (Ram)	

Distributed System – Lab Manual

EXPERIMENT – 1

Objective: The design and implementation of RMI using java?

Theory and concept: Remote Method Invocation (RMI) facilitates object function calls between Java Virtual Machines (JVMs). JVMs can be located on separate computers - yet one JVM can invoke methods belonging to an object stored in another JVM. Methods can even pass objects that a foreign virtual machine has never encountered before, allowing dynamic loading of new classes as required. This is a powerful feature.

Consider the following scenario:

- Developer A writes a service that performs some useful function. He regularly updates this service, adding new features and improving existing ones.
- Dcvcloper B wishes to use the service provided by Developer A. However, it's inconvenient for A to supply B with an update every time.

Java RMI provides a very easy solution! Since RMI can dynamically load new classes, Developer B can let RMI handle updates automatically for him. Developer A places the new classes in a web directory, where RMI can fetch the new updates as they are required.

Figure 13.1 shows the connections made by the client when using RMI. Firstly, the client must contact an RMI registry, and request the name of the service. Developer B won't know the exact location of the RMI service, but he knows enough to contact Developer A's registry. This will point him in the direction of the service he wants to call..

Developer A's service changes regularly, so Developer B doesn't have a copy of the class. Not to worry, because the client automatically fetches the new subclass from a web server where the two developers share classes. The new class is loaded into memory, and the client is ready to use the new class. This happens transparently for Developer B - no extra code need to be written to fetch the class.

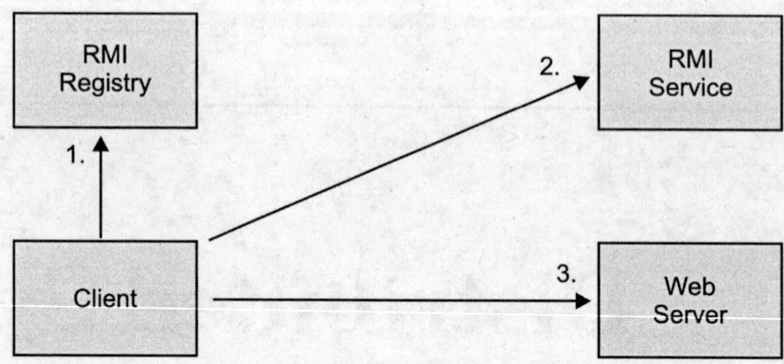

Fig. 1 Connections made when client uses RMI

Writing an interface: The first thing we need to do is to agree upon an interface, An interface is a description of the methods we will allow remote clients to invoke. Let's consider exactly what we'll need.

1. A method that accepts as a parameter an integer, squares it, and returns a BigInteger public BigInteger square (int number_to_square);
2. A method that accepts as a parameter two integers, calculates their power, and returns a BigInteger public BigInteger power (int num1, int num2);

Implementing the interface: Implementing the interface is a little more tricky - we actually have to write the square and power methods! Don't worry if you're not sure how to calculate squares and powers, this isn't a math lesson. The real code we need to be concerned about is the constructor and main method.

We have to declare a default constructor, even when we don't have any initialization code for our service. This is because our default constructor can throw a java.rmi.RemoteException, from its parent constructor in UnicastRemoteObject.

Writing a RMI client: What good is a service, if you don't write a client that uses it? a client has to do is call the registry to obtain a reference to the remote object, and call its methods. All the underlying network communication is hidden from view, which makes RMI clients simple.

Our client must first assign a security manager, and then obtain a reference to the service. Note that the client receives an instance of the interface we defined earlier, and not the actual implementation. Some behind-the-scenes work is going on, but this is completely transparent to the client.

1. **Start the RMI registry:** To start the registry, Windows users should do the following (assuming that your java\bin directory should be the current path than run):-

   start rmiregistry
2. **Compile the server:** Compile the server, and use the rmic tool to create stub files.
3. **Sart the server:** From the directory in which the classes are located, by typing the following:-

   java PowerServiceServer

Problem: Design the client and server using the RMI ?

EXPERIMENT – 2

Objective: The design and implementation of a Task Bag Server using CORBA or Java RMI?

Theory and concept: Task Bag is a Distributed System using the .NET Framework and Remoting

Introducing Remoting system using

- Framework for remote method invocations in a .NET application
- Similarities to CORBA and Java RMI
- Can integrate with non-.NET applications using SOAP over HTTP
- Replaces Microsofts DCOM

Remoting Example using C#

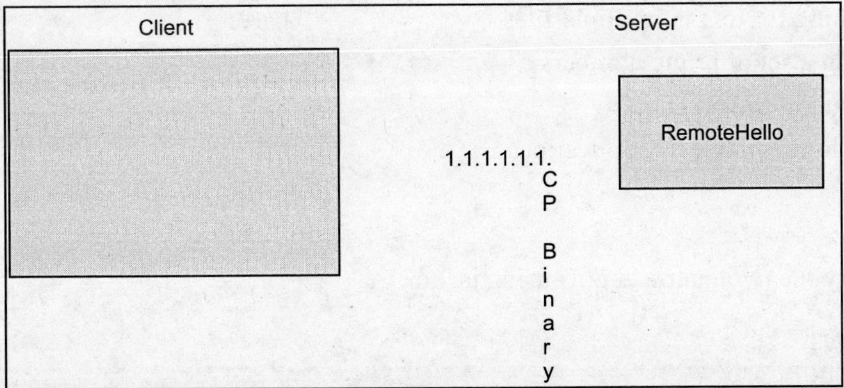

Fig. 2

Task Bag Overview

- Distributed system based on master/slave paradigm
- Master produces Tasks for Workers to complete
- Task Bag is a repository for Tasks and Results

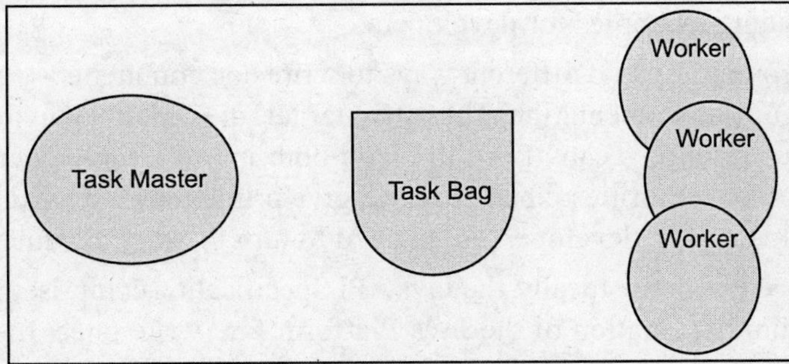

Fig. 3 Task Bag Operations

Task Masters Void

RegisterMaster (string masterName, TaskMasterCallback callback)

void RemoveMaster(string masterName)

void AddTask(Task task)

int GetResult(string taskId)

Workers

void RegisterWorker(Worker worker)

void RemoveWorker(string workerName)

Task GetTask(string workerName) (asynchronous callback)

void AddResult(Task task)

Tasks for Task Bag: Any problem that can be divided into sub-tasks and solved in parallel:

- Searching for text in multiple files
- Finding a set of prime numbers
- Computing fractal images
- Performing matrix multiplication
- Etc.

Problem:

1 Multiply the two matrix A & B using task bag?

EXPERIMENT – 3

Objective: Design and implementation API using JAVA application

Theory and concept: At Java Software, we have several guidelines that might make our documentation comments different than those of third party developers. Our documentation comments define the official Java Platform API Specification. To this end, our target audience is those who write Java compatibility tests, or conform or re-implement the Java platform, in addition to developers. We spend time and effort focused on specifying boundary conditions, argument ranges and corner cases rather than defining common programming terms, writing conceptual overviews, and including examples for developers.

Thus, there are commonly two different ways to write doc comments — as API specifications, or as programming guide documentation. These two targets are described in the following sections. A staff with generous resources can afford to blend both into the same documentation (properly "chunked"); however, our priorities dictate that we give prime focus to writing API specifications in doc comments. This is why developers often need to turn to other documents,.

Writing API Specifications: Ideally, the Java API Specification comprises all assertions required to do a clean-room implementation of the Java Platform for "write once, run anywhere" — such that any Java applet or application will run the same on any implementation. This may include assertions in the doc comments plus those in any architectural and functional specifications (usually written in FrameMaker) or in any other document. This definition is a lofty goal and there is some practical limitation to how fully we can specify the API. The following are guiding principles we try to follow:

The Java Platform API Specification is defined by the documentation comments in the source code and any documents marked as specifications reachable from those comments.

Source Files: The Javadoc tool can generate output originating from four different types of "source" files:

Source code files for Java classes (.java) - these contain class, interface, field, constructor and method comments.

Package comment files: These contain package comments

Overview comment files: Tthese contain comments about the set of packages

Miscellaneous unprocessed files: These include images, sample source code, class files, applets, HTML files, and whatever else you might want to reference from the previous files.

Documenting Unchecked Exceptions: It is generally desirable to document the unchecked exceptions that a method can throw: this allows (but does not require) the caller to handle these exceptions. For example, it allows the caller to "translate" an implementation-dependent unchecked exception to some other exception that is more appropriate to the caller's exported abstraction.

Since there is no way to guarantee that a call has documented all of the unchecked exceptions that it may throw, the programmer must not depend on the presumption that a method cannot throw any unchecked exceptions other than those that it is documented to throw. In other words, you should always assume that a method can throw unchecked exceptions that are undocumented.

Problems:

1. Write a program in Java which reads the contents of a file whose name has been passed by the user in the form of a command line argument and prints the contents of the file on the screen.
2. Write a program in Java that reads the contents by using System.in and writes into a file specified on the command line.

EXPERIMENT – 4

Objective: Using the Java Streams

Theory & concept: The following table lists java.io's streams and its description. In this many times, java.io contains character streams and byte streams that perform the same type of I/O but for different data types.

I/O Streams		
Type of I/O	**Streams**	**Description**
Memory	CharArrayReader CharArrayWriter ByteArrayInputStream ByteArrayOutputStream	Use these streams to read from and write to memory. Create these streams on an existing array and then use the read and write methods to read from or write to the array. Use StringReader to read characters from a String in memory.
	String Reader String Writer String Bugger Input Stream	Use StringWriter to write to a String. StringWriter collects the characters written to it in a StringBuffer, which can then be converted to a String. StringBuffer Input Stream is similar to StringReader, except that it reads bytes from a StringBuffer.
Pipe	Piped Reader Piped Writer Piped Input Stream Piped Output Stream	Implement the input and output components of a pipe. Pipes are used to channel the output from one thread into the input of another.
File	File Reader File Reader File Input Stream File Output Stream	Collectively called file streams, these streams are used to read from or write to a file on the native file system.
Concatenation	N/A Sequence Input Stream	Concatenates multiple input streams into one input stream.
Object Serialization	N/A Object Input Stream Object Output Stream	Used to serialize objects.
Data Conversion	N/A Data Input Stream Data Output Stream	Read or write primitive data types in a machine-independent format.
Counting	Line Number Reader Line Number Input Stream	Keeps track of the numbers while reading.
Peeking Ahead	Pushback Reader Pushback Input Stream	These input streams each have a pushback buffer. When reading data from a stream, it is sometimes useful to peek at the next few bytes or characters in the stream to decide what to do next.
Printing	Print Writer Print Stream	Contain convenient printing methods. These are the easiest streams to write to.
Buffering	Buffered Reader Buffered Writer Buffered Input Stream Buffered Output Stream	Buffer data while reading or writing, thereby reducing the number of accesses required on the original data source. Buffered streams are typically more efficient than similar nonbuffered streams and are often used with other streams.
Filtering	Filter Reader	These obstract classes define the interface for filter

Type of I/O	Streams	Description
	Filter Writer Filter Input Stream Filter Output Stream	streams, which filter data as it's being read or written.
Converting between bytes and characters	Input Stream Reader Output Stream Writer	A reader and writer pair that forms the bridge between byte streams and character streams. An Input Stream Reader reads bytes from an Input Stream and converts them to characters, using the default character encoding or a character encoding specified by name. An output Stream Writer converts characters to bytes, using the default character encoding or a character encoding specified by name and then writes those bytes to an Output Stream.

Problems:

1. Write a program in Java which copies the contents of one file into another file.
2. Write a program in Java using swings which creates an Applet containing two command buttons labeled as "First Button" and "Second Button". Both the command buttons should contain two pictures along with the text. On clicking on the button marked as "First Button" a message "You like carrots" should be displayed on the screen while on clicking the second button a message "You like corn" should be displayed on the screen.

EXPERIMENT – 5

Objective: Create an applet by using swings.

Theory & concept:

Using Images in a Swing Applet: The Applet class provides the getImage method for loading images into an applet. The getImage method creates and returns an Image object that represents the loaded image. Because Swing components use Icons rather than Images to refer to pictures, Swing applets tend not to use getImage. Instead Swing applets create instances of ImageIcon — an icon loaded from an image file. ImageIcon comes with a code-saving benefit: it handles image tracking automatically.

Problems:

1. Write a program in Java to create an Applet by using swings which displays an image marked as "This is an image" on the screen.?
2. Write a java program using swings which displays a tree like structure for the following data?

Physics

  Metaphysics

  Astrophysics

Biology

Microbiology

Biotechnology

Chemistry

Organic

Inorganic

3. Write a program in java using swings which displays a simple menu based on the above data (For instance physics is the main menu option, below it display Metaphysics and Astrophysics)?

EXPERIMENT – 6

Objective: Create an applet by using record database.

Theory & concept: By using Jdbc and odbc bridge driver we connect the java applets .By SQL query run the table record and connect with jdbc & odbc bridge driver and run tha java applets.

Problems:

1. Create a database with table product having columns prod_code, prod_name and quality. Write a java applet that updates the record whose prod_code is accepted through a text field in the applet.?
2. Write a prgram to create an applet, which deletes a record from the above mentioned table whose prod_code is given in a text field in the applet.?

EXPERIMENT – 7

Objective: Create an swing GUI and connect java that retrieved HTML file..

Theory & concept:

Embedding an Applet in an HTML Page: The recommended way to include an applet in an HTML page is using the APPLET tag. Here's the APPLET tag for the cartwheeling Duke applet:

```
<applet code="TumbleItem.class"
codebase="example-1dot4/"
archive="tumbleClasses.jar tumbleImages.jar"
width="600" height="95">
<param name="maxwidth" value="120">
<param name="nimgs" value="17">
<param name="offset" value="-57">
<param name="img" value="images/tumble">
</applet>
```

Problems:

1. Write a program to create a Swing GUI that accepts login name and password. Then the login name and password must be validated against the names and passwords present in a table. If they match display a message "Access granted". If the login name and password do not match with those present in the table, then display a message "Invalid user name/password Access is denied!"?
2. Write a program in java that connects that retrieves an HTML file from your machine and displays its contents in the browser window.?

EXPERIMENT – 8

Objective: Create an socket based client and servelet.

Theory & concept: Create a socket ba client and server with the help of JAVA. also connect java program with HTML file that display that contents.

Problems:

1. Write a program in java that connects that retrieves an HTML filefrom your machine and displays its contents in the browser window.?
2. Create a socket based client and server in java for implementing a Quiz application.?
3. Create a servlet that accepts your name, address and date of birth. Display the information only after the user confirms that the entry is complete. Accept the information through a form.?

EXPERIMENT – 9

Objective: Create an applet by using swings and servlet..

Theory & concept:

Images in HTML Destination

Naming of doc images in HTML destination - Images would have the same name as they have in the source tree. Example: Button-1.gif

Location of doc images in HTML destination: With hierarchical file output, such as Javadoc 1.2, directories would be located in the package directory named "doc-files". For example:

api/java/awt/doc-files/Button-1.gif

With flat file output, such as Javadoc 1.1, directories would be located in the package directory and named "images-<package>". For example:

api/images-java.awt/
api/images-java.awt.swing/

Problems:

1. Create a servlet that allows the user to enter two numbers. The servlet should display the result sending on the operator selected by the user. The operator could be one of the following:
   Addition
   Subtraction
   Multiplication
   Division
2. Write a program in Java using swings which creates an Applet containing two command buttons labeled as "First Button" and "Second Button". Both the command buttons should contain two pictures along with the text. On clicking on the button marked as "First Button" a message "You like carrots" should be displayed on the screen while on clicking the second button a message "You like corn" should be displayed on the screen.
3. Write a program in Java to create an Applet by using swings which displays an image marked as "This is an image" on the screen.

EXPERIMENT – 10

Objective: Create an applet by using record database.

Theory & concept : Create a record in excess and connect that with java applets and run SQL query on that and connect with JDBC & ODBC.

Problems :

1. Write ram to create an applet, which deletes a record from the above mentioned table whose prod_code is given in a text field in the applet.
2. te a program to create a Swing GUI that accepts login name and password. Then the login name and password must be validated against the names and passwords present in a table. If they match display a message "Access granted". If the login name and password do not match with those present in the table, then display a message "Invalid user name/password Access is denied!"

Questions Bank

1. Draw and explain architecture of **distributed** system.
2. List and explain motivation behind development of **distributed** systems.
3. List and explain in detail design issues in **distributed** systems.
4. Draw and explain Remote Procedure Call concept.
5. What are the drawbacks of absence of **global** clock and **global** time in **distributed** systems.
6. Explain Lamport's Logical clocks with example.
7. Explain Vector clocks.
8. Explain difference between logical clock and vector clock with the help of example.
9. Define virtual time.
10. What are the limitations of Lamport's clock.
11. What do you mean by causal ordering of messages.
12. Explain Birman-Schipher-Stephenson protocol.
13. Explain Schiper-Eggli-Sandoz protocol.
14. Define the **global state** with the help of neat diagram.
15. Define local **state**.
16. Explain the difference between **global state** and local **state**.
17. Explain Chandy-Lamport's **Global State** Recording algorithm.
18. What is collected **global state**.
19. Explain cuts of a **distributed** computation.
20. What do you mean by termination **detection**.
21. Explain Huang's termination **detection** algorithm.
22. What do you mean by mutual exclusion.

23. Explain the requirements of mutual exclusion algorithm.
24. Explain with example Lamport's Non-taken **based** algorithm for mutual exclusion.
25. Explain with example Ricart-Agrawala Non-token **based** algorithm for mutual exclusion.
26. Explain the difference between Token-**based** and Non-token **based** mutual exclusion algorithm.
27. Explain the Suzuki-Kasami's broadcast algorithm with proof of correctness.
28. Explain Singhal's Heuristics algorithm.
29. Discus the comparative performance analysis for **distributed** mutual exclusion **algorithms**.
30. Show that in Lamport's algorithm the critical section is accessed according to the increasing order of timestamps.
31. In Lamport's algorithm condition L1 can hold concurrently at several sites. Why then is L1 needed to guarantee mutual exclusion.
32. Discuss the issues in **deadlock detection** and resolution.
33. List and explain any one centralized **deadlock detection** algorithm.
34. List the **distributed deadlock detection** algorithm.
35. Explain Path-pusing **distributed deadlock detection** algorithm.
36. Explain Edge-Chasing **distributed deadlock detection** algorithm.
37. Explain Diffusion Computation **based distributed deadlock detection** algorithm.
38. Explain **Global State Detection Based distributed deadlock detection** algorithm.
39. Discuss the model of processor failures in Agreement protocols.
40. List and discuss classification of agreement problems.
41. List solutions to the Byzantine agreement problem and explain any one.
42. Explain the interactive convergence algorithm for fault tolerant clock synchronization.
43. Explain the interactive consistency algorithm for fault tolerant clock synchronization.
44. What is atomic commit in DDBS.
45. Show that Byzantine agreement cannot be always be reached among four processors if two processors are faulty.
46. Draw and explain architecture of a **distributed** file system.
47. List and explain in short various design issues related to **distributed** file system.
48. Draw and explain architecture of a Sun Network File System (NFS).
49. Draw and explain architecture of **distributed** shared memory.
50. Define memory coherence.
51. List and explain various forms of memory coherence.
52. Explain Write-invalidate and write-update coherence protocols.
53. Explain with neat diagram cache coherence in the PLUS system.

54. What is Granularity.
55. Explain page replacement.
56. Discuss IVY (Integrated Shard Virtual Memory at Yale) as a **distributed** shared memory.
57. Discuss Mirage as a **distributed** shared memory.
58. Discuss Clouds as a **distributed** shared memory.
59. Explain issues in Load Distribution for **Distributed** scheduling.
60. List load distributing **algorithms** for **distributed** scheduling.
61. Explain Sender-Initiated **algorithms** for load distribution.
62. Explain Receiver-Initiated **algorithms** for load distribution.
63. Explain Symmetrically Initiated **algorithms** for load distribution.
64. Explain Adaptive **algorithms** for load distribution.
65. Explain Load sharing policies for the V-System.
66. Explain Load sharing policies for The Sprite System.
67. Explain Load sharing policies for The Condor System.
68. Explain The Stealth **Distributed** Scheduler.
69. Explain task migration in **distributed** system. Also explain general steps involved in task migration.
70. What are the various issues related to task migration.
71. Explain structure of a migration mechanism.
72. Discuss performance of a various task migration mechanisms.
73. Explain the concept of recovery in **distributed** systems.
74. What do you mean by backward and forward error recovery.
75. Discuss the two phases of the Checkpoint Algorithm.
76. Explain the example of the Checkpoint Algorithm.
77. Explain with example The Rollback Recovery Algorithm.
78. Discuss scheme for Asynchronous Check pointing and Recovery.
79. Discuss the algorithm for Asynchronous Check pointing and Recovery with example.
80. Explain the characteristics of atomic actions.
81. Explain the concept of Generals Paradox for commit protocols.
82. Explain the Two-Phase commit protocol.
83. What do you mean by static voting.
84. Explain in detail The Voting Algorithm.
85. Explain Data Encryption Standard (DES) with the help of neat diagram.
86. What is Cipher Block Chaining.

87. Write short note on public key cryptography.
88. Explain in detail The Rivest-Shamir-Adleman (RSA) method for public key cryptography.
89. Write short note an authentication in **distributed** systems.
90. Define Authentication servers.
91. Explain the protocol for private key system.
92. Explain the protocol for public key system.
93. What do you mean by digital signatures.
94. Discuss digital signature in private key system.
95. Discuss digital signature in public key system.
96. Draw and explain Kerberos authentication protocol.
97. Explain the three phases of Kerberos authentication protocol.

Index

D

E

F

G

H

I

K

L

M

N

O

P

Q

R

S